A CULTURAL HISTORY OF FAIRY TALES

VOLUME 3

A Cultural History of Fairy Tales
General Editor: Anne E. Duggan

Volume 1
A Cultural History of Fairy Tales in Antiquity
Edited by Debbie Felton

Volume 2
A Cultural History of Fairy Tales in the Middle Ages
Edited by Susan Aronstein

Volume 3
A Cultural History of Fairy Tales in the Age of the Marvelous
Edited by Suzanne Magnanini

Volume 4
A Cultural History of Fairy Tales in the Long Eighteenth Century
Edited by Anne E. Duggan

Volume 5
A Cultural History of Fairy Tales in the Long Nineteenth Century
Edited by Naomi J. Wood

Volume 6
A Cultural History of Fairy Tales in the Modern Age
Edited by Andrew Teverson

A CULTURAL HISTORY OF FAIRY TALES

IN THE AGE OF THE MARVELOUS

VOLUME 3

Edited by Suzanne Magnanini

BLOOMSBURY ACADEMIC
LONDON • NEW YORK • OXFORD • NEW DELHI • SYDNEY

BLOOMSBURY ACADEMIC
Bloomsbury Publishing Plc, 50 Bedford Square, London, WC1B 3DP, UK
Bloomsbury Publishing Inc, 1359 Broadway, New York, NY 10018, USA
Bloomsbury Publishing Ireland, 29 Earlsfort Terrace, Dublin 2, D02 AY28, Ireland

BLOOMSBURY, BLOOMSBURY ACADEMIC and the Diana logo
are trademarks of Bloomsbury Publishing Plc

First published in Great Britain 2021
Paperback edition published 2025

Copyright © Suzanne Magnanini, 2021

Suzanne Magnanini and Contributors have asserted their right under the Copyright, Designs and Patents Act, 1988, to be identified as Author of this work.

Series design by Raven Design
Cover image: The Sea Monster © duncan1890 / Getty Images

All rights reserved. No part of this publication may be: i) reproduced or transmitted in any form, electronic or mechanical, including photocopying, recording or by means of any information storage or retrieval system without prior permission in writing from the publishers; or ii) used or reproduced in any way for the training, development or operation of artificial intelligence (AI) technologies, including generative AI technologies. The rights holders expressly reserve this publication from the text and data mining exception as per Article 4(3) of the Digital Single Market Directive (EU) 2019/790.

Bloomsbury Publishing Plc does not have any control over, or responsibility for, any third-party websites referred to or in this book. All internet addresses given in this book were correct at the time of going to press. The author and publisher regret any inconvenience caused if addresses have changed or sites have ceased to exist, but can accept no responsibility for any such changes.

A catalogue record for this book is available from the British Library.

A catalog record for this book is available from the Library of Congress.

ISBN:	HB:	978-1-3500-9465-9
	PB:	978-1-3505-9412-8
	ePDF:	978-1-3502-8752-5
	eBook:	978-1-3502-8590-3
	set:	978-1-3505-9409-8

Series: A Cultural History of Fairy Tales

Typeset by Integra Software Services Pvt. Ltd.
Printed and bound in Great Britain

For product safety related questions contact productsafety@bloomsbury.com.

To find out more about our authors and books visit www.bloomsbury.com
and sign up for our newsletters.

CONTENTS

List of Illustrations · vii
Series Preface · ix

Introduction: Fairy Tales in the Age of the Marvelous · 1
Suzanne Magnanini

1 Forms of the Marvelous: Ring and Riddle in the Shakespearean Marriage Tale · 25
 Kevin Pask

2 Adaptation: Prose Stories Dressed in Ottoman Attire · 49
 N. İpek Hüner Cora

3 Gender and Sexuality: Gender and Sexuality in the Fairy Tales of Straparola and Basile · 71
 Cristina Mazzoni

4 Humans and Non-Humans: Animal Bridegrooms and Brides in Japanese *Otogizōshi* · 95
 Laura Nüffer

5 Monsters and the Monstrous: Witches and Werewolves in Early Modern French and Italian Tales · 119
 Kathleen P. Long

6 Space: Geographies of the Fairy Tale in Giambattista Basile's *The Tale of Tales* · 149
 Davide Papotti

7 Socialization: Civilizing the Fairy Tale in Early Modern Italy   169
   Suzanne Magnanini

8 Power: Abuse of Power, Gender, and Race in Tales by
   Straparola and Basile   191
   Armando Maggi

NOTES   213
REFERENCES   229
NOTES ON CONTRIBUTORS   245
INDEX   247

ILLUSTRATIONS

0.1 Hercules and his nephew Iolaus slay the hydra, by German printmaker Hans Sebald Beham (1545) — 3

0.2 A hydra brought from the Ottoman Empire to Venice in 1530, from Conrad Lycosthenes, *Prodigiorum ac ostentorum chronicon* (1557) — 4

0.3 The title page of *History of Queen Stella and Mattabruna,* an anonymous nineteenth-century chapbook printed in Naples — 14

1.1 "Here take my ring" by James Hopwood, printmaker (1799) — 36

1.2 Louis Rhead, "Softly unloosening the bracelet from her arm" — 43

1.3 Arthur Rackham, *Lament for Imogen* (1899) — 45

2.1 A Turkish translation of the Persian epic Şehnāme with the figures dressed in Ottoman attire — 54

2.2 Dog-headed people and pygmies in a Turkish version of *Wonders of Creation,* made for the seventeenth-century Vizier Murtaza Pasa — 63

3.1 Straparola's prince sheds his pig skin before his wife Meldina, by E. R. Hughes, from *The Italian Novelists: The Pleasant Nights* (1901) — 78

3.2 Four of Basile's heroines illustrated by George Cruikshank in *The Pentamerone, or The Story of Stories, fun for the little ones* (1848) — 84

4.1	Tosa Hirochika (1439–92), Amewakahiko's wife being locked in the castle of snakes by her father-in-law, the ogre, in *The Tale of Amewakahiko*	101
5.1	"The Berkeley Witch," from the Nuremberg Chronicle (*Liber chronicarum*, 1493)	129
5.2	"Witch Being Abducted," from Olaus Magnus, *Historia de gentibus septentrionalibus* (1555)	130
5.3	"Witches Flying," from Ulrich Molitor, *De lamiis et phitonicis muliebris* (1489)	134
5.4	"Half-Human, Half-Dog Hybrid," from Pierre Boaistuau, *Histoires Prodigieuses* (1560)	143
5.5	"Animal-Human Hybrids," from Fortunio Liceti, *De Monstris* (1665)	144
5.6	"Half-Human, Half-Dog Conjoined Twins," from Fortunio Liceti, *De Monstris* (1665)	144
6.1	Abraham Ortelius's map of "The Kingdome of Naples" (1603)	161
6.2	*Il Paese di Cuchagnia*, a fanciful eighteenth-century print of the land of plenty with capons that rain down from the sky, a mountain of cheese, and a wine-spouting fountain	167
7.1	Gabrina casts a spell over Isabella as a devil enters the room from *Le tredici piacevolissime notte* (1608)	179
7.2	Master of the Die (1530–60), Lucius the ass overhears the old woman recounting the tale of Cupid and Psyche, sixteenth-century engraving	182
8.1	Costantino Fortunato and his enchanted cat from *Le tredici piacevolissime notte* (1608)	197
8.2	A second slave named Lucia, from Basile's "The Three Citrons," mistakes the fairy's image for her own in the fountain, by Warwick Goble in *Stories from the Pentamerone* (1911)	209

SERIES PREFACE

Taking a transnational approach, *A Cultural History of Fairy Tales* seeks to deepen our appreciation for and knowledge about a type of *text* (understood in the broadest sense of the term) that is often taken for granted due to its association with children's literature, old wives' tales, and oral peasant culture. Whether we think of the Brothers Grimm or films by Walt Disney Studios, fairy tales are often viewed as naïve and timeless stories with universal appeal, which suggests they are ahistorical, innocent narratives. This series brings together scholars from a diversity of disciplines to challenge many of these preconceptions about the fairy tale, shedding light on its very complex cultural history.

The chapters included in these six volumes foreground how the fairy tale was deployed in different historical periods and geographical locations for all kinds of cultural, social, and political ends that cross categories of class, age, gender, and ethnicity. "Fairy tale" here serves as a broad umbrella term for what more generally could be referred to as "wonder tale," which encompasses but is not limited to texts that feature fairies, witches, enchanters, djinn, and other beings endowed with magical or supernatural powers; anthropomorphized animals; metamorphosis (humans transformed into animals or other objects and vice versa); magical objects; and otherworlds and liminal spaces. "Fairy tale" also refers to texts that may not include any of these qualities but have been received as—that is, read or categorized as or are generally considered to be—a fairy tale.

By moving from antiquity to the present and transnationally, chapters crossing the six volumes foreground, for instance, how ancient animal fables present both continuities and discontinuities with the representation of animals in later wonder tales; how conceptions of fairies, djinn, and other magical characters change across historical periods and geographical locations; and how the very notion of what is marvelous, natural, or supernatural is understood differently across space and time. Chapters showcase the range of different types of characters and themes one can find in wonder tales as well as the multiple forms and functions tales can take. Together these volumes paint a broad picture of the ways in which different national tale traditions interact with and mutually influence each other, giving us a transnational and transhistorical understanding of the fairy tale. Indeed, readers will discover the rich, complex, and often ideologically charged cultural history of texts that can seem so familiar to us, which helps us understand them in new and exciting ways.

All six volumes cover the same eight themes for the reader to gain a sense of continuities and discontinuities between types of characters, narratives, and traditions over time. Readers will move from *forms* of the fairy tale and the ancillary genres that fed into it to the history of *adaptations*, revealing the ways in which tales are always already a blend of multiple local, regional, and national traditions. A genre often focusing on questions related to development and initiation into adulthood and sometimes (less than we might think) concluding with marriage, tales often feature the norms of *gender and sexuality* grounded in a particular culture. Through the prevalence of non-human characters and problematic human figures, the fairy tale allows for the exploration of the boundaries between *the human and the non-human*, as well as between what is considered normal and *monsters or the monstrous*. As a nonmimetic genre, generally speaking, the fairy tale also plays with the delimitations between real and imaginary *spaces*, opening up both utopic and dystopic possibilities. Tales have often been used in the processes of *socialization*, for both children and adults, men and women, articulating class, gender, and ethnic differences. As such, tales cannot be separated from questions of *power* and ideology.

This cultural history of the fairy tale is divided into the following historical periods:

Volume 1: A Cultural History of Fairy Tales in Antiquity (500 BCE–800 CE)

Volume 2: A Cultural History of Fairy Tales in the Middle Ages (800–1450)

Volume 3: A Cultural History of Fairy Tales in the Age of the Marvelous (1450–1650)

Volume 4: A Cultural History of Fairy Tales in the Long Eighteenth Century (1650–1800)

Volume 5: A Cultural History of Fairy Tales in the Long Nineteenth Century (1800–1920)

Volume 6: A Cultural History of Fairy Tales in the Modern Age (1920–2000+)

Readers will come away with a new and fresh understanding of the fairy tale, which indeed enhances our appreciation for a genre that has touched many of us since childhood. Far from being naïve, innocent, timeless texts, *A Cultural History of Fairy Tales* foregrounds the ways wonder tales are embedded in sophisticated social, cultural, political, and artistic practices across history, anchored in specific cultural contexts that shape their meaning as tales are adapted from one cultural and historical context to another.

Anne E. Duggan, *General Editor*

Introduction

Fairy Tales in the Age of the Marvelous

SUZANNE MAGNANINI

As any reader of the genre knows, fairy tales brim with marvelous motifs: animal helpers who speak readily; revivifying waters and restorative elixirs; cloaks of invisibility and seven-league boots; and magic that turns people into frogs, pigs, and serpents and back again. Enchantment also propels the plots forward. Fairies and other magical beings create or remove obstacles; ogres and dragons serve as foils to heroes and heroines and their defeat proves the protagonists' worthiness; astounding metamorphoses alter characters' physical form or social and economic status. For these reasons, no matter their theoretical orientation or field of study, contemporary scholars have distinguished the fairy tale from other sorts of stories by the presence and function of marvels and magic in the plot. For example, among the Russian formalist Vladimir Propp's thirty-one functions, or characters' actions, that comprise all fairy-tale plots, we find listed for function seven regarding tricksters, magical agents (witches), and the marvelous metamorphosis of characters (a dragon becomes a golden goat) ([1928] 1996: 29). In his classification of folktales that builds upon the work of folklorists Antti Aarne and Stith Thompson, Hans-Jörg Uther classifies the majority of fairy tales in the category named "Tales of Magic," although some plots can be found in "Religious Tales," where God, angels, and devils do the work of fairies, blessing or condemning, bestowing gifts, or facilitating transformations that usher in happy endings (Uther 2004). In the volume *Wonder Tales: Six French Stories of Enchantment* Marina Warner notes that "more than the deeds of fairies, wonders characterise fairy tales" ([1994] 2004: 4). In endeavoring to answer the question "What is a fairy tale?" Maria Tatar observes that "the presence of enchantment is perhaps the defining feature of the genre" (2019: 16).

It is perhaps not surprising, then, that histories and anthologies of the European literary fairy tale often begin in the age of the marvelous (1450–1650), a period during which scientific, economic, religious, and aesthetic upheavals spurred an intense fascination with marvels and wonder.[1] Of course, humans' interest in marvels transcends geographical and historical boundaries, and wonder tales proliferated in this period in other parts of the world such as the Islamicate Mediterranean and Asia, as N. İpek Hüner Cora and Laura Nüffer demonstrate in Chapters 2 and 4 in this volume. In these two centuries, however, Europeans experienced a heightened fascination with marvels and the marvelous, the very elements often cited to distinguish fairy tales from other sorts of narratives. New World encounters brought together European and indigenous peoples and cultures of the Americas for the first time (Greenblatt 1991). Wondrous flora and fauna entered early modern European museums and cabinets of curiosities where they were placed beside artifacts held to be unicorn horns or the skins of dragons (Findlen 1994). During the fifteenth century, humanists' impulse to recuperate the texts of the classical world revived interest in the wonders that abounded in scientific and literary works of ancient Greece and Rome, such as Pliny's monstrous races. By the seventeenth century new modes and methods of inquiry were challenging the wisdom of the ancients. Improvements in optics brought previously unseen worlds into view: through their telescopes astronomers, for instance Johannes Kepler and Galileo Galilei, perceived new features on heavenly bodies, while primitive microscopes revealed tiny life-forms that the ancient Greeks and Romans never imagined. Both innovative optical devices and travel would eventually radically change the maps of Earth and the universe, and new notions of humanity's relation to space on earth and in the heavens would slowly emerge, as Davide Papotti explains in Chapter 6. In literary academies, the rediscovery and translation into European vernacular language of Aristotle's *Poetics*, which called for both mimesis and the marvelous in literary texts, sparked debates on what should be the proper balance of the two in literature (Hathaway 1968: 9). Eventually, a new baroque poetics of the marvelous emerged according to which creating wonder in the reader was the explicit goal of the poet. Throughout Europe, Catholics and Protestants warred over the presence and function of the miraculous in religious life, but shared disdain for what they perceived to be the diabolical—but marvelous—practices of witches and necromancers, who, like the fairies in fictional tales, seemed to possess the power to induce shape-shifting and to bring the dead back to life, subjects that Kathleen Long explores more fully in Chapter 5. Fueling the proliferation and circulation of all these marvels was a wonder of information technology: the printing press with moveable type. Printed texts moved images, descriptions, and discussions of marvels with greater speed across a wider geographic area.

The mobility of marvels, however, was not just across geographical borders but also across what today often seem impassable boundaries dividing intellectual fields of inquiry from each other. At a time when "science" often simply meant "knowledge," less narrowly defined fields of study helped marvels to flow easily across what are today entrenched epistemological boundaries. For example, hydras, multi-cephalic dragons with regenerative powers, appeared as formidable foes to the heroes of classical myths: Hercules slays the hydra of Lerna as one of his labors (Figure 0.1).[2]

In these same years, hydras appeared as portents and objects of trade in prodigy books such as the Alsatian humanist Conrad Lycosthenes's *Prodigiorum ac ostentorum chronicon* (1557). Without mentioning the portent's significance, Lycosthenes describes the hydra as having been carried from Turkey to Venice in 1530 and then to King Francis I of France; he estimates its worth at 6,000 ducats (Figure 0.2). This same story was retold in Pierre Boaistuau's

FIGURE 0.1: Hercules and his nephew Iolaus slay the hydra, by German printmaker Hans Sebald Beham (1545). From The New York Public Library, https://digitalcollections.nypl.org/items/1ac90330-64a4-0133-d359-00505686a51c.

FIGURE 0.2: A hydra brought from the Ottoman Empire to Venice in 1530, from Conrad Lycosthenes, *Prodigiorum ac ostentorum chronicon* (1557). Courtesy of the Newberry Library, Chicago. Public domain.

Histoire Prodigieuses (1560), a prodigy book aimed at spiritually reforming its readers, and volumes of natural history written by physician Konrad Gesner in Switzerland (1558), Edward Topsell in England (1608), and the naturalist and collector Ulisse Aldrovandi in Italy (1640). Early modern scientists such as Aldrovandi occasionally attested to having examined dragons caught just outside their city's walls, but more often than not refuted the existence of hydras in nature in their illustrated tomes of natural history, where they also attested to the existence of "fake" hydras and dragons, creative taxidermy displayed in early modern museums and court collections, or by charlatans at the fair. Giambattista Basile plays with these multiple identities of this monster in his tale "The Merchant" in his *Lo cunto de li cunti* (*The Tale of Tales*, 1634–6), which was written in Neapolitan dialect and published under his pseudonym Gian Alessio Abbattutis. Basile's hapless hero Cienzo decapitates a creature whose description more closely resembles that of an artificial hydra crafted by a taxidermist and displayed in a court collection than a fearsome beast (Magnanini 2008: 117–43).

While fairy-tale creatures such as dragons and hydras moved fluidly across diverse spaces and texts, scientific and literary marvels blended together in equally interesting ways. When Johannes Kepler sought to circulate his scientific findings regarding lunar astronomy and avoid the Catholic Church's censorship of ideas that supported Copernican theories, he incorporated his calculations and observations in a fantastic Latin novel, *Somnium* (*Dream*) that features witches, daemons, and marvelous travel from the earth to the moon (Kepler [1634] 1965). The poet and literary theorist Emanuele Tesauro titled his treatise on wondrous metaphors *Il cannocchiale aristotelico* (The Aristotelian Telescope, 1654). The title page featured an engraving of a woman, an allegory of Poetry, gazing through a telescope at sunspots as the Greek philosopher Aristotle stands beside her, while her companion Painting paints an anamorphic image that is legible in a reflecting cone depicted on the canvas.[3]

At the same time, the borders circumscribing literary fairy tales were not yet firmly established, the rules for their creation or identification were not yet definitively written.[4] In fact, a number of different literary genres shared plots and motifs with the fairy tale. For example, dragon-slayer plots appeared in fairy tales such as Basile's and Jocabus de Voragine's thirteenth-century *Legenda aurea* (*The Golden Legend*), a collection of saints lives still widely read during the Renaissance. In the biographies of the Saints George and Martha, the dragon slayer is rewarded by the conversion of infidels rather than a royal marriage (Voragine [13th c.] 2012: 238–42, 409–12). Tales of virtuous maidens without hands were performed as *sacre rappresentazioni* (religious dramas), included in prose tale collections, and printed in verse in chapbooks. Many of the magic motifs so central to fairy tales—magic rings, sorcerers, and dragons—also appeared in chivalric epic poems created in Italian courts that were elaborations of the popular tradition of tales of knights and ladies found in medieval romances. And at least one poet, the Florentine Lorenzo Lippi, inserted three of Basile's fairy tales into his comic epic *Il Malmantile racquistato* (Malmantile Reconquered, 1676). In the first chapter of this volume Kevin Pask shows that fairy-tale motifs of riddles and rings also found their way onto English stage through Shakespeare's plays. And, of course, in other parts of the world, fairy tales assumed diverse forms, such as the Japanese *otogizōshi* (see Chapter 4, this volume) and the prose tales of the Ottoman Empire (see Chapter 2, this volume).

Although, as Volumes 1 and 2 in *A Cultural History of the Fairy Tale* attest, fairy tales existed long before the age of the marvelous, contemporary anthologies and histories of the European fairy tale—despite presenting differing views on the genre's origins—often locate its beginnings in Italy in this period with the publication of Giovan Francesco Straparola's *Le piacevoli notti* (*The Pleasant Nights*) (Venice, 1550–3) and Giambattista Basile's *Lo cunto de li cunti, overo lo trattenemiento de peccerille* (*The Tale of Tales, or Entertainment for the Little Ones*) (Naples, 1634–6), also known as the *Pentamerone* (Bottigheimer 2002, 2009; Canepa 1997, 1999; Zipes 2000c). If French tales dominate the long eighteenth century, and the German tales of the Brothers Grimm inform many discussions of fairy tales in the nineteenth century, the years 1450 to 1650 were the centuries when Italian authors made their mark on the genre.

All canons are created by a backward glance firmly planted in a present. And when the nineteenth-century folklorists and tale collectors who helped shape the contemporary fairy-tale canon looked back, they recognized familiar forms and tale types in Straparola's Italian and Basile's Neapolitan dialect tales, even if the context and some of the content might have appeared alien. Both Straparola and Basile penned short prose narratives embedded in frame tales animated by narrators who used their stories to entertain and to illustrate moral lessons or proverbs. Their tales included stories belonging to tale types that are still well known today: "Puss in Boots," "Cinderella," "Sleeping Beauty," "Beauty and the Beast," and "Rapunzel." For contemporary readers, however, Straparola's and Basile's versions of these familiar plots are often shocking: Straparola's beastly King Pig murders his first two wives before falling in love with his "Beauty"; Basile's Cinderella murders her first stepmother by breaking her neck, and his Sleeping Beauty marries the king who had raped and impregnated her while she slept, but only after he executes his first wife. Armando Maggi has referred to these violent and sexually explicit stories as "dirty" tales, as opposed to the sanitized tales we often encounter today, such as those created by Walt Disney (Maggi 2015: 9–10). It is in this Italian dirt that the French and German tales that would become popular worldwide in subsequent centuries, as well as other European national traditions, took root and grew. In Chapter 5, Kathleen Long provides a nuanced discussion on how Straparola's tales were transplanted on French soil, as she explores representations of monstrosity.

The Italian Peninsula proved such fertile ground for the literary fairy tale to blossom in this period for a number of reasons. First, from the fourteenth to the sixteenth centuries, prominent members of Italian literary culture such as Cardinal Pietro Bembo, author of *Prose della volgare lingua* (On the Vernacular Language, 1525), promoted Giovanni Boccaccio's *Decameron* as both the literary and linguistic model for authors wishing to write in prose. The *Decameron* (c. 1353) is a collection of one hundred novellas, or realistic tales, circumscribed by an overarching narrative in which a group of ten young Florentines quarantine during the plague of 1348 and amuse themselves by telling stories for ten days. Though the *Decameron* contains no fairy tales, the twin impulses of writers in this period to imitate and experiment brought new frames for storytelling and new sorts of stories, including fairy tales, into print. Boccaccio's shadow looms large in both Straparola's and Basile's texts. Straparola copies phrases and paragraphs, as well as an entire tale (night 9, tale 2), from the *Decameron* in *The Pleasant Nights*.[5] Basile reworks elements from Boccaccio's novellas for his own fairy tales, albeit in a distorting and parodic manner (Ansani 1997). For this reason, as well as the five-day structure of the frame narrative, the first editor of *The Tale of Tales*, and perhaps Basile himself, referred to the collection as the *Pentamerone*, which would become the title of some subsequent editions. It was Straparola's and Basile's innovation of including fairy tales, however, that made readers cherish their texts. Finally, many Italian cities, such as Venice, boasted a thriving print trade with printers who were always on the lookout for novel works to capture readers in an expanding literary marketplace.

In the pages that follow, I examine three Italian persecuted maiden tales: the blacksmith poet Francesco Corna da Soncino's verse tale *Historia della Regina Oliva* (History of Queen Oliva, 1487), the sixteenth-century anonymous verse tale *Historia della Regina Stella e Mattabruna* (History of Queen Stella and Mattabruna), and Basile's "Penta la mano-mozza" ("Penta with the Chopped-Off Hands," day 3, tale 2), in *The Tale of Tales*. My aim is to provide readers of this volume with a better idea of the contours of the fairy tales created in the age of the marvelous. Fairy-tale wonders were not limited to our contemporary repertoire that includes glass slippers, magic potions, and enchanted and enchanting fairies, but extended to the sorts of marvels that could also be found in medical or scientific treatises, religious texts, and handbooks on baroque poetics of the marvelous. These three tales illustrate clearly the blurring of boundaries circumscribing fairy tales, saints' legends, and chivalric epics. Although often associated with children in this period—Basile's text was subtitled "Entertainment for the Little Ones"—the fairy tale was not yet primarily a didactic literature, as I explain in Chapter 7. Finally, my analysis focuses on how fantastic fairy tales examined the very real issues of physical, psychological, and sexual violence, as they related to gender, race, power, and religious faith through a close reading of Basile's persecuted maiden tale. The chapters that follow this introduction continue this work in greater depth and reveal the malleability of a genre that assumed diverse forms and utilized the marvelous to explore society's pressing issues from various angles.

THREE PERSECUTED MAIDENS: ADAPTATIONS AND FORMS

In Basile's fairy tale "Penta mano-mozza," when Penta's brother insists on marrying her, she has her hands chopped off to avert his incestuous desire. Enraged, he puts her in a chest and throws her into the sea. Now handless, she will begin to change hands. First, she is found by a fisherman whose jealous wife Nuccia casts Penta back on the waves. Next, the king of Green Earth finds her adrift and takes her in. To fulfill his dying wife's wish, the king will eventually, begrudgingly, marry Penta who is for him "a writing box full of amorous joys" without "handles" (Basile [1634–6][2007] 2016: 218). When the king travels abroad, Penta gives birth to a male heir. The fisherman's wife Nuccia manages to intercept the correspondence carried by a messenger between the king and his courtiers. She first misinforms the king that his wife has birthed a wolf dog and then, with another falsified letter, makes the courtiers believe they must burn the mother and child at the stake. Taking pity, the courtiers instead banish Penta and her child. When she arrives at Torbid Lake and tells her sad tale to the sorcerer, he graciously provides her with shelter and support. Moved to tears by her tragic tale, the sorcerer then yearns to hear more sad stories and offers a scepter and crown to whomever will tell the greatest tale of misfortune. Penta's brother and husband appear before the sorcerer and tell their own stories. Reunited happily with her family, Penta then regains her hands thanks to the sorcerer's magic.

Stories of persecuted maidens such as Basile's allow us to consider how what are today considered classic fairy-tale marvels tumbled and mixed with religious miracles, scientific wonders, and poetic marvels in tales created during the age of the marvelous. Basile's tale belongs to a long tradition of persecuted maiden tales that includes a number of different tale types and stretches back to antiquity, such as the tale of Cupid and Psyche in Apuleius's *The Metamorphoses, or The Golden Ass.* Psyche endures much suffering at the hands of her jealous mother-in-law Venus, including being beaten, being forced to venture into the underworld, and to complete other impossible tasks. Like Penta, the serpent-god Amewakahiko's wife in the Japanese tale *The Seventh Night* (*Tanabata*) similarly underwent a series of trials at the hands of her ogre father-in-law, as Laura Nüffer describes in Chapter 4. And, as N. İpek Hüner Cora describes in Chapter 2, in one Ottoman tale from this period, it is a prince, rather than a princess, who is forced to endure numerous hardships as he travels from island to island. Medieval romances recounting the trials of suffering maidens, such as *La Belle Hélène de Constantinople, Roman de la Manekine,* and the Middle English Constance saga, enjoyed great popularity throughout Europe, and their literary lineage has been well documented (Beecher 2012: 1:434–55; Marchi 1998: 18–33; Ronco n.d.: 5–6). Many of these medieval and early modern persecuted maidens, who patiently endure a torrent of physical, sexual, and psychological abuse, closely resembled the female martyrs of saints' legends. Indeed, in Uther's classification of folktales, the tale type of "Maidens Without Hands" (ATU 706) includes both secular and religious variations: "The Father Who Wanted to Marry his Daughter" (706C), "The Chaste Nun" (706B), and "St. Wilgefort and Her Beard" (706D) (Uther 2004: 284, 378–82). Sometimes seemingly secular tale types, for instance ATU 707, "The Three Golden Children," to which the story of Queen Stella and Mattabruna examined here belongs, included religious miracles, as well as marvelous motifs typical of the chivalric epic.

Marina Warner has called fairy tales "second order narrative," for the genre is more about retelling a story rather than inventing something new (2014: xvii). Thus, all fairy-tale authors are to some extent adaptors, reinterpreting, salvaging, in order to create a different text, to use Linda Hutcheon's terms (2006: 8). While N. İpek Hüner Cora's Chapter 2 provides many fascinating insights into how adaptation functioned in the Ottoman Empire, here I will examine how Basile adapts what was the widely known story of Queen or Saint Oliva (or Uliva), which was recounted frequently during the age of the marvelous in various genres, including as a *sacra rappresentazione* or religious play (D'Ancona 1863); as a prose legend (Wessolofsky 1866); and as verse tale chapbook that was reprinted in different versions at least sixteen times between the fourteenth and seventeenth centuries (Marchi 1998: 44–50).

Chapbooks in verse, called *cantari* in Italian, were short narratives cheaply printed on a few pages oftentimes with one or two woodblock illustrations (see Figure 0.3). All sorts of tales circulated in this format, including religious texts, stories of the exploits of knights drawn from medieval romances, classical myths, ghost stories, news of world events, and a number of fairy tales. Beside the two fairy tales examined below, this latter group included the tale of Lionbruno with his seven-league boots, the story of the rustic trickster Campriano, and tales of the marvelous land of plenty, Cuccagna or Cockaigne, where sausage trees, macaroni mountains, and rivers of wine kept everyone well fed without working at all (Rubini 2007: 437–9). Chapbooks moved tales from more learned collections of tales modeled on the *Decameron* into public squares and across national borders in a more affordable format. Many of Boccaccio's tales, including those of patient Griselda and wily Masetto who seduces an entire convent of nuns, were reprinted in verse throughout the sixteenth century in Italy (420).[6] Straparola's fairy tale about Dionigi, a sorcerer's apprentice who bests his master Lattanzio, was adapted by the English actor Robert Armin and printed as a verse chapbook in London in 1609, entitled *The Italian Tailor and His Boy*. Chapbooks enjoyed popularity with readers from all strata of society, and thus ensured the multidirectional flow of tales from the public square to the royal court and back again, crossing class and cultural lines. For example, the learned female interlocutors in Moderata Fonte's proto-feminist dialogue *Il merito delle donne* (*The Worth of Women*, 1600), show their knowledge of both canonical tales and chapbooks by easily referencing tales from Boccaccio's *Decameron* and the fairy-tale chapbook *Lionbruno* using only the characters' first names, assuming that their listeners will immediately identify the references (Fonte [1600] 1997: 59, 73).

MARVELOUS MACHINES AND HOLY MIRACLES

Although many chapbooks were printed anonymously, some bore the names of their authors. Such was the case for the *Historia di Regina Oliva* (History of Queen Oliva), which reveals the identity of the author in the final octaves, Francesco Corna da Soncino. Corna was a blacksmith and poet whose only other extant text chronicled the history and treasures of his adopted city, Verona (Marchi 1998: 9). Although Corna refers to his protagonist Oliva as a "precious saint" in the opening lines of his poem, it is first and foremost the maiden's mechanical ingenuity, not prayer, that saves her from her father's incestuous desire. When the emperor Juliano proposes marriage to his daughter Oliva, claiming that the Pope will grant a dispensation for this incestuous union, she is desperate to deflect his advances. After learning that her beautiful hands have ignited his perverse yearnings, and finding that her words fail to deter him, she enters the kitchen and constructs a marvel of engineering that will cleanly lop off both her hands with one blow: "with certain counterweights she knew to make / the knife slide in the frame / and chopped off both hands from her arms " (Corna [1487] 1998: 55).[7] Perhaps Corna's own experience as a blacksmith helped him imagine such an ingenious machine, for it does not appear in other versions of the tale. In the fifteenth-century anonymous prose legend, *La figlia del re di Dacia* (The Daughter of the King of Dacia), after praying, the persecuted Eilisa has a vision in which she is instructed to slice off the hand that was defiled when her father made her touch him after being tempted by a devil (Wesselofsky 1866: 5). In the first act of the sixteenth-century religious drama, *La rappresentazione di Santa Uliva,* Uliva manages the amputation herself after praying to Jesus Christ and the Virgin Mary. With this holy assistance, she cuts off both hands in one blow to counter her father's incestuous desires, which she terms "the work of the devil" (D'Ancona 1863). Corna's protagonist invents her own ingenious device for the amputation, a testament to both her wit and agency. The marvelous miniature guillotine that Oliva constructs recalls the Renaissance machines invented by Leonardo da Vinci that similarly employed counterweights, such as his catapults, clocks, and cranes. Despite her engineering prowess, throughout the rest of the poem Oliva depends primarily on divine intervention, miracles wrought by prayer, to save herself. When Corna's Oliva revives after fainting post-amputation, she immediately prays to Christ, who along with the Virgin Mary will answer her prayers by providing protection and safe passage as she moves from one trial to the next.

If persecuted maidens such as Eilisa, Uliva, and Corna's Oliva can depend heavily upon prayer and divine intervention, Basile's Penta is bereft of such spiritual comforts. The Brothers Grimm, who greatly admired Basile's text and saw it as a precursor of their own collection of tales, were surprised to find that the Neapolitan's tales were devoid of Christian references (Maggi 2015: 66). Although God and the saints abandoned Basile's tales, the devil remains, albeit in a more literary than spiritual form. In fact, "Penta with the Chopped-off Hands" begins with a demonic possession of sorts. A "farfariello," or little devil, puts the idea to wed his sister in the head of the king of Dry Rock. Devils named "Farfariello" appear in an array of Italian literary texts from Dante's *Inferno* (Canto 26) to Luigi Pulci's chivalric epic *Morgante* (1483) to Straparola's *The Pleasant Nights* (night 7, tale 1) (Bonomo 1958: 368), and thus Basile imparts to his nameless demon (farfariello is a common noun here) an impressive literary, rather than spiritual, genealogy.

MARVELOUS LANGUAGE

The king's declaration of his perverted intentions toward his sister Penta, however, seems less lustfully demonic than purely practical, and he describes their future union through a series of decidedly unromantic metaphors related to the combinatory work of artisans, merchants, lawyers, and apothecaries: "Be content, then, to make this inlay, this shopkeeper's agreement, this *uniantur acta,* this *misce et fiat potum,* and both of us will see good days" (Basile [1634–6][2007] 2016: 215). Penta's response is swift, strong, and indignant and she counters his metaphors of productive, profitable unions with another series of images of inappropriate admixtures. After this outburst, she locks herself in a room for more than a month, and then, still perplexed by his demands, she reappears to question her brother's incestuous desire. Penta says, "I have looked long and hard at myself in the mirror, and I have found nothing in this face that could merit your love, since I am not such a delectable morsel that I send people into fits" (216). As in all the "Maiden Without Hands" tales examined here, the king dismisses her assessment, stating that Penta is beautiful and flawless from head to toe, but her hand is the cause of his infatuation. Now, we might expect an ode to her white, delicate hand to follow, one based on Petrarch's versified fetishizing of Laura's hands and the gloves that cover them in sonnets 199 to 201, or something akin to what we find in private letters written in the period praising a beloved's ivory hands (Feng 2017: 170–1). The king of Dry Rock, however, compares Penta's hand not to ivory but to quotidian utensils that manipulate his heart and soul: a serving fork, a hook, a vise, a ladle, pincers, and a bat or stick (Basile [1634–6][2007] 2016: 216).

These complex metaphors with which the siblings spar represent yet another wonder in Basile's text: his baroque literary aesthetics. One of the greatest poets in Basile's day, fellow Neapolitan Giambattista Marino (1569–1625) opined that "marvel is the poet's objective" (cited in Battistini 1997: 479).[8] In the literary treatise *Il cannocchiale aristotelico* (The Aristotelian Telescope, 1654), Emanuale Tesauro championed the "metafora ingegnosa" (ingenious metaphor) arising from the poet's keen wit, which juxtaposed two seemingly unrelated objects or concepts in a surprising way. For Tesauro, it was these unexpected juxtapositions, of the sort we have seen in Basile's text, that generated wonder in the reader (Battistini 1997: 479). Thus, Basile creates a sense of wonder through both the marvels contained in his tales—fairies, dragons, speaking animals—as well as through the language with which he describes them. As Nancy Canepa remarks, the function and presence of metamorphosis in Basile's tales "also extends to the figural level, where Basile's exuberant use of metaphor reworks the familiar language of literary tradition into a marvelous 'new' literary language" (Canepa 1999: 24–5).

Although Penta's verbal exchanges with her brother generate wonder, the scene of amputation does not. No marvelous metaphors describe the violent act; no miracles occur; and no wonderful contraption is employed, despite the fact that technological wonders—automatons, telescopes—appear in many other of Basile's tales. Instead, in the midst of their discussion, Penta abruptly interrupts her brother, promising to return in a minute:

> And she went back to her room and called for a slave who didn't have much of a brain, handed him a large knife and a handful of old coins, and said, "My dear Ali, you cut my hands, me want make nice formula and get more white!" The slave, thinking he was doing her a favor, cut them clean off with two blows. She had them placed on a Faenza platter and sent them, covered with a silk cloth, to her brother, with the message that he should enjoy what he most desired, along with good health and baby boys.
> (Basile [1634–6][2007] 2016: 216)

Quite an insult for a man whose own title, king of Dry Rock, points toward sterility. In response, Penta's brother will cast his handless sibling into the sea in a chest, condemning her to an uncertain future.

DISABILITY AS WONDER

In Corna's poem Oliva's lack of hands figures as a disability that limits her activities. Furthermore, her mutilated body makes her the credible target of false accusations. After amputating her own hands to avoid her father's incestuous advances, Oliva escapes death by convincing her father's servants who have brought her into the woods to spare her life rather than carry out the king's death sentence. Wandering alone in the forest, she is eventually found by the king of Catelonia, thanks to the will of the Virgin Mary. The king sends her to his wife the queen, who finds her to be very knowledgeable about various arts, and although her disability prevents her from practicing these skills, she teaches them to others: "trained in many arts and trades, / and because she could not work / she taught the young girls to embroider" (Corna

[1487] 1998: 58).⁹ When the queen gives birth to a male heir the virtuous Oliva is chosen to oversee the newborn prince's care while he is at the wet nurse far from the castle. There, a vicar falls in love with beautiful Oliva and assaults her when she refuses to yield to his advances. During the attack she drops the infant, who dies. First the lying vicar and then the king both blame the tragedy on her disability. Although the true cause for the boy's death is the vicar's lust and violence, Oliva's lack of hands is twice depicted as the defect that leads to the child's death.

Penta also experiences similar trials once she leaves her brother's kingdom, but Basile turns her disability into a sort of marvel. Penta instills wonder and admiration in those who watch her complete tasks that usually require hands: "she did every imaginable job with her feet, even sewing, threading a needle, starching collars, and combing the queen's hair, and for this she was held as dear as a daughter" (Basile [1634–6][2007] 2016: 218). Penta's actions are akin to those marvelous performances of armless individuals described in the French surgeon Ambroise Paré's *On Monsters and Marvels* (1573), including an armless woman from Paris "who cut cloth and sewed and performed several other actions" ([1575] 1982: 37) and a man who "performed almost all the actions that another might do with his hands … he could make a carter's whip snap … and with his feet he ate, drank, and played cards and dice" (36).

Although in many other handless maiden tales, the woman's hands are restored before her marriage to the king, Basile leaves Penta handless until the very end of the story. In Basile's tale, Penta remains a sort of freak, with all the ambiguity that status implies. Her ability to perform tasks with her feet marks her as a wonder, but her lack of hands renders her less desirable than other women. Although the queen loves Penta like a daughter and extracts a promise from her husband that he will marry the handless maiden should she die, he only begrudgingly promises to marry Penta, saying, "'it does not matter to me that she is scrawny and without hands, for one should always take only a small amount of the unpleasant.' But he mumbled these last words under his breath so that his wife wouldn't hear them" (Basile [1634–6][2007] 2016: 219). After the queen's death, on their wedding night, the king "grafted a baby boy onto" Penta (219). It is the birth of this child that will bring about Penta's next trial, for when she gives birth and the king is away at war, Penta will be accused of having given birth to a wolf dog.

THE BIRTH OF MONSTERS

It is this accusation of monstrous birth on the part of a jealous woman that links Basile's and Corna's maidens without hands to the suffering protagonist in *The Story of Queen Stella and Mattabruna*, an anonymous chapbook reprinted multiple times between the fifteenth and seventeenth centuries, and into the nineteenth (Figure 0.3).¹⁰

FIGURE 0.3: The title page of *History of Queen Stella and Mattabruna*, an anonymous nineteenth-century chapbook printed in Naples. Public domain.

In the tale of Queen Stella, God, Jesus, and angels intervene as they did in the tale of Queen Oliva, to further the progress of the persecuted maiden and her children toward a happy ending that restores justice by punishing the evildoer. While these aspects of the tale resemble a saint's legend, the marvels in this story range from typical fairy-tale motifs (children born with silver necklaces) to accusations of bestiality and the birth of animal-human hybrids that could be found in medical texts and prodigy books printed in the period.

The tale begins with King Orcano married to beautiful Queen Stella who is despised by her mother-in-law Mattabruna. One day the king spies a woman walking hand in hand with her children in the street and wishes that his wife were pregnant, a wish that the Virgin Mary grants. When Stella is about to give birth, Mattabruna dismisses all the servants in the household to carry out her evil plan. Stella gives birth to four children born with silver chains about their necks, three boys and a girl, whom Mattabruna removes immediately after their birth and replaces with four puppies. Mattabruna gives the babies to a servant named Guido whom she instructs to drown the children. Unable to commit the atrocity, Guido prays, makes the sign of the cross, and abandons the children on a riverbank where they are found by a religious hermit. Back at the court, Mattabruna informs the king that his wife has given birth to four dogs. The king can't quite believe his mother's words and resists her suggestion that he kill his wife. Instead, after praying to God, the king decides to imprison Stella.

Persecuted maidens are often accused of having given birth to deformed offspring or animal-human hybrids, an act that suggests some sort of reproductive crime which is rarely explicitly articulated, but instead simmers just beneath the surface of the tale. In Corna's poem, Oliva's mother-in-law first substitutes the court's letter that joyfully announces the birth of a healthy male heir with a letter declaring the Queen has given birth to a deformed child "laido, mal facto e tutto sfegurato" ("filthy, deformed, and completely disfigured," Corna [1487] 1998: 64). Next she substitutes the king's measured response to the false letter announcing the anomalous birth that the courtiers should await his return, with another false missive ordering that the mother and child be burned. Basile's king of Green Earth takes an even more generous approach to the falsified letter he receives, which states that Penta has given birth to a "wolf dog." Rather than denounce her, he placidly writes back "that they should keep the queen in good spirits and that she should not have a dram of displeasure, since these things happened by license of the heavens and a respectable man must not try to rearrange the stars" (Basile [1634–6][2007] 2016: 220). In the story of Queen Stella, the accusation of bestiality becomes an explicit charge rather than a conclusion suggested by somatic abnormality.

And those puppies she placed at her side
Screaming loudly with harsh words,
Saying "Whore, with whom did you reproduce?
You've been adulterous with a dog
I promise you that by blessed God above,
I'll kill you with my own hands!"
And in this way, so enraged,
She left the room screaming.
(*Historia della Regina Stella*, sixteenth century)[11]

Mattabruna's excoriation of Stella continues once the king has agreed to imprison her, for she enters Stella's chamber pulling the beautiful queen from the bed by her hair, kicking and punching her while yelling "falsa meretrice" (false harlot), causing Stella to weep copiously.

Mattabruna's accusations that bestial copulation brought forth animal offspring to a human mother might seem ludicrous to contemporary readers, but these charges of sexual impropriety were often repeated in scientific texts of the period, with illustrations of the monstrous offspring visually testifying to the mother's sins (see Figures 5.4, 5.5, and 5.6). No consensus existed, however, regarding whether such births were possible either by biological or demonic means. Some, such as the humanist Sperone Speroni, viewed the female body as capable of bringing forth all sorts of monstrosities, as capable of making *favole*, fables or fairy tales, come true by giving birth to up to seventy offspring at once, elephants and snakes, minotaurs and hippocentaurs (Speroni 1558: 53r). Others, such as Benedetto Varchi, invoking Aristotle's theories on generation, doubted that such unions between creatures with wildly diverse somatic types could ever produce offspring. For Varchi, those who claimed such things to be true had been deceived by appearances (Varchi [1548] 1858: 2:666). Regardless of their scientific stance on interspecies generation, the authors of these works unanimously denounced bestiality, a sin viewed as far worse than other sexual transgressions. To some degree Christianity distinguished itself from pagan religions by redefining the relationship between the animal and the human. By the thirteenth century, Thomas Aquinas viewed bestiality as the most grievous of unnatural sexual sins, while the theologian Alexander of Hales argued that both the animal and human partners must be killed to "erase the memory of the act with the participants" (Salisbury 1994: 99). Thus, suggestions or accusations of improper coupling, seemingly supported by the presence of malformed offspring, proved a highly effective tool for envious women who wished to discredit their daughters-in-law. As Laura Nüffer shows in Chapter 4, for Buddhists, tales of animal-human marriages evoked a different set of concerns.

AMAZING ENDINGS: SAINTS, GIANT KILLERS, AND SORCERERS

It is often said that in fairy tales magic brings about the happily ever after, and each persecuted maiden tale examined here provides a different sort of marvelous end to the female protagonist's suffering. Perhaps because Stella's story includes an open denunciation of her character—Mattabruna calls her a *puttana* (whore) and a *meretrice* (harlot)—her happy ending demands an explicit, clear defense and restoration of her good name. The ending of the tale veers away from the religious tale or magic tale, to embrace a motif typical of the chivalric epics and popular chapbooks of the period featuring the exploits of knights: a duel with a giant. The giant Triadasse, who Stella's son Tasso must defeat to defend his mother's honor, binds this fairy tale in verse to the chivalric epic tradition in which giants were plentiful, as both friends and foes. Such is the case in Luigi Pulci's *Morgante* (1583), a poem he wrote based on popular *cantari* at the suggestion of his patron Lucrezia Tornabuoni de' Medici. After his fellow giants are slain by the knight Orlando, the giant Morgante converts to Christianity and becomes Orlando's squire. Matteo Maria Boiardo's *Orlando Innamorato* (*Orlando in Love*) (1483–95) begins with four giants arriving at the court of Charlemagne. Giants are also linked to defending female honor in another chivalric epic, Moderata Fonte's *Floridoro* (1581). In the first canto of Fonte's poem, the giant Macandro arrives at the court of King Cleardo and challenges the knights there to a joust to defend his beloved lady's reputation as the most beautiful woman alive (Fonte [1581] 2006: 59–63).

In the story of Queen Stella, the king's giant Triadasse one day happens upon three of the four children as the hermit and the fourth sibling are out gathering food. Triadasse tells Mattabruna of his discovery and she, realizing they must be Stella's offspring, orders him to return to the hermit's cell and kill the children. Moved by pity, the giant merely steals their silver chains and brings them back to Mattabruna as proof that he has completed the task. When the hermit returns home and learns what has transpired, he prays that the children's identity will be disclosed to him. An angel reveals the details of their birth to the hermit just before Mattabruna plans to have Stella burned at the stake. The hermit baptizes the three boys Tasso, Oriano, Villian Furiam, and their sister Belpome. The brothers and the hermit head to the kingdom after leaving Belpome in a convent. Once Mattabruna invites anyone who wishes to defend the disgraced Stella's honor to a duel with Triadasse, the strongest of the three boys, Tasso, does battle with the giant. The moment that Triadasse insults Stella, Tasso kills him. The hermit then reveals what has happened, Stella is restored to her position as queen and the king decides to execute Mattabruna by having her drawn and quartered. It is ultimately Tasso's strength and skill, rather than his mother Stella's saintly suffering, that brings about the happy ending. The tale closes with a simple, rather generic moral message: "chi male fa non speri daver bene," whoever does evil should not expect any good to come of it.

In Corna's poem, Oliva's hands are reattached miraculously through divine intervention. Her fervent prayers are answered as she floats in a chest after being cast out of the convent on false charges of having stolen a chalice. Only then, with her hands reattached, is she fished from the sea and brought to the king of Castiglia who will become her husband. She is thus restored to her former (whole) self before she marries and must face her final trial: her mother-in-law falsifying correspondence between the king at war and his court, so that Oliva is condemned to death for having birthed a deformed infant. The viceroy who receives the falsified letter ordering him to burn mother and child places Oliva and her baby in a chest and burns another woman and her child in Oliva's stead. Oliva is, once again cast upon the waves and floats with her son to Rome and is taken in by two kind elderly women. When the king returns home to discover his mother's deception, he burns her alive in the convent where she lives. Twelve years later, Oliva hears that her husband the king has come to Rome to do penance and sends their son to meet him. In the end, Oliva's good name is restored, and she is reunited with her husband, and her father repents and asks for her forgiveness. In the final octaves of the poem, Oliva is depicted as a saint and Corna urges his readers to pray to her for intercession. God and prayer, not fairy magic, bring Oliva and her family to their happy ending. Basile's tale is resolved by a totally different and wholly fairy-tale type of marvel: the magic of a sorcerer.

RACE, GENDER, AND POWER IN WONDER TALES

Social historical approaches to the fairy tale highlight the ways in which fantastic narratives reflect and critique the very real issues and values of the society in which they were created. The two chapbooks examined here, for example, highlight intergenerational competition among women for family favor and resources, a common component of many fairy tales, as Warner has shown (1994: 218–40). They also champion heroines who conform to normative gender roles, who in their quiet, patient resistance to persecution, and preference for self-harm over harming others, embody the role of the female martyr. The rewards they receive, a return to their wifely status and/or sanctification, are similarly traditional, although, as Cristina Mazzoni persuasively argues in Chapter 3, fairy tales in this period did not always embrace such normative gender roles.

Basile's persecuted maiden tale takes on a different set of issues that regard not only gender but also race and power. Although his protagonist Penta is also long-suffering, rather than celebrate her saintly perseverance, Basile relates the sad tale of her loss of agency. Instead of being raised up after a false accusation of having birthed a wolf dog, by the end of the tale Penta herself becomes a dog, at least metaphorically. This tale begins with a threat of an incestuous union that Penta denounces through a series of metaphors about inappropriate mixtures. But the tale also points toward anxiety about a different sort of joining: interracial, interreligious unions first introduced in the frame tale of Basile's collection.

By calling on the Muslim slave Ali to chop off her hands, Penta stages her amputation as a grotesque farce of the martyrdom of Saint Olivia of Palermo. In this way, Basile's secular tale provides a distorted echo of the religious roots of his tale. That fifth-century virgin martyr was sent from Sicily by Vandal invaders to Tunis where she would be martyred by the Muslim governor after converting many of his citizens to Christianity. In Penta's staging, it is an enslaved Muslim who mutilates a Christian maiden, though not out of religious conviction, but for money and at her request. Furthermore, in her struggle to repel her sinful sibling, Penta remains without spiritual guidance or assistance. At the same time, through her command to Ali, "you cut my hands, me want make nice formula and get more white!" Penta reverses their roles and positions herself as a slave, both through the way she speaks and her expressed desire to be whiter. Of course, such master-slave reversals were a real possibility in Basile's Mediterranean context where slavery was marked by reciprocity, with Christians enslaving Muslims and Muslims enslaving Christians (Fiume 2009: x–xi). During Basile's lifetime, Naples was a city with a Muslim community and where up to 7 percent of the population was comprised of slaves coming from all around the Mediterranean including the Middle East, Eastern Europe, and North and sub-Saharan Africa (Boccadamo 2010: 144–51). He served at Neapolitan courts under the rule of Spanish viceroys, the counts of Lemos, whose former slaves had converted to Christianity and still worked at the court (179). In short, Basile's Naples was a multiethnic, multi-confessional, and multilingual city where Neapolitans under Spanish rule lived alongside free and enslaved people of color, many of whom were Muslim, and this is the context in which we must read his tale. Basile's insistence here on color and slave speech also redirects his readers to other representations of slavery in *The Tale of Tales*.

Penta speaks to Ali using a Neapolitan-Moorish patois, a language that Michele Rak calls "parlar turchesco" and "napoletano-moresca" and tells us was both a spoken and a literary language in seventeenth-century Naples (Rak 1986: 29n17). No other characters in Basile's text speak to slaves using the slaves' own language. In doing so, Penta aligns herself with two other black, female slaves in *The Tale of Tales* who speak the same way and are both named Lucia, which was a typical name for enslaved women in Italy (Epstein 2001: 27). The first Lucia appears in the overarching narrative, or frame tale, where she cries the final tears necessary to awaken Prince Tadeo from his enchanted slumber and marries him, deceitfully taking the place of melancholy Princess Zoza. To eventually unseat her rival, Princess Zoza uses a marvelous machine she received from a fairy, an enchanted automaton that breathes the desire to hear tales into Lucia's ears, a desire that the slave expresses in this same patois: "If people no come and with my ears fill, me punch belly and little Georgie kill" (Basile [1634–6] [2007] 2016: 10). This Lucia, Zoza's antagonist, will meet a violent death at the end of *The Tale of Tales*, thus allowing Princess Zoza to wed Tadeo. Before her downfall, Lucia will hear the tale of "The Three Citrons," the penultimate tale in the collection, which tells of another black slave named Lucia who speaks the same patois and kills a white fairy to marry a prince. For example, while gazing into a fountain and mistaking the fairy's reflection for her own, this Lucia says "What you see, unfortunate Lucia, you be so beautiful and mistress send you to get water and me put up with this, O unfortunate Lucia?" (Basile [1634–6][2007] 2016: 448). So, by speaking in Neapolitan-moresca, Penta not only marks herself as a slave but also associates herself with these two Lucias, who both suffer violent deaths at the hands of men in power.

Penta also suggests that she is dark-skinned or black, like the two Lucias, when she convinces Ali that amputating her hands is part of a "secreto," a recipe or formula, to make herself whiter. While this might appear to be sure confirmation of Ali's limited intellectual ability, there was no shortage of such "secrets" or recipes for whitening skin circulating in early modern Italy. For example, in *Gli ornamenti delle donne* (The Adornments of Women, 1562), the physician Giovanni Marinello dedicates a disproportionate amount of space to such whitening recipes, indeed more space than he dedicates any other kind of beauty secret or cure, indicating his culture's obsession with whiteness. And undoubtedly, having her hands amputated will make Penta whiter, if only through blood loss. Indeed, in the fifteenth-century prose legend, *La figlia del Re di Dacia* (The Daughter of the King of Dacia), Eilisa amputates her hand, but hides the wound from her father; it is her extremely pale face that leads him to discover her defiant act (Wesselofsky 1866: 6).

Penta's expressed desire to be whiter verbally juxtaposes light and dark skin by implying that she herself is dark-skinned, a discursive move that once again associates her with other enslaved women in Basile's text. Although records of sales indicate an array of skin colors of slaves sold in Italy, and slaves came to Italy from Eastern Europe, the Middle East, as well as North and sub-Saharan Africa (Epstein 2001: 79), in *The Tale of Tales,* slaves are always depicted as dark-skinned or black, even when they are presumably white. For example, in the tale "La Schiavetta" ("The Little Slave Girl"), when the protagonist Lisa's cruel aunt wants to pass off her niece as a slave, the aunt literally beats Lisa black and blue. She cuts Lisa's hair, puts her in a ragged dress and every day "unloaded lumps on her head, eggplants on her eyes, brands on her face and gave her a mouth that looked like she had eaten raw pigeons" (Basile [1634–6] [2007] 2016: 182). The two Lucias are not only described as black, but their skin color is also often noted through negative comparisons to white objects. For example, in the frame tale, "the prince got out of his coffin of white stone as if he were awakening from a long sleep, took hold of that mass of black flesh, and carried her off to his palace." In "The Three Citrons," the white fairy helps the slave Lucia climb up beside her, and "as the slave scrambled up [the fairy] put out her little white hand, which grasped by those black sticks looked like a crystal mirror in an ebony frame" (449). Through her unique staging of the amputation, which emphasizes her desire to be whiter, Penta performs the multiple forms of harm she endures due to her brother's threats of sexual violence. To thwart his assault, she must endure not only physical mutilation but also a loss of her liberty and subjectivity as she is (metaphorically) enslaved. Although she avoids succumbing to his desires, she is nonetheless punished, crippled, as well as silenced by them. Although Penta began the tale by boldly opposing and verbally sparring with her brother, we do not hear her speak until the end of the tale when she tells her story to the sorcerer.

Unlike other handless maidens who publicly recount their suffering and spur incestuous relatives to repent and reclaim their rightful positions as royal spouses, Penta tells her story in a very different moment and to very different effect. It is her disability that requires narrative and her story is told not to her husband or lecherous brother, but to the sorcerer of Torbid Lake, who seems to know her tale before he hears it:

> When he saw this lovely cripple who crippled hearts and waged a fiercer war with the stumps of her arms than Briareus with his hundred arms, he wanted to hear the whole story of the misfortunes that had befallen her: from when her brother was denied a meal of meat and wanted to make a meal of fish out of her, up to the day that she had set foot in his Kingdom.
> (Basile [1634–6][2007] 2016: 220–1)

Here David T. Mitchell's and Sharon L. Snyder's idea of "narrative prosthesis" from their study *Narrative Prosthesis: Disability and the Dependencies of Discourse* (2000), which Ann Schmiesing employs in her own compelling analysis of the Grimms's "Maiden Without Hands" tale, seems to be at work: "all narratives operate out of a desire to compensate for a limitation or to reign in excess" (cited in Schmiesing 2014: 2). Penta will tell her tale to explain her lack of hands, but from that point forward the sorcerer will desire to be inundated by a sea of sad stories.

Penta's "bitter tale" causes the sorcerer to weep copiously and feel profound compassion, her story of suffering earns her "a beautiful apartment in his palace," and he takes care of her like a "daughter" (Basile [1634–6][2007] 2016: 221).

She receives economic and emotional compensation for this account of her suffering that she relates in a private, instead of a public, setting. Rather than repentance or conversion, Penta's tale engenders in the sorcerer the desire to hear of more tales of woe. The next day he issues a proclamation throughout Europe: "anyone who came to his court and told of a misfortune would be given a golden crown and scepter worth more than a kingdom" (221). The response is overwhelming.

Penta's story of female suffering is then displaced by the tales told by men, including those of her husband and brother, who both head to Torbid Lake to compete for the prize. The first four men who recount their travails, a courtier, a merchant, a poet, and a servant, all tell of occupational tragedies—scant or no earnings, sunk ships, imperious masters—before Penta's brother and husband arrive and recount their own stories in detail. Her brother feels anguish and affliction for his actions, and although he recognizes his errors, he does not repent or ask for anyone's forgiveness. Penta's husband then tells of the tragic loss of his wife and child. The sorcerer quickly realizes that he has Penta's brother and husband before him and calls her son forward to greet his uncle and father. When asked if the boy is his son, the Sorcerer replies they should ask his mother and Penta appears. But she doesn't tell her story again. In fact, the woman who began the tale as an articulate, fierce defender of her own virtue and independence has been reduced to a lap dog, figuratively if not literally: "And, like a little dog that has been lost for many days and then finds her master and barks, licks, wags her tail, and gives him a thousand other signs of her happiness, so she ran first to her brother and then to her husband" (Basile [1634–6][2007] 2016: 223). Bound by his word, indeed he describes himself "like a slave in chains" before the two men, the Sorcerer then gives not only his scepter but also his crown to the king of Green Earth, Penta's husband, judging him to be the one who "truly came close to bursting with sorrow." The only thing marring the happy ending now is Penta's disability. The Sorcerer says, "And so that there remains nothing left to desire for Penta's happiness, let her put the stumps under her apron, and she'll pull out hands that are more beautiful than they were before" (224). This ending, the narrator tells us, was happiest for Penta's husband who considered Penta's miraculous transformation, from mutilated body to whole woman, as "far greater fortune than the other kingdom given to him by the sorcerer" (224). In the final lines of the tale, rather than being held up as an exemplum of female virtue and perseverance, Penta and her story disappear: "After they had spent a handful of days in great festivities, the king of Dry Rock returned to his kingdom, and the king of Green Earth, having stayed on with the sorcerer, paying off fingers of suffering with arm's length of delight, and testifying to the world that *you cannot find sweetness dear if you have not first known bitterness*" (224, emphasis in the original).

Penta's tale begins with her vigorous denunciation of the incestuous union her brother proposes, but her adoption of the speech and color of the enslaved women of the frame tale and "The Three Citrons" links her story to tales that belie anxiety surrounding a different sort of mixing, interracial marriages or unions in which black slaves temporarily displace white brides. Because Basile never completely conflates metaphorical and actual slaves, these depictions demonstrate how power functions at the intersection of gender, race, and class. Unbridled male desire temporarily mutilates the white princess Penta and ultimately robs her of her voice and agency, though both her hands and social status are restored to her. In Basile's godless universe, Penta's story of hardship and abuse does not serve as a saintly example but becomes instead a private entertainment that creates the desire to hear more tales of suffering. But in this racist world, the black women's desire for white spouses, and the wealth and power acquired through such unions, leads to their violent deaths at the hands of their husbands. At the end of "The Three Citrons," the black Saracen Lucia is burned alive, her ashes scattered to the wind. At the end of the frame tale, Lucia tumbles from the throne and awaits corporeal disintegration, buried alive so that the worms may devour her flesh as Princess Zoza takes her place as Tadeo's wife. In Chapter 8, Armando Maggi will more thoroughly examine Basile's troubling representations of the gendered and racialized abuse of Others by those in power.

CONCLUSION

The age of the marvelous was a marvelously unstable time. It was a moment when scientific discoveries challenged beliefs held since antiquity about what the world was and how it worked. Men and women in Europe were rethinking gender roles, and specifically the place of women in society, in a debate unfolding on the printed page called the *querelle des femmes*, a battle in which fairy-tale authors such as Straparola participated (Magnanini in Straparola 2015: 23–30). The once unified Catholic Church was splintering into different Protestant sects, sparking religious wars. Europe's colonization and subsequent enslavement and exploitation of people in Africa and the Americas destabilized indigenous societies. As the chapters that follow show, early modern fairy tales offered a way to view these very real instabilities and ambiguities regarding gender, race, religion, and the division between animals and humans through a fantastic, wondrous, and miraculous lens. Many more marvels await the readers of this volume in the chapters that follow this introduction. The majority of images in this volume were created during the age of the marvelous, but others testify to the visual legacy of these early modern tales in subsequent centuries in the hands of well-known illustrators of fairy tales. Together the eight chapters show the variety, malleability, and mobility of marvels in the fairy-tale tradition during the age of the marvelous.

CHAPTER ONE

Forms of the Marvelous

Ring and Riddle in the Shakespearean Marriage Tale

KEVIN PASK

Shakespeare's theatre is a kind of cultural clearinghouse through which some of the elements of the folktale and romance tradition, from a variety of European sources, entered into the modern formation of English literature, including its skepticism regarding the marvelous. In this respect, he was not a direct participant in the creation of the European literary fairy tale, which was a phenomenon that was most decisively shaped by the transformation of the Boccaccian novella in the work of Giovan Francesco Straparola (*c*. 1480– *c*. 1557) and Giambattista Basile (1575–1632). Both Straparola and Basile continued the framework of Giovanni Boccaccio's *Decameron* (*c*. 1353) as the exchange of tales over the course of a delimited time frame, but they also charged their narratives with a much higher degree of magical incident than was on offer in Boccaccio.

Boccaccio's own adaptations of folktales and Eastern sources favored cunning over magic, but Straparola followed the general format of *The Decameron* to produce literary fairy tales in *Le piacevoli notti* (*The Pleasant Nights*, 1550–3).[1] Shakespeare was probably at least indirectly acquainted with some of Straparola's tales, if not the fairy tales from his collection. William Painter's *The Palace of Pleasure* (1566, 1575), the repository of translated Italian and French tales and novellas for English readers, was full of Boccaccio, Marguerite of Navarre (1492–1549), and Matteo Bandello (*c.* 1480–1562), but it included only one tale of erotic double-crosses and humiliations from Straparola, the second tale of the second night. *Tarleton's News Out of Purgatory* (1590) contained an adaptation of the fourth tale of the fourth night. Close to the end of Shakespeare's writing career, his theatrical associate (chief clown of the King's Men) Robert Armin published *The Italian Taylor and His Boy* (1609), based on the fourth story of the eighth night, which included magical powers and fairy-tale motifs.

Translations of Italian *novelle* remained consistently popular with English readers and playgoers. By 1570, Roger Ascham's *The Scholemaster* condemned such tales as "the inchantementes of *Circes*, brought out of *Italie* to marre mens maners in England" (1570: 229). The concern was the enticing lewdness of Boccaccio and his followers rather than the representation of magic. Adaptations of such enchantments for the stage were the subject of similar unease. Stephen Gosson's *Schoole of Abuse* (1579) comments on the wide-ranging and promiscuous "ransacking" of source materials and indicates something of the literary catchment of the Elizabethan playwrights, including an expansive range of marvels and romances: "I have seen it that the *Palace of Pleasure*, the *Golden Ass*, the *Ethiopian History*, *Amadis of France*, the *Round Table*, bawdy comedies in Latin, French, Italian and Spanish have been thoroughly ransacked to furnish the playhouses in London" (Clubb 2002: 32). Apuleius's *Golden Ass*, from the late second century CE, was the source of the interpolated narrative of Cupid and Psyche, a kind of liminal narrative between classical mythology and European fairy tale, and Lorenzo Selva adapted Apuleius as a vehicle for fairy tales in his *Metamorfosi* (1582) (Magnanini 2011). *The Golden Ass* also provided Shakespeare with the Bottom plot in *A Midsummer Night's Dream*. Shakespeare was no stranger to the staging of the supernatural, including the fairies of *A Midsummer Night's Dream*, the witches of *Macbeth*, or Prospero's magic in *The Tempest*; but the Shakespearean examples are generally engaged with a high, cosmic magic rather than the fairy-tale magic connected to the vicissitudes of ordinary human desires and needs. Even the transformation of Bottom is only the collateral damage of the cosmic struggle between Oberon and Titania.

This, however, was not the only mode in which Shakespeare worked with the marvelous. In three plays that represent some of the transformations of Shakespearean comedy into tragicomedy over the course of his career—*The Merchant of Venice, All's Well That Ends Well,* and *Cymbeline*—the action of the plays assumes something of the aura of the marvelous, generally without overstretching the credulity of the Protestant skepticism that increasingly characterized English narrative. In these plays, the aura of the marvelous comes from the talismanic character that Shakespeare attaches to a woman's ring, itself associated with the binding power of marriage, and which is not present or less emphasized in the sources, which are all Italian *novelle*, two by Boccaccio.[2] Protestant emphasis on the spiritual centrality of marriage no doubt inflected Shakespeare's choices, but not without a countervailing skepticism about marriage that is equally characteristic of Shakespeare. Magic might be one name for the force that holds together contradictory attitudes regarding marriage in these plays.

The association of such magic with the fairy tale is a strong one. Charlotte Artese has recently argued for the role of folktale sources in several of Shakespeare's plays, partly by carefully sifting the numerous variants of the individual tales that might have influenced Shakespeare, and which, she claims, were known by his audience. This changes our sense of how the original audience might have responded to plots that relied on folktales. The evidence, although suggestive, often remains speculative. Some of the folktales instanced by Artese are not known to have circulated in England during Shakespeare's time, even if more tales circulated than are attested in print or manuscript references (Artese 2015).

In any case, it is often difficult to distinguish folktale sources from romance or fabliau ones in the formation of what might appear retrospectively as fairy tale. In, for example, his discussion of the sources of *Cymbeline*, Roger Warren notes that it is difficult to pin down romances that influenced the play "partly because of the way in which romance motifs are so widely disseminated among folk-tales and oral traditions" (1998: 16)—and vice versa. The high and popular cultures shared elements of the marvelous in the period before elite culture began to distinguish itself from popular beliefs.[3] As Adam Fox has written (and as Artese has approvingly cited), "Any crude binary opposition between 'oral' and 'literate' culture fails to accommodate the reciprocity between the different media by this time; just as any crude dichotomy between 'elite' and 'popular' fails to illuminate a spectrum of participation" (Fox 2000: 6; cited by Artese 2015: 5). *The Winter's Tale*, for example, highlights its connections to the popular and oral in the idea of the tale; the aura of marvelous events is "like an old tale still" (*WT* 5.2.60). The events themselves, however, are not primarily drawn from the world of oral tales but from the literary one of pastoral romance, in particular Robert Greene's *Pandosto* (1588), the primary source for the play.

But if Shakespeare's theatre largely derived from sources in the literate culture, its playhouse production was an aural and visual event, maintaining its connections to a popular and oral culture in which tale-telling was central and which anticipated the form of the fairy tale, narrated by an "old wife." George Peele's *The Old Wives' Tale* (published 1595) uses tale-telling as the frame for the play; an old wife entertains three visitors, who appear by their names (Anticke,

Fantastike, and Frolicke) to be courtly players. The staging of the tale allows it to "come to life," highlighting the power of theatrical form in remediating the older oral world of the tale for a popular audience.[4] Shakespeare's early play, *The Taming of the Shrew*, includes an induction, or theatrical frame, that, unlike Peele's, is simply abandoned after the opening scene of the play, but which, like Peele's, testifies to the role of theatre in presenting popular subjects in a new medium. Here, the self-referential medium of professional theatre brings a kind of cultural struggle to the fore: between the obstreperous Christopher Sly and the anonymous Lord who commissions the performance of the shrew story—itself based on a ballad version of a common European folktale concerning the subjugation of supposedly "unruly" women—as part of a practical joke on Sly. Sly belongs more clearly to Shakespeare's world of Stratford-upon-Avon than any other character in the Shakespeare canon, referencing places and common names from the vicinity. Shakespeare's abandonment of the induction plot as the play progresses (Sly probably sleeping uninterrupted in the gallery after his final spoken lines after the first scene) perhaps registers the reversal of an initial theatrical decision that would have emphasized elite condescension to popular characters and plots (Artese 2015: 41–2).

CIRCE AND THE WIFE: *THE MERCHANT OF VENICE*

The Merchant of Venice reveals something of the distinction of the Shakespearean—and English—handling of such materials. The main plot of the play probably derives from a novella in Ser Giovanni's *Il Pecorone* (The Simpleton), traditionally dated to the late fourteenth century but unpublished until 1558, and untranslated into English in Shakespeare's time.[5] In Giovanni's version of the tale, the young man, Giannetto, who is the equivalent of Shakespeare's Bassanio, accompanies his seafaring friends on a trading voyage to Alexandria, and his adoring godfather, Ansaldo, agrees to provide him with an expensively furnished ship. On the way, however, Giannetto hears of an unnamed lady who has issued a standing challenge to any male visitor to her domain: he who can have his way with her in bed will have her and her belongings; if, however, he fails to do so, then he must give up all of his possessions. Giannetto loses the challenge once—the lady provides her male visitors with a drink that contains a sleeping potion before taking them to bed—and then, resupplied by his godfather, loses yet again.[6] The third time is the charm, however, thanks to the intervention of a serving woman who warns Giannetto to avoid the drink provided by the lady of the house. Having finally won the lady, Giannetto lingers with her until suddenly remembering, at the last possible moment, the dire necessity of Ansaldo, who had been able to outfit him for his third voyage only through taking a loan from an unnamed Jew; the penalty for failure to meet the terms of the loan is a pound of Ansaldo's flesh.

No attempt is made to explain the Jew's malignancy; his Jewishness seems to function in the story as entirely sufficient explanation. By contrast, Shakespeare's attempt to build up a set of psychosocial motivations for Shylock—who bitterly resents Antonio's anti-Semitism—is one of the aspects of the play that separates it from its sources.

Perhaps the most striking transformation of this source is the handling of the lady who serves as the basis of Shakespeare's Portia. In the Italian story, the heroine is an avatar of Circe, linking the story to one of the motifs of the European romance: the powerful temptress (Quiller-Couch [1926] 1969: x–xi) and enchantress echoed in Ludovico Ariosto's Alcina (*Orlando furioso*, 1516), Torquato Tasso's Armida (*Gerusalemme liberata*, 1581), and Edmund Spenser's Acrasia (*The Fairie Queene*, 1590), as well as in tales by Straparola (3.4) and Basile (1.7). Shakespeare's Portia is apparently without any such magical or enchanting power. Her entrance is marked by her melancholy lament at her immobilized situation, the prize of the lottery set up by her deceased father, who now apparently controls her marriage from beyond the grave. The lottery concerns the need for Portia's future husband to select the correct casket containing the appropriate riddle, a plot device Shakespeare may have borrowed from the medieval *Gesta Romanorum* (a new English translation appeared in 1595), which he re-genders by having the future husband and not wife undergo the trial.[7] In Shakespeare's handling, Ser Giovanni's three voyages of Giannetto, along with their frank avowal of the value of sexual cunning, are replaced by another version of the folktale "Law of Three" (Olrik [1909] 1965: 133): the three scenes of male attempts to choose the correct casket, in which the woman exercises neither choice nor cunning, although Portia arguably begins to exercise both when she seems to offer hints about the correct choice in her extended instructions to Bassanio—her preferred suitor—before his moment of decision.

The sexually powerful aura of Ser Giovanni's lady is replaced by the apparently diminished wifeliness of Portia, who announces after Bassanio's successful choice of the leaden casket that everything she owns will henceforth belong to him. The one proviso, however, is the ring that she gives him, a token of his fidelity whose talismanic quality Portia exploits to the fullest—short of assigning magic to it—thus playing on the power rings held in the long history of both romance and folklore, including both Geoffrey Chaucer and Edmund Spenser.[8] In doing so, she asserts the literal significance of the bond produced by the ring—with the ring goes her fidelity and even her body—that demonstrates her debt to Shylock's insistence on the literal word of Antonio's bond—that he will allow Shylock to take a pound of his own flesh if he does not meet their agreed upon date for repayment—and even her ability, like a good Calvinist, to exceed it in logical rigor. Disguised as the (male) doctor of law, Balthazar, Portia's triumph over Shylock in the courtroom scene is not the application of the Christian principle of mercy (although Balthazar/Portia offers him the choice of mercy, which he refuses) but rather the Old Testament insistence on the letter of the law: the failure of the bond to specify the taking of Antonio's blood as well as his flesh. God, wrote St. Paul, "hath made us able ministers of the New Testament, not of the letter, but of the spirit: for the letter killeth, but the spirit giveth life" (2 Corinthians 3:6). Portia, like Shylock before her, weaponizes the letter.

As Sigurd Burckhardt (1962) argued long ago, Shylock's bond becomes in her hands the "gentle bond" between husband and wife, both "gentle" in the sense of well born and gentile, and one that she wields powerfully, having in some sense learned from Shylock himself.[9] To activate the talismanic bond of the ring, Shakespeare has Portia enact the folktale motif of the cross-dressed woman (ATU 514), shared with Straparola (4.1) and Basile (4.6), but most directly following from the earlier disguise of Jessica—Shylock's daughter—as a page to elope with Lorenzo, which Jessica experiences as a source of shame. With Portia, however, Shakespeare seems to discover the motif, for the first time in his career, as a source of power. "Pardon me, Bassanio," she says to her husband in the final scene of the play, "For by this ring, the doctor lay with me" (*MV* 5.1.258–9). The ring's symbolic function as the bond between husband and wife has become a literal token of possession and a blending of faith and flesh: "riveted with faith unto your flesh" (5.1.169), as she scolds Gratiano about his loss of his own ring to his disguised, cross-dressed beloved. She appears to claim that any man with the ring can occupy the place of her husband before revealing that the claim is a kind of riddle spoken by a suddenly practiced and subtle trickster (she "lay with" herself, in her role as the doctor). She has become familiar with the uses of the letter of the law, unfolding what Catherine Belsey terms a "festival of riddles" (2007: 168) in the fifth act and concentrated on the talismanic ring. Her doubleness, Burckhardt argued (1962: 261), perhaps most especially her double role as both man and woman, allows the literalism of the riddles to produce distinctively Shakespearean comedy, with a twist. Phyllis Gorfain aligned disguise and deception, particularly in the form of the boy actor playing a female part, with the Renaissance culture of riddles and paradox, "used to penetrate otherwise inaccessible realities" (1976: 271). Portia thus herself acquires the identity of a riddle that needs to be solved. As Gorfain likewise explains, the riddle can allow a relatively less powerful person (the wealthy heiress who has now given all to her new husband) to "embarrass an opponent who holds a position of greater power outside the riddling context" (1977: 151).

The trickery behind the riddle of Portia also suggests Shylock, whose usury aligns itself, at least in his mind, with folktale motifs that Portia also seems to exploit. Shylock affiliates himself with the biblical Jacob at the beginning of the play (*MV* 1.3.73–87), specifically with Jacob as the cunning folklore trickster who outwits his father-in-law, Laban (Niditch [1987] 2000: 106–10). Jacob is able to accumulate a great share of the herd of goats that he tends for Laban in an arrangement that allows him to keep the striped kids (Genesis 30:25-44). He fashions striped poles for the goats to see while they are mating, and this produces, in a kind of sympathetic magic, striped offspring. Both Jacob himself and, in the play, Antonio attribute this result to the will of God, but Shylock himself is resolutely focused on Jacob as trickster-magician, modeling his own ability to make his gold and silver "breed as fast" (*MV* 1.3.93) as Jacob's goats.

Crucially for the symbolic bond between Shylock and Portia, both find themselves, just before her complete defeat of Shylock, responding along similar lines to Bassanio's and Gratiano's protestations of homosocial fidelity to Antonio, swearing that they would sacrifice their wives for Antonio's life. Portia comments, "Your wife would give you little thanks for that / If she were by to hear you make the offer" (*MV* 4.1.286–7). Shylock adds disparagingly, "These be the Christian husbands" (4.1.293), before lamenting his daughter's marriage to the spendthrift Lorenzo: "Would any of the stock of Barrabas / Had been her husband rather than a Christian!" (4.1.294–5). Shylock himself is strikingly uxorious, devoted to his deceased wife, Leah. Unlike the countless absent and/or deceased and unnamed mothers in Shakespeare's plays, Leah is named. She is, moreover, linked to the story of Jacob, as the first wife that Laban has substituted for Jacob's choice, Rachel, in a bed trick. Shakespeare's choice of the name Leah underlines that Shylock, the trickster, can be tricked (as Laban tricked Jacob into taking Leah), but his fidelity to his first wife symbolically differentiates Shylock from both Jacob and, at least potentially, Bassanio and Gratiano. The spendthrift nature of the relationship between Lorenzo and Jessica amplifies this connection between Shylock and Portia even as she prepares his downfall. Jessica, after all, has purchased a monkey by pawning the ring that her mother once gave to Shylock. "I would not have given it for a wilderness of monkeys" (*MV* 3.1.113–14), exclaims Shylock. Jessica's alienation of the ring joins her marriage to the potential for profligate sexual (and monetary) expenditure on the part of the Christian husbands, which is the reason for the prophylactic against male infidelity that Portia administers in the last scene of the play. This connection between Shylock and Portia, then, paves the way for Portia's extension of the relentless logic of the bond from the courtroom into her marriage to Bassanio.

The Circean power that seems to invest Ser Giovanni's lady, even if removed from the supernatural nature of Circe herself, is denied to Portia, but the remainder of the play, after she is "won" by Bassanio, shows her gaining a new form of pragmatic power inside marriage, partly through the cunning she has learned from Shylock and partly through the use of cross-dressing to redescribe her relationship with Bassanio as both homoerotic and marital bond, contained in the talismanic power of the ring. "If you had known the virtue of the ring" (*MV*

5.1.199), she begins her catechism of Bassanio in the final scene, a remarkable epistrophe in which she concludes four consecutive lines with the word "ring" in response to Bassanio's epistrophe of the same word over the course of five lines (5.1.193–7). Shortly afterward, she brings Antonio news of the sudden return of three of his argosies and thus his wealth and has Nerissa, her maid, inform Jessica and Lorenzo of the inheritance they will receive from Shylock (which, in the trial scene, had been arranged by Antonio). "Sweet lady, you have given me life and living" (5.1.286), responds Antonio. "Fair ladies, you drop manna in the way / Of starvèd people," says Lorenzo. The aura of salvific fairy tale draws upon the power of enchantresses like Circe even while it also points forward to the subsequent tendency of the English novel—Samuel Richardson's *Pamela* (1740) would be a central example—to emphasize feminine virtue and power in the domain of marriage.

ALL'S WELL THAT ENDS WELL?

The potency of the ring as the marker of a wedding bond returns in *All's Well That Ends Well*, a play that has also been widely acknowledged to possess fairy-tale motifs, but without any illusions about marital love. Its affiliations with *Measure for Measure*, most prominently in the use of the bed trick—in which "a sexual encounter occurs in which at least one partner is unaware of the other partner's true identity" (Desens 1994: 11)—would appear to date the play to roughly the same period, around 1604–5. After healing the king of France, the wily Helena gains the latter's approval to marry the man she loves, Bertram, against his will, who then sets seemingly impossible conditions that Helena must fulfill to legitimate their marriage. In this play, the efficacy of a woman's appropriation of the power of a ring—in this case, her husband's rather than her own—to affirm a marriage bond reaches a limit. The play cannot assure a modern reader, or a modern audience, that Helena has fully captured her husband, Bertram, at the end of the play. This is partly because the play focuses so squarely on a woman's use of cunning to pursue her own desire in the face of her object's rejection. There is, as Susan Snyder has argued ([1993] 2008: 31–2), no equivalent example elsewhere in Shakespeare (although Helena's namesake, the Helena of *A Midsummer Night's Dream*, pursues an unmoved object of desire and obtains him, spellbound, at the end of the play), and partly for this reason it has elicited the disapproval of many critics. Perhaps for that very reason, the play tends to highlight the aura of the fairy tale and the supernatural where the primary source for Shakespeare's plot, Boccaccio's *Decameron* 3.9 (translated in Painter's *Palace of Pleasure*), is remarkably pragmatic in its treatment of the equivalent events, in keeping with the ultimate sources of the story in Sanskrit literature and folktale (Lee [1909] 1966: 101–3). Shakespeare stretches the possibilities of the form to produce a kind of "magic realism" that resonates with the mixture of verisimilitude and magic in variations of the bed trick practiced in Bandello (1890: vol. 2, tale 43), Straparola (3.1, 7.1), and Basile (1.3, 5.6, 1.10).

Helena is a riddle from her first words in the play, "I do affect a sorrow indeed, but I have it too" (AW 1.1.53–4), where the implied riddle is untangled by the distinction between her pretense of mourning for her father and her genuine sense of lovesickness for Bertram. But she is also quite capable of the reflections on fate and human nature that more usually belong to characters such as Iago from *Othello* and Edmund from *King Lear*—although couched in rhyming couplets that suggest the incantations of fairy tale:

> Our remedies oft in ourselves do lie
> Which we ascribe to heaven. The fated sky
> Gives us free scope, only doth backward pull
> Our slow designs when we ourselves are dull.
> What power is it which mounts my love so high,
> That makes me see, and cannot feed mine eye?
> (AW 1.1.214–19)

The speech finally merges the individualism of the (male) malcontent with the entrepreneurial (here female) hero of folktale: "Who ever strove / To show her merit that did miss her love?" (1.1.224–5).

This odd positioning of the fairy-tale ideal within a larger and more complex plot continues into the folktale logic of the cure of the king, in the female version of "Doctor She," as Lafew calls her.[10] In the first scene of the play, Helena asserts the almost shockingly modern claim to her own sexuality. In response to Parolles's teasing banter about losing her virginity, based on the assumption that all young women are dedicated to preserving it before marriage, Helena responds, "How might one do, sir, to lose it to her own liking?" (AW 1.1.151–2). Parolles hardly knows how to respond and soon resumes his posturing on the topic of virginity. By the time of her arrival at the court of France, however, Helena has assumed some of "the traditional association of virginity with magic power and priesthood" and "is also involved in the priestess-like incantations for the recovery" of the king (Hunter 1962: xlii). Her status as a female doctor, moreover, seems to align her with the Christian reversal of the humble and the powerful, children and wise men:

> He that of greatest works is finisher
> Oft does them by the weakest minister.
> So holy writ in babes hath judgment shown
> When judges have been babes.
> (AW 2.1.137–40)

And she explicitly claims the power of heaven in her healing even after she has initially made it clear to the king that her power of healing comes to her directly from her father's medical research: "Dear sir, to my endeavors give consent; / Of heaven, not me, make an experiment" (2.1.154–5). The king first dismisses her offer of aid based on her father's expertise (which, we are to assume, is the actual source of her ability to cure him), but he is persuaded by the incantatory, divinizing discourse, as well as her willingness to wager her own life on his recovery. Boccaccio's king briefly muses on Giletta's possibly heaven-sent cure, but the knowledge gained from her father remains at the center of Boccaccio's narrative. Shakespeare's king is more persuaded by magic and risk, the logic of the fairy tale.

Helena's successful cure of the king does not produce the expected folktale reward for striving and merit that she invokes at the beginning of the play. Even those members of the audience familiar with Boccaccio's tale or its English translation would not be fully prepared for the somber affective atmosphere in which Helena wins her goal. In Boccaccio, the accomplishment of the seemingly impossible tasks is considerably more straightforward than it is in Shakespeare's plot. Unlike Shakespeare's "poor" Helena, Boccaccio's Giletta is a wealthy woman even before her marriage to Count Beltramo. She is an accomplished manager of her husband's estates in his absence, and his people are distraught when she leaves them to search out a means to accomplish the tasks. Her negotiation and setting in motion of the bed trick requires no apparent consultation of the young woman with whom she changes place to sleep with Beltramo. Everything is accomplished through the young woman's mother, and the response of the young woman to the chain of events is not addressed. Only Boccaccio's brief mention that the mother "was troubled at the idea of compromising her daughter" (1993: 238) discloses one unsettling aspect of the proposed trick that will occupy a good deal of Shakespeare's treatment. Giletta's final encounter with Beltramo is relatively uncomplicated. She reveals the twin sons born of their couplings (in the case of Helena it is a single sexual encounter that produces a still unborn child at the end of the play), and Beltramo, impressed by "how artful and tenacious she had been" (240), quickly decides to recognize her as his wife and the babies as his own.

Giletta, then, is the meritorious and cunning heroine imagined by Helena at the beginning of Shakespeare's play. Helena achieves the same basic tasks as her precursor, but in a fashion that calls every aspect of her actions into question. At the same time, however, Shakespeare continues to amplify the riddling, magical aura of the actions well beyond the scope of Boccaccio's tale, and different in kind from the often bawdy riddles that follow each story in Straparola's *Pleasant Nights*. The riddle, in André's Jolles's influential formulation of its role as a "simple form," possesses links to trial and initiation that would be appropriate to the women (and men) of *The Pleasant Nights*: "From the riddler's point of view the riddle is both a test of the guesser's equality and a matter of forcing the guesser to demonstrate his equality" ([1929] 2017: 105). This is relevant to Portia's riddling use of the ring in *The Merchant of Venice*, and it will also play a role at the end of this play, but it is first a kind of self-testing that reveals—and then quickly banishes—her own moral qualms about the bed trick:

> Why then tonight
> Let us assay our plot, which if it speed,
> Is wicked meaning in a lawful deed,
> And lawful meaning in a wicked act,
> Where both not sin, and yet a sinful fact.
> But let's about it.
>
> (*AW* 3.7.43–8)

Artese writes that the extensive use of riddles throughout the play, and especially after the introduction of the idea of the bed trick, is "a form of folk discourse that serves to naturalize the trick to the folktale plot" (2015: 131). The bed trick was not common in the "Deserted Wife" folklore plot, which typically concerned a husband refusing to consummate a marriage, and then departing on a journey; the wife then follows him in disguise, manages to gain his love and sleep with him to bear a child. However, the bed trick was an ancient and widespread plot device of Indo-European folklore and literature. It does not necessarily require much acculturation to the folktale of the "Deserted Wife," as Boccaccio realized when he made it central to Giletta's task without any fussiness. Shakespeare's use of riddle, however, goes beyond folktale cunning to an ongoing, self-questioning anguish within the play. Helena confronts the chiasmus that links her to Bertram. If Bertram's act during the bed trick is lawful (wedded intercourse) even when his intentions are bad, Helena acknowledges that her own actions are "wicked" (the sexual deception of her husband, possibly the use she has made of Diana to serve as her "bait") despite her "lawful" intention. "But let's about it" is the almost jaunty conclusion of her reflections, taking her back to the persona of the plucky folktale heroine that she tries to assume at moments when the burden of her plot weighs particularly heavily. "All's well that ends well," is the slogan of this aspect of Helena, spoken twice after the bed trick (*AW* 4.4.35–6; 5.1.25). Part of the interest of the play is that such affirmations, which can work well enough in a folktale context or in Boccaccio, are made to feel like temporizing responses to the overwhelming sense of the bleakness of the marriage game as revealed by the play.

We are thus presented with the systematic debasement of Bertram, for which there is no precedent in Boccaccio. Diana herself, meanwhile, experiences the full, coruscating force of this spectacle organized by her benefactor, Helena. In addition to obtaining Bertram's ring, already part of Boccaccio's plot, Diana

FIGURE 1.1: "Here take my ring" by James Hopwood, printmaker (1799). Courtesy of the Folger Shakespeare Library. Public domain.

gives Bertram her own ring (which is from Helena, and given to Helena by the king himself), which gives her, and Helena as well, some of the power associated with Portia's ring in *The Merchant of Venice* (Figure 1.1).

Portia's ring comes from Ser Giovanni's *Il Pecorone*, but the ring that travels from the king to Bertram is Shakespeare's invention, although Straparola's tale of Ortodosio and Isabella Simeoni (7.1) provides an analogous instance of female jewelry (a necklace in Straparola) used to verify the claim of a wife who has tricked her husband (with the aid of a sorceress) into sleeping with her and making her pregnant. In the first appearance of Helena's ring, it is associated with Diana's riddle, "Adieu till then; then, fail not; you have won / A wife of me, though there my hope be done" (*AW* 4.2.64–5). The audience recognizes the force of the riddle: Diana renounces her own marriage even while he "wins" not Diana but his actual wife, Helena. "Marry that will, I live and die a maid" (4.2.74). Here, the name Diana (goddess of virginity) is affirmed by her decision to avoid marriage. Diana's choice is one of disillusionment, in which Helena is necessarily implicated. (In the final scene, Diana's last name is revealed to be "Capilet," which seems to make her a cynical Juliet Capulet of *Romeo and Juliet*.)

The bed trick pushes Helena to an equally bleak picture of men, but one that she immediately deflects in the interest of pursuing her fairy-tale goal of marriage:

> But, O strange men!
> That can such sweet use make of what they hate
> When saucy trusting of the cozened thoughts
> Defiles the pitchy night; so lust doth play
> With what it loathes, for that which is away.
> But more of this hereafter.
>
> (*AW* 4.4.21–6)

And, in one spectacular and equivocal scene, she obtains her goal. The final scene continues the moral degradation of Bertram, revealing the full extent of his intended treatment of Diana to the key court figures, who had been content to let bygones be bygones and marry him to Lafew's daughter. He sinks low, it seems, to be raised by Helena—without much real choice when it is revealed to the court that she is alive and pregnant with his child. Unlike Beltramo's genuine appreciation of Giletta's pluckiness in Boccaccio's handling of the story, Bertram is not in a very good position to do anything but accept the salvific aura with which Helena invests her arrival. The "victory" of Helena, her fairy-tale achievement, is a kind of zero-sum game that comes with his almost total humiliation, nicely summarized by Samuel Johnson's comment that Bertram is "dismissed to happiness" at the end of the play.[11]

The final scene multiplies the significance of the ring exchange between Bertram and Helena, including the information that Helena's ring, which she gave to Bertram in bed, and which Bertram now produces as a kind of engagement ring to Maudlin, Lafew's daughter, had been given to Helena by the king as a token to send back to him if she were in need. The two rings bind the central characters in marriage, but they also bind the representative courtly society of the play (the countess, the king, and Lafew) as givers and/or recipients of the rings, implicating them in the vicissitudes of the rings' movements but also enforcing their participation in the correct disposition of the affections associated with the rings. As with Portia's use of the ring that she gives Bassanio, the general sense is that a woman's cunning use of the talismanic and binding qualities associated with a ring enforce male love and fidelity in a world in which that quality is rare or, as in this play, practically nonexistent. "He loved her, sir, as a gentleman loves a woman," riddles Parolles concerning Bertram's relationship to Diana. "He loved her, sir, and loved her not" (*AW* 5.3.244–5, 247).

The final scene amplifies the riddling quality of both Helena's and Diana's language, concluding with the presentation of Helena as the answer to Diana's paradoxical "neck riddle"—a riddle in which someone evades punishment or even death through an unsolvable riddle—of the dead and the "quick":

> [Bertram] knows himself my bed he hath defiled,
> And at that time he got his wife with child.
> Dead though she be, she feels her young one kick.
> So here's my riddle: one that's dead is quick—
> And now behold the meaning.
>
> (*AW* 5.3.297–301)

The "meaning" is Helena herself, pregnant, and "quick" in the sense both of alive and pregnant.[12] Neither Bertram, nor anyone else, is given the opportunity to answer the riddle before receiving the "meaning." The testing of equality and membership, which Jolles aligns with the riddle, is denied to Bertram, but extended to the audience, which would be in a position to know the answer before the presentation of Helena herself. The *bund*, or association, that is the result of the riddle in Jolles's account, is not the association formed by the marriage of Helena and Bertram, but rather that of audience and spectacle, an aspect of the "conversation" concerning the Italian novella tradition that Melissa Walter (2019) identifies in Shakespeare's adaptations of elements of that tradition.

The audience also witnesses a spectacularized but also rationalized version of the resurrection from the dead, which also characterizes Shakespeare's late plays. Like *Measure for Measure*, with which it is often rightly twinned, *All's*

Well includes a final act of restoration to life, and some version of happiness is accomplished in terms that throw the role of marriage into high relief. In *Measure for Measure*, the Duke doles out marriages at the end of the play as forms of punishment—and then offers his hand in marriage to Isabella. *All's Well* is less triumphant, partly because a "poor" woman, rather than Duke Vincentio, whose name signals power and victory, is the agent who effects the marriage. Helena's consolidation of her own marriage is not a multiplier for other marriages (notably breaking off the arrangement of Bertram's marriage to Maudlin and of course souring Diana on the idea of any marriage), and she remains acutely conscious of the vulnerability of her own engagement, promising Bertram "deadly divorce" (AW 5.3.315) should her story be found untrue. She is responding to Bertram's equivocal acceptance of the marriage: "If she, my liege, can make me know this clearly, / I'll love her dearly—ever, ever dearly" (5.3.312–13). The king, on the other hand, steps into the traditional Shakespearean role of multiplying marriage, promising Diana her choice of husband as her reward for her unstained virginity. Instead of augmenting the general happiness, his action instead seems to promise yet another iteration of the same cycle in which a woman chooses an unwilling partner promised by the king. "All yet seems well" (5.3.329), remarks the king in the final lines of the play, glancing at the provisional nature of the happy ending and hoping for future clarification. Both *All's Well* and *Measure for Measure* add the aura of magic and resurrection—of the sort that will come to the fore in the late tragicomedies (*Pericles, Cymbeline, The Winter's Tale, The Tempest*)—to the comic conclusion. *All's Well* is particularly insistent on this aspect of the conclusion, which is a clear departure from the traditionally folkloric account of the reconciliation of Beltramo and Giletta in Boccaccio in which Beltramo happily recognizes his wife's virtue. Riddles and (seeming) resurrection, affiliated with both folktales and the Christian *mythos* at the end of the play, produce compensatory effects of comedic conclusion that the marriage plot itself calls into question. It is, then, a bridge between problem comedy and late Shakespeare, but one in which the role of riddles and rings is particularly fraught.

FELLOWSHIP AND THE RING: *CYMBELINE*

With *Cymbeline*, the ring plot has fully entered the romance world of the late Shakespeare, but without abandoning some of the equivocal forms of resurrection and reconciliation that have more usually marked a play like *All's Well* as a problem comedy. When the central lovers of the play, Imogen and Posthumus, are finally reunited at the conclusion, Posthumus does not recognize Imogen in her male attire, and strikes her when she attempts to comfort him in his conviction that he has already killed her: "Shall's have a play of this? Thou scornful page, / There lie thy part" (*Cym* 5.5.231–2). "O my lord Posthumus, / You ne'er killed Imogen till now" (5.5.233–4), cries his faithful servant, Pisanio. Posthumus's scornful and violent rejection of the cross-dressed Imogen compromises any sense of the joyful reconciliation of the two lovers at the end of the play. Imogen is closer to the shame of Jessica dressed as a page than to the power of Portia dressed as a lawyer.

The plot of *Cymbeline* stitches together stories about wagering on the fidelity of a wife, which derives from both Boccaccio's *Decameron* and the *Historie von vier Kaufmännern* (Tale of Four Merchants), first published in Nuremberg in 1478, and translated into English, as *Frederyke of Jennen* (Genoa), in 1518; and elements constitutive of the tales of Snow White— particularly with respect to the figure of the evil stepmother and a potion that leads to death-like sleep—although there are no records of the tale's circulation in England during Shakespeare's time. Even without the possible direct influence of a tale resembling Snow White that could have been circulating, some of its essential elements were available in the romance tradition, with which the folktale versions no doubt intersected, some of it extending all the way back to Heliodorus's *Aethiopica*, some of them closer to hand in the Elizabethan popular drama, *The Rare Triumphs of Love and Fortune* (1582), or even slightly after Shakespeare's time, in the Italian version of Basile's "The Little Slave Girl" (2.8). Martin Butler argues that Shakespeare found in the *Aethiopica* "intertwined narratives, lost children, a wicked stepmother, an imprisoned hero, a sexually threatened heroine, and identities recovered through oracles and tokens" ([2005] 2012: 9). Geoffrey Bullough and Roger Warren identify *The Rare Triumphs* as the source of the names Hermione (from *The Winter's Tale*) and Fidele as well as

> the unequal match between a Princess and young orphan brought up at her father's court ... the banishment of the young lover by an angry King and the latter's desire to marry his daughter to another courtier [a version of Shakespeare's Cloten, where the preferred suitor is the king's own stepson]; the dweller in the wilds, exiled years before through a false accusation; his meeting with the King's daughter; the intervention of Jupiter to bring about happy discoveries and reunions.
>
> (Bullough 1957–75: 8:23)

Both plots are woven into a late version of the history play, which, like *Lear*, might be called a British myth play rather than an English history play.[13]

As with *The Merchant of Venice* and *All's Well*, Shakespeare heightens the role of rings, and, as with the other two, the ring wields a talismanic power in the plot and in the symbolic register of marriage. In both *The Decameron* and *Frederyke of Jennen*, merchants gather and discuss the lives of their women at home, who, they speculate, are most likely sleeping with other men. In

Boccaccio's tale, in particular, this conviction is combined with the indulgent sexual morality characteristic of the book:

> And one of them jovially remarked: "I've no idea how mine gets by; what I do know is that if I get my hands on a wench who takes my fancy, why, I don't let my love for my wife stand in the way—I have my fill of the girl in hand."
>
> "That's just what I do," said another. "Suppose I believe my wife makes hay while the sun shines: so she does. And what if I don't believe it? She'll do it just the same! What's sauce for the goose is sauce for the gander; as a man sows, so does he reap."
>
> (Boccaccio [c. 1353] 1993: 147)

Dioneo, the "wild card" among the storytellers of *The Decameron* (having obtained the license to tell whatever story most pleases him whatever the topic of the day, and also the male storyteller most inclined to tease the women), begins the following story, which he says that he has selected instead of his planned story at the last minute, as a rejoinder to Bernabò's (the Boccaccian precursor for Posthumus) assumption of his wife's fidelity "and the absurdity of all those men who are ready to believe what he evidently did, that as they go roaming about and enjoy a romp with one woman after the next as occasion serves, their wives just sit at home with their thumbs tucked into their belts" (Boccaccio [1353] 1993: 158). Dioneo's story is a classic fabliau about an old and impotent man who marries a young wife, only to have her stolen away by a young pirate—whom she much prefers to her staid life at home.

To the extent that he borrows from Boccaccio, then, Shakespeare demonizes the assumptions of Dioneo in the figure of Iachimo, who articulates the Dioneo position in Shakespeare's play; Imogen, meanwhile, becomes a model of absolute female virtue, close to tragic heroines such as Desdemona or Cordelia or to Lucrece from Shakespeare's narrative poetry. Imogen's virtue, like that of Cordelia, seems designed to carry some of the weight of a new configuration of Britishness that is retrospectively assigned to the ancient past. When Iachimo first troubles her with his insinuations about Posthumus's behavior with the Italian women, her response, "My lord, I fear, / Has forgot Britain" (*Cym* 1.6.112–13), conflates his fidelity to her with his fidelity to Britain. (He himself is referred to as "the Briton" [1.4.25] rather than named as Posthumus when we first meet him in exile.) If the assumption of greater female constancy is a given of Shakespearean characterization, then the late Shakespeare seems to elevate that quality to a metaphysics of female virtue that encompasses state and nation as well as family.

The transcendental spirit of female virtue, however, is still tied to the domestic space of marriage, and the ring remains the talismanic "gentle bond" of marriage. Neither Boccaccio's nor *Frederyke of Jennen*'s version of the wager tale revolves around the possession of a ring. In both tales, discussion of the fidelity of wives occasions a money wager on the chastity of one particular wife. In *Cymbeline*, on the other hand, the wager is for a ring given to Posthumus by Imogen at the beginning of the play. As with Portia, the ring given by the wife is the emblem of male fidelity:

> Look here, love;
> The diamond was my mother's. Take it, heart,
> But keep it till you woo another wife
> When Imogen is dead.
>
> (*Cym* 1.1.111–14)

Posthumus, in return, gives her a bracelet that he calls "a manacle of love" placed upon "this fairest prisoner" (*Cym* 1.1.121–2). He is both her "adorer" (1.4.65) and her jailor, perhaps enough of a comment on the status of the husband in the play.

When Iachimo challenges the fidelity of Imogen in Italy, it is expressly occasioned partly by the ring, which he equates, without any specific knowledge, with both the body and reputation of Imogen: "If she went before others I have seen, as that diamond of yours outlusters many I have beheld, I could not but believe she excelled many; but I have not seen the most precious diamond that is, nor you the lady" (*Cym* 1.4.68–72). Proposing a wager on the fidelity of Imogen, Iachimo asks Posthumus to stake the ring against ten thousand ducats on his own part. Posthumus initially refuses in terms that bind it to his own body: "I will wage against your gold, gold to it. My ring I hold dear as my finger; 'tis part of it" (1.4.129–30). Iachimo's further insinuations about Imogen are enough—and here we have a preview of the power of Iachimo's cunning language on Posthumus—to bring Posthumus quickly to the point of staking the ring on the wager: "I shall but lend my diamond till your return" (1.4.139–40). There is no particular need to "lend" his diamond—which might mean that the diamond is dramatically brought forward for display before the audience before some form of safekeeping—but it highlights the extent to which Posthumus has already betrayed his own fidelity, which Imogen explicitly associates with his possession of the ring.

The crucible of Posthumus's transformation from adoring husband to virulent misogynist is thus not such a long journey as it might first appear to those who have not fully assimilated the symbolic force of his staking of the ring in the initial scene with Iachimo. When Iachimo returns to Italy with his "proofs" of Imogen's infidelity, his production of the bracelet, Imogen's "manacle," stolen from her chamber, is the tipping point for Posthumus. Iachimo's language underlines the way in which the jewels metonymically represent the bodies with which they are associated: "It [the bracelet] must be married / To that your

FIGURE 1.2: Louis Rhead, "Softly unloosening the bracelet from her arm." Courtesy of the Folger Shakespeare Library. Public domain.

diamond" (*Cym* 2.4.97–8) (Figure 1.2). His possession of the "manacle" binds him, not to Imogen but to Posthumus, in a kind of marriage. This illusion is possible because Posthumus has already strayed in willingly alienating Imogen's ring from himself, and then finally handing it over to Iachimo. Instead of wooing another wife, as Imogen foretold in giving the ring, it becomes another kind of bond, his homosocial one with Iachimo (like the bond between Antonio and Bassanio in *Merchant*).

The quasi-magical powers invested in the ring and bracelet are echoed in the aura of female resurrection central to late Shakespeare. Imogen goes to bed with a prayer to the pagan gods: "To your protection I commend me, gods. / From fairies and the tempters of the night / Guard me, beseech ye!" (*Cym* 2.2.8–10). Fairies, and perhaps their tales, seem to be more than usually present in the language of the play, especially in the scenes of Imogen with her brothers in Wales. When Belarius and his "sons" encounter Imogen as they return to their cave—a moment that might recall tales closely related to

Snow White in which a young woman lodges unknown with her brothers or rescues her brothers (Artese 2015: 181-3)—Belarius says that he would be inclined to call her a fairy but for the fact that she eats their food, like a human (*Cym* 3.6.39–41). After her apparent death from the potion that the queen (the evil stepmother) believes to be poison, but which the audience knows to be a sleeping potion, Guiderius bids Fidele farewell in terms that suggest the possibility of awakening:

> Why, he but sleeps.
> If he be gone, he'll make his grave a bed;
> With female fairies will his tomb be haunted,
> And worms will not come to thee.
>
> (*Cym* 4.2.215–18)

Shakespeare invests Wales in particular with the aura of fairies inhabiting the ancient Britain of Cymbeline as if to highlight a mythic/folkloric British antiquity (Figure 1.3).

When Imogen awakens, she immediately encounters the dead Cloten, slain and beheaded by her brother Guiderius. Cloten happens to be wearing the attire of Posthumus, since, outraged by her earlier stray remark about the great value of Posthumus's meanest apparel in comparison with him, Cloten had planned to rape Imogen while he wore Posthumus's clothing to exacerbate her injury. This macabre piece of stagecraft, the headless body of Cloten wearing the clothing of Posthumus, concludes the symbolic logic of the wager plot, the equation of Posthumus with Cloten. Even at the play's conclusion, Posthumus is somewhat insecurely rehabilitated, as his striking of Imogen in the final scene indicates. As in the sources for the wager story, Imogen is central to the unraveling of the deception, but in Shakespeare it comes from her sighting the ring that Iachimo, now a prisoner of the Britons, still wears. Iachimo himself, unlike his equivalent in the sources, is stricken with guilt and wishes his own death, so powerful has been the recognition of Imogen's virtue. His final words in the play combine the desire for ultimate punishment along with the handing back of the ring and bracelet to Posthumus:

> Take that life, beseech you,
> Which I so often owe; but your ring first,
> And here the bracelet of the truest princess
> That ever swore her faith.
>
> (*Cym* 5.5.417–20)

The lines presumably accompany the return of the ring and bracelet into Posthumus's hands, which, once again, operates as talismanic bond between husband and wife.

FIGURE 1.3: Arthur Rackham, *Lament for Imogen*, 1899. Courtesy of the Folger Shakespeare Library. Public domain.

The recognitions at the end of the play, however, are even more familial than oriented to the romantic love of Posthumus and Imogen. The restoration of the brothers to both Cymbeline and Imogen is more powerful in many respects than the awkwardness of the relationship between the two lovers. The last three acts of the play, as the action switches from the British court and Italy to Wales, is a kind of extended lesson in the natural nobility of the brothers, independent of the court, combined with the leveling spirit of pastoral retreat that becomes a form of universal brotherhood:

> Arviragus
>   Brother, stay here.
> Are we not brothers?
> Imogen
>   So man and man should be,
> But clay and clay differs in dignity,
> Whose dust is both alike.
>
> (Cym 4.2.2–5)

This might seem like an odd lesson from the top of the aristocratic world order, but it is characteristic of late Shakespeare. Brotherhood is indeed the general spirit of the final scene, presided over by a Cymbeline who rejoices from the position of the mother rather than the patriarchal tyrant: "O, what am I? / A mother to the birth of three? / Ne'er mother / Rejoiced deliverance more" (Cym 5.5.371–3). Cymbeline names Belarius as brother (5.5.402). Posthumus, having fought with Arviragus and Guiderius in the battle, becomes their brother through marriage, confirming a previous act of brotherhood: "You holp us sir," says Arviragus to him, "As you did mean indeed to be our brother. / Joyed are we that you are" (5.5.425–7). Siblinghood, even hints of universal siblinghood, is the strongest note of the end of the play, combined with the complex set of negotiations that make Britain and Rome into fraternal empires rather than competitors. (The newly "maternal" Cymbeline decides to yield to Rome even though he has just defeated Rome in battle.) The fairy-tale aspect of the plot is transferred, as G. Wilson Knight long ago implied, to the "majestic marriage [of Britain and Rome], where we are to imagine that the partners 'lived happily ever afterwards'" ([1947] 1966: 139).

The condensation of romance/folktale motifs into political arrangements thus appears to subsume the more exclusive focus on marital bonds in the earlier Shakespeare plays examined here. The afterglow of the wife's uncanny power, however, is increasingly diffused: extended to the fraternal bonds between family, countrymen, and ultimately, myths of origin (the *translatio imperii* from Rome to Britain). The play seems to adumbrate the path to national identity as the *fraternité* later elaborated by the French Revolution. It is difficult to read these plays together without the sense that the final play of the three, *Cymbeline*, generalizes the "marriage tale" as a metaphysics of nationhood.

CONCLUSION

In many respects Shakespeare works close to the development of the European fairy tale, without directly participating in it. In the three comedies/romances examined here, Shakespeare seems to revel in the use of plots, devices, and motifs that suggest folktale and romance. The use of devices such as cross-dressing, riddles, and bed tricks—here, as in elsewhere in Shakespeare—suggests a playwright consistently working close to cultural forms of inversion that are equally important to the fairy tale, as well as to folklore and romance. In plays focused on marriage, as these plays are, the talismanic ring represents the spiritual power ascribed to marriage, especially true in a newly Protestant country, but also traces the trajectory of exchanges (male to male, husband to mistress) that undermine the same "magic." The uncanny qualities that Shakespearean comedy often grants to its heroines is not, then, simply to be equated to the elevation of marriage but rather to a kind of prophylactic against any naïve trust in marriage. This is the Shakespearean "magic realism" of the marriage plot: resolutions that border on the magical while revealing a strikingly disenchanted, psychologically nuanced perspective on "happ'ly-ever-aftering."

CHAPTER TWO

Adaptation

Prose Stories Dressed in Ottoman Attire

N. İPEK HÜNER CORA

INTRODUCTION

Writing about adaptations of tales and related genres in Ottoman literature and storytelling is an intriguing challenge, as it requires a somewhat clear definition of adaptation and translation in the Ottoman context, as well as a comprehensive overview of Ottoman literature and storytelling. Since many studies on the Ottoman literature focus on case studies or trace specific themes, we lack a bird's-eye view of the corpus of Ottoman fiction analyzed comparatively alongside Islamicate and Mediterranean literatures.[1] The present attempt, therefore, stands as an exploratory effort to understand the complexity and richness of Ottoman literary production, its translations and adaptations, by asking questions and tracing some examples in the form of prose stories.

After a short introduction on prose fiction and storytelling in the Ottoman Empire, this chapter will discuss the fluid world of translations, adaptations, and versions in Ottoman Turkish. It will then discuss how the stories were adapted—or in other words, how they donned Ottoman attire. In doing so, the chapter challenges the quest for an "original" to every Ottoman story. Then, continuing to think about adaptations in context, the discussion turns to three stories, each with several versions, and speculates on how the stories changed according to their respective audiences and contexts.

Storytelling has always had many forms in the Ottoman literary tradition. Ottoman literati used different genres to tell stories; prose fiction was only one of them. Storytelling in verse (in *mesnevī* form)[2] was equally (if not more) common, as poetry seems to have been the preferred form of higher literary production. Both the Ottoman authors and modern scholars following their instructions have declared prose secondary to poetry—in quality and in popularity. This attitude granted prose fiction a rather marginal status.[3] However, the sheer number of prose stories in manuscripts and of references to oral culture speaks for a broader corpus. Thus, this chapter will limit itself primarily to prose fiction.[4]

The categorization of Ottoman prose fiction is fluid, as is that of its adaptations and translations. Scholars have attempted to organize stories in Ottoman Turkish according to their themes (for example, religious, mystical, heroic, love, historical, metaphorical, adventurous), their characters (for example, love stories with two heroes), or their origins (stories from the Quran, Arabic or Persian literature, "national" or "local" stories, anonymous stories).[5] An overarching binary that has often been used is that of folk vs. high literature, and the primary indicators of that division have been the language, patrons, and places of reading. Yet the stories that were in circulation in the Ottoman Empire themselves defy neat attempts at categorization, as versions of the same story can be found in manuscripts spanning several centuries with only minute updates.

On top of the universal difficulties of defining the genre of literary fairy tales (Zipes 2000b), the Ottoman context had its own complication. As the category of fairy tale is primarily studied by folklorists in search of "Turkish" tales, the primary material focus has been on collecting and recording stories in oral circulation. The genre has been seen as primarily oral, since it belonged to the "folk." Consequently, such tales are treated as timeless productions of the Turkish nation, instead of being the literary productions of an Ottoman literary elite.[6] The binary between folkloristic studies and historicist approaches, as well as the classical vs. folk dichotomy, made a holistic view of the fairy tales difficult to achieve. Pertev Naili Boratav, a key figure in fairy tale studies and folklore, has brought attention to the written sources of the tales and emphasized the significance of including works by the Ottoman literati when tracing the history of literary fairy tales (Boratav 1969: 399–413). This chapter attempts to do just that, by focusing on stories in writing.

Another difficulty is the applicability of the term "literary fairy tale" to the Ottoman context. Discussions on the fairy tale genre primarily belong to the Western context, while the "Oriental Tale," especially *The Thousand and One Nights*, has been one of the principal sources of the fairy-tale corpus (Marzolph 2000: 370–2). These "Oriental" tales coming from the popular corpora, such as *Ferec Bad'eş-Şidde* (*Relief After Hardship*), *Forty Viziers*, and *The Thousand and One Nights*, as well as their many translations and adaptations, were in circulation in the Ottoman lands, both in manuscript and—presumably—oral forms. With their focus on "high" literature and limited interest in storytelling, the literary scholars of the Ottoman Empire preferred "realist" stories over all others, and stories with unrealistic elements were regarded simply as marginal. They have also been treated under the category of *mirabilia* (*'acā'ib* and *garā'ib*). Folkloristic approaches instead regarded the stories primarily as timeless, looking at adaptations to find archetypes (Boratav 1982: 274).

Considering all the layers of the question of Ottoman prose fiction and the Turkish literary fairy tale, it is still difficult to categorize the stories that have been selected for discussion in this chapter. However, I believe that they serve an important purpose, as they provide a fruitful base for comparison with other cultures and exemplify how tales were adapted by and for Ottoman audiences. Thinking of the establishment of the European fairy-tale tradition, the first story discussed below, with its pear tree, may be familiar to readers of Giovanni Boccaccio and Geoffrey Chaucer; the second to readers of Petronius and Jean de La Fontaine, and the last to devotees of *The Thousand and One Nights*. In short, to use a cautionary phrasing, this chapter will look at the examples of Ottoman literary prose fiction and the stories in question have been recorded in the pages of the manuscripts by Ottoman literati while they might have been also circulating among Ottoman people orally.

Over its nearly 600-year life span, the Ottoman Empire's subjects produced a significant amount of literary fiction. The time period that this volume covers (1450–1650) overlaps roughly with the "Classical Age" of the empire, which has been seen in the traditional scholarship as the "Golden Age."[7] During this epoch, the Ottomans were extremely successful on the battlefields and in diplomatic endeavors. This period also abounded in literary patronage, which facilitated the production of many works that have been celebrated for centuries.[8] The artistic productions of the period have been characterized as canonically "imperial" or "Ottoman."[9]

There are possible pitfalls to accepting such a neat categorization of the classical or golden age. The first issue is that the historical and political chronology is expected to fit in neatly with the literary production—and the historical chronology has been debated.[10] This is not to say that the literary culture was static, but rather to emphasize that political changes do not necessarily overlap with changes in literary production and patronage. Furthermore, many stories in circulation are in no way limited by the (fluid) boundaries of the Ottoman Empire, and of its many languages. The stories are an integral part of a larger Islamicate and Mediterranean world where people told and retold stories—possibly inscribing different desires in them and providing different morals for them. Belonging to a shared culture over many centuries, however, does not make the stories any less "Ottoman."[11]

There are different ways in which the "imperial" and "Ottoman" characteristics of literary production can be understood. Some scholars have used such terms to refer to a specific Ottoman production that is unique and different from that of other cultures. This attitude, which by its definition leaves translations and adaptations of tales out of the picture, is especially dangerous as it runs the risk of excluding many works that Ottomans appreciated and deemed their own. A second attitude, which treats translations, adaptations, and versions also as "Ottoman" works, is more productive, as they reflected Ottoman choices and expectations as much as—if not more than—the "original works" by the Ottoman authors.[12] Like the Ottoman Empire itself, Ottoman literature was built on the heritage of other civilizations. The Ottomans grounded their literature in this rich literary legacy to create an imperial culture that was a vibrant and unique amalgamation of many cultures.

The emphasis on seeking the origins of the "Ottoman" story or identifying the original Turkish story—or rather, categorization of stories into groups that are broadly labeled as translations from Arabic, Persian, Indian, or other languages—and the ways in which it has been dealt with strongly relates to the topic of this chapter, as it speaks to the rather unsuccessful attempts to label the stories as originals (read "ours"), translations (read "theirs"), and adaptations (read "it was theirs, but now it may be considered somewhat as ours"). The traditional scholarship on Ottoman prose fiction generally favors the so-called "originals" over the adaptations and translations, and thus a significant body of stories are simply left at the margins of academic attention.[13] However, the translations, adaptations, and versions are key to the Ottoman literary corpus—be it prose or poetry—and Ottomans' contemporaneous relationship to these concepts should be regarded in context.

"DRESSED IN RŪMĪ ATTIRE": ADAPTATIONS, TRANSLATIONS, AND RETELLINGS IN OTTOMAN CONTEXT

For the centuries under examination, it is very difficult to distinguish between translations, adaptations, and versions. Ottoman literary choices, which are of course different from modern ones, also complicate the question. One of the most important pillars of the Ottoman literary tradition is *nazire* (imitatio)—which means providing a literary response to a work or engaging in a dialogue with a work, a practice most frequently encountered in poetry. The motivations behind writing a *nazire* are numerous: it may be an appreciation of the work and its author, a desire to engage in a conversation with the author, or a claim to show superiority. Perhaps difficult to understand in our contemporary literary environment that celebrates originality, the *nazire* tradition created a literary corpus that was profoundly "intercultural" (Paker 2002: 120–1).[14] In that respect, originality has been discussed mostly with respect to poetry, but this chapter will limit itself to literary prose as yet another venue for discussing intertextuality, fluidity, and how different works have been adapted across centuries and geographies.

Many classical works of the Islamicate literatures, especially the tales of love and adventure—such as Layla and Majnun, Yusuf and Zulaikha, Khusraw and Shirin, and so on—have been translated from and retold in Arabic, Persian, Ottoman Turkish, and other languages of the wider Islamicate lands repeatedly over the centuries, being adapted and appropriated for different audiences.[15] These stories, while treated commonly as "translations," were an indispensable part of the Ottoman literary canon, and many references, metaphors, and allusions invoking these stories and/or their elements confirm their canonical position. In this respect, the circulation of these stories—be they translation, adaptations, or oral retellings—in Islamicate and Mediterranean cultures affirms that "adaptation becomes a veritable marker of canonical status" (Sanders 2016: 9). Scholars today have sometimes simply regarded these works in Ottoman Turkish as translations. Sometimes, they celebrated the authors by noting that they had actually written the story anew. Creativity and originality in translation is in the foreground of these appraisals; they are definitely not being appreciated for their fidelity to the original text. The bias toward originality seems to persist also in translators' favoring retellings instead of verbatim translations.[16]

Defining the set boundaries of adaptations, translations, retellings, versions, etc. is impossible and surely not unique to the Ottoman case.[17] With respect to defining translations, Ottomans used a variety of phrases, and an apt metaphor the Ottomans have used is that of dressing in *Rūmī* attire, so the authors/translators are presented as the agents clothing the text in local dress (Paker 2014: 44).[18] During the time period under consideration, *Rūmī* is used with reference to the core lands of the Ottoman Empire.[19] Thus, the authors'/translators' act of clothing the text (namely, translation/adaptation) is not merely a simple translation, but also an adaptation and contextualization so that the text will be at home in its new attire. In other words, the readers/audience will be able to recognize the characters—and as an extension thereof, the topic—as they will be familiar with them already. Serpil Bağcı observes the same in miniatures. For example, the translated copies of the famous Persian epic *Şehnāme* (*Shahnama*), have their figures painted in Ottoman attire. Not only the text is translated but also the images (Bağcı 2000) (Figure 2.1).[20]

The boundaries between adaptation and translation have been vague since the very early works penned in Ottoman Turkish. For instance, Gülşehrī (late thirteenth/early fourteenth century) adapted *The Conference of the Birds*—a Sufi epic poem concerning birds on a quest for their ideal king as a metaphor to the Sufi path of life by Ferīdūn ʿAṭṭār (twelfth century)—translating from Persian to Ottoman Turkish, while preserving the work's original title.[21] Gülşehrī's work, however, includes around thirty stories, in comparison to the 186 original stories that were chosen by ʿAṭṭār—and of those thirty stories, only

FIGURE 2.1: A Turkish translation of the Persian epic *Şehnāme* (*Shahnama*) with the figures dressed in Ottoman attire. From The New York Public Library, https://digitalcollections.nypl.org/items/510d47e3-7600-a3d9-e040-e00a18064a99.

about a third are taken from ʿAṭṭār. While keeping the frame tale but changing the number of birds, he replaces individual stories with ones that his readership are familiar with, primarily from the canonical books of his time.[22] In that respect, his translation follows the same method that ʿAṭṭār used in compiling his book—the stories he placed within the frame tale were ones that had already been in circulation (Sak 2012: 658–9). From a modern perspective, the idea is challenging: he sticks with the old and the known. One can speculate as to the reasons, but transmitting the moral of the story to his audience may have been the main motivation. According to Yıldız, the choices by ʿAṭṭār went beyond simply addressing an Anatolian audience. While confirming that Gülşehrī's protagonists must have been residents of Anatolia, she also shows that Gülşehrī was actually addressing ongoing religious polemics between Muslims and Christians in the fourteenth century in that local context; the work thus differed significantly from ʿAṭṭār's original (Yıldız 2015: 332–8).

With the same bias toward originality, Gülşehrī's translation/adaptation to Ottoman Turkish is commonly praised as "almost-an-original." Many Ottoman authors followed suit with adaptations of canonical works in the subsequent centuries. Contemporary scholars are also on the same page with Gülşehrī. In *Adaptation and Appropriation*, for instance, Julia Sanders, referencing Susan Basnett's argument that all translations are a "form of rewriting," notes, that "all adapters are translators, then, and all translators are creative writers of a sort" (2016: 9).[23]

THE "QUEST" FOR THE ORIGINAL STORY

The quest for the "original" story is not unique to Ottoman studies. In *A Theory of Adaptation* (2006), Linda Hutcheon criticizes the "case-study model," which privileges or prioritizes "the source" or "the original" text and consequently gives it a higher value. Instead, she argues, challenging its "authority" or "priority" and arguing that the "adapted text" can be "plural" with many versions is a more productive approach (2006: xiii). This approach is especially appropriate with respect to Ottoman literary culture, as the "adapted text" may just as well be oral, circulating freely in reading circles as its different versions are kept in writing. Another benefit of this approach—accepting plural versions across time and space—is that it also makes it easier to deal with the manuscript culture. Many stories are recorded in story compilations and miscellanea that cannot be dated, and many that are dated simply provide the date of the copying and compiling, not the date of the stories within. This "silence of the sources, the problem of lacunae in the manuscript traditions" as Karla Mallette puts it, affects all scholars working on manuscripts (2014: 130). In addition, the versions in the manuscripts were—very probably—rarely read silently, but would instead be read in literary gatherings called *majlis*.[24] In all these performances, the storytellers continuously "adapted" the stories according to the audience, taking their reactions and expectations into consideration. While some of these adaptations might have been recorded in writing, others have simply been lost. This possibility of further adaptations shows the interactive and lively world of early modern Ottoman literature and the—almost—futile search for "the" original.

Considering the fluidity of the literary tradition, locating, or even before that, defining the original is difficult, if not impossible. The word *te'līf* (literally, "the act of compiling a book") is commonly translated today as "original."[25] In her attempt to contextualize translations and original works, Saliha Paker instead defines *te'līf* as "a work that relies upon a source or sources that can be considered foreign, a work that is produced partially by the author's contributions" (2014: 39).[26] In an article in English, she translates *te'līf* as "creative mediation," and underlines that in translation studies the word *te'līf* is commonly translated into English as "'indigenous' rather than as 'original'" (Paker 2015: 27, 37). Paker's intervention to the *"te'līf* = original" debate is significant, as it problematizes what modern readers expect from an original work and what premodern readers expected from *te'līf* works. Many *te'līf* works bear strong intertextual links to other texts, as the examples below will show. However, we need further studies digging into primary sources comparatively to understand what the Ottoman authors meant when they claimed that a work was their own *te'līf*. Were they thinking of their "original" contribution or an "original" adaptation? What were the boundaries between *te'līf* and *nazire* (imitatio)?

Some sources claim that the "first" known original prose story by an Ottoman author was the story of "Anabacı" by Vahdī Çelebi, written in the first half of the sixteenth century (Kavruk 1998: 85). Contemporary sources also state that the story is his creation.[27] But this claim is rather difficult to prove. The plot is a classical—even cliché—example of the women's wiles stories, in which female characters prove to be (often sexually) deceitful, a prevalent genre in Islamicate literatures. In this story, a merchant is devastated by the love (and deception) of a beautiful and clever woman, only to learn that he is but one of the many victims of her vicious tricks.[28]

A remarkable feature of the story is its similarity to an episode of the frame tale of "The Story of King Shahriyār and His Brother" in the *Arabian Nights* compendium.[29] In the story in the *Nights*, a woman famously collects the rings of the men with whom she has managed to sleep while being kept under close surveillance by a djinn who tries to keep her away from all men. The sheer number of the rings she collects represents the impossibility of keeping women away from their desires—and their unfaithfulness. The protagonist of the "Anabacı" story likewise collects memorabilia from her lovers: she asks for one of their teeth as a token of their love (hence the story is also known as "The

Story of the Teeth" (*Hikāye-i Dendāniyye*). The details of the plots and the ends of both stories differ—yet the use of the same motif is striking. Even though the story cannot be called a translation, it may be considered adaptation or an inspiration, as Vahdī Çelebi might have heard or read the story from the *Nights* or one of its many other versions that must have been in circulation throughout the Islamicate world.[30]

Stories circulated beyond boundaries, languages, and class barriers: a story may be found in different languages with subtle changes, and the characters, as well as their religious and ethnic affiliations, change according to where the stories were told. In addition, the same story may appear both in a manuscript that has been prepared for the Sultan and in a low-quality production that might have been in circulation in the city. Of course, in a world of literary production that was primarily fueled by the patronage system, the palace and the sultan's taste mattered. Sultan Murad III's (r.1574–95) fondness for stories, for example, is well known and the story of one of the collections he commissioned shows the many facets of its circulation.

A set of stories usually referred to as *te'līf* is Cinānī's (d.1595) story collection, *Bedāyi'ü'l-āṣār* (*Embellished Works*).[31] He compiled these stories at the request of Sultan Murad III, who asked for stories yet untold. His quest to earn praise and honor from the sultan for his efforts proved vain as one of Sultan's booncompanions took his compilation while it was at the bookbinder and told them to the sultan. Thus, when presented it, the sultan was not impressed because he had already heard the stories. His quest for originality failed—though in this case it did not really matter who had created the story, the originality was based on having heard the story. In the end, Cinānī was disappointed because his efforts were poorly rewarded (Kavruk 1998: 90–3). What the sultan did not know—or even if he did, it did not become part of the discussion—was that Cinānī had included several translations and adaptations in his collection (Ünlü 2009: 108–16). Two of the stories he included in his compilation require a closer look, as they are adaptations of stories that had circulated widely for centuries, but appeared now in "Ottoman" attire.

ADAPTATIONS BEFITTING THE CONTEXT AND THE AUDIENCE: AN OTTOMAN IN THE (PEAR) TREE

The adaptations in Cinānī's compilation indicate an "Ottomanization" of the stories. Here, with Ottomanization, I do not refer to an imperial or nationalist agenda. "Ottomanization" of the stories is a process that can be better explained with the metaphor of the story and its characters' donning an Ottoman attire. Of course, with the limited information at hand and the disadvantages inherent in working with manuscripts, it is impossible to pinpoint Cinānī as the sole person behind the changes in the narrative or as the creative mind behind the adaptation. It is possible that Cinānī recorded stories that he had heard or read. Yet this uncertainty does not change our main argument: these stories were adapted for their Ottoman audiences.

The first example of an adaptation is recorded as the thirty-second story in Cinānī's collection ([16th c.] 2009: 121–3). The story, another example of women's wiles, is set in the past and features a pretty trickster, her husband, and her lover. Broadly summarizing, the story goes as follows: the lover could not possibly meet the woman because her husband was always at her side. One day, unable to endure the pain of separation, the lover sent her a threatening message giving her no chance to refuse: she should make their union possible, if not, he would kill her first, and himself later. Seeing the urgency of the situation, she invited him via a messenger to come to a promenade and instructed him to hide there. At dawn, she convinces her husband to go for a romantic stroll on the same promenade. Her husband, portrayed as a simple-minded man, complies. While they are wandering around, the woman climbs to the top of a big tree. Suddenly, she looks down at her husband and starts crying and accusing him of having intercourse under the tree. Her husband, perplexed, denies the accusations, yet the woman quickly comes down and implores him to go to the qadi so that they can get a divorce. The husband then has a brilliant idea: what if it is the tree that causes the person sitting in it to see the people below in such a way? To test this argument, he climbs the tree, looks down and sees a man take his wife and copulate with her. He cheerfully declares his superior intellect and says that if he were deficient in intellect like her, he would have slandered her—but he has understood the peculiar qualities of the tree.[32] Meanwhile, the couple below the tree have finished their dalliance, the man leaves and the married couple return home with peace of mind. Cinānī ends his story with a couplet calling the husband a panderer and chastising him for his imbecility.

While Cinānī has defined his own compilation as a collection of rare stories, this story had surely been in circulation for at least a few centuries—and it was to be retold by Ottomans and later by subjects of the Turkish Republic.[33] Before Cinānī's version, it is possible to locate several different versions of this tale and, looking across those adaptations, it is possible to see how the Ottomans adapted the story according to its audience. Below, I will first introduce an earlier Ottoman version of the text in the story collection *Forty Viziers*, and then I will try to locate the Ottoman adaptation within the larger Mediterranean framework as other versions in Persian and Arabic are introduced and discussed, with reference to Franklin Lewis's comparison with episodes in Boccaccio and Chaucer (Lewis 2012).

A fifteenth-century version of this story in Ottoman Turkish is found in the collection *Forty Viziers*.[34] The *Forty Viziers* consists of a set of stories embedded in a frame tale. The frame tale goes as follows: the sultan's son has been advised by his instructor not to talk for forty days, as he has seen an inauspicious time period in the young man's life. Just as the prince starts his period of silence, the new and young wife of the sultan opens up to him about her feelings toward him, but meets with silence and rejection. The wife then tries to convince her husband, the sultan, to kill his son, accusing him of having attacked her. Each night, the woman tells a story to the sultan that aims to convince him to kill the disloyal son, and in response, one of the forty viziers tells a story about women's wiles and why one should never listen to women. A version of the tree story is told by the thirty-first vizier, and while the plot runs parallel to Cinānī's version, there are a few key differences. For instance, the woman does not come up with the plan because her lover has threatened to kill her. Instead, the lover is concerned that the husband may kill them if he gets wind of the affair, and the woman takes up the challenge: she shall fulfill his desires in front of her husband's eyes. In this version, unlike the later Ottoman versions, women's lack of mental capacity is not referred to. One of the important details is that the woman does not simply assume that her husband will blame everything on the tree; she actually suggests the idea to him by asking if the tree has a mystery. Another motif that is unique to this version is that both husband and wife are high on intoxicants (*bengī*), as the woman makes her husband enjoy *bengī* with her on the way to their outing ("Kırk Vezir Hikâyeleri İnceleme-Metin-Sözlük" ["The Story of Forty Viziers, Analysis, Text, Dictionary"] 2012: 318–19).

In "One Chaste Muslim and a Persian in a Pear Tree," Lewis discusses the "pear tree episode" by elaborating on the use of the pear tree by Boccaccio, Chaucer, Rūmī, and an Arabic narrator. The story, always an alarming example of women's wiles, has changed among versions and I will not summarize them all in detail here, as Lewis has already done so (2012: 137–64). To give the background very succinctly, in Boccaccio's pear tree episode, the wife successfully engages in sexual intercourse with her lover before her husband's eyes by using a pear tree and the so-called misperception it causes. In Chaucer's "The Merchant's Tale," the wife engages in an encounter in the tree but her husband's blindness is cured just at that moment so that she can be punished. However, she convinces her husband that he, having just regained his sight, is not seeing things clearly. In both stories, the authors emphasize the age difference between an old husband and an inappropriately young bride. The Persian version of the story, narrated by Rūmī, the thirteenth-century poet and mystic, predates Boccaccio's, and the wife, again, convinces her husband that it is the tree that makes the person on top see the person below as if they were copulating. However, the wife blames the husband for having sex with a boy (*amrād*), not a woman. The clueless husband rejects all the claims arguing, righteously, that he is all alone. Rūmī's version also entails a mystical interpretation of the story, instead of a purely bawdy one. For him the pear tree is not an actual tree but symbolizes existence, and the human ego is deceptive, causing people to see things wrongly. So one should abandon selfishness to see without deceptions (Lewis 2012: 152). In all these versions, climbing the tree has a logical motivation: to pick the fruit. The Arabic version Lewis introduces, which predates all the other versions, changes the tree into a date tree, yet the fruit-plucking remains and the imagined partner of the husband is a woman. But it is the man who threatens the wife with divorce (137–64).

The Ottomans adapted the story for their own audiences. In turning the story into part of the women's wiles canon, they give the woman more agency—presumably not to empower her but to showcase women's deceptive tendencies. In the version in the *Forty Viziers*, the woman arranges the encounter in the pear tree as a challenge. In all the versions in Ottoman Turkish, it is the woman who asks for divorce when faced with the so-called adultery scene. Cinānī even puts words into the man's mouth that ridicule and emasculate him further, as he says that he is not deficient in intellect, like his wife ([sixteenth century] 2009: 26).

While empowering women—or carried away by the excitement of events—the narrators drop a logical step from the plot: the women in all the Ottoman versions simply climb the tree, no fruit or fruit-picking is even mentioned. Why would a woman climb up a tree? In the version in the *Forty Viziers*, do the exhilarants (*bengī*) create an explanation for this action? Do they help the husband to assume that he is simply hallucinating because of the tree? Need one look for logical elements in plots?

A reader who has encountered the versions in Ottoman Turkish before all the others (like the author of this chapter) does not realize this gap in the plot and simply assumes that women climb on trees on a whim if they are up to mischief. Within the canon of Ottoman women's wiles stories, this one reads like just another example showing the extent to which women can go in debauchery or wittiness.[35] What the story in its Ottoman garment might have meant for its various Ottoman audiences is an intriguing question that is beyond the purposes of this chapter; with the lack of reader's responses and our inability to access the oral circles of those days, the answer must remain pure speculation. Instead, I will turn my gaze to another story that has donned Ottoman dress.

AN OTTOMAN WIDOW

Another enduringly popular story that made it into Cinānī's compilation also showcases how the authors adapted the stories for Ottoman audiences and made them an internal element of the women's wiles corpus, this time by changing the motives in the story in tune with the anxieties of the Ottoman readership and their perceptions of honor. Story number 5 in Cinānī, a version of the *Widow of Ephesus* story, which dates back to the first century, tells the story of an apparently faithful wife who, now a widow, dishonors her deceased husband by having intercourse on top of his grave, removing his body from his grave, plucking the hairs from his beard, and substituting his body for the missing body of a hanged criminal.[36] The fact that she does all these actions to save her future husband, the guard who was supposed to watch the missing corpse (instead of enjoying himself with the recent widow), is not stressed by Cinānī. In comparison to many other versions of this story, Cinānī's retelling, as well as other Ottoman versions in subsequent centuries, has three interventions that the Ottoman audience would readily relate to. First of all, the woman plucks the deceased's beard hair by hair so that he will look like the stolen corpse. Second, the story continues beyond the disinterring of the body, with the guard and the woman going on to marry. Third, after a few years of marriage, the guard is on his deathbed and he provides her with the remainder of her dowry and an additional 3,000 silver coins (*aqçe*).[37] In the presence of witnesses, he declares that the 3,000 *aqçe* is *to prevent her from plucking his beard* after his death so as not to suffer like her deceased husband ([16th c.] 2009: 121–3).

While there are differences in the plotline and in other details, all the Ottoman versions of the story stick with the beard-plucking—which has been a mutilation motif in other versions beyond the Ottoman realms. Also, the wedding of the couple and the payment in addition to the dowry seem to be choices on the part of the narrator intended to make the story more relevant to the audience. Plucking the beard of a man is a symbolic emasculation and can be considered worse than the initial disinterring of the body, considering the social and moral codes in the Ottoman Empire.[38] The marriage may represent a feasible end to the couple's intercourse in the cemetery, but more importantly, it leads the plot to the deathbed of the guard, who there emphasizes the evil and disloyal nature of the woman in front of the witnesses. Thus, this age-old story is made into an Ottoman women's wiles story ending in a couplet warning men not to believe in women or their love. Ottoman narrators made sure that the moral codes in the story were adapted accordingly.

SIGNIFICANCE OF VERSIONS: LOST AND FOUND IN TRANSLATIONS

The two stories I have discussed above are examples of stories in circulation that became a part of the Ottoman storytelling tradition in their Ottoman attire. Their adaptation, thus, was done with an Ottoman audience in mind. The last story I will discuss in detail has different versions for various audiences and changes accordingly. Below, I will tell the story as it was narrated in the *Forty Viziers*, in an Ottoman manuscript compiled centuries later (TDK A 142, see Untitled Manuscript n.d.), and in a German translation of *The Thousand and One Nights*.[39] In this case, thinking of the audience (instead of the moral) seems to be more telling, especially considering the different turns that the narration takes, especially when it meets its German readers in the nineteenth century.

Relief attained after years of suffering is a popular theme in the Islamicate storytelling tradition and this story is a prime example thereof.[40] The version of the tale in the *Forty Viziers* is told by the fourteenth vizier as an exemplum to show the shah the significance of patience and endurance (*The Story of Forty Viziers* 2012: 207–17). The story is as follows: a grand *pādişāh* (sovereign, ruler) rules over all the seven climes of the world. Alas, he is not blessed with children. One day, his sacrifices and prayers are accepted by God and he is blessed with a son comparable in beauty only to Joseph. To celebrate, he gathers a *majlis* (a joyful assembly) in which astrologers take part alongside other members of the court. Bestowing gifts upon them, the *pādişāh* seeks to learn the newborn's fortune. The astrologers prognosticate that at the age of thirty his fate will turn inauspicious and he will suffer until he reaches the age of sixty.

The *şehzāde* (crown prince) grows up as a crown prince should, well educated and trained in the martial arts. When he reaches adulthood, he is married off to a princess and they have two beautiful boys. One day, the *şehzāde* takes his boys out for a trip by sea, but they encounter a *Frenk* corsair—*Frenk* being a blanket term commonly used to refer to people from Western Europe.[41] The *şehzāde* is enslaved along with his sons and forty men and sold to *seg-sārs*, creatures who have one side of their faces as that of a dog, while the other side is human (Figure 2.2).[42]

The *seg-sārs* place the *şehzāde* and his men in a house and feed them regularly with raisins. Every day, the dog-headed people slaughter one of the men, prepare him in the kitchen as a meal and eat him. When all his forty men have been eaten, they bring the *şehzāde* himself to the kitchen to be slaughtered. Observing the situation, the *şehzāde* asks for God's help and he is granted divine support, so that he is able to reach for a large knife and start killing each of the *seg-sārs* as they approach him. He kills all those in the kitchen and those who attempt to come in. Hearing this, their *şāh* comes to observe what is going on. Seeing the *şehzāde* skillfully slaughtering all his men, he asks him not to fight him and offers to give his daughter to him in marriage. Helpless, the *şehzāde* accepts the offer.

After a few years of marriage, his wife dies. Those dog-faced people also have a peculiar death ritual: if a person dies, his or her partner accompanies the deceased into a well with a piece of bread and a jug of water. The entrance to the well is blocked by a stone and the living partner is left to die alongside the corpse. Accordingly, the *şehzāde* is left in the well alongside his partner's body. Astonished by the turn of events, he again asks for God's help and prays. He then begins to investigate his surroundings. When he reaches the bottom of the well, he finds there a very beautiful woman who has just lost her husband and been left alongside him to die. While sitting alongside many corpses, he sees a candle light. A beast then comes and drops a human corpse into the well. The

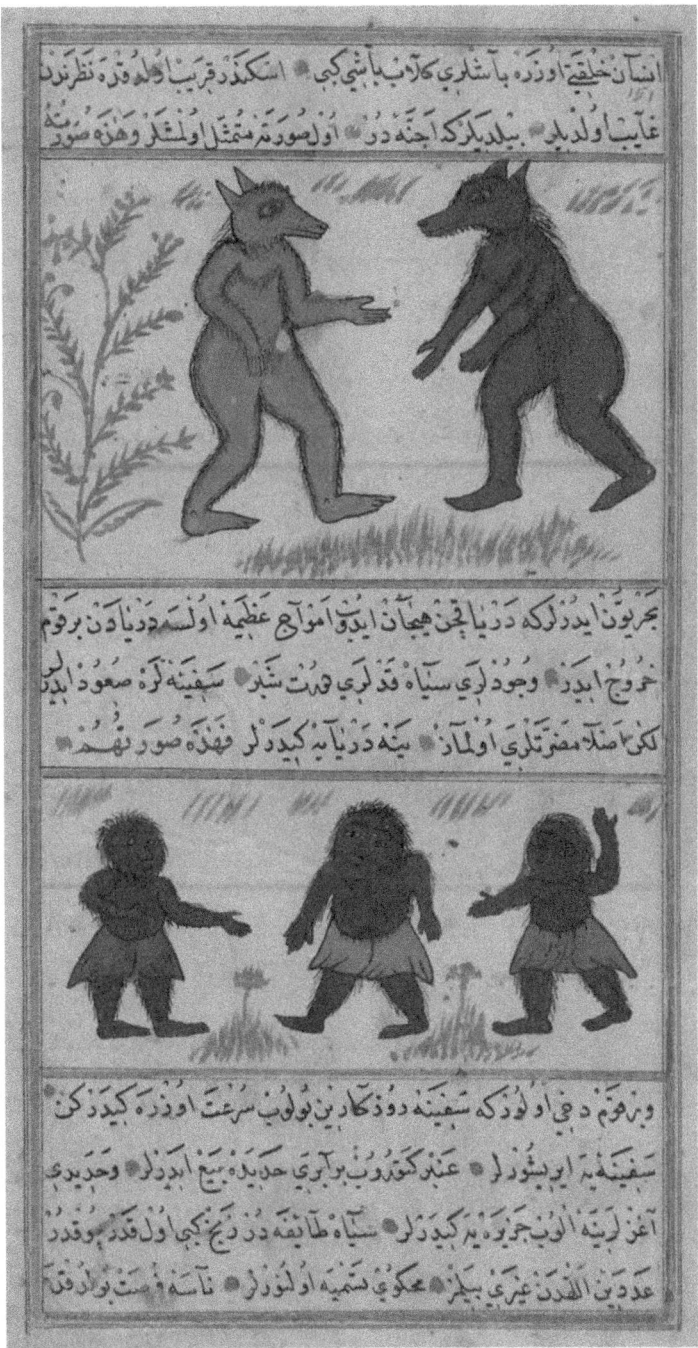

FIGURE 2.2: Dog-headed people and pygmies in a Turkish version of *Wonders of Creation*, made for the seventeenth-century Vizier Murtaza Pasa. Courtesy of the Walters Art Museum. Public domain.

şehzāde thus deduces that the beast must have come from outside, so they start to follow his trail. When they run out of water and bread, the *şehzāde* prays to God, and soon after a light appears at the end of the path.

After passing through a hole, they end up on a mountainside next to a shore. Thanking God, they spend a few days there, picking fruits from the trees. Next, they go aboard an abandoned ship they discover on the beach. Moved by the current, the ship disappears into a hole under the mountain and they spend their time in darkness praying, unable to distinguish the passing days from the nights.

After three days of travel filled with hardship, the sustenance they had found in the ship is exhausted, so they again take refuge in God. Finally, they sail out of this pit and reach shore again. There, they see a grand fortress, but its entrance is securely locked. Before its entrance there is a marble column with an inscription that informs the visitors that they must kill a monster with five feet in front of this door to enter the fortress. Marveling over the idea of the monster with five feet, they settle before the gate and spend the night there. Overnight they are infested with lice and in the morning, the prince kills one of them. Thereupon, the door opens, and they realize that the monster with five feet is a louse.

Upon entering the fortress, they see a beautiful garden, in which the trees are of gold and their fruits of precious stones. Then they reach a dome, also adorned with stones, and in the middle find a corpse lying over a wooden board. The ornamented inscription above his head informs the visitors that he was a *pādişāh* called *Rubūy Perī*, and ruled over all humans for thousands of years. Realizing that he was about to die, he had the dome built in three days to serve as his tomb. The two fountains above his head were built to provide nourishment for his visitors and to receive their blessings. The *şehzāde* turns each tap and finds that one pours a sugar syrup and the other milk. The *şehzāde* and the woman spend some time in that dome, nourishing themselves with sugar and milk. They then pick from the trees as many precious stones as they can fit in the ship and sail away.

Next, they come ashore on another island, where they are captured by men without heads. These people have their eyes in their shoulders and their mouths in their chests. When they talk, they sound like birds. The adventurous couple are taken to their *pādişāh*, but the *şehzāde* recites the glorious names of God and all the beasts run away. They spend thirty years at sea, going from island to island—including the islands of the pig-headed, the elephant-headed, and the bird-headed people. Each time they are saved by reciting the names of God.

The *şehzāde* thus is tormented for many years and is saved through his faith in God. Once while he is on the run, he loses his companion and, despite all his efforts, cannot find her. So, he is left alone on the ship. The woman, arriving at the beach to board the ship, sees that both the ship and the *şehzāde* are gone.

She spends the night on the shore, crying and sleeping. In the morning, she runs into a group of seven people who have been shipwrecked on the island by a storm. After introductions, they ask for food and she tells them that she will guide them—but they shall treat her as a girl—implying that they should not make any sexual advances toward her. The men promise so she leads them to the mountains. Then they all leave the island with the ship.

Meanwhile, the *şehzāde* comes ashore at another island. Seeing him, the local people immediately bring him to their *pādişāh*. The *pādişāh* listens to his adventures and treats him kindly and offers him his daughter's hand in marriage. He himself retires from his duties as a ruler and leaves the throne to the *şehzāde*. After the *pādişāh*'s death, the *şehzāde* becomes the sole ruler.[43] One day, a ship of captives is brought to be sold to the *şehzāde*. The *şehzāde* decides to keep them overnight to see if he likes them. Thus, he asks each of them their story. Listening to their adventures, he realizes that these are his sons, so he tells them his own story and sleeps alongside them overnight.

In the morning, he assembles his *dīvān* (court of assembly), and the Frenk slave-merchant comes over. At the *şehzāde*'s orders the Frenk slave-merchant is tortured and killed. Then a ship comes along. When the men see a pretty concubine in the ship, they inform the *şehzāde*. He questions the woman and realizes that she was his traveling companion. The *şehzāde* rewards the men for their good treatment of the woman. He then goes to his own lands and those who know him come and celebrate.

The vizier concludes the story by explaining why he has related it to the ruler: blessed and cursed times follow each other, and anyone may be afflicted by misfortunes. His son's fortune may be inauspicious for a few days, but the *pādişāh* should not kill him, as remorse would not bring him back.

I will briefly introduce two other versions of this story to speculate on the adaptations and how they change in different contexts. Another version in Ottoman Turkish appears in a manuscript located at the library of *Türk Dil Kurumu El Yazması ve Nadir Eserler Kütüphanesi* under catalog number A 142 (Untitled Manuscript n.d.). The manuscript is an interesting combination of a travelogue, collection of *ʿacāʾib* and *ġarāʾib* (marvelous and wondrous anecdotes, mirabilia), and a story collection. There is no introduction or dedication, nor any information about the aim or reason for the compilation. The first piece in this miscellanea, a short travelogue, dates the manuscript to the nineteenth century. Different prose works and stories follow this short travelogue. While the travelogue dates the compilation to the nineteenth century, the subsequent texts and stories can be traced back to earlier centuries.

While there are slight differences in several details between these two Ottoman versions, two dissimilarities demand further attention. First of all, while the version in the *Forty Viziers* (over)emphasizes putting one's trust in God, the story in TDK A 142, originally titled "A crown prince who was a traveler for thirty years and became *pādişāh* after all his torment and suffering,"⁴⁴ emphasizes this less. The moral of the story is the same—about trusting in God—but, for instance, calling God's names to escape danger is not as frequently mentioned in this version.

The most important difference is the story of the woman who accompanies the *şehzāde* throughout his adventures. The invisibility and triviality of the female protagonist is epitomized by her unceremonious disappearance after spending thirty years with the crown prince. In the version in TDK A 142, she is simply lost in the narrative without a trace. The phrasing is too vague even to understand whether she is lost at sea or on land (TDK A 142, see Untitled Manuscript n.d.: 334a4–6). She is simply and vaguely lost and her absence is neither remarked nor commented upon. Except for their thirty-year-long (compulsory) companionship and their involvement in numerous adventures, we are not privy to the nature of their relationship. The readers know almost nothing about her, except that she was once married on the island of the dog-headed people, her partner passed away, and she is strikingly beautiful (332a15–16).

In the version in the *Forty Viziers*, her story—albeit in brief—is told and the readers do learn that she arrives to the lands of the *şehzāde* safe and sound. While, again, we lack information about the nature of their relationship, the *şehzāde*'s attempts to look for her and his reward to the men chaperoning her indicate that theirs was a companionable relationship. Alas, the readers do not learn what happens to her after the arrival in the *şehzāde*'s domains.

The version in Maximilian Habicht's translation of *The Thousand and One Nights*, titled "The Story of the Prince of Khwarazm and the Princess of Georgia," is remarkably different in that respect. In the early nineteenth century, Habicht published a German translation of *The Thousand and One Nights*. His edition is primarily based on Antoine Galland's French edition, but he added stories from other sources including a Tunisian manuscript.⁴⁵ A version of this story was also included in the French translation of the *Forty Viziers* by Pétis de La Croix and translated into English in the early eighteenth century.⁴⁶

In Habicht's version, which addresses a German readership, whereas the main plot line is similar enough to call this story yet another adaptation, some of the tale's plot elements, the tale's length, the time line of events, and the style are significantly different. Most significant for my purposes is the fact that the role of the woman changes drastically: she becomes one of the two main protagonists of the story alongside the crown prince. Remarkably, she is the only person named in the tale—the fourteen-year-old princess of Georgia, Dilārām—whereas the man is described only by his title, crown prince.

In this version, the inauspicious events do not wait until the prince reaches the age of thirty, but start when he is fifteen and end when he is thirty. So, at the beginning of his adventures the prince is not married and does not have any children yet. The woman he meets on the island of dog-headed people will become his wife and the mother of his two boys. After being kidnapped and his first marriage in the island of the dog-headed people, he meets Dilārām, who has also been captured by Samsars and forced to marry a Samsar who has also become sick and died. She is the one who offers to rescue him (on the condition of marriage).

As her offer of marriage indicates, Dilārām has her own voice, as well as her own story. The sealed fate of the couple is even carved on a marble stone in the well with an inscription stating: "When the prince of Khwarazm and the princess of Georgia come here together, they may lift this stone and descend the stairs" (Habicht, van der Hagen, and Schall 1826: 10). Thus, going out of the well, they embark on a series of adventures. A significant difference between this version and the Ottoman versions is that on the first island, they do not find a corpse but a very old king alive and well, who has discovered the secret of immortality. He asks them to keep him company in this luxurious palace and promises to share the secret of immortality in time. The couple thus peacefully settles on the island, gets married there, and has two sons. However, after a while, Dilārām is bored with isolation and wants to see her family. When they ask the king for permission to leave, stating that they will return in a few years, he becomes so sad that he loses his desire to live and dies upon calling for the angel of death.

When the king dies, the miraculous palace disappears and the couple leaves on their ship, this time with their boys—but they are soon attacked by corsairs. The corsairs drop the *şehzāde* off at the island of headless people. Unlike the versions in Ottoman Turkish, the adventures he engages in on different islands are narrated in considerable detail. After a series of military successes, the king of the headless people wants him to marry his daughter and become his heir—and he has no choice but to accept. The princess, however, is already in love with a genie. On their wedding night, the genie makes the newlywed couple escape the island while they are sleeping. He leaves the *şehzāde* on another island, where Dilārām has already become queen. With their two boys, the couple rules over the people and their realm is called the happiest of all.

There is no possibility to show a direct link between the versions and even the chronology might be wrong, considering the gaps and lack of information on the manuscript TDK A 142. So, what to do with these three versions? I am aware of the risks of reaching conclusions based on a limited sample, but the differences among versions leave ample room for speculation. The protagonist of the story of the "Crown Prince" travels from one marvelous place to another for thirty years and, like many other characters who stumble across marvels, he does not marvel at what he sees (a feature common in the Western fairy-tale tradition).[47] Merely noting the different customs and characteristics of the monstrous races in passing, he heroically escapes from difficult situations. Throughout his travels, which are more fairy-tale-like compared to the rather factual Ottoman narrative, he encounters dog-headed, pig-headed, and bird-headed people, people without heads, a miraculous palace, trees of gems, and so on. Most of the elements in the story can be traced back to the ancient traditions; the dog-headed people and the people without heads, for example, can be traced back to Herodotus. In that regard, Habicht's version is closer to the earlier translation by Pétis de La Croix. Remarkably, the introduction to the eighteenth-century *Forty Vizier* collection, which includes a version of this story, indicates that these tales are not French inventions but are original and "have all the Beauties, without the extravagance of our own Tales of the Fairies" (Philips and Pétis de La Croix 1708).

Leaving aside the Ottomans' disinterest in this particular female protagonist—to the extent that they lose her entirely in the version in TDK A 142—the naming of Dilārām seems to be a feature of the versions that are in circulation in the Western world, namely that of Pétis de La Croix and Habicht, who are familiar with storytelling and fairy-tale traditions in Western Europe, as well as with readers' expectations. While fairy-tale characters are not always named, the female characters tend to be the ones with the memorable names.[48] In this story, one presumes an adaptation/appropriation of an Ottoman/Oriental story to a Western audience. While the characters and the story are still in their oriental attire, the plot follows the expectations of a Western audience, in which the married couple lives happily ever after with their sons.

IN LIEU OF A CONCLUSION

Robert Darnton rightfully warns his readers against falling into the trap of over-reading by making comparisons based on a limited number of versions and adaptations (1984: 18–19). However, I still believe that close reading of these versions is a useful exercise to think about translation and adaptation and how audience-centered approaches might help literary historians to understand the complexities of circulation.

The adaptations and translations in the Ottoman literature portray the richness of the canon, as well as its intertextual relationships to the larger Islamicate and Mediterranean literary tradition. Thus, as Hutcheon mentions in her *Theory of Adaptation*, "seen from the perspective of its process of reception, adaptation is a form of intertextuality" (2006: 7). A closer look at adaptations and the ways in which Ottoman authors have chosen to adapt their texts tells us not only about Ottoman literary tastes and expectations but also about the context and the readership. For instance, the ways in which the tree story has changed show the Ottoman emphasis in foregrounding women's agency and thus highlighting women's wiles; the emphasis on the beard-plucking and marriage in the widow story showcases the Ottoman codes of morality and masculinity; and the changes in the crown prince story depict how a story may change while traveling to the West becoming more fairy-tale-like. To have a more inclusive overview of adaptations in the Ottoman world, however, we need many more studies that trace stories—without seeking an original.

Acknowledgment

I want to thank to Michael Pifer, Yaşar Tolga Cora, and the editors of the volume for their careful reading and insightful comments on this chapter. I have discussed these stories with Helga Anetshofer, Hakan Karateke, and Franklin Lewis and their comments were very helpful in shaping my ideas. Different versions of this chapter have been presented at Boğaziçi University and Toplumsal Tarih Ankara Tartışmaları. I am thankful to the audiences and their useful comments.

CHAPTER THREE

Gender and Sexuality

Gender and Sexuality in the Fairy Tales of Straparola and Basile

CRISTINA MAZZONI

INTRODUCTION

Are fairy tales good or bad for women? To nuance this blunt question, one might ask instead: do fairy tales portray and promote an oppressive patriarchal agenda that helps keep women subordinate to men, or do they imagine a world where women are free to act in ways they believe to be life-affirming? This debate gained prominence some fifty years ago and continues to this day. Against Alison Lurie's 1970 claim that fairy tales "suggest a society in which women are as competent and active as men, at every age and in every class" (1970: 42), Marcia Lieberman rebutted two years later that "an analysis of those fairy tales that children actually read indicates instead that they serve to acculturate women to traditional social roles" (1972: 383). Three years after that, Kay Stone noted that while Disney's and the best-known fairy-tale heroines are indeed judged by their looks or meekness, there are many fairy tales out there with "active heroines" who "are not victims of hostile forces beyond their control but are, instead, challengers who confront the world rather than waiting for success to fall at their pretty feet" (1975: 46). At the conclusion of her classic 1979 article, critical of the negative impact of fairy tales on "female expectations of their role in patriarchal cultures," Karen Rowe asks, "do we have the courageous vision and energy to cultivate a new fertile ground of psychic and cultural experience from which will grow fairy tales for human beings in the future?" (1979: 256, 257). The study of fairy tales has since included examinations of women characters as potential role models; social and cultural issues important to women and frequently at the center of fairy tales, such as pregnancy and childbirth; as well as theoretical questions about the construction of gender and heterosexuality in these texts. And certainly numerous feminist fairy tales have been published since Rowe's question, including by major authors such as Margaret Atwood and Angela Carter; but many of the literary features Rowe sought and did not find in traditional fairy tales are in fact alive and well in some of the magical stories penned in Italy during the sixteenth and seventeenth centuries.

These early modern fairy tales often feature female protagonists and provide readers with numerous opportunities to explore such topics as the representation of gender and sexuality, including femininity and masculinity and how they are manifested in fairy tales; the ways in which women may claim narrative agency in its multiple configurations; and the pressures of heteronormativity, with some of the implicit scenarios that queer interpretations allow readers to glimpse. As Donald Haase puts it so well, "Awareness of the fairy tale as a primary site for asserting and subverting ideologies of gender is evident throughout the genre's history. This is especially evident and most readily documented in the development of the literary fairy tale" (2004: vii). When it comes to gender and sexuality, early modern Italian literary fairy tales are both very clearly connected to later and better-known examples of the genre, such as tales by seventeenth-century French writer Charles Perrault and the nineteenth-century collections by Jacob and Wilhelm Grimm. These Italian collections regularly challenge our stereotypes of what the representations of gender and sexuality look like in fairy tales. In this tension they force readers to confront the fact that literary fairy tales have a history and a geography, and are not the unchanging, atemporal, and seemingly universal narratives that some believe them to be. At the same time, the changing representation of gender and sexuality in the history of the fairy-tale genre is not always, and in fact not usually, an unequivocal positive progress toward increased agency, equality, and freedom.

Fairy tales have been traditionally associated with women: women tell fairy tales, women listen to fairy tales, women are featured in fairy tales. This is true despite the fact that all but one of the tales constitutive of the contemporary fairy-tale canon—which includes, among others, "Little Red Riding Hood," "Cinderella," "Sleeping Beauty," and "Rapunzel"—are authored and edited by men, the main exception being Jeanne-Marie Leprince de Beaumont, author of "Beauty and the Beast."[1] Perrault puts an old woman who is spinning even as she tells stories to a spellbound young audience on the frontispiece of his collection; the Grimm brothers' informants, and the informants of many a nineteenth-century fairy-tale collector, were notoriously older women; and within the collections by Giovan Francesco Straparola (c. 1485–c. 1557) and Giambattista Basile (c. 1575–1632) tellers of fairy tales are women. The association of women with the telling of fantasy stories, whether it is based on actual practice or is a cultural construction handed down in written and visual texts, has a long tradition that well precedes these early modern Italian literary fairy tales. The representation of this bond goes back to antiquity and to the connection between spinning, weaving, and speaking, between caregiving and the handing down of language and oral traditions, as part of socialization, from generation to generation, through the hands and mouths of women. In her study *From the Beast to the Blonde*, Marina Warner noted that, "One salient aspect of the transmission of fairy tales has not been looked at closely: the female character of the storyteller"; since then, this aspect has been a regular part of critical readings of fairy tales (1994: 16). As Michele Rak put it, "The fairy tale is an invention of Modernity and within it flow many ancient materials and techniques of a narrative tradition by women and for women" (2007: 50).[2]

THE TALES AND THEIR TELLERS

As she lies dying, a young and wise princess in the southern Italian city of Salerno asks her beloved husband Tebaldo that he only remarry if he finds a woman whose finger fits her own ring. He loves her and agrees, but the only one who allows him to fulfill his wife's deathbed wish is the couple's own daughter, Doralice, who must then engage in a series of adventures, including travel to a distant land across the sea, accusations of filicide, and live burial, to escape her father's incestuous proposal. Thus begins the first fairy tale in *Le piacevoli notti* (*The Pleasant Nights*, 1550–3) by Straparola, the earliest significant collection of fairy tales to be printed in Europe. Doralice's is the fourth story told during the first of thirteen nights of storytelling in this book. Published in Venice in two volumes in the 1550s, Straparola's book includes seventy-three short narratives; in several of these stories readers will recognize the genre we call the European literary fairy tale—and although Straparola's narrators include some men, his fairy tales are all told by women (Straparola [1550–3] 2015). Almost a century later, between 1634 and 1636, *Lo cunto de li cunti* (*The Tale of Tales*) by Basile was published posthumously in Naples, under the anagrammatic pseudonym Gian Alessio Abbatutis. This book consists of forty-nine fairy tales within a narrative frame, again told by women in the course of five nights—hence the book's subtitle, *Pentamerone*; the fiftieth tale is the frame itself. Written in the Neapolitan language in an overwrought baroque style, Basile's is regarded as the first European collection consisting exclusively of fairy tales.

After these two early collections, the fairy-tale genre is thought to have languished in Italy and, for a variety of reasons, these two authors' early work inspired more imitators in France, including prolific women writers of fairy tales such as Marie-Catherine d'Aulnoy and Henriette-Julie de Murat, than in their native land. For *The Pleasant Nights* and *The Tale of Tales* contain some of the earliest printed classics of the European fairy-tale tradition, with most of them featuring, especially in these early Italian versions, female protagonists. Perrault clearly derived his famous "Puss in Boots" (1697) from Straparola's "Costantino Fortunato" and Basile's "Cagliuso," where the cat is gendered as female, and connections between Perrault's "Donkey Skin" and Straparola's story of Doralice and Basile's "The She-Bear" are more subtle but equally clear. Perrault's beloved "Sleeping Beauty" and "Cinderella" evidently find their predecessors in Basile's "Sun, Moon, and Talia" and "The Cinderella Cat," respectively. Tales by the Brothers Grimm also have earlier models in Straparola and Basile. For instance, "The Golden Goose" recalls the story of Adamantina's magical doll in Straparola, and "The Goose" in Basile, and the Italian versions—unlike the Grimms' male-centered one—are set in worlds peopled largely by women. The Grimms' "Simple Hans" finds a precedent in the story of Crazy Peter in Straparola and that of "Peruonto" in Basile; "Hans My Hedgehog" and "The Handless Maiden" appear in Straparola's collection as "The Pig King" and "Biancabella," respectively; finally, the Grimms' "Rapunzel," "Snow White," and "Hansel and Gretel" have much in common with earlier versions by Basile titled "Petrosinella," "The Little Slave Girl," and "Nennillo and Nennella."

Like Giovanni Boccaccio's celebrated *Decameron* (c. 1353), whose tales—dedicated by the author to women in love and described as especially useful and delightful to women—are told over the course of ten nights by as many young people gathered in a country villa after fleeing plague-infested Florence, the tales by Straparola and Basile are told within clearly defined narrative frames developing over the course of a specific number of days. Straparola's collection is set on the island of Murano, in the Venetian lagoon, where the aristocratic companions of Lucrezia Sforza—a noblewoman who, with her father, had to flee her home in Milan for political reasons—tell their tales as entertainment during the last thirteen nights of Carnival, just before the beginning of Lent. That the earliest fairy tale should be about a father-daughter relationship gone wrong is especially significant, then, given that the hosts in the frame holding these stories together are also a father-daughter pair. In their shared exile, the daughter asks her father for the company of ten young women and two older matrons.

Likewise, Basile's tales are told within a framing device. Basile's frame however, unlike Boccaccio's and Straparola's idyllic yet also real-world set up, is itself a fairy tale, featuring a women's world where the popular motif of the princess who would not laugh is paired with that of the powerful and spell-casting old crone. In Basile's frame tale, when Princess Zoza finally laughs, it is at the expense of an old woman, who exposes her genitals after a young man plays a trick on her; the crone, in anger, curses Zoza to fall in love with a prince she could only awaken with a bucket of her own tears.[3] Just as Zoza is about to complete her task, in this first part of the frame tale, the Moorish slave Lucia steals the bucket, finishes filling it, and marries the prince. The impostor becomes pregnant and to satisfy her insatiable desire for stories—the early modern theme of pregnant cravings, intensified by magical spells, repeatedly returns in Basile's book—the prince hires the ten best storytellers in the land, "the ones who appeared to be the most expert and quick-tongued" (Basile [1634–6] 2007: 41), among whom hides the disguised true bride. At the end of the five days, the last fairy tale in the collection is told. Titled "The Three Citrons," it indirectly yet unmistakably reveals the impostor's plot and leads Lucia to condemn herself to being buried alive. Her pregnant craving has turned back against herself, as her desire for stories eventually leads to the telling of the story that will unmask and condemn her. Ultimately, Basile's collection of tales is born, so to speak, of Lucia's cravings: without her desire to hear stories we would not have the fairy tales that make up *The Tale of Tales*.

Straparola's and Basile's tales are told in a fictional context of oral transmission, for within their frame narratives, as we have seen, are many storytellers. Straparola's tellers of fairy tales are aristocratic ladies addressing themselves primarily to women like themselves. Thus, for example, the teller of Doralice's tale is named Eritrea and, as many of her peers also do, she even genders her audience as feminine in her introductory remarks when she begins to speak with the address, "Loving ladies" (Straparola [1550–3] 2015: 74). On the opposite end of the aesthetic spectrum and a parody, rather than an imitation, of Boccaccio's elegant, storytelling *brigata* in the *Decameron*, are Basile's tellers, ten lower-class, grotesque crones that are reminiscent of the old woman who curses the princess within the frame tale and who, in their comical deformity, are well embedded in Basile's baroque style. These tellers are, as the author describes them, "lame Zeza, twisted Cecca, goitered Meneca, big-nosed Tolla, hunchback Popa, drooling Antonella, snout-faced Ciulla, cross-eyed Paola, mangy Ciommetella, and shitty Iacova" (Basile [1634–6] 2007: 42).

MONSTROUS SEX

Women have been associated with storytelling since well before Europe's first literary fairy tales, and although Doralice's story is often described as the earliest printed literary fairy tale in Europe, important elements of the genre her story inaugurates, including the gendering of fairy-tale telling as female, certainly precede Straparola's own work. The best-known antecedent to the European literary fairy-tale tradition is the story of Cupid and Psyche, embedded in Lucius

Apuleius's second-century Latin novel *The Golden Ass*, or *The Metamorphoses*. This text, lost for centuries and rediscovered in manuscript form in the fourteenth century, was one of the very first printed books in Italy, its first edition having been published in Rome in 1469; the popularity of Apuleius's work finds evidence in successive editions in that same century, as well as translations and verse paraphrases into Italian during that time period. Its influence on the new genre of the literary fairy tale is evident and enduring (Bottigheimer 1989). Within Apuleius's book, the love story between the god of love and the most beautiful of mortal women is told by an old woman to a young woman, to distract the latter from the horror of having been kidnapped on her wedding day by a band of robbers (the novel's male protagonist, Lucius, overhears it and retells it: already men are represented as eavesdroppers on women's narrative business, not unlike nineteenth-century folklorists such as the Grimm brothers). It features the adventures of a female protagonist, Psyche, whose love life is regularly interrupted by the envious intrusions of other women—specifically, her two sisters and her future mother-in-law, who happens to be Venus herself, the goddess of love. The elements that "Cupid and Psyche" present in common with many of Straparola's and Basile's fairy tales, and with numerous later ones as well, are clear and include a narrative frame with a woman telling the story to another woman; a persecuted and beautiful female protagonist who must go through life-threatening trials; envious, mean-spirited sisters and a jealous as well as envious older woman; an active heroine not above taking murderous revenge on her enemies—in this case, her own malevolent sisters; magical helpers that allow for seemingly impossible tasks to be accomplished; romantic love and a happy ending, including the birth of a child, leading to the protagonist's rise in social status—in Psyche's case, from mortal to divine.

Although the presence of gods and goddesses makes it read more like myth than a fairy tale, the story of Cupid and Psyche has been classified under the ATU 425 tale type, "The Search for the Lost Husband," and connected to the "Beauty and the Beast" tales—even though the god Cupid, far from being a beast (he is only described as such by Psyche's envious sisters), is actually the most handsome of bridegrooms. Psyche's lover, Venus's son, was also known as the personification of Love: in Italian, the most common way to refer to Apuleius's famous couple is as "Amore e Psyche," "Love and Psyche." It is worth noting therefore that Straparola's tale of Doralice opens with a description of this very personification:

> I do not think that there is one of us who has not felt firsthand how great are the power of Love and the urges of the mortal flesh. He rules as a powerful lord and governs over his empire not with a sword, but with a single wave of his hand, as you will understand by the tale that I intend to tell you.
>
> (Straparola [1550–3] 2015: 74)

The earliest of Europe's printed fairy tales, then, begins with an invocation of Love and a nod to Apuleius's story.

The story of Cupid and Psyche has much in common with the Beauty and the Beast cycle, but in Basile's collection there are tales with even closer ties to Apuleius's narrative and its complicated representation of gender and sexuality.[4] In his mysterious and somewhat fractured tale "The Padlock," the ninth tale of the second day, Basile clearly invokes some of Apuleius's narrative elements. Here too are three sisters and when the youngest, Luciella—more helpful than the older two—agrees to fetch water for her mother at the fountain, a slave invites her into a marvelous palace where she is given everything she might want; every night, while she sleeps deeply because of a potion she is surreptitiously given, an unseen man lies with her. Luciella regularly visits her family and eventually her envious sisters, informed by an ogress, tell her about her nightly visitor, convincing her to stay awake and discover the identity of her lover. When he realizes what curious and mistrustful Luciella was up to (through a magical padlock that leads Luciella to shout out loud, rather than Psyche's sharp razor and scalding drop of oil), he sends her home. Her sisters also kick her out of the house. Luciella is now "pregnant and big-bellied" (Basile [1634–6] 2007: 201) without even having been aware of her own sexual activity—for it took place while she was unconscious. Excluded by society as pregnant, as unmarried women of her time and place would have been, she wanders as a beggar until she reaches the city where her lover now resides. There is no fairy godmother to guide her, or divine providence to help her carry her burden; the only help comes from a compassionate lady-in-waiting. Luciella gives birth, her lover finds his son, the queen becomes aware that her own child, Luciella's lover, is also in town, and eventually all are reunited as a family.

The prince, in this tale, is cursed; he is silent and sad, with a silence and a sadness that are typically gendered in fairy tales as female–as they are in fact in Basile's own frame tale, featuring a princess who could not laugh. It is only to his infant son that the prince speaks, whereas Luciella herself does not communicate with her child. This gendering of the prince as motherly and feminine continues with his affectionate connection to his son, whom he addresses as "O lovely son of mine" (Basile [1634–6] 2007: 201); no sign of Luciella's affection toward her child, on the other hand, is ever mentioned. His feminine sadness is a curse, though the reasons behind his nightly rape of an unconscious woman are left untold; for impoverished Luciella in the end becomes a queen and perhaps the ways to such a rise in status must necessarily come through hardship and pain. Basile retells Apuleius's story of Cupid and Psyche again in another tale of his *Pentamerone*, "The Golden Trunk," also featuring the youngest of three sisters who is victimized by the envy of the older two; in a magnificent setting, Parmetella has nightly sex with a mysterious man who chases her away as soon as she attempts to discover his identity; like Psyche, Parmetella then has to undergo trials and accomplish seemingly impossible tasks before she is reunited with her lover.

Luciella is not the only pregnant woman to wander across the lands in search of her bridegroom, in Basile's collection (we will meet another such wanderer, Betta, below), and more generally, European literary fairy tales repeatedly address issues of pregnancy and childbirth, with narratives that by turns celebrate the reproduction of life or ponder infertility as the worst of all curses. The arrival of children in these texts is, by turns, expectantly desired by frequently infertile couples, or tremblingly feared by those not ready to deal with its consequences—whether such consequences involve unbearable financial strains, the mother's own death, and/or the child's monstrosity. In Straparola's collection, the animal bridegroom tale is known as "The Pig King" (Figure 3.1). Unlike Cupid and Luciella's lover, the beast featured in this story is a real and not an imagined one, resembling the somewhat similar and far more famous Grimm brothers' "The Frog King." In both cases a disgusting animal eventually turns into a handsome young man in the presence of a beautiful woman who breaks the spell that had turned him into a beast.

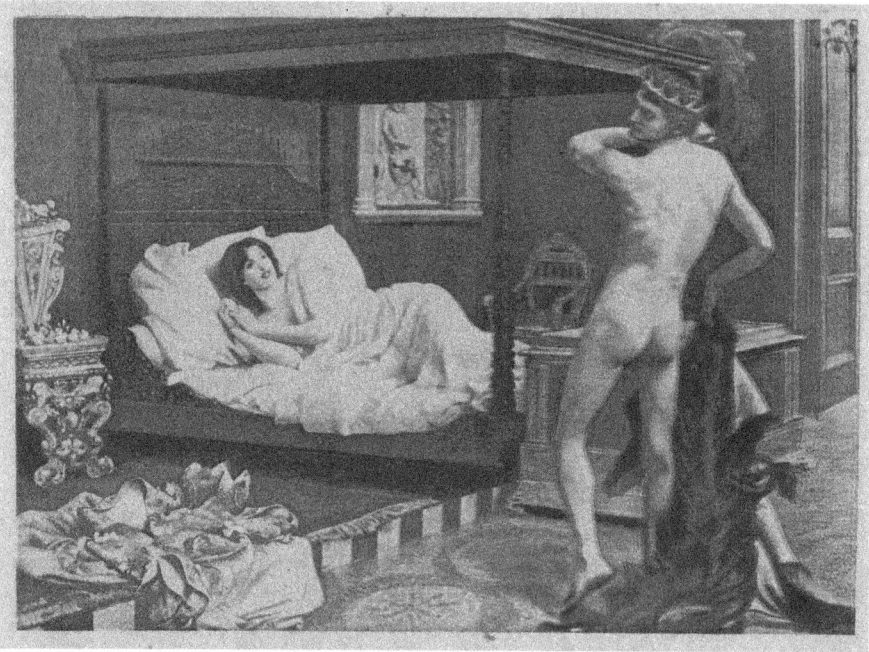

FIGURE 3.1: Straparola's prince sheds his pig skin before his wife Meldina, by E. R. Hughes, from *The Italian Novelists: The Pleasant Nights* (1901). Courtesy of the University of Colorado Boulder Libraries. Public domain.

Straparola's version features a porcine protagonist who marries below his station, in succession, three sisters who do not want a pig for a husband but are entreated to accept him by their mother (unlike later "Beauty and the Beast" tales, it is the mother not the father who arranges the daughter's future), for their recompense would be queendom. The pig kills his first two wives because, disgusted by his appearance, they were in their turn plotting to kill him. Sex and violence are closely bound together in this tale type (remember that, contrary to popular belief, the Grimms' frog becomes a king not after the princess kisses him but only after, full of disgust, she slams him against the wall). As we might expect, the youngest sister, the pig's third wife, survives. The reader may think it is because of her kindness, since unlike her sisters she does not plan to kill her own husband out of disgust on their wedding night, and indeed she appears to have enjoyed it, having woken up covered in mud and smiling contentedly. However, the fairy tale relates that it is at the pig king's third marriage that the spell will be broken: the third wife's survival is not only about her personal kindness but also about the ineluctable nature of (female) fairies' magic spells. Moreover, the tale importantly attributes the breaking of this spell to the active cooperation of the two women in the pig king's life, his wife and his mother, who ensure that the skin is cut into pieces (and although technically it is the king who issues this order, he is portrayed as a secondary character, with the wife and her mother-in-law making all the decisions). The specific geographical and historical context of this tale suggests that the pig king may represent as well a male sexuality viewed as dangerous in early modern Venice because it was not subject to rules as women's sexuality was, and was therefore menacing to the civic order—much as the monstrous hybrid, that is, the pig king is a threat to the stability of biological categories.[5]

Our modern sensibility, however, is more likely to describe as monsters characters such as the father in Doralice's story, who, enraged by his own daughter's rejection of his sexual advances, finds out her whereabouts, disguises himself to approach her, kills her infant children, and succeeds in laying on Doralice the blame for this gruesome double murder. In the tales of the "Donkey Skin" folktale cycle (ATU 510B)—named after its most famous version by Perrault, a tale type that is classified as a subtype of "Cinderella" (ATU 510A) and that includes Basile's "The She-Bear" as well as Straparola's Doralice—the mother and father seem to be conspiring in the incest plot, with the effect of decreasing the father's culpability and emphasizing the mother's collusion with the father's incestuous desire. The incest theme, a central motif in this tale-type, has been interpreted psychoanalytically, as a representation of the daughter's desire for the father, and psychologically, as an expression of the feeling of abandonment from the mother into the father's incestuous clutches. From a historical perspective, incest in these tales has been viewed as a form of preserving absolute power on the part of the patriarchal figure—the king—through the rejection of exogamy. Alternately, from the viewpoint of the queen, the tales have been seen as a means of maintaining a female line of power, of making sure that one's daughter becomes, like oneself, a queen. The strategy works and the queen's wish is realized: although they manage to elude their father's sexual advances, these heroines do become queens (or comparably powerful rulers) in the end, also thanks, in some of the tales including "The She-Bear," to the other queen in the tale: the prince's mother, the protagonist's mother-in-law—a surrogate of sorts for the now dead mother (Carney 2018: 128; Ferraro 2008: 29–30; Jorgensen 2012: 101–2).

In these tales, the protagonist's mother's protective role is taken over at her death by an older woman—not a fairy as in Perrault but, rather, the protagonist's beloved nurse in Straparola and a makeup seller in Basile, both powerfully connected to the life cycles—who safeguards the heroine by preventing incest through magical means. In Straparola's version, the nurse gives Doralice a liquor that allows her to survive without food and tells her to hide inside a wooden wardrobe, which her father in anger sells to a merchant who then brings it to England, where King Genese buys it. The wardrobe is meant as a repellent covering to shelter Doralice's beauty from her father's desire (and it succeeds, as he is annoyed by the very sight of it), but this piece of furniture itself becomes imbued with Doralice's sexual attractiveness: the merchant "who had spotted the beautiful and richly carved wardrobe fell deeply in love with it" (Straparola [1550–3] 2015: 76); King Genese, "who has already noted the beautiful and finely carved wardrobe, felt such a desire to possess it that every hour seems a thousand to him"; he was "quite enamored with this precious object" (76). Although in most examples of this tale-type the father is not punished, this is not the case in Straparola's version, where he is drawn, quartered, and fed to the dogs—not only for his incestuous proposals but also because, in his vengeful pursuit of Doralice after she is already married to the English king, he slaughters his own grandchildren and makes his daughter appear to be the murderer. It is the elderly nurse who rides alone all the way from Salerno, in southern Italy, to England, and saves Doralice from her slow and painful death (she had been buried alive). The elderly nurse is the character who performs the most heroic deed in the tale.

Rather than hide inside and transmit her sexuality to a wooden wardrobe (which repulses her father on the one hand and attracts the English king on the other), Basile's protagonist literally becomes a beast, a frightening she-bear, with a furry covering intended once again to repel her father's desire and give her the power to show herself. A bestial appearance is more transparent for the identity concealed inside it than a wooden wardrobe, and rather than hide, as Doralice must, Preziosa is able to flaunt her new form, provoking terror in the other instead of experiencing it herself. Significantly, she first becomes a bear just as her father is about to rape her:

But when he called the bride to bring him the register in which to settle their amorous accounts, she put the stick in her mouth and took the shape of a terrifying bear, and then went in to him. Terrified by this marvel, he rolled himself up in the mattress and wouldn't stick out his noggin even when it was morning.

(Basile [1634–6] 2007: 180)

Unusually, this same animal is one that the prince Preziosa will eventually marry actually enjoys: his initial fear subsides quickly thanks to the bear's tame and friendly behavior. Thus, before the prince even realizes that the bear is a woman, "he brought it home and ordered that it be taken care of as if it were he in person, and he had it put in a garden next to the royal palace so that he could see it whenever he wanted to from his window" (Basile [1634–6] 2007: 181). The prince briefly sees Preziosa's true form but she changes back into a bear before he reaches her in the garden, and "he was so bewildered by the deception that a great melancholy came over him, and in four days he fell ill, repeating over and over again 'My dear bear, my dear bear!'" (181). His mother imagines that the bear has hurt him, orders the animal killed, the servants spare her life, and the prince finds her—only to fall terribly ill again and take to his bed when he realizes that she is not resuming her human form. His mother tries to console him at length but he requires that the bear take care of him, make his bed, and cook his meals—a test of domesticity, through which Preziosa may eventually reenter human society (like Doralice who also leaves her wardrobe in the prince's absence so as to clean and adorn his room). But this does not happen before she kisses the prince at length while she is still in the form of a bear, incited by the prince's mother herself: "'Kiss him, kiss him, my lovely animal ...' the prince grabbed her cheeks and couldn't get enough of kissing her, and as they stood there muzzle to muzzle, I don't know how but the stick fell out of Preziosa's mouth" (183), and she turns into a beautiful woman again. The climax of the tale is in this intimate oral touch between a man and an animal, with a mother, rather than a father, overseeing the wedding. This desire for a bear on the part of a human prince underscores how desire, in fairy tales is often queer: strange and peculiar, yes, but also non-normative (more on queerness and fairy tales below).

MASCULINE AND FEMININE

Feminist readings of fairy tales have from the start focused on the representation of fairy-tale heroines, a representation often criticized for its emphasis on physical beauty and a quiet passivity, in contrast with male characters whose chief attribute is bold activity and even aggression.[6] Doralice is an excellent example of this literary emphasis: she is a beautiful and patient protagonist who must rely on outside help to be saved. The shape in which such help comes, however, is not that of a man—men are evil or gullible in this tale—but, instead, that of an old woman: Doralice's fiercely and lovingly protective nurse, who rides alone for days and across several countries to save her charge (in this, she is most reminiscent of the protagonist's mother in Angela Carter's "The Bloody Chamber"). Aside from Doralice, however, some of the other tales of the Donkey Skin cycle, starting with Basile's "The She-Bear," are invoked by critics as providing counterexamples of strong fairy-tale heroines, particularly in relation to the representation of the male love interest, the prince. While he languishes sad and silent, twice absorbed in his own pain and melancholy and dependent on his mother's help to heal and find love and the desire to live, the protagonist is active and resourceful, and faces adversities alone, bravely putting up with pain and suffering to hold on to her own self-determination—rather than give in to her father's wishes; for these reasons, one critic calls her "a spunky, self-reliant female character" (Goldberg 1997: 41). The princess who does not laugh of Basile's frame tale becomes a melancholy prince both in "The Padlock" and in this tale of the fearsome she-bear, where the prince is paralyzed perhaps by the queerness of his own desire—a romantic if not downright sexual attraction to a bear resulting in a passionate kiss between the two.

A melancholy, listless prince also features at the start of Basile's last tale in the collection, "The Three Citrons," particularly important not only because it is the last tale but also and especially because it unveils the frame tale's impostor. Melancholy may be gendered as feminine in the classic fairy tales, but it is an ailment that often attacks males in Basile's collection. In "The She-Bear," the prince falls into a deep melancholy when he cannot reach the bear he loves, and his mother must intervene. In "The Padlock," the curse attached to the feminine prince, silent and sad, may be broken only through the interruption of the passage of natural time, figured by the queen's killing of all the roosters in the kingdom—a way of preventing the sun from rising and a new day from starting. In "The Three Citrons," a prince's listlessness prevents him from marrying, much to his parents' dismay; and it is only when he sees his own blood on a piece of ricotta that he begins to desire a woman as red and white as that bloodied cheese.

There are determined, active women and melancholy, passive men in these early fairy tales, but there is also no paucity of misogyny in the tales of Straparola and especially Basile, with repeated references to women's envy, cunning, and curiosity and greed for pretty things—traits that apply to protagonists and not only to antagonists: "And women truly have so many different forms of cunning," we read in Basile's introductory remarks to "The She-Bear," "that you could thread them by the hundred on each hair of their head, like little chips of garnet. Fraud is their mother, falsehood their wet nurse, flattery their teacher, duplicity their counselor, and deceit their constant companion; and they twist and turn men in whatever manner they please" (Basile [1634–6]

2007: 177) (Figure 3.2). The attributes defining good women in classic fairy tales such as "Cinderella" by the Grimm brothers and Perrault, and the virtues for which they are rewarded and that are usually associated with femininity—kindness, above most others, and of course physical beauty—appear and disappear in unusual ways in the work of Straparola and Basile, where the female protagonists' shrewd and violent actions are typically rewarded rather than punished, and where beauty often plays a secondary role (Canepa 1999: 155–73). Basile's "Cinderella," the earliest European version of this tale type, is an eloquent example of this challenge to the feminine stereotyping of women in canonical fairy tales. This heroine, whose birth name is Zezolla, soon becomes known as "Cinderella the Cat"—an animal, after all, known for its fierce independence. This Cinderella is not the meek and gentle character typically evoked by that name; nor do we know much about her goodness or beauty. Zezolla is never described as good or kind; at her first appearance we simply read that she was very dear to her father (Basile [1634–6] 2007: 83) and it is only at the ball, after she has been physically transformed by magic, that someone—the prince—mentions her great beauty (86); it is the fairies that come out of her magic date tree, in fact, who, with very practical means such as jewels, accessories, and, especially, makeup and beauty treatments (remember how in "The She-Bear" the makeup seller has access to magic?), "made her as beautiful as the sun" (87).

Because her widowed father "had taken a fiery, wicked, and demonic thing for his wife" (Basile [1634–6] 2007: 83), Zezolla, requiring minimal encouragement from her beloved sewing teacher, kills this evil stepmother by slamming the lid of a chest onto her neck; she then convinces her father to marry her sewing teacher who, within a few days, turns into a second evil stepmother (this teacher also turns out to have six daughters she had kept hidden). Cinderella is visited by a magic dove who offers the services of the dove of the fairies in Sardinia. So, when her father travels to Sardinia and asks what his stepdaughters and daughter might wish for as gifts, Cinderella wants her father to just give her regards to the dove of the fairies and to ask the dove to send her something. But her request is not the meek and humble one of the fairy-tale heroines most people remember. Cinderella's request, in Basile, revolves around an open threat: "and if you forget," she tells her father, "may you be unable to go forward to backward. Keep in mind what I say: your arm, your sleeve" (85; the last four proverbial words mean, "If you don't keep your word, all the worse for you"). Sure enough, the father forgets and just as surely his boat is stuck until the ship's captain is visited in a dream by a fairy who tells him the reason why they cannot budge, and the negligent father must obey his daughter's request. Cinderella receives from the fairies as a gift a date tree and the objects needed to cultivate it and it is this tree that magically and magnificently readies her for the balls, where the king falls in love with her and

FIGURE 3.2: Four of Basile's heroines illustrated by George Cruikshank in *The Pentamerone, or The Story of Stories, fun for the little ones* (1848). Courtesy of the Newberry Library, Chicago. Public domain.

eventually finds her thanks to the slipper she leaves behind in her haste to flee. That this is the same story as Perrault's and the Grimms' version is clear; that the title character is an entirely different person is just as evident.

Lisa, the young protagonist of Basile's "The Little Slave Girl," an early version of the Snow White story, has a personality similar to Cinderella's. This character's physical appearance, too, is barely described, and the older woman in the tale is jealous because she thinks Lisa is her husband's lover, rather than being envious of her greater beauty, as in the Grimms' "Snow White." "The Little Slave Girl" begins with a baron's sister who becomes pregnant by eating a rose petal after cheating at a game with her friends; the fairies to whom the baby girl is sent give her many gifts, but the last fairy twists her foot on her way to seeing the child and, distraught by her pain, curses the baby to perish at seven years of age through a comb accidentally stuck in her head by her own mother. This is just what happens and the mother dies of grief, but not before she encases her daughter's body in seven crystal caskets that she places in a distant room of the palace, under lock and key—which she gives to her brother with the injunction to never open the door to that room. And he doesn't, but his wife does as soon as she has the chance, "impelled by jealousy and consumed by curiosity, which is woman's first attribute" (Basile [1634–6] 2007: 196; this motif, already present in "Cupid and Psyche," returns frequently in fairy tales). The seven-year-old child had in the meantime grown, the crystal caskets had grown with her, and the baron's wife, assuming the young woman to be her husband's lover and therefore filled with jealousy, beats her savagely and makes a slave of her. When the baron goes on a trip, he asks everyone what they want him to bring back—unlike any of the women in the tale, he is described as "courteous" (197)—and Lisa's threatening request is reminiscent of Cinderella's: "I want nothing but a doll, a knife, and a pumice stone; and if you forget them, may you never be able to cross the first river you come to on your journey" (197). This father too, however, forgets, and needs to learn the effectiveness of Lisa's threat and retrace his steps so as to fulfill her request. Lisa recounts her misfortunes to the gift doll, but when she realizes that "the doll was not answering, she took the knife, sharpened it on the pumice stone, and said, 'You'll see; if you don't answer me, I'm going to stick myself, and the party will be over!'" The doll reacted appropriately and, with a similarly impertinent tone, "finally answered, 'Yes, I heard you, and better than a deaf person!'" (198). Eventually her uncle overhears the exchange and, in the care of a relative, Lisa becomes "as beautiful as a goddess" and is given "a nice husband," whereas the baron's wife is kicked out of the house (198). The outspoken nature of Zezolla and Lisa is shared by many others of Basile's heroines. Thus also Preziosa in "The She-Bear," when her father proposes to marry her, "flew off the handle and gave him a piece of her tongue, and I'll let the heavens tell you about it in my place" (180).

It is a commonplace of fairy tales that the most important attribute of positive female characters is physical beauty—an attribute that is believed by contrast to be unimportant in the case of male characters. While that may generally be the case, we find that in several of these early modern Italian tales male beauty is emphasized much more than female beauty. Cinderella's beauty is a side effect of magic, not an initial attribute of her physical description. Furthermore, because in Italian the same adjective is used for male and female physical attractiveness—"bello/bella" means both handsome and beautiful—less gender differentiation is implicitly evoked in descriptions of male and female physical beauty. Male more than female beauty matters in Straparola's tale of Livoretto—a tale that repeatedly differentiates women from men and thus places issues of gender at its heart. Beloved by his mother for being the youngest and helped by animals because of his kindness, Livoretto's physical beauty is frequently described; but his elderly master's object of desire, Bellisandra, a "perfidious and wicked woman" (Straparola [1550–3] 2015: 144) that Livoretto had kidnapped as his master the sultan had ordered, cuts off Livoretto's head and proceeds to mince his flesh and mix it with his powdered bones, "just like women usually do when they make a hash from cured ground meats" (145), fashioning a man after her desire, "and immediately the young man was resurrected from the dead and brought to life, and became more handsome and charming than before" (145). The lecherous and vain sultan, eager to become young and handsome again, asks Bellisandra to do the same to him, and she kills him but then has him thrown out the window into a pit. Far from being punished for her repeated murderous acts, Bellisandra marries Livoretto, and she is "respected and feared by all for her marvelous deeds" (145). The stereotypes of femininity and masculinity are challenged in this tale, where Livoretto's beauty and kindness are foregrounded and Bellisandra's explicitly and creatively vengeful nature is rewarded.

Basile's tale "Pretty as a Picture," the third tale of the fifth day in *The Tale of Tales*, likewise reprises the motif of a woman who does not wish to belong to a man, or to be married in a traditional way, and prefers to fashion a husband to her own liking: much to her father's dismay, Betta "banned the passage of any man through her territory as if it were a no-trespass zone or a private hunting ground" (Basile [1634–6] 2007: 399). Instead, she creates with her own hands "a splendid young man" (400)—though Basile's protagonist uses kitchen ingredients such as sugar, almonds, and flour, along with precious minerals such as gold, garnets, rubies, and sapphires, instead of minced human flesh and bones as Straparola's Bellisandra. Betta, whose physical appearance is never described, instills life into this statue by imitating Pygmalion and praying to Venus, and when her father sees "this beautiful young man," he "remained speechless," struck by a "beauty so great that he could have charged a coin a head to come and admire it" (400). Betta names her husband "Pretty as a Picture" but he is stolen by an unknown queen smitten by his beauty.

Like Psyche and Luciella, pregnant Betta must wander far and wide in search of her husband and manages to spend two nights with him, but the queen had drugged him and he is unaware he has company; on the third night this beautiful and passive male character is told to avoid the sleeping potion, hears his true bride's and creator's tale, and together they go back to her father's house.

Cinderella and Lisa become beautiful through careful ministrations; Betta is nowhere described as physically attractive. Likewise, we know nothing about the looks of the princess in Basile's tale of "Peruonto," though we do know she is melancholy and had never laughed before seeing the ridiculous protagonist riding a bundle of sticks. The good-for-nothing Peruonto is not sexually attracted to her but, angered by her laughter, he wishes that she should become pregnant by him from a distance; his wish is granted and eventually they and their child are condemned to death by her family. The tale type to which Basile's "Peruonto" belongs has been called a male tale (ATU 675, "The Lazy Boy"), not only because it features a male protagonist—who, socially and sexually humiliated by a woman, takes his revenge on her both socially and sexually—but also because it contains humor, physical violence, and sexual themes (though all three of these traits are common throughout Basile's book).[7] We may not know about this princess's looks but we do know that she appreciates physical beauty because, once she realizes Peruonto's magical power, she asks him "to obtain the grace of becoming handsome and well groomed ... for although the proverb says, 'Better to have a dirty little husband than an emperor for a friend,' nonetheless if he changed his face she would consider it the greatest fortune in the world" (Basile [1634–6] 2007: 68). The magic works and Peruonto "was transformed from a flycatcher into a goldfinch, from an ogre into a Narcissus, from a grotesque mask into a lovely little doll" (68). In the similar tale of Crazy Pietro by Straparola, the princess is indeed "very beautiful and lovely" (Straparola [1550–3] 2015: 130)—but she is also only ten years old and not at all melancholy; in fact, she laughs regularly and so hard at Pietro that "she felt herself dying from laughter ... laughing uncontrollably ... as young children are wont to do" (130). But when she has the power to ask the magical fish for anything she wants, the first thing she asks is that "he make it so that Pietro would transform from a filthy madman into the most handsome and wise man living in the world then" (134)—wise, yes, because she is not stupid and wants a wise husband, but handsome first.

CLAIMING AGENCY

The related tales of Crazy Pietro by Straparola and Peruonto by Basile (ATU 675) are particularly eloquent on the matter of gender in the history of the literary fairy tale. When comparing the older tale with the newer, some of the traits typical of the fairy-tale genre gain more prominence: doubling and tripling, for example, and in terms of gender, a reduction of women's role and agency from the earlier tale to the later one. Whereas in Straparola the king's advisor is his wife, Basile's king is counseled by a group of men; and although Straparola's princess cleverly asks the protagonist to transfer his wish-fulfilling powers to herself, proceeding to make things right through smart decisions that her male partner seemed incapable of, the princess in Basile's version has to keep asking Peruonto to change things, by feeding him wine and figs. Finally, the heroine's intelligent plot of hiding an apple in her father's cloak to make him realize that not all of our mistakes are of our own free will (she was no more responsible for her pregnancy than he was of the apples in his coat), so memorable and prominent in Straparola's conclusion, is completely absent in Basile—where it is the male protagonist's wealth that brings the royal father's change of heart, not a realization brought on by his daughter's clever behavior. The daughter, in fact, even asks for her father's forgiveness, with the implication that she is somehow in the wrong (Bottigheimer 1993). Other heroines that claim agency in these tales include Betta in "Pretty as a Picture," who rejects the husbands her father proposes and chooses instead to create one for herself; and, to the extent that their more dire situation allows them, the earliest incarnations of Cinderella (who actively kills her first stepmother) and Snow White (featuring Basile's demanding Lisa).

Among the canonical fairy tales, the changing representation of female agency in the history of this genre is especially evident in tale-type ATU 310, "The Maiden in the Tower." The best-known example is the Grimm brothers' "Rapunzel," but the earliest known version is Basile's "Petrosinella," where the name of the title character evokes a different herb from the German rapunzel: Italian parsley, "petrosino" or "petrosello," in Neapolitan (*Petroselinum crispum*), replaces, or rather precedes, the more northern rampion, or rapunzel (*Campanula rapunculus*)—as it does as well in the French "Persinette" (1698), by Charlotte-Rose de Caumont de la Force.[8] While the Grimms' Rapunzel may be easily cited as an icon of fairy-tale female passivity—the title character is abducted as a small child, seduced as a young woman, and abandoned as a new mother—Basile's Petrosinella is a clever and resourceful young woman who physically and emotionally embraces her own desire rather than fall victim to someone else's. She takes after her mother, perhaps, who, unlike Rapunzel's—who has her husband pick the herb she craves, and lets him make the deal with the magical garden owner—picks the parsley she craves all by herself (there is no husband in this story to do it for her), and alone deals with the ogress who owns it. The strength of the mother's desire for parsley shows up on her daughter's parsley-shaped birthmark, explained through the early modern belief that a pregnant woman's cravings would leave a mark on the body of the child she was carrying: "when the time came, Pascadozia gave birth to the most beautiful baby girl, a joy to behold, and she gave her the name of Petrosinella, for on her breast was a mark like a fine sprig of parsley" (Basile [1634–6] 2007: 136).[9] So also Petrosinella is the one to invite the prince to visit her in the tower after several days of intense and mutual courting (in the Grimms, the prince tricks Rapunzel instead and shows up uninvited and terrifying). Petrosinella drugs the ogress who keeps her prisoner and knowingly hoists up the prince. Once together, their love-making is related to her name and its origin in desire: "he sprang into the room and there feasted with that sprig of parsley at the banquet of love" (137). The parsley in this tale signals the mother's desire as well as Petrosinella's own and significantly appears on an erogenous zone, the younger woman's breast. And whereas the pregnant Rapunzel is discovered by her captor, who sends her off into the wilderness and then pushes the prince off the tower, blinding him in the process, Petrosinella's fate is altogether different. She does not get pregnant at all, and before the ogress can do anything to her after discovering her tryst thanks to one of Basile's many nosy and gossipy female neighbors, Petrosinella outwits the ogress with three magical acorns the hiding place of which she had discovered by eavesdropping. And versed in the magical arts like her captor, Petrosinella destroys the latter by dropping behind her the magical acorns as she runs away with her lover.

MARVELOUS AND QUEER

Clearly, many of the early modern fairy tales of Straparola and Basile, including the first versions of beloved stories featuring female protagonists, such as "Rapunzel," "Cinderella," and "Snow White," invite readers to wonder about the applicability of those gender norms that we normally associate with the canonical fairy tales. This genre is usually thought of instead as containing shining examples of gender orthodoxy, namely, unambiguous instances of masculinity and femininity clearly mapped onto characters who are biologically male or female. Likewise, readers typically expect from fairy tales an affirmation of heteronormativity, that is, of a coherent and privileged heterosexuality. These stories are supposed to conclude with an unequivocally happy ending, most commonly consisting in the marriage between a man and a woman and their shared happily ever after. Although fairy tales are indeed and understandably thought of as resolutely heterosexual, critics in recent years have noted the numerous and more or less veiled queer elements within them—elements, that is, which when noticed and analyzed, uncover and then challenge expectations of fairy tales as setting forth a simple and binary view of sexuality and gender expression. As Lewis Seifert puts it, "queer reading practices work against the expected, the familiar, the predictable—of gender, sexuality, and structures of domination more generally—exposing their unexpected, unfamiliar, and unpredictable sides ... there is nothing inevitable about the link between the fairy tale and heteronormativity" (2015a: 17).

The tale in Straparola that most explicitly questions masculinity and femininity as unambiguously attributed to men and women, respectively, is surely the story of Costanza/Costanzo. Born in her parents' advanced age after their royal inheritance had already been divided among her three adult sisters, the biologically female protagonist of this tale, rather than marry below her station, "mounted a powerful horse [and] left Thebes alone and set off in the direction where fortune led her. Riding about aimlessly, Costanza changed her name and called herself Costanzo rather than Costanza" (Straparola [1550–3] 2015: 175). Costanza was educated as both a woman and as a man, having been taught the skills appropriate to both genders: needle arts, as well as arms and letters—just the sort of education seen as essential, in the context of the Renaissance intellectual debate about the role of women known as the "querelle des femmes," if women were to obtain equality with men. A king "who very much liked the looks of the young man" (176) took Costanzo as his personal servant. The king appreciates the protagonist's male appearance, that is, and this appreciation, homosocial and not explicitly sexual, is made acceptable by the reader's knowledge that Costanzo is biologically female. The queen, however, falls in love with Costanzo and, when rejected, tries to get him killed by sending him to capture a satyr; this satyr is the only magical element of the tale, a creature whose ability to discern reality beneath appearances eventually reveals both Costanzo's biological gender and the fact that the queen's handmaidens were all biologically male. A possibly transgender protagonist (for there is more to Costanzo's masculine identity than male clothing), male-to-male attraction (though not based on biological sexual identities), and a group of heterosexual transvestites: only the latter are represented in negative terms, and that is because they are assumed to be the queen's adulterous lovers, not because of their clothing choices. In Basile's "The Three Crowns" we also have a cross-dressed female protagonist, Marchetta, whose male appearance physically appeals to a king as well as to his wife the queen (Basile [1634–6] 2007: 341); in this character's case, too, the gender uncertainty goes deeper than just the donning of masculine attire. Before Marchetta was conceived, her childless royal parents had been given a choice about the gender of their child and they hesitated for a long time before deciding on a girl (337).

There are also tales where same-sex bonds, though not necessarily romantic, are stronger than heterosexual ones. The connection between sisters, for example, can be the most powerful one in a story and go deeper than the perfunctory marriage in each. In Straparola's tale of beautiful Biancabella, the protagonist is saved by her "sister," the formidable snake-woman Samaritana, who was born as a snake coiled around Biancabella's neck. Samaritana forgives her sister's neglect, restores Biancabella's eyes and hands that had been gouged out and chopped off at her stepmother's orders, and returns her rightful husband to her. Basile's "The Old Woman Who Was Skinned" features two grotesque elderly sisters who attract the lustful king's attention through their melodious voices; one becomes young and beautiful again through magic and in a huff tells her curious sister that she had herself skinned—but when the sister imitates her and gets someone to actually skin her, she dies.

Likewise, Straparola's "Adamantina's Magical Doll" features a women's world, where a mother dies leaving two daughters in poverty; the younger sister obtains a magical, female doll from an elderly woman and becomes rich with the gold the doll excretes—until a female neighbor steals the doll from her. The king is the victim of the doll's bite and needs the protagonist's help to be freed—upon which, he marries her. Basile's tale "The Goose" follows a similar storyline but instead of a doll it is a goose that excretes gold (the Grimms surmised that the switch from doll to goose was due to the linguistic similarity between the northern Italian word for doll and the Neapolitan word for goose, which is grammatically feminine). Basile's and Straparola's narratives unfold in a female world of mothers and daughters, maternal practices and filial devotion, curious and envious female neighbors, and sisterly solidarity. It is only with the Grimm brothers that the female world of the Italian versions of ATU 571, "All Stick Together," is turned into a male one in "The Golden Goose," with a male protagonist, a male magical helper, and a female object of desire, a royal spouse; the women in the Grimms' version are curious and greedy, when not passive. Whether through a doll or through a goose, the early Italian tales feature an object that substitutes itself for the deceased mother by appearing upon the latter's death even as the female protagonist comes to enact practices of maternity over it: Adamantina massages the doll's belly every night with oil, and the doll calls her "mamma" and rewards her by excreting money.[10]

In Basile's "The Enchanted Doe," the bond between two boys born at the same time from different mothers is stronger than any other: "The two boys grew up together with such love that they became inseparable, and their fondness for each other was so intense that the queen began to feel a bit of envy, since her son showed greater affection for the son of one of her servants than for herself" (Basile [1634–6] 2007: 111). One of the boys calls the other "heart of mine" (111) and they feel "anguish" in the other's absence (112). "The Enchanted Doe" is one of three tales that Italian film director Matteo Garrone chose (but also fundamentally changed) for his film version of *The Tale of Tales* (2015), along with "The Flea" and "The Old Woman Who Was Skinned." Together they form a trilogy of women's life span, from the marriageable young woman whose father is more concerned with a pet flea than with herself and who must quite literally slay an ogre to take charge of her own life; to the mother whose possessive love and jealousy turn her into a monster that her own son must kill to save himself and his beloved friend; to the old woman so desirous to become young and beautiful again that she asks a barber to flay her alive.[11]

Same-sex bonds provide rich material for queer interpretations of fairy tales, but it is also at a narrative level that some of these texts may be read queerly. For example, the disruption of chronological time in fairy tales has been interpreted as a break in the heteronormative nature of the "happily ever after"—as a significant disturbance, that is, in the steady narrative (and entirely unrealistic) move toward the happy ending consisting in marriage and the birth of children. This is the thesis of Seifert's influential queer reading of Perrault's "Sleeping Beauty" (Seifert 2015b). Although in Perrault's "Sleeping Beauty," as in many early Italian fairy tales, the "happily ever after" binds together heterosexuality and time, the temporal irregularities of the Sleeping Beauty tale disrupt the sequential progression anticipated by the reader: sleep obeys its own temporal rules, the past intrudes into the present, and the second plot emerging after the wedding indicates that marriage is not in itself a happy ending, or even an ending at all.

Perrault's beloved classic finds an antecedent in Basile's "Sun, Moon, and Talia." Talia is the sleeping or, more accurately, the temporarily dead beauty in Basile's version. She is abandoned by her father in their locked-up country palace after she falls dead because of a piece of flax stuck under her fingernail, as male fortune-tellers had simply predicted, for there is no known curse; she is then raped and impregnated while she is sleeping by a passing king with a penchant for necrophilia ("since her beauty had inflamed him, he carried her in his arms to a bed and picked the fruits of love," Basile [1634–6] 2007: 414); and she is finally awoken when one of the twins she gives birth to nine months later, while seeking her nipple, sucks instead on her finger and thus dislodges the piece of flax that had caused her to fall asleep. The king finds her by accident, while following his falcon during a hunt; there is no invocation of the kiss of true love here, much less a romantic awakening: the dead princess is not brought back to life by love or a man, but by the urgent need of an infant. Talia's lover, who eventually remembers her and seeks her out, taking up a relationship with her, is in fact already married—so much for romantic fantasies—and his jealous wife orders the children killed, cooked, and served to her husband (as is common in fairy tales, a compassionate servant spares the children and serves up two goat kids instead). The jealous queen then prepares a fire to burn her rival in, but clever Talia delays her own execution through a slow, deliberate, and noisy striptease: "Talia began to undress, letting out a shriek with every piece of clothing she took off. And when she had taken off her dress, her skirt, and her jacket, and was about to take off her petticoat, she let out the last shriek while they dragged her off" (416). This gives the bigamous and necrophiliac king time to arrive and have his wife burned in the great fire instead. Is it a "happily ever after" for Talia to spend the rest of her life with such a man? It is perhaps not surprising that this tale is one of the few in Basile's collection not to have a moralizing introduction by its teller, for the move toward the happy ending that rewards goodness with marriage is disrupted throughout this narrative: a father leaves her daughter for dead; a married king rapes a seemingly dead woman; said royal rapist proceeds to forget about his victim, then repeatedly cheats on his wife when the woman comes back to life, leading in fact a double life in bigamy. In this tale, the queen's jealous rage may well be the most relatable feeling of all.

CONCLUSION

As we marvel at the fluidity and diversity of the representations of gender and sexuality in the stories of magic written by Straparola and Basile, we must also keep in mind that theirs are among the very first instances of a new genre, the European literary fairy tale. At the time of these two authors' writing, this genre was not defined the same way it is today, which makes interpretive generalizations about many topics in these tales, including gender and sexuality, not especially helpful. The criticism typically leveled against fairy-tale stereotypes on this subject—that in fairy-tales the women are always beautiful and passive, the men brave and active, and desire monolithically heterosexual and reproductive—is quite difficult to sustain, however, when we read closely the diverse stories told by the women narrating Straparola's and Basile's tales, where gender identities and sexual desire are far from flatly predictable. Surely there is plenty of misogyny in both texts, with female characters defined by greed, envy, and duplicity; and certainly, as one does expect in fairy tales, many marriages are celebrated and numerous children born. It is also true that both authors are male. Yet it is on female figures that they rely in their narrative frames to tell their tales, tales where we meet beautiful men and beautiful women but also plain, ugly, or nondescript examples of both genders; we observe the actions of smart women and dim-witted men, and of dumb women and clever men; we marvel at women presenting as men and men who are attracted to these characters' male appearance; there are passive women and passive men—though in Basile very few characters are anything less than willful and vocal; some same-sex bonds go much deeper than some marriages and negative characteristics such as ugliness, passivity, aggression, and vengefulness apply to protagonists and not just antagonists, be they male or female. Gender and sexuality in Straparola's and Basile's early modern collections are ambiguous and shifting, and complicated indeed; and it is precisely for this reason that these stories continue to speak to and about gender and sexuality in our own ambiguous, complicated, and ever-shifting world.

CHAPTER FOUR

Humans and Non-Humans

Animal Bridegrooms and Brides in Japanese Otogizōshi

LAURA NÜFFER

Once upon a time, there lived a rich man with three daughters. All of them were beautiful, but the youngest was kind-hearted as well, and her father loved her best of all.

So begins the fifteenth-century Japanese tale *The Seventh Night* (*Tanabata*). Anyone acquainted with Western fairy tales will immediately sense a familiar pattern and suspect that the third daughter is destined for extraordinary things. As it happens, this is very much the case: she marries a giant snake who transforms into a handsome god. But more on that later.

The Seventh Night—also known as *The Tale of Amewakahiko*, the name of the youngest daughter's serpent husband—numbers among a large body of tales from medieval Japan prominently featuring animals. (Historians generally identify 1185 as the beginning of Japan's medieval period and 1603 as its end date.) The roles that animals play in these tales are many: they can be benefactors, foes, or allegorical figures—and sometimes, they can be lovers. This chapter explores medieval Japanese narratives of animal-human marriage, with a focus on the fraught and sometimes fatal relationships between animal grooms and human brides. Readers acquainted with Western fairy tales will find familiar echoes here—beauties and beasts, princesses and frogs—but the romances of these odd couples do not always develop in the direction Western readers might expect. Be warned: happy endings are a scarce commodity. Unfortunately, English-language scholarship on the subject also remains scarce, but translations and analyses of several medieval Japanese tales of animal-human marriage can be found in *Monsters, Animals, and Other Worlds* (2018), edited by Haruo Shirane and Keller Kimbrough.[1]

The works discussed here belong to a group of roughly four hundred tales known as *otogizōshi*, or "companion tales," illustrated prose narratives produced from the fourteenth to the seventeenth centuries. The term *otogizōshi* derives from *Otogi bunko*, or *The Companion Library*, the title given to a collection of twenty-three medieval stories reproduced as printed booklets in the early eighteenth century.[2] In the words of the publisher, Shibukawa Seiemon, "I have collected, without omission, all the ancient scrolls and tales and assembled them here as a convenient guide for women's self-improvement" (Fujikake 1982: 26). In other words, *The Companion Library* was intended as a "companion" to women, although as the literary historian Barbara Ruch archly observes, "How stories of maiden-eating monsters and suicides were to be construed as convenient guides on self-improvement remains for further scholarly examination" (1971: 594). Most of the tales reproduced in *The Companion Library* were originally aimed at a general audience of both sexes, all ages, and varying levels of education; if their earlier tellers had intended to do anything other than entertain, they primarily sought to inculcate Buddhist piety rather than cultivate feminine virtues. Nonetheless, Shibukawa succeeded in his attempt to rebrand medieval fiction as edifying texts for women. *The Companion Library* proved an enduring favorite and went through multiple reprintings. By the early nineteenth century it had acquired the alternate title *Otogizōshi*, and over time, this term expanded to include not only the tales in the original *Otogi bunko* but medieval tales in general.[3]

The people who first created and consumed these tales would not have called them "*otogizōshi*," and the use of this term in literary scholarship has been a bone of decades-long contention.[4] Detractors object to the term "*otogizōshi*" for numerous reasons, but one common complaint is that it is an obvious cognate of "*otogibanashi*," the Japanese word for "fairy tale."[5] This criticism originates in part from the unfair assumption that kinship with fairy tales tarnishes literary merit. However, even if we discard the notion that *otogizōshi* are devalued by association with fairy tales, a simple conflation of these categories would be badly misleading. In Europe, literary fairy tales emerged within the highly eclectic novella tradition, which also encompassed romance, tragedy, comedy, history, and religious didacticism. *Otogizōshi* span a similarly broad range of genres. Certainly, some would strike both Japanese and Western readers as fundamentally of a kind with fairy tales. *The Seventh Night* is one such work; other examples include *The Stuck-on Bowl* (*Hachikazuki*), often compared to

"Cinderella"; and *Little One-Inch* (*Issun bōshi*), whose pint-sized but daring hero recalls Tom Thumb. But these represent only a select subset of a highly heterogeneous corpus of texts: *otogizōshi* can also take the form of love stories, miracle tales, and literary parodies, among others.

The diversity of *otogizōshi* extends beyond their subject matter. Some are the work of elite ateliers patronized by the imperial court; others are the products of commoner artisans marketing to a growing class of literate urbanites. Some were designed for professional storytellers to present to an audience; others were intended for private, silent reading. Some are illustrated scrolls, others are picture books, and yet others are woodblock-printed volumes. This variety permits few meaningful generalizations; *otogizōshi* are typically defined simply as mid-length illustrated prose fiction produced between the fourteenth and seventeenth centuries. Arguably, the term *otogizōshi* does not denote a coherent genre at all. Literary historian Ichiko Teiji made an early and influential attempt to systematize this messy miscellany. His scheme of classification, still widely used, divides *otogizōshi* into six categories: tales about aristocrats, tales about warriors, religious tales, tales about commoners, tales about inhuman beings, and tales of foreign lands (Ichiko 1955: 70). The term I have translated here as "tales about inhuman beings," *irui mono*, might also be translated as "tales about animals," although this is less precise: *irui* literally means "other kind." While most *irui mono* are indeed stories about animals, "other kind" characters may also be plants, fantastical creatures, or even inanimate objects. Many *irui mono* derive their interest from playful depictions of anthropomorphic animals. In *The Tale of the Jewel Beetle* (*Tamamushi no sōshi*), insects hold a poetry contest to compete for the heart of Lady Jewel Beetle; in *The Fishes' Chronicle of the Great Pacification* (*Uo Taiheiki*), freshwater fish wage war against saltwater fish in a parody of a martial epic; and in *The Tale of the Cat* (*Neko no sōshi*), a cat and a mouse debate the Buddhist prohibition against the taking of life (the cat, while properly pious, feels that exceptions ought to be made). Ichiko calls works of this kind "pure *irui mono*," in contrast to another kind of narrative about inhuman beings: *kaikon-tan*, or "tales of supernatural marriage." A more widely used near-synonym for *kaikon-tan* is *irui kon'in-tan*, meaning "tales of marriage between kinds" or "tales of interspecies marriage." (In keeping with the diversity of conjugal practices throughout Japanese history, "marriage" refers to a variety of relationship structures, ranging from nocturnal visitation to cohabitation.) *Otogizōshi* about interspecies marriage may be sites of play and parody, but more often they imagine a marvelous and dangerous world in which monkeys abduct maidens, foxes seduce emperors, and third daughters marry giant snakes.[6]

Narratives of interspecies marriage boast a long history in Japan, predating even the earliest *otogizōshi* by at least six centuries. Japan's oldest surviving text, the 712 mytho-historical chronicle *Records of Ancient Matters* (*Kojiki*), recounts the romance between an ancestor of the imperial line and a sea monster. Slightly later eighth-century myths feature equally odd couples: a fisherman and the turtle-goddess he catches in his net, a hunter and the bird-maiden whose feathered cloak he steals, a woman and the gentleman caller who turns out to be a snake.[7] Animal-human pairings did not remain confined to the realm of ancient mythology but found their way into later literary genres, beginning with the short anecdotal tales known as *setsuwa*. Like *otogizōshi*, *setsuwa* vary widely in theme and tone, but the subset of *setsuwa* concerning interspecies liaisons generally reflects the shift toward a "Buddhist episteme" (LaFleur 1983: 13), framing the relationship in terms of sin and salvation or virtue and karmic repayment. *Otogizōshi* about interspecies marriage draw freely on myth and *setsuwa*, but to a greater or lesser extent, they transform their source texts rather than simply transmitting them.

Both in *otogizōshi* and elsewhere, narratives of interspecies marriage unfold along different lines depending on the respective sexes of the human and inhuman spouses. This chapter will focus on the inhuman grooms of *otogizōshi*, which broadly speaking fall into one of two categories: they may be fearsome beasts who demand a human bride, or more frequently, they are seemingly heaven-sent suitors hiding a shocking secret. By contrast, inhuman brides most often serve as a kind of recompense for their human husbands. Some offer themselves to repay a debt of gratitude—for instance, in *The Tale of the Crane* (*Tsuru no sōshi*), a crane freed from a snare returns to her rescuer in the form of a beautiful woman. Others are granted by gods or buddhas to reward the extraordinary virtue of a human man. Not all animals who take the guise of women do so for benevolent reasons; they may also lure men—usually Buddhist monks—to their destruction. The reverse scenario never occurs; no beasts masquerade as beaus to seduce nuns. The rigidly gendered nature of these animal temptresses testifies to the "medieval misogyny" of Japanese literature (Tonomura 1994: 154),[8] as does the perception of brides, human or otherwise, as commodities to be given and gained.

Otogizōshi about interspecies marriage serve as fantastical mirrors of the all-too-real tensions and anxieties surrounding relations between the sexes: the fraught and fragile union between human and animal reflects the distance between men and women, husbands and wives, in a society where matches were most often made on the basis of family advantage rather than individual preference. But at the same time, these tales also work to map the messy boundary between human and animal, a site of deep ontological anxiety in premodern Japan. Buddhism conceives of humans and animals as neither separate nor equal: humans have been reborn into a higher realm than animals, but both exist within the same cycle of transmigration. Accordingly, human treatment of animals is a matter of deep spiritual concern; in particular, it is a grave sin to take animal life (and, as happens in medieval morality tales, those who commit this sin may find themselves in the horrifying position of having murdered their reincarnated parents). From its introduction to Japan in the sixth century, Buddhism has coexisted and often commingled with the complex of cults and ritual practices broadly known as Shinto and described, not entirely accurately, as Japan's "native religion." It is also an oversimplification to describe Shinto as an animistic religion, but it does ascribe numinous qualities to the natural world, meaning that animals may be the messengers of gods or even gods themselves, although not necessarily benevolent ones; they must be approached with caution. This syncretism of Shinto and Buddhism situates animals simultaneously above, below, and alongside humans; in all cases, interactions across the species line are a high-stakes proposition.

In contrast to Buddhism, Christianity traditionally draws an absolute distinction between humans and animals, and perhaps this explains why Western fairy tales almost never entertain the possibility of a truly interspecies marriage. Beauties may be betrothed to beasts and princesses to frogs, but these appalling mésalliances resolve into ideal matches when the seemingly inhuman spouse is returned to his (or, less commonly, her) original human form. An early Italian example of this appears in Giovan Francesco Straparola's *The Pleasant Nights* (1550–3): in the tale "The Pig King," the heroine accepts her porcine husband, warts and all, and is rewarded for her forbearance when he becomes a handsome prince. Although the specter of bestiality lurks at the edges of these stories, the threat to the animal-human boundary is ultimately averted. By contrast, in *otogizōshi*—and in Japanese lore in general—interspecies marriage occurs between a human and an actual animal, not a fellow human under an enchantment. At times, the couple may even produce offspring, who are typically destined for greatness: the legendary magician Abé no Seimei was said to be the son of a fox, and if one believes the myths, the Japanese emperor is the distant descendant of a sea serpent.[9] This generally positive valuation of animal ancestry contrasts with European tales from this period, in which transgressions of the animal-human boundary beget monstrous hybrids.

But while Japanese tales of interspecies marriage permit the temporary union of human and animal in a way that European fairy tales do not, they seldom sanction it in the long term. Often the relationship follows the opposite trajectory as in Western fairy tales: what initially appears to be matrimonial bliss between two humans abruptly dissolves when one of the spouses is revealed to be an animal and subsequently departs. Sometimes this revelation occurs when the human spouse succumbs to typical human perversity and opens a forbidden box, looks in a forbidden chamber, or violates some other taboo. In other cases, it is the animal spouse who chooses to drop the disguise. For instance, in the *otogizōshi The Tale of the Crane,* a crane-bride brings wealth to her human husband, then returns to her feathered form and flies away. Animal spouses who do not leave of their own accord must die instead. In oral folklore, this outcome is typically presented as triumph over a menacing beast: boar grooms are set on fire, monkey grooms are drowned, and snake grooms are stabbed to death with needles. Buddhist principles of nonviolence generally do not extend to animals who take human wives. While several *otogizōshi* follow this pattern, others depart from it by aestheticizing the tragedy of the animal spouse's death. Unions between humans and animals may dissolve in many ways, but their dissolution verges on inevitable. With rare exceptions, the best the characters can hope for is a bittersweet ending—and this is exactly what awaits the youngest daughter in *The Seventh Night*.

MAGIC SKINS AND STOLEN WINGS: THE INHUMAN GROOM AS OTHERWORLDLY BEING

Back to the rich man and his three daughters. One day, a giant snake appears in front of his house and issues a blunt demand: give me one of your daughters or I will kill you. The elder two daughters refuse to marry a snake; only the youngest consents to the match for the sake of her father. Trembling, she goes to meet her husband-to-be. He is every inch as terrible as she had feared: a serpent seventeen fathoms long. But far from attacking her, the snake urges her to cut off his head with a sword. She only has a blade meant for trimming fingernails, but nonetheless she obeys. A handsome youth emerges from the snakeskin, which he folds and puts away in a wooden chest. Her fear forgotten, the woman exchanges vows of love with her now-human husband.

At first the couple live happily, wanting for nothing, for the wooden chest that holds the snakeskin provides them with endless wealth. But one day the man declares that he is in fact Amewakahiko, the dragon king of the sea, and he has business to attend to in heaven. He promises to return in seven days—but just in case, he teaches his wife how to travel to heaven if he does not come back. Above all, he warns her never to open the wooden chest or he will be unable to return to earth. After Amewakahiko's departure, the woman's sisters come to visit. Now resentful that *they* did not marry the serpent, they poke and pry through all the fine things in her house, and so stumble across the wooden chest. The woman refuses to unlock it, but her sisters steal the key and open it. To their disappointment—and the woman's despair—there is nothing inside but a wisp of black smoke.

The appointed time for Amewakahiko's return comes and goes, and so his wife sets out in search of him. Following his instructions, she buys the seed of a magical gourd and rides its leaves up to heaven. There, she asks directions from a series of celestial bodies, finally arriving at Amewakahiko's palace. The couple are happily reunited, but their troubles are not over: Amewakahiko reveals that his father is a fearsome ogre who will not accept a human daughter-in-law. At first he conceals his wife by transforming her into various objects—an armrest, a fan, a pillow—but at last the secret comes out. The enraged ogre makes his son's wife a servant in his household. First, he orders her to herd a thousand cattle, then to move a thousand bushels of rice from one storehouse to another; after this, he locks her for seven days in a chamber full of centipedes and another seven days in a castle full of snakes (Figure 4.1). However, Amewakahiko secretly gives her a magical sleeve, and by waving it, she overcomes all these trials. The ogre grudgingly decrees that she and Amewakahiko may meet once a month; unfortunately, the woman mishears this as "once a year," and the ogre quickly retracts his original bargain. He throws a melon, which bursts open to release the Milky Way—a great river running between the two lovers.[10] Amewakahiko and his wife can still be seen on opposite sides of heaven: they are the stars Altair and Vega, fated to meet only once a year on the seventh night of the seventh month.

Out of all the interspecies couples in *otogizōshi*, Amewakahiko and his wife will likely feel the most familiar to Western readers. Snake grooms appear in

FIGURE 4.1: Tosa Hirochika (1439–92), Amewakahiko's wife being locked in the castle of snakes by her father-in-law, the ogre, in *The Tale of Amewakahiko*. Bpk Bildagentur, Museum fuer Asiatische Kunst, Berlin. Photograph by Jürgen Liepe, Art Resource, NY.

several European fairy tales, beginning with "The Serpent" in Giambattista Basile's *The Tale of Tales* (1634–6). *The Seventh Night* also bears a striking resemblance to "Cupid and Psyche" in Apuleius's *The Golden Ass,* one of the earliest animal bridegroom tales from the West. Although Japanese scholars have recognized this similarity since the late nineteenth century, it is unclear whether it is the result of direct influence or cross-cultural convergence (Katsumata 1997). The earliest extant manuscript of *The Seventh Night* (which bears the tale's alternate title, *The Tale of Amewakahiko*)[11] can be confidently dated to the mid-fifteenth century; it is generally accepted that the calligrapher was Emperor Go-Hanazono (1419–71) and the artist was the court painter Tosa Hirochika (1439–92). This postdates Apuleius by over a millennium— more than enough time for "Cupid and Psyche" to travel eastward. However, if this transmission occurred, it left no paper trail, and most of the motifs that *The Seventh Night* shares with "Cupid and Psyche" are also shared with sources closer to home.

Just like their Western counterparts, third daughters in Japanese folklore show a marked tendency toward self-sacrificing virtue. Japanese folklore also offers many examples of spouses—usually husbands, but occasionally wives— who must complete a series of seemingly impossible challenges. This motif, known as *nandai muko* or "the groom's tasks,"[12] makes an early appearance in a myth from *A Record of Ancient Matters*. When Ōkuninushi courts the daughter of the god Susanoo, his prospective father-in-law orders him to sleep first in a chamber of snakes and then a chamber of centipedes. Ōkuninushi fends them off by waving a magical scarf given to him by Susanoo's daughter, just as Amewakahiko's wife survives the same ordeal by waving the sleeve given to her by her lover.

The most proximate source of *The Seventh Night* is "The Tale of the Rich Man Qian Luwei,"[13] a nearly identical tale recorded among Fujiwara Tameie's (1198–1275) extensive annotations to the classic poetry collection *Poems Ancient and Modern* (Mitani 1952: 451). Crucially, Tameie's version of the tale lacks one of the motifs that seems most indicative of a genetic relationship between *The Seventh Night* and "Cupid and Psyche" (Katsumata 1997: 21). In *The Seventh Night*, ants come to the aid of Amewakahiko's wife when she must empty a storehouse of rice, much as they assist Psyche in sorting a pile of grains. But no equivalent task exists in "Qian Luwei"; instead, the heroine is charged with weaving a feathered robe while her husband is made to herd cattle.

The motif of a weaver woman marrying a cowherd does not hail from Greek mythology, but neither is it native to Japan. Both "Qian Luwei" and *The Seventh Night* exist within a complex constellation of pan-East Asian lore about the stars Altair and Vega—the Cowherd and the Weaver, respectively. The two are imagined as husband and wife trapped on opposite sides of the Milky Way and permitted to meet only once a year on the seventh night of the seventh lunar month—the night celebrated as the Star Festival.[14] The plight of these star-crossed lovers has inspired many tales, all interwoven in a tangled network of variations and recombinations. The myth of Altair and Vega arrived in Japan by at least the seventh century CE (Como 2009: 138), but it has a much longer history in China, where it is first referenced in a poetry collection from the seventh century BCE. The oldest documented form of the tale, which is probably closest to the original, casts both husband and wife as human—a cowherd and a weaver forbidden to meet after they neglect their work for romance. At some point, this simple story of lovers parted became a tale of interspecies marriage, perhaps because the sad fate of the cowherd and the weaver fit well with the typical unhappy outcome of animal-human unions.

Amidst the kaleidoscopic profusion of star-festival legends, *The Seventh Night* stands out as an anomaly in that it is the husband who is the inhuman spouse. In China, the most widespread form of the star-festival tale casts the wife in this role: she is a bird or heavenly maiden—the two are not entirely distinct—who marries the cowherd who stole her feathered robe. The two are separated when the woman recovers her robe and flies away, and although her husband follows after her, they are separated again by the creation of the Milky Way. Feathered-robe tales circulated independently of the star-festival tale for many centuries, both in Japan and throughout Asia, and they exist within an even more widespread folkloric complex centered on an archetypal figure known as the swan maiden. Broadly defined, swan maidens need not be swans: they are bird-women who shape-shift by doffing and donning a magical skin, and they are bound to marry the man who steals it.[15] Swan-maiden tales may ultimately originate in "shamanistic and totemistic conceptions" (Hatto 1961: 327), but their power lies in their polysemy: they are concerned with the otherworldly endeavor of negotiating passage between heaven and earth, but they also express earthly tensions and anxieties surrounding sex and marriage. From the female perspective, the swan maiden embodies the "estrangement" underlying conjugal configurations in which "woman was a symbolic outsider ... and marriage demanded an intimate involvement in a world never quite her own" (Fass-Leavy 1994: 2). From the male perspective, she gives form to fears about the secret selves of women, who may at any time slip beyond the bounds of their husband's control.

Japan's oldest feathered-robe tales, preserved in eighth-century provincial records, convey only the barest bones of the narrative: first a bird-woman loses her feathered robe and the man who took it gains a wife, then the bird-woman regains her robe and the man loses his wife. One version adds a brief coda stating that the man later became an immortal and flew up to heaven, but provides no further details.[16] However, swan-maiden tales have a "tendency to attract or be attracted by other motifs and symbolic elements" (Miller 1987: 55–6), and so these ancient minimalist formulations became a prologue to the quest to regain the lost wife. In the first half of the twentieth century, pioneers of Japanese folk studies such as Yanagita Kunio (1875–1962) and Seki Keigo (1899–1990) collected a rich and varied body of feathered-robe lore from across the country. Significantly, this includes tales that merge the feathered-robe motif with the star-festival motif and the groom's tasks motif, which speaks to the enduring legacy of *otogizōshi* in Japanese cultural history. A version collected in the village of Iyayama in the 1950s presents a striking parallel to the medieval text, *The Seventh Night*.

One day in the seventh month, three heavenly maidens come to earth to bathe in a river. They hang their robes on a tree, and a hunter carries one off as he passes. When he returns to the river that evening, he finds one of the heavenly maidens still there, earthbound without her robe. He takes her as his wife, hiding her robe in a hollow in the central pillar of his house. Every day before he goes hunting, he checks to make sure the robe is still there. The heavenly maiden gives birth to two children, and when they grow older, they ask her why their father looks inside the pillar every morning. She looks for herself and finds her long-lost robe. Putting it on, she flies away, carrying her children with her. The hunter pursues his runaway wife, climbing a tree up to heaven. There, he goes to her house and asks her father to accept him as a son-in-law. Her father consents on the condition that the hunter completes three tasks: cut down a forest in one day, burn the cut-down trees on the next day, and sow three bushels and three pecks of buckwheat on the third day. The hunter manages this by waving a magic fan received from his wife. Her father thereupon agrees to the match and charges his new son-in-law with guarding the melons in the storehouse. Although the hunter's wife warns him not to eat the melons, he grows hungry and cuts a slice from one. When he does, a river comes bursting out, leaving him and his wife stranded on opposite banks. This happens on the sixth day of the seventh month; the hunter and his wife are now worshipped as the god and goddess of the Star Festival, the seventh night of the seventh month (see Seki 1953: 243; Shinoda 2007: 101).

Both *The Seventh Night* and the oral tale begin with a marriage between a human and a heaven-dwelling entity, made possible by the latter removing a magical skin or garment. This item, which possesses the power to transport its owner between heaven and earth, is kept in a container that upholds the household, either literally or figuratively: the heavenly maiden's robe is hidden in the house's central pillar, while the chest holding the snakeskin supplies its owners with wealth. When the secret of this container is breached, the inhuman spouse vanishes and the formerly stable union collapses. In both cases, curious relatives are the catalyst for this catastrophe; although the jealous sisters in *The Seventh Night* do not perfectly correspond to the innocently inquisitive children in the tale from Iyayama, the shared implication is that a wife's ties by blood pose a lurking threat to her ties by marriage.

By climbing a plant, the human spouse travels to heaven in search of the lost partner. There, the inhuman spouse's father demands that his prospective in-law complete a series of impossible tasks, some or all of which relate in some way to agriculture. The human spouse accomplishes these tasks by waving a magical object received from the inhuman spouse. Just when it seems that the couple has been reunited, a final separation occurs through the error of the human spouse: Amewakahiko's wife mishears her ogre father-in-law, while the hunter eats when he is told not to. As a consequence, husband and wife are separated by a river that bursts out of a melon, and the pair are thereafter associated with the Star Festival on the seventh night of the seventh month.

At points, the parallel seems to falter. Unlike *The Seventh Night*, the tale from Iyayama does not purport to explain the origin of the Milky Way, and although the hunter and the heavenly maiden are named as the deities of the Star Festival, they are not said to meet on this night. Other tellings, however, fill in these blanks. According to a similar tale collected in Kagoshima, "a great flood rushed out of the melon, forming the Milky Way and separating husband and wife. Because of this, they can only meet on the day of the Star Festival when it does not rain" (Seki 1953: 239). A variant from Kōchi also incorporates the motif of the misheard date: "As the man was being washed away [by the flood from the melon], he said 'let's meet on the seventh day of every month.' The woman misheard this as 'the seventh day of the seventh month,' and so it is that they meet on the day of the Star Festival" (Seki 1953: 241). These hybrid feathered-robe/star-festival tales cluster around Japan's Seto Sea (Fukuda 1997: 270–1; Seki 1943: 457), which connects to the East China Sea and has long served as a corridor for cultural interchange with mainland Asia. It is no coincidence that very similar tales can be found in China; indeed, in many Chinese versions, the groom's trials include being locked in a chamber of snakes, centipedes, or other venomous creatures (Kimijima 1999: 47, 58), mirroring the trials undergone by Amewakahiko's wife.[17]

By now it should be apparent that *The Seventh Night* shares a lengthy sequence of key motifs with folklore about heavenly maidens and their human husbands. Prominent folklorist Komatsu Kazuhiko also notes the resemblance between *The Seventh Night* and feathered-robe/star-festival tales and concludes "it seems certain that one influenced the other" (2003: 103), although he declines to make a firm pronouncement as to the direction of this influence. The question of chronology is a thorny one: because of the difficulty of dating orally transmitted narratives, we cannot definitively state that tales first recorded in the twentieth century existed in the thirteenth century, when "Qian Luwei" was written. However, ethnographers have recorded feathered-robe/star-festival folklore in multiple languages across large expanses of East Asia (Kimijima 1967). This broad geographic and linguistic distribution suggests a correspondingly deep history: the older a story is, the further it spreads. By contrast, *The Seventh Night* has not been documented as an oral folktale. As Komatsu writes, "it is entirely conceivable that [the hybrid feathered-robe/star-festival narrative] had taken shape and was in popular circulation by the medieval era, and this served as reference in the creation of the story of Amewakahiko" (2003: 103). Although Komatsu does not discuss "Qian Luwei," here too we find evidence for a link with heavenly maiden tales: the heroine is specifically tasked with weaving "a heavenly feathered robe."

Amewakahiko's wife is not a heavenly maiden, but her story is a feathered-robe story flipped on the axis of gender. This does not mean simply that the sexes of the characters have been swapped while their roles remain the same; the reversal of male and female demanded a more profound reworking, beginning with the species of the animal spouse. Tales of interspecies marriage tend to consistently code a given species as either male or female, and as a general rule birds fall in the latter category. Nonetheless, bird husbands were not an unimaginable proposition to the authors and audiences of *otogizōshi*, as will be seen in the discussion of *The Tale of the Wild Goose* (*Kari no sōshi*) below. However, the bird wives of the feathered-robe tales are also heavenly maidens, who are, as the name suggests, fixedly female, lacking a male counterpart (Yamamoto 2008: 89). And thus, the heavenly maiden became not a heavenly man but rather a serpent groom.

The substitution is more logical than it may initially appear. Amewakahiko is not only a snake but also a dragon—in Japanese lore, the two are inextricably intertwined—and as such, he can travel between heaven and earth in the same manner as a heavenly maiden. When heavenly maidens descend to earth, they come to bathe in ponds and rivers—an explanation for their vulnerable state of undress, but also a remnant of their original identity as migratory waterfowl (Hatto 1961: 332–3). Likewise, both dragons and snakes have strong aquatic associations. In *The Seventh Night*, the snake first approaches a washerwoman by the river in front of the rich man's house, and on his wedding night, he slithers out of the lake to greet his human bride. Perhaps most crucially, snakes resemble heavenly maidens in that they shed their skin. In the earliest feathered-robe tales, disrobing entails a transformation from bird to women; in later iterations, the heavenly maiden's avian alter ego fades away, recalled only by her power of flight and her feathered robe (Kimijima 1969: 420). In either case, however, her marriage to her human husband rests on his possession of her feathered robe. In *The Seventh Night*, the skin of the serpent groom plays an equally vital role in determining the course of the relationship, but it functions within a very different power dynamic.

To uncover the significance of the snakeskin, we must first unravel the meaning of the snake himself. Like swan maidens, serpent grooms trace back to ancient myth, but unlike Amewakahiko, these mythical serpent grooms come courting in human guise. The woman's first glimpse of her lover's true form marks the end of the relationship, and often the end of her life. In *The Chronicles of Japan* (*Nihon shoki*, 720), Princess Yamato-Totohi-Momoso receives nightly visits from a mysterious suitor. She asks to see him in the daylight, and he tells her to look inside her comb box in the morning, warning her not to be alarmed. When she opens the box, she finds a little snake coiled there. She recoils, and the snake transforms into a man—her lover, now revealed as the god Ōmononushi—who berates her for shaming him and disappears. The princess stabs herself in the genitals with a chopstick and dies. An even more sinister snake groom appears in the records of Hizen province, also from the eighth century. The tale opens in the usual way: an unknown man comes every night to a woman named Otohi, who grows curious about his identity. But rather than asking to see her lover, Otohi ties a thread to his robe before he leaves. When she follows the thread the next morning, it leads to a serpent basking in a swamp—the same swamp where her body is later found.

These ancient snake-groom myths make no clear distinction between marriage and sacrifice, and their shadow hangs over *The Seventh Night*. Although human sacrifice was never practiced in Japan, it enjoyed a storied history in the cultural imaginary; deities displaced by rival cults, particularly snake gods, were recast as demons demanding human offerings (Sasaki 1982). As most famously exemplified by Gabrielle-Suzanne de Villeneuve's "Beauty and the Beast" (1740), Western animal-groom tales reproduce the logic of arranged marriage: daughters are the capital with which fathers repay debts and uphold bargains. But a different, darker logic underlies *The Seventh Night*. There is no pretense of a fair transaction to legitimize the interspecies union; the rich man is simply propitiating a monster. However, the threat of violence abruptly reverses direction when the Amewakahiko orders his wife to behead him. It is the terrible serpent, not his trembling human bride, who assumes the role of sacrificial victim, if only momentarily; in the end, she must still suffer greatly on her husband's behalf.

While Amewakahiko's wife is as self-sacrificing as any Western fairy-tale heroine, she is spared the usual burden of accepting her inhuman husband as he is and the attendant punishment for failing to do so. Unlike Psyche (or Yamato-Totohi-Momoso and Otohi), she violates no taboo in discovering her husband's true form; the narrative uncouples this revelation from the transgression that results in his departure. And unlike Beauty, she does not forgo a "passionate coupling" in favor of a "companionate pairing" with an outwardly hideous creature (Tatar 2017: xxvi); her horror becomes love only after the serpent becomes a handsome man. In this regard, Amewakahiko's wife resembles the princess in Jacob and Wilhelm Grimms' "The Frog King," who, far from achieving happy domesticity with her amphibian partner, finds him so revolting that she throws him against a wall, upon which he becomes a handsome king. According to psychoanalyst Bruno Bettelheim, the discomfort of the princess's sexual awakening—represented by her compelled intimacy with the slimy, vaguely phallic frog—culminates in "an instant of violent self-assertion," and only afterwards can her initial repugnance give way to pleasure (1976: 291). However, the similarity between the princess and Amewakahiko's wife extends only so far. In his serpent form, Amewakahiko—while unmistakably phallic—inspires terror rather than disgust. Unlike the frog, he is vulnerable only because he chooses to make himself so, and his wife, far from asserting herself, assaults him on his orders and against her own wishes. And while the frog becomes a human king—a member of the same species and social class as the princess—Amewakahiko becomes a dragon king, albeit one with a human appearance. His wife is hopelessly overmatched both before and after his metamorphosis.

Japanese folklore establishes its own precedent for beastly grooms becoming men when assaulted by their human wives. For instance, the title character of the oral tale "Rich Man Mudsnail" (*Tanishi chōja*) is transformed from mudsnail to rich man in much the same way that the frog king is transformed from frog to king: his wife throws him against a rock.[18] (In fact, in some variants of the tale replace the mudsnail groom with a frog groom.) But while Amewakahiko's wife is not alone in taking arms against her animal husband, she is alone in taking his skin; we must look outside of Japan to find this motif with husband and wife in the same roles. Geographically speaking, the nearest example appears in the Korean oral folktale "The Rat-Snake Groom." Like Amewakahiko's wife, the rat snake's wife is a third daughter whose inauspicious marriage becomes an ideal match when her husband sheds his serpentine guise on their wedding night. Also, like Amewakahiko's wife, she makes the mistake of letting her sisters see her husband's snakeskin and so must undergo a lengthy journey of atonement. Scholars have plausibly suggested a genetic relationship between *The Seventh Night* and "The Rat-Snake Groom," although the latter has not been documented in Japanese folklore and the two diverge in several key respects; notably, "The Rat-Snake Groom" has no connection to the star-festival narrative (Kawamori 2000: 76–7). One subtle but significant difference lies in how the animal husband's skin is removed. In *The Seventh Night*, this feat is accomplished with the assistance of Amewakahiko's wife, who faces the unenviable task of decapitating a serpent seventeen fathoms long. By contrast, the rat-snake—small enough to fit into a bucket of water—politely washes off his own skin before joining his bride in bed.

Amewakahiko's transformation finds a closer analog in the traditional Danish tale "King Lindworm," in which a shepherd girl is reluctantly betrothed to an enchanted snake king. As in *The Seventh Night*, it is the wife's task to humanize her beastly husband, an undertaking that is simultaneously violent and reminiscent of the rituals of hygiene—Amewakahiko's wife beheads her husband with a nail trimmer while the lindworm's wife scrubs him bloody with lye. This choice of implements is not accidental; grooming tames the unruly organic—*animal*—aspects of the human body. But this shared symbolism operates within very different power dynamics. In "King Lindworm," the wife must initiate the process of transformation, coaxing her husband through the removal of his skin as she was taught to do by an elderly woman. Feminine wiles and feminine wisdom, the tale implies, hold the secret to turning monsters into men. Amewakahiko's wife works no such womanly craft; when she wields her nail trimmer, she does so in obedience to her husband's instructions.

On one level, the beheading of Amewakahiko fulfills the same function as the battering of the frog king or the brutal scrubbing of the lindworm: it presents a marvelous parallel to the mundane predicament of a wife in an arranged marriage, who must somehow make an undesired husband into a desirable one. But although Amewakahiko's wife accomplishes this feat through the same violent means as the heroines of "The Frog King" and "King Lindworm," she never achieves the same agency as they do. Indeed, it is never clear why— or even if—Amewakahiko requires his wife's assistance to shed his skin. No enchantment binds him to his animal form, as it does for the frog king and the lindworm king; the casting and breaking of spells is not the mechanism of transfiguration in Japanese fairy tales. In *otogizōshi* and other medieval works, lustful or covetous humans may spontaneously become snakes, after which they can only be saved by the intercession of Buddhist forces. However, this also fails to explain Amewakahiko's situation: somewhat unusually for literature of its day, *The Seventh Night* does not make even token reference to Buddhism.[19] Far from being a man under a curse or a sinner in need of salvation, Amewakahiko is a divine being. Although he seeks his wife's assistance to bring about his transformation, as if to refute any loss of power that this may imply, he later transforms *her* into a sequence of inanimate objects.

As we pick apart the riddle of Amewakahiko's snakeskin, we glimpse the shape of the feathered-robe narrative that lies beneath. Amewakahiko's wife must remove his skin because the men who marry heavenly maidens must first take their feathered robes, which were originally bird skins. However, the loss of the feathered robe entails captivity, and the role of the captive could not be transferred from the wife to the husband; such a reversal lay outside the range of marital circumstances conceivable in medieval literature. Men might be lured into the lairs of foxes in the guise of beautiful women or pursued to their death by lustful she-serpents. However, while *otogizōshi* and other works of medieval literature express much anxiety about women harming men through romantic or sexual attachment, they do not consider the possibility that a husband might be forced into marriage in the same manner as a heavenly maiden. Thus, one sort of tale about a woman forced into marriage—a heavenly maiden trapped on earth—became another sort of tale about a woman forced into marriage—a daughter sacrificed to a giant snake. *The Seventh Night* replaces the subtle but real violence of the feathered-robe tales—in which the theft of the feathered robe may plausibly stand in for abduction and rape—with overt but unreal violence. Amewakahiko's beheading does him no more injury than the unfastening of a garment; unlike the lindworm king, who emerges from his snakeskin bloody and naked, Amewakahiko springs out clad in court robes. Significantly, his first act is to lay claim to his own cast-off skin; it does not pass into the possession of his spouse as do the robes of the heavenly maidens. But in both cases, regardless of its original owner, the inhuman spouse's magical covering must remain in the husband's control. When the wife (re)gains ownership, disaster befalls the marriage.

In her monograph on swan-maiden lore from around the world, Barbara Fass-Leavy astutely notes that, despite their apparent heroic enterprise, Psyche and other fairy-tale brides who embark on quests for lost animal grooms do not necessarily subvert patriarchal norms any more than the swan maidens who take flight from their human husbands: "Psyche's so-called victory places her at the end of her story where the swan maiden is near the beginning of hers—a dutiful wife" (1994: 105). *The Seventh Night* offers perhaps the perfect illustration of this principle. The narrative proceeds through all the same plot points as the feathered robe tales, but what were originally feats of masculine audacity—the theft of the heavenly maiden's robe, the pursuit of the lost wife— are rewritten as acts of feminine obedience. Amewakahiko's wife beheads her serpent-husband because he tells her to do so, and she makes the journey to heaven following the instructions that he gave her. Her course is set for her, and even her missteps are not truly her own. She does not have the satisfaction of opening the forbidden box for herself; that crime is committed by her sisters. Nor does she steal a taste of forbidden fruit, as does the husband in the tale from Iyayama; it is an innocent mishearing that leaves her stranded on the wrong side of the Milky Way. She can fail, but she cannot rebel.

Amewakahiko's wife is both beautiful and dutiful, and by the logic of Western fairy tales, this ought to guarantee her a happy ending. However, Japanese fairy tales—in *otogizōshi* and in other forms—show no consistent commitment to rewarding virtue or (in Proppian terms) resolving lack.[20] As the prominent folklorist Ozawa Toshio observes, whereas "Western fairy tales tell about the good fortune of an individual … Japanese fairy tales are often nothing more than accounts of something experienced by the protagonist" (1989: 39). Elsewhere, Ozawa contrasts the resolution-oriented structure of Western fairy tales with the circularity of Japanese fairy tales and notes that, while the former "lead to a conclusion within the human world, namely the acquisition of an opposite-sex partner," the latter are "concerned with human existence within nature" (1994: 219–22). Another noted scholar, Kawai Hayao, expresses much the same idea more succinctly: Japanese fairy tales, he declares, "come to nothing"

(1982: 29); their protagonists end up back where they began. This is not precisely the case for Amewakahiko's wife, who begins on earth and ends in heaven, but hers is not a tale of ideal couple-formation in the same way as the Western animal-groom tales discussed here. Instead of going from single to blissfully wed, she goes from single to eternally pining. Out of all the *otogizōshi* about interspecies marriage, only one begins with a woman betrothed to a beast and still ends with an unambiguous happily ever after: *The Tale of the Wisteria Basket* (*Fujibukuro no sōshi*), in which a monkey falls in love with an old man's daughter.

APING ROMANCE: THE INHUMAN GROOM AS ABDUCTOR

The heroine of *The Tale of the Wisteria Basket* is not a third daughter, but she is a figure no less marked by destiny: a foundling miraculously granted to an elderly childless couple. Predictably, she grows to be a beautiful young woman—but her beauty does not guarantee an equally desirable mate. One day, her adoptive father grows weary while hoeing the fields, and mutters to himself that he would marry his daughter to anyone who would do the work for him. Rash promises are a staple of folklore around the world, and this particular rash promise ends as poorly as usual: a monkey who happened to be listening nearby appears and hoes the fields. Then he leaves, but not before warning the old man to uphold his end of the bargain.

The old man and his wife try to hide their daughter, but to no avail; the monkey comes back the next day and carries her off into the forest. He treats his human bride with the utmost ceremony, but on the wedding night she only sobs, unreceptive to the advances of her nonplussed husband. In the morning, the monkey goes to gather fruit for her—but first, for safekeeping, he hangs her from a tree in a basket woven from wisteria. Meanwhile, the old man and his wife enlist the aid of a hunter and his men, who rescue the monkey's captive bride and put their hunting dogs inside the wisteria basket instead. When the monkey returns and opens the basket, the dogs leap out and slaughter him and the rest of his troop. (Perhaps I should have specified: the happily ever after is not for the monkey, only the old man's daughter.) Struck by the beauty of the woman he has rescued, the hunter marries her and keeps her and her parents in wealth and comfort thereafter—a blessing from the bodhisattva Kannon, the narrator piously declares.

Like her counterpart in *The Seventh Night*, the human bride in *The Tale of the Wisteria Basket* does not choose her animal groom but is given away by her father. To Western readers, the match between the old man's daughter and the monkey might initially appear more promising than that between the rich man's daughter and the serpent, which bears a disquieting resemblance to human sacrifice. Although *The Tale of the Wisteria Basket* carries distant echoes of old tales about monkey gods demanding virgin offerings, the monkey groom earns his wife honestly by the standards of the day: human men, too, might be expected to perform agricultural labor for their prospective in-laws before being allowed to formally marry (Mukasa 2008: 39–40). The monkey not only pays a proper bride price but also performs all the other prescribed nuptial rituals: he carries his new wife away in a palanquin and fêtes her with a fine wedding feast, complete with music and poetry. Beauties have reconciled themselves to marriage with fouler creatures under crueler circumstances; ought not the monkey's solicitude be rewarded with the transformative love that turns fairy-tale beasts into princes?

Alas, the monkey remains a monkey and nothing more. In Japanese folktales, initially repulsive animal grooms may occasionally transform into ideal human husbands, as demonstrated by "Rich Man Mudsnail." However, it is far more common for an animal groom to either assume a human disguise or simply remain in animal form throughout the course of the relationship, which in either case seldom lasts long: the majority of animal grooms perish. A contemporary Japanese reader of *The Tale of the Wisteria Basket* would never expect the monkey to find happiness with his human wife, for he strongly recalls the doomed title character of "The Monkey Groom" (*Saru mukoiri*), one of the best-known folktales in modern Japan.[21] Like his counterpart in *The Tale of the Wisteria Basket*, the folkloric monkey groom wins a human bride by working in her father's fields only to be killed for his overambitious choice of mate. However, the culprit is not a hunter but his own beloved wife, who tricks him into falling into a river while carrying a heavy load. Modern commentators on "The Monkey Groom" struggle to make sense of the tale's brutal ending; why does the monkey, who has been kind to his wife and fair in his dealings with her father, deserve to die? *The Tale of the Wisteria Basket* invites the same question, which has much the same answer. One scholar who asked elderly villagers to explain "The Monkey Groom" was repeatedly told, "it's outrageous for a monkey to take a human wife; of course he had to be killed" (Ozawa 1989: 32). Komatsu similarly notes that "hostility toward non-humans runs through the tale," and concludes that its meaning cannot be understood in terms of virtue and vice, only cleverness and foolishness (1995: 156–7).

In *The Tale of the Wisteria Basket*, too, the monkey falls victim to human guile, although it is not his bride who bests him. Unlike her folkloric counterpart, she remains utterly passive throughout the tale, transferred unresisting from her father to the monkey to the hunter. Like feathered-robe tales, "The Monkey Groom" is at its core a story about a woman rejecting an unwanted husband, and thus it invites potentially subversive readings about relations between the sexes. By contrast, *The Tale of the Wisteria Basket* implicitly affirms the traditional hierarchy of sex just as it affirms the hierarchy of species. The female protagonist's fate rests wholly in male hands (or paws) and her feelings on the matter are at most a footnote. Indeed, the narrator grants the monkey greater psychological interiority than his human bride; throughout much of the tale, the reader is given a ringside seat to the monkey's thoughts, which center around the care and feeding of his new wife. The monkey's fumbling attempts to please may invite a limited sympathy, as viewers might have felt for King Kong many centuries later, but mostly they underscore his fatal folly—his belief that he is a suitable match for a human woman. The monkey-groom folklore that circulated among rural villagers establishes human superiority over animals, but it also suggests the superiority of certain kinds of humans over others. The monkey can be read as the kind of man who might be duped into working in another man's fields in hopes of earning a bride, only to be rejected after all his troubles (Mukasa 2008: 39–40). The division of agricultural labor would have held little concern for the original audience of *The Tale of the Wisteria Basket*; the earliest manuscripts of the tale, which date to the sixteenth century, were illustrated by artists of the eminent Tosa school and enjoyed an elite readership (Ryūsawa 2005: 41). However, *The Tale of the Wisteria Basket* encodes its own commentary on human society. Standard Japanese historiography regards the sixteenth century as an era of the low overthrowing the high (*gekokujō*), and many scholars read the literature of the day as a reflection of this scramble for wealth and status. However, in the words of the noted scholar of *otogizōshi* Barbara Ruch, "the main agent of medieval fiction is fate, not ambition; the essential core ... is restoration of the proper world order, not *gekokujō*" (1971: 284). While this claim does not hold universally true, it certainly applies to *The Tale of the Wisteria Basket*. During the fifteenth and sixteenth centuries, wealthy commoners increasingly pursued poetry, tea ceremony, and other arts that had traditionally been the purview of the aristocracy. The monkey apes the conduct of his betters in much the same way: he composes poetry, listens to music, wears court robes, and even rides in a palanquin made of sticks and leaves. But for all his accomplishments, he cannot escape the circumstances of his birth, and his arrogant attempt to marry above his station earns him a brutal comeuppance.

Unlike "The Monkey Groom," in which the heroine drowns her simian husband and walks away as the merriest of widows, *The Tale of the Wisteria Basket* does not accept the severance of the animal-human marriage as a happy ending unto itself; the heroine must also acquire (or be acquired by) a suitable human husband. Significantly, one of the eight surviving manuscripts of *The Tale of the Wisteria Basket* may have been created for the trousseau of a woman who married into the powerful Owari clan (Ryūsawa 2005: 42–3). Books and scrolls featured prominently among the wedding goods that upper-class brides brought to their new households; the works selected for this purpose either carried auspicious associations or cultivated feminine virtues. At first, *The Tale of the Wisteria Basket* may appear to be an odd choice for inclusion in a bridal trousseau, given that the heroine's arranged marriage ends in bloody murder rather than blissful matrimony. *The Seventh Night* is listed among the contents of another trousseau—this one belonging to the wife of the first lord of the Mito clan—but this seems more fitting: the sad fate of Amewakahiko and his wife notwithstanding, the tale assures readers that an apparently monstrous husband may turn out to be the perfect man.

However, despite their surface dissimilarities, both *The Seventh Night* and *The Tale of the Wisteria Basket* celebrate "the virtues of obedience to the law of the father" (Tartar 1987: 147). In *The Seventh Night*, the rich man's ready capitulation to the serpent's threats looks very much like cowardice, but—even if inadvertently—he has in fact arranged a fine match for this daughter. It is her own error, not her father's, that sours her happily ever after. Likewise, although the old man in *The Tale of the Wisteria Basket* seems to commit a grievous mishap by inadvertently promising his daughter to a monkey, this unpropitious betrothal is the prelude to a perfect marriage. Granted, the monkey is murdered and replaced by an ideal husband rather than becoming one himself, but—except from the monkey's perspective—the outcome is much the same.

UNSUITABLE SUITORS: THE INHUMAN GROOM AS TRAGIC LOVER

Not all of the women who marry beasts are given away by their fathers. Some choose their animal husbands for themselves, although never knowingly—they do not realize who (or what) they have wed until it is too late. This broad outline unites a group of three *otogizōshi* produced among the aristocracy and warrior elite during the late fifteenth and sixteenth centuries. Although these tales originated within much the same context as *The Seventh Night* and *The Tale of the Wisteria Basket*, they develop the theme of the animal groom in a very different direction, foregrounding the emotions of the human woman as her reckless love affair takes her from longing to apparent fulfillment to painful revelation and loss.

Tales of Things Transformed (*Bakemono no sōshi*) begins in a desolate mountain village where a lonely woman longs for a husband—"even that scarecrow in the field would do," she says. Some time later, a man comes courting; he vanishes in the morning, but night after night, he faithfully returns. The woman eventually grows curious and ties a thread to her lover's robes. To her horror, she discovers that the thread leads to the scarecrow in the field. Her lover never comes again. *The Tale of the Wild Goose* opens in much the same way: one autumn night, a woman prays for a husband, "even a wild goose." That night, a mysterious traveler appears at her door, and the two quickly fall in love. Spring arrives, and her lover announces that he must return to his hometown, promising to return in the fall. When he departs, she glimpses a wild goose flying away, and for the first time realizes the truth. Some months later, she dreams that a goose brings her a letter, and awakens to find a letter on her pillow. It is from her lover, telling her that he has been killed by a hunter's arrow. The woman becomes a nun to pray for the goose in his next life and eventually achieves enlightenment herself. A grimmer ending awaits the protagonist of *The Tale of the Mouse* (*Nezumi no sōshi*): she wishes for "someone, anyone" to love her, finds a seemingly perfect husband, and loses him when he is eaten by her mother's cat. Someone, as it turns out, was a mouse.

These tales resist straightforward interpretation. They are evocative rather than declarative, seemingly more concerned with aesthetics than didactics. With its themes of asceticism and salvation, *The Tale of the Wild Goose* imbues its tragic romance with a Buddhist flavor; however, while it does reflect the general principle that worldly attachments lead to suffering, it does not articulate an explicit moral. Ought one or ought one not enter into affairs with strange men who come knocking in the middle of the night? The answer is surprisingly ambiguous. The other two works lack a religious dimension and conclude inconclusively, with final scenes that seem crafted to elicit an emotional response rather than impart a lesson. *Tales of Things Transformed* closes with its heroine reeling at the discovery of her husband's identity: "Over and over, she felt shame and horror; she must have believed that it was a monster that had appeared to her. She never saw him again after that." The heroine of *The Tale of the Mouse* ends her story in a similar state, although her horror is complicated by longing for her lost husband: "How shameful, that she had pledged herself to that! And yet ... all those months and those years, all those deep words of love that he had spoken ... she thought of it all again and again, and despaired. Truly, theirs was a bond not of this world." Scholarly discussions of these *otogizōshi* have tended to emphasize their aesthetic and allusive qualities, which are seen as the result of tales of interspecies marriage "being drawn into the domain of courtly literature"; within this rarefied context, the pathos of the inevitable parting of the human and animal spouses became the most appealing aspect of the interspecies narrative, and thus the tales "were simplified into a single storyform" as the focus shifted to "drawing out the lyricism of the separation" (Yoshida 2009: 19).

Without question, *Tales of Things Transformed*, *The Tale of the Wild Goose*, and *The Tale of the Mouse* are literary inventions in a way that *The Seventh Night* and *The Tale of the Wisteria Basket* are not. While the latter two tales have not been documented as orally transmitted folklore, as we have seen, both tap into a dense network of folkloric influences; indeed, snakes and monkeys are the archetypal animal grooms. On the other hand, the folkloric line-up of inhuman husbands does not include scarecrows, geese, or mice—these are not the usual suspects, and they do not follow the usual modus operandi. The animal grooms of folklore most often present themselves in their undisguised form; while the ancient snake-gods come to their wives in human guise, in later tales such transformation would become the hallmark of animal brides (Nakamura, Yumira, and Mamiya 2001: 98–100). The scarecrow groom, the goose groom, and the mouse groom are novel creations, but their pattern of incognito nocturnal visitation is an archaism, hearkening back to old myths and obsolete marital customs. But while the ancient snake gods vanished when they were unveiled, this newer cohort of inhuman grooms die instead. (The exception is the scarecrow, which, being an inanimate object, cannot die.) In this regard, they resemble the animal grooms of folklore who are killed at the end of the tale, as exemplified by the monkey groom in *The Tale of the Wisteria Basket*. However, the *otogizōshi* discussed here radically reframe the death of the inhuman husband, presenting it as not a triumph but a tragedy.

The treatment of the inhuman husband's demise would seem to support the argument that these tales are primarily about sentiment—but if we press them, they yield meaning as well as mood. The most obvious reading is a cautionary one. *Tales of Things Transformed* stands apart from the other *otogizōshi* in this group inasmuch as it has a clear mythic basis: the woman follows the thread tied to her husband's robes in the same manner as Otohi did centuries before, although this ancient motif is defamiliarized (and desacralized) by the substitution of a scarecrow for a snake god. The tale might be read as an injunction against imprudent curiosity, although unlike Otohi—whose grisly fate would make Bluebeard's wife flinch—the scarecrow's lover suffers no punishment beyond returning to her former lonely state; her original sin lies in having vowed to accept a scarecrow as a husband in the first place. The heroines of *The Tale of the Wild Goose* and *The Tale of the Mouse* do not violate any taboos against looking, but they too suffer for their carelessly worded wishes, which betray a dangerous openness to the wrong sort of suitor.

When we read these works as cautionary tales, they form a complement to *The Seventh Night* and *The Tale of the Wisteria Basket*, which employ the motif of the animal groom to teach that arranged marriages more or less work out for the best. By contrast, *Tales of Things Transformed*, *The Tale of the Wild Goose*, and *The Tale of the Mouse* illustrate the perils of *un*arranged marriage. The union with the inhuman groom is not a stepping-stone on the way to conjugal bliss, but rather irrefutable proof that a woman has erred in her choice of mate. But viewed from another angle, these tales do not warn against taking illicit lovers, but rather lament the circumstances that leave women vulnerable to such attentions in the first place.

The heroines of these tales are not beautiful princesses or even rich men's daughters; they are in dire straits even before they encounter their inhuman suitors. The scarecrow's wife lives in a rundown house in a remote village, as does the mouse's wife, who worse yet has passed marriageable age and is no great beauty. Similarly, the goose's wife is an orphaned noblewoman of low rank living on the outskirts of the capital. Spatially and socially, these women inhabit the periphery—the liminal places where the uncanny creeps in—and their marginalized status puts them in a double bind. Their illicit affairs lead to heartbreak, but waiting chastely for a properly arranged marriage will not bring them any closer to a happy ending. And in these tales, a happy ending is as much a matter of economics as emotions; for all three women, the longing for a husband is explicitly bound up in a desire for someone to rely upon.

The heroine of *Tales of Things Transformed* gains nothing from her involvement with the scarecrow, and she herself brings about the dissolution of the affair. The narrator withholds judgment about this outcome—did the woman outwit a sinister creature or drive away a faithful lover?—saying only that the woman herself believed she had been visited by a monster. *The Tale of the Wild Goose* and *The Tale of the Mouse* take an even more ambivalent view of the end of the interspecies romance. The heroines of these tales profit from the gifts that their husbands bring to them (although the goose's wife finds his offerings of rice fresh from the fields to be rather odd). While they are horrified to discover their husbands' true identities, unlike the heroine of *Tales of Things Transformed*, they nonetheless continue to long for them. Indeed, even after realizing that he is a bird, the heroine of *The Tale of the Wild Goose* impatiently awaits her lover's return.

In folklore, if the human women who find themselves married to animal grooms cannot transform them into men—and they seldom can—then they must escape them; thus, the severance of the marriage constitutes a happy ending. The dissolution of the interspecies relationship is only presented as a loss when a human man is deserted by his animal bride, who frequently brings wealth to her husband's household and then leaves after he violates some taboo. (Several *otogizōshi* follow this paradigm, although discussion of these works falls beyond the scope of this chapter.[22]) The interspecies relationships in *The Tale of the Wild Goose* and *The Tale of the Mouse* share some of these traits, although the parallel is not perfect. As we have already seen, the mouse groom and the goose groom come to their lovers at night—a uniquely masculine prerogative—and the marriage ends not when they depart, as an animal bride would, but rather when they die. Their unmasking and subsequent death intermingle the poignant sorrow more usually associated with the departure of an animal bride with the abject misery of a human bride who has found herself wed to an animal. By contrast, men who learn that their beloved wives are cranes or foxes do not experience shame or horror, only grief at parting.[23] Finally, crucially, the marriages in *The Tale of the Wild Goose* and *The Tale of the Mouse* do not fail because of the error of the human spouse; no taboo is violated. The wives of the goose and the mouse may gain their inhuman husbands because of their rash wishes, but they lose them through no fault of their own.

An uncharitable reader might view these women as pathetic figures whose desperation drives them into the arms (or wings, or paws) of bestial lovers, but they possess a deep subjectivity that we do not see in the heroines of *The Seventh Night* and *The Tale of the Wisteria Basket*. What they want is the point of the tale, even if they don't get it. By contrast, the animal husbands' motives for entering into relationships with human women remain a mystery—it is not their desires but those of their wives that drive the narrative. The ability of the goose and the mouse to assume human form goes unexplained and unremarked. There is no magical robe or skin that allows them to shape-shift; they just do. Apart from animals masquerading as men, the tales do not stray far beyond the confines of mundane reality. No seventeen-fathom-long serpents are beheaded, no constellations are created, nobody journeys to heaven or even into the deep forest where the monkeys live. The events unfold on a stage almost completely circumscribed by the heroines' households, and the deaths of the animal grooms are suitably quotidian. A hunter kills a goose; a cat eats a mouse. This is the ordinary course of things, and although we can glimpse the workings of a world arrayed against the happiness of the heroines, no one in particular is to blame. The end does not need to answer the questions it poses: it is simply the end.

CHAPTER FIVE

Monsters and the Monstrous

Witches and Werewolves in Early Modern French and Italian Tales

KATHLEEN P. LONG

INTRODUCTION: MARVELOUS STORIES AND FAIRY TALES

Fairy-tale monsters that appear in the formative period of the genre are an eclectic group of figures that can be separated into a number of categories and subcategories: the supernatural, including demons, witches, and magical animals (shape-shifters, dragons, and other beings that exceed the capacities of the natural); the biological, encompassing monstrous births and other physiological differences such as giants and dwarves; and the social, with wild men and women, and evil princes or princesses. What all of these categories have in common is transgression of rules or laws, whether theological, natural, or social, and effacement of the boundaries that uphold these laws, between human and animal, male and female, demonic and human, or normal and pathological.[1] Needless to say, these categories all blur and overlap at certain points, with, for example, the werewolf and the wild man existing in close proximity, conceptually speaking. Because this rich array of figures is too vast to examine in a single essay, and because the biological or teratological aspects of the marvelous in fairy tales have been amply examined elsewhere, this chapter will focus on how narratives of witchcraft served as a repository of magical figures from which fairy tales could draw, with witches and demons becoming fairies, and shape-shifters like the werewolf becoming humans either born as animals or transformed into animals. The wild man will also be considered relative to these human-animal hybrids, particularly as his dual status, at once more savage and more noble than the "civilized" humans, complicates distinctions between the human and the animal.

An examination of fairy tales in the period 1450–1650 reveals a broad range of sources for their representations of monsters: ancient and medieval legends and myths, chivalric epics and romances, and the early modern science of monsters, linked to that of teratology (the study of abnormal development), offer a broad array of monstrous types adopted by this genre. Scholars such as Lewis Seifert and Suzanne Magnanini have addressed the complex science of the marvelous and monstrous relative to fairy tales (Seifert 1996: 21–42; Magnanini 2008: 19–47). Other scholars, most prominently Ruth B. Bottigheimer, have written extensively on the long history of magic tales, linking ancient and medieval sources to the early modern fairy tale (Bottigheimer 2014). Still others, such as Holly Tucker, have analyzed the connections between fairies, midwives, and witches (2003: 63–70).[2] Much attention in this scholarship has been devoted to monstrous births, and certainly the frog-boy, dog-boy, and pig-men that appear in scientific/medical treatises, for instance the French physician Ambroise Paré's *On Monsters and Marvels* (1573), inform tales of pig kings, monkey princesses, and other royal animals (Paré [1575] 1982, 1971; Canepa 2001; Hoffman 2005).[3] For Paré, "Monsters are things that appear outside the course of Nature ... such as a child who is born with one arm, another who will have two heads, and additional members over and above the ordinary" (Paré [1575] 1982: 3). Paré's prodigies or marvels are probably more pertinent to the development of fairy-tale characters: "Marvels are things that happen that are completely against Nature as when a woman will give birth to a serpent, or to a dog" (Paré [1575] 1982: 3; 1971: 3). For Paré, monsters remain natural, and prodigies reside in the domain of the supernatural. However, outside of the realm of medical treatises, this distinction is somewhat blurred as, over time, monsters and prodigies become associated with each other.

All of these monstrous images take on a more sinister tone in the context of widespread persecution of witchcraft. With the dissemination of the diabolical version of witchcraft, which presented the witch as an ally of Satan in his quest to destroy God's creation by corrupting human souls, by means of the publication of many witchcraft treatises over the course of the early modern period, widely available imagery of the monstrous human-animal hybrid raises a number of ontological and epistemological questions. In particular, the figure of the shape-shifter, a being that can move back and forth between human and (mostly) animal forms, embodies debates over the relationship between the mind and the body, the human and the animal, and physical reality and illusion. Transformation between human and animal forms also elicits questions concerning agency and responsibility: who makes this new form possible, and how does it relate to the previous identity and behavior of the individual involved?

This chapter will explore how a wide range of monstrous figures used in sixteenth- and seventeenth-century fairy tales also appear in texts related to witchcraft and demonology: witchcraft treatises, some medical treatises, and popular stories known in France as *histoires prodigieuses*, or prodigy tales. Witches themselves inform the representations of fairies, with their supernatural means of travel, their involvement in childbirth, and their capacity for shape-shifting. This last trait links witches to werewolves, which figure prominently in early modern discussions of demonology and which evolve in fairy tales into other human-animal transformations, such as deer, snakes, cats, monkeys, and birds. These transformations also owe something to Ovid's *Metamorphoses*, with its numerous humans changed into deer or birds, as well as to Apuleius's work of the same title, with its human trapped in the body of an ass after an act of magic gone wrong. The setting of omnipresent witchcraft in this latter work—as the protagonist Lucius's obsession with magic causes him to seek it out in Thessaly and then seek the remedy for the effects of his excessive curiosity once he is transformed—makes it a particularly important source for early modern fairy tales. But in the wake of a sustained obsession with witchcraft in this period, they are also touched with the stigma of demonic transformation. Fairies transform humans into animals as a form of punishment, often for the sins of the parents that must be expiated.

This moral aspect of human-animal transformations links them to another form of monstrosity in the early modern era: the human-animal hybrid, discussed in monster treatises and in marvel tales, and thought to be the result of bestiality, itself considered a monstrous act in the period. The ambiguous nature of these creatures, caught somewhere between the human and the non-human, becomes an important aspect of many of the human figures transformed into animals in fairy tales. Whether in speech, dress, or behavior, the shape-shifted protagonists of fairy tales never fully abandon their human aspect. Helpful animals in fairy tales might be linked to witches' animal familiars, but seem closer to the shape-shifters or hybrids in that they consistently demonstrate human qualities such as human language and behavior, even more than protagonists known to be metamorphosed humans. The various versions of Puss in Boots by Giovan Francesco Straparola, Giambattista Basile, and Charles Perrault, the serpent sister in Straparola's tale of "Biancabella" ([1550–3] 2015: 147–55), and Marie-Catherine d'Aulnoy's "Beneficent Frog" ([1698] 2008b: 83–122) and "Green Serpent" ([1697–8] 2008a: 631–68) all fit this model of the helpful animal.

The wild man, a popular monster in both prodigy tales and fairy tales, shares this ambiguity, also calling into question the frontiers between human and non-human. More than this, the wild man also calls into question the assumption of human superiority and the importance of what we call civilization. He is either the figure of man fallen from the state of grace because of his arrogance, or that of a man better connected to nature, capable of speaking truth to power. This latter, more positive, quality is evident in the truth-telling satyr in Straparola's story of Costanza/Costanzo, the penniless princess who disguises herself as a man to travel freely and enters the service of a king. It is this wild satyr who reveals her true gender to the king, as well as the queen's infidelity (Straparola [1550–3] 2015: 173–81). In fairy tales generally, as in this example, the wild man is generally a beneficial figure.

The publication of the first fairy tales in Italy and France, Straparola's *The Pleasant Nights*, published in two parts in 1550 and 1553, and then translated by Jean Louveau[4] and Pierre de Larivey,[5] occurs in the context of the long period of persecutions for witchcraft. Bottigheimer considers these the first French fairy tales, a claim justified by the popularity of these translations and by the imitations of these stories in the 1690s by Perrault, d'Aulnoy, and Henriette-Julie de Murat.[6] For this reason, this chapter will focus on Louveau's and Larivey's versions of Straparola's tales, as well as the tales of d'Aulnoy, which frequently appropriate or imitate Straparola's work and feature monstrous human/animal transformations.

While these translations were published well into the seventeenth century, their popularity paled in comparison to that of the wonder tales known as *histoires prodigieuses* (*prodigy tales*), first published by Boaistuau in 1560,[7] and continuously republished well into the seventeenth century.[8] The *histoires prodigieuses* featured diabolical activities and monstrous humanity, as well as natural disasters and strange animals, thus uniting the material of witchcraft treatises with that of medical treatises and natural philosophy, and offering a wealth of imagery and ideas to authors of fairy tales. Over the course of the seventeenth century, many pamphlets were produced under the titles *Histoire prodigieuse*, *Histoire mémorable*, or *Histoire admirable*, thus spreading the genre to a much broader audience. The material of this genre overlapped with that of the *histoires tragiques* (or *tragic tales*).[9] Both featured ghosts, demonic or divine intervention, sinful human behavior, and spectacular punishments. But the *histoires tragiques* were firmly focused on human misbehavior and its terrible consequences, while the *histoires prodigieuses* were more capacious in their scope, relating anything that might elicit wonder or horror, including monsters of all sorts. The reception of these tragic and prodigy tales remained far more extensive than that of fairy tales in France until the latter part of the seventeeth century.[10]

Their darker take on human behavior and the role of evil in the world is related to the period of witchcraft persecution in Europe, and perhaps even intensified by the long period of the Wars of Religion in France. According to Mack Holt, the Wars of Religion lasted from 1562, the year of the Massacre at Vassy—in which the duc de Guise and his men killed Protestant worshippers in a barn, settting off the first war—until 1629, after the second siege of La Rochelle, which resulted in the dismantling of the last Protestant stronghold in France (Holt 2005: 3–4, 173–89). The massacres of Saint Bartholomew's Day, extending over several months in the late summer and fall of 1572, leave their somber mark on this period. As Andrea Frisch has carefully demonstrated, the suppression of this very negative history is related to literary forms that seek to move their audience toward greater support for their community and their king (Frisch 2015: 1–25). Fairy tales, by taking the negative narratives of the period of the Wars of Religion, and banishing them to the realms of the imagination, while putting a more positive spin on these stories, offer narratives in support of the monarchy and all of the institutions that uphold it (patriarchal marriage and social hierarchies feature most prominently). This escapism might well explain the popularity of translations and adaptations of Straparola's tales, as well as the rise of the French fairy tale toward the end of the seventeenth century.

The focus of this chapter will be the persistence of the darker themes of the early modern period as subtexts for the fairy tales that proliferate in the sixteenth to the early eighteenth centuries, present not only in descriptive details and characterizations, but also in direct references to witchcraft and other diabolical activities. The negative moralizing aspect of witchcraft treatises and the *histoires prodigieuses*, echoed by the closely related form of the *histoires tragiques*, carries over into the seventeenth century in the stark contrast between bad fairies, who more closely resemble witches and who threaten lineage and render the birth of princes and princesses problematic, and good fairies, who protect the wealthy, worthy, and beautiful. These reassuring narratives thus have troubling subtexts revealed by monsters, those ambiguous figures that call into question epistemological categories.

FAIRIES AND WITCHES

Prior to the early modern period, fairies appear in medieval romances and shorter tales such as Marie de France's *lais*. In "Lanval," one of her *lais* based on Arthurian legends, the main character falls in love with a fairy (Marie [12th c.] 2018: 162–95). Medieval fairies are not represented as demonic; they are associated with another realm, represented as having supernatural qualities, but generally detached from human affairs. Their interventions can be good or bad, depending upon the behavior of the humans with whom they are interacting. At one point Lanval's fairy beloved fails to come to his assistance because he inadvertently betrayed their secret, but in the end she saves his life. Similarly, fairies in many fairy tales appear and disappear, harm or help depending on a range of circumstances. They are not a constant presence, nor is their behavior entirely predictable. Whereas in tales from the end of the seventeenth century, good fairies reward good people and punish the bad, while bad fairies are cruel to all, fairies from earlier tales do not always exercise their magic in such morally charged ways. In Marie de France's story, "Yonec," the fairy lover is a shape-shifter, transforming from a hawk to a human and back at will (2018: 210–39); this attribute is also linked to Morgan le Fay, King Arthur's magical sister, in Geoffroy of Monmouth's *Life of Merlin* (Hebert 2013: 21–2). Once again, this attribute is not portrayed as good or bad, but simply seen as a sign of magic qualities.

REPRESENTATIONS OF THE WITCH: 1450–1650

The period of witchcraft persecution in Switzerland, Italy, and France serves as the context for more negative representations of fairies. The concept of diabolical witchcraft was first officially disseminated by the Council of Basel (1431–49).[11] Thomas Malory's influential representation of Morgan le Fay in *Le Morte d'Arthur* was probably composed in the 1460s, in the wake of the diabolization of witchcraft. While Malory's Morgan can heal, she also does considerable harm (Hebert 2013: 71, citing Malory 1967: 90–1). Rather than being portrayed as a complex fairy, in Malory's representation, she becomes a practitioner of black magic, and an adversary of King Arthur and his knights, even using her magic to try to kill the King, her brother (see Malory 1967: 138–42). As Maureen Fries asserts, "Female wizardry in a more malevolent form emerges in Malory's subsequent treatment of Morgan, where his earlier neutral mentions yield to a catalog of her deceits and entrapments, seductions and attempted seductions, triumphant shapeshiftings and chastity-testing gifts, all designed to bring shame upon Arthur, Guinevere, and their court" (Fries 1994: 10).[12] Malory's longest account of Morgan's evil is the tale of her attempt to trick her lover, Accolon, into killing Arthur (11). Thus, in Malory's account, Morgan transforms from a Celtic goddess into a witch, with some of the trappings of witchcraft described by post-Basel treatises: shape-shifting, seduction, and deadly meddling via magic in human affairs.

According to Hans Broedel, in this period, "the concept of the witch remained extremely fluid, while generalized fear of witches grew" (2013: 32). Broedel also points out that flight and animal transformation are widely understood to be fundamental characteristics of witches in this period (33). While details in the accounts of witchcraft vary a great deal from one geographical location to another, the concept of *maleficium*, or magical harm, is central (34). Broedel suggests that "generalized anxiety associated with wars, pestilence, famine, and religious turmoil may have led to increasing fears of the devil's occult powers," and this fear was focused on the figure of the witch (36). Healing practices were also often associated with witchcraft in this period, sometimes linking midwives and witches (38–9). Witchcraft persecutions rose in parallel to persecutions for heresy; Waldensians, adherents of the most prevalent movement accused of heresy by the Catholic Church in the medieval and early modern periods, were particularly targeted as witches (37–40). This connection may well explain the widespread nature of persecution for witchcraft in the early modern period.

William Monter notes that the influence of the Paris Parlement, in its role as an appellate court, was important for limiting witchcraft persecution in France. While other regional courts might have used judicial torture, the Paris Parlement put limits on the use of judicial torture, and controlled the process much more carefully in witch trials. It did not allow ecclesiastical tribunals to make final judgments in areas under its jurisdiction, which resulted in far fewer condemnations. Also, it was easy to appeal a condemnation (Monter 2013: 219). Thus, the horrific spectacles of torture and burning of those accused of witchcraft were less frequent in France than in Germany and other regions. Nonetheless, theories of witchcraft proliferated in France, and the images they propagated of witches found an afterlife with fairies. The separation between theories of witchcraft, which generated numerous publications in France in the early modern era, and the practice of persecution may have made it easier to detach the imagery of magic from the horrors of the trials, thus making its appropriation for use in fairy tales less problematic.

While some belief in "white magic" remained, the focus after the Council of Basel was on black magic or diabolical witchcraft (connected to heresy). By the time the *Malleus maleficarum* (*The Hammer of Witches*) was first published in 1487, black magic was the dominant representation of the occult in treatises. Practitioners of diabolical, also called demonic, witchcraft were thought to have made a pact with the devil in exchange for supernatural powers; these powers in turn were to be used to undermine God's power by interfering with reproduction and killing babies, harming people's health and well-being (so, bringing on tempestuous weather and destroying crops as well as making people sick), and transforming both witches and others into animals.[13] White magic, generally called natural magic for its use of natural elements, mineral and botanical, sought to improve health and restore order in the universe, as well as to improve the practitioner's understanding of that universe. These goals linked it to the field of natural philosophy. While diabolical magic was considered to be supernatural, natural magic worked within the confines of nature and thus in accordance with God's will and not the Devil's (see Zambelli 2007: 13–34, esp. 17–18). The negative view of magic as predominantly diabolical was particularly pervasive in the wake of the Reformation. Many authors on the subject took magic to be real, and morally repulsive, rather than a subject of fiction. But not all authors agreed with this view. Ambroise Paré's discussion of demons and sorcerers reflects the skepticism toward these theories of witchcraft and calls into question the reality of witches (and demons). He raises the question of whether transformations really occur, or whether they are merely appearances or hallucinations (Paré [1575] 1982: chs. 26–33, 85–105; 1971: chs. 25–32, 80–99). These questions most likely echo the work of Johann Weyer, whose treatise *On the Illusions of Demons, and on Spells and Poisons* (*De praestigiis daemonum, et incantationibus ac veneficiis*, 1563) was translated into French in 1567.[14]

As Richard Kieckhefer suggests, the mythologies and learned discourses of witchcraft are quite varied, but certain images dominate in interrogations during the early modern period: travel to assemblies of witches, killing and eating of infants, worship of Satan, and denial of God (2013: 161–4). These representations of the characteristics of witches then permeated popular culture throughout Europe. Examples of this are evident in both the *histoires prodigieuses* and the *histoires tragiques* traditions.[15]

REPRESENTATIONS OF SORCERY AND MAGIC: TRAVELING WITCHES AND FAIRIES

At first, the region of the Alps, Switzerland, southeastern France, and northern Italy was the epicenter of witchcraft trials and executions, as well as publications and proselytizing concerning witches (Broedel 2013: 36–40). Tamar Herzig observes that the "bloodiest phase of Italian witchcraft trials occurred in the period generally associated with the Italian Renaissance," beginning in 1385, even before the Council of Basel, and reaching "their climax during the Italian Wars (1494–1530)" (2013: 249). Straparola's tales thus appear in the context of the aftermath of the worst of these persecutions, when some skepticism had already entered into discussions of magic. Thus, a number of the stories reflect an interest in sorcery, yet do not seem to emphasize the diabolical nature of this practice. For example, in the first tale of the seventh night, that of the wayward Ortodosio, his faithful wife Isabella turns to magic when her prayers for the return of her long-lost husband do not work:

> So, seeing that neither by fasting, nor prayers, nor by almsgiving, nor by other good deeds had she been granted what she wanted, she decided to change her ways and take the opposite path. And whereas before she had been devout and fervent in her prayers, now she gave herself over entirely to incantations and spells, hoping that things would turn out better for her.
>
> (Straparola [1550–3] 2015: 283)

The theological aspects of this passage are striking; the acceptable religious methods of supplication are represented as inefficacious, although they are being misused in a superstitious manner. Sorcery is presented as a potentially much more useful alternative to orthodox religion. So, it is not surprising that Isabella seeks out the aid of a sorceress, who summons helpful demons:

> When the hour the sorceress had chosen arrived, she took her little book and made a circle on the ground that was not very large and surrounded it with certain symbols and characters. Then she took a fine liqueur, drank a drop of it, and gave the same amount to Isabella to drink. And when she had drunk it, she spoke to her like this, "Isabella, you know that we have met here to cast a spell so that we can learn something of your husband, but it is necessary that you be steadfast and not fear anything you hear or see, even if it is frightening. Nor should you give yourself courage by invoking God or the saints or by making the sign of the cross, because you would not be able to come back and you would risk your life."
>
> (Straparola [1550–3] 2015: 284)

There are some details worth noting here. The usual invocations of Christian intervention must be rejected as potentially very harmful. While the sorceress suggests that what Isabella will see might be very frightening, there is little sustained description of the demons or their characteristics. They seem to serve at the pleasure of the sorceress, and her agency is crucial.

Larivey offers a somewhat more troubling version of these actions and words:

> Meanwhile, night having fallen, this old sorceress took a little book, in which she mumbled some secret words, made a circle of medium size on the ground, which she surrounded with certain magical figures and characters. Afterwards, she took a little vial of I don't know what kind of delicate liqueur out of her bosom, and drank a drop of it, and having made Isabella take just the same amount, said to her: "My daughter, you know that we are not here to string pearls, but to pull spirits from the deepest of the infernal abysses, and by virtue of my words force them to do what the strength of men cannot achieve, something which is of no little difficulty nor easy to bring to completion. Therefore, my friend, it is necessary here that you arm yourself with a great and assured constancy, without taking fright at all at anything which you might see or hear, however horrible it might be. And above all, make sure that you are not taken by the desire to invoke the name of God or of his saints, nor even make the sign of the cross, because, if you do any of these things, you will put yourself in great danger of dying."
>
> (Straparola [1550–3] 1882: 76–7)

This sorceress fits better with the image of the old lady muttering spells. Her emphasis on the "infernal abysses" is an embellishment that underscores the evil nature of her actions, whereas Straparola's witch is more delicate in her language and behavior. Nonetheless, this brief gesture toward the diabolical version of witchcraft is not borne out by the rest of the story, which emphasizes the happy outcome of enforcement of the husband's marital fidelity.

In both versions, one of the demons, Farfarello, is transformed into a horse and flies with Isabella on his back to visit her husband, disguising her to look just like the courtesan the husband is madly in love with, and disguising the courtesan herself as an elderly lady (Straparola [1550–3] 2015: 285). Isabella becomes pregnant by her husband, returns home, gives birth, and the scandalized family calls Ortodosio back to deal with his wife. She proves her fidelity by showing him objects taken from the courtesan's house, and the baby, who resembles him completely, down to a missing toe. She credits God's intervention, brought on by her frequent prayers and good works, for this happy event, and they all live happily ever after. Isabella covers over what she has done by claiming divine, not diabolical, intervention, and no commentary ensues concerning the morality of this move, whereas in witchcraft treatises, this behavior was severely condemned. By amplifying the negative representation of the old sorceress, Larivey gestures toward witchcraft treatises; still, he sidesteps overt condemnation. Both versions of this story seem to thus present sorcery as an acceptable practice, one potentially even approved of by God.

The form of travel Isabella takes, that of a flying animal, was considered one proof of witchcraft, as is clear from certain treatises and images. Both Hans Baldung Grien and Albrecht Dürer represent witches traveling to the diabolical sabbath on the back of a flying goat; the Nuremberg Chronicle offers an image of the Berkeley Witch being carried off by a devil on the back of a horse (Schedel 1493) (Figure 5.1), as does an image from a sixteenth-century edition of Olaus Magnus's *History of the Northern Peoples* (Magnus 1555: 126) (Figure 5.2).

Perhaps by examining modes of travel in late seventeenth-century fairy tales we can see how representations of witches inform the portrayal of fairies. At first, fairy travel seems much more elaborate than that of witches. In d'Aulnoy's "La Princesse Carpillon" (2008a: 36), the fairy Amazone first appears in a fiery globe, which holds her chariot drawn by swans, perhaps an allusion to Venus's chariot in Ovid's story of Adonis in the *Metamorphoses*.[16] This mode of transport signals the divine nature of the goddess, offering an image in stark opposition to Medea's more infamous chariot. Medea, who, along with Circe, serves as the ancient model for medieval and early modern representations of witches, is portrayed as frequently flying through the air in her dragon-drawn chariot in the *Metamorphoses*, and this form of travel is always connected to her nefarious deeds, either as a prelude or as a form of escape from punishment for them.[17]

FIGURE 5.1: "The Berkeley Witch," from the Nuremberg Chronicle (*Liber chronicarum*, 1493). Courtesy of the Division of Rare and Manuscript Collections, Cornell University Library. Public domain.

FIGURE 5.2: "Witch Being Abducted," from Olaus Magnus, *Historia de gentibus septentrionalibus* (1555). Courtesy of the Division of Rare and Manuscript Collections, Cornell University Library. Public domain.

At the end of the d'Aulnoy's tale, Amazone appears suddenly on horseback, flying through the air as the witch of the Nuremberg Chronicle had done (d'Aulnoy [1698] 2008b: 80), ready to set the situation right. Both the divine and diabolical forms of transport are thus associated with a fairy who maintains order in the realm of humans. Perhaps d'Aulnoy feels free to combine the fairy and the witch in her imaginary realms, as her work comes in the wake of Louis XIV's 1682 edict dissolving the special court created to deal with the "Affair of the Poisons," a scandalous series of events involving supposed sorcerers' and witches' interference in court affairs. This edict reflected contemporary skepticism concerning the existence of witchcraft, which informed subsequent prosecutions. While witch-hunting continued in scattered parts of the realm, in the wake of this edict, legal proceedings in most parts of France focused on criminal behavior such as poisoning, or heresy, rather than witchcraft (Monter 2013: 225–6).

D'Aulnoy embellishes these forms of transport in "La Biche au Bois" ("The Doe in the Woods"), as the fairies descend upon the palace to bestow blessings (and perhaps a harsh curse) on the newborn princess:

> Each one had her own chariot in a different style: one was ebony pulled by white pigeons, another ivory guided by little crows, yet others of cedar or calaba. This was their mode of transport for alliances and for peace, for

when they were angry, it was only flying dragons, or snakes which threw fire from their mouths and eyes, only lions, or leopards, or panthers, on which they transported themselves from one end of the world to the other, in less time than one needs to day "good day" or "good night."[18]

In her study of the centrality of childbirth to fairy tales, and the connections between midwives and fairies in these tales, Tucker uses this passage to underscore the inherent duality of fairies that is signaled by these different modes of transport, arguing that the role of the midwife is transformed into the intervention either of good fairies or of evil ones who resemble witches (2003: 63–5). When doves or even crows pull their chariots, the fairies are benevolent; when they intend evil, they travel with flying dragons, snakes, lions, leopards, or panthers.[19]

The duality of these fairies evokes some of the most significant sources for these tales. While Venus is transported in a swan-drawn chariot in Ovid's *Metamorphoses*, her iconography is more closely associated with one pulled by doves, an attribute inspired by the tale of Cupid and Psyche in Apuleius's *Metamorphoses* (also known as *The Golden Ass*). Venus uses this chariot to ascend to Jupiter in her quest for revenge after Cupid's injury:

> But Venus, after that she was weary with searching over all the earth for Psyche, returned towards heaven and commanded that one should prepare the chariot which her husband Vulcanus had most curiously shaped and given unto her as a marriage gift ... Four white doves, out of all those that stood sentinel to the chamber of their lady, stepped very briskly in front and bowed their rainbow-coloured necks to the yoke of precious gems, and when Venus was entered in, bore up the chariot with great diligence. After her chariot there followed a number of sparrows chirping about, making sign of joy, and all other kind of birds sang very sweetly with honeyed notes.
>
> (Apuleius 1977: 257–9)[20]

While this image thus connects the fairies of "La Biche au Bois" with a powerful divinity, this representation is one of a goddess who is not in her benevolent mode. This intertext suggests the potential for harm even in fairies traveling to do good. Thus, while the sixteenth-century fairy tales stay closer to the imagery of witchcraft treatises, d'Aulnoy complicates this association by augmenting the choices and the descriptions of these means of transport, thus bringing the potential for divinity into the realm of the diabolical, and complicating what might seem like a dualistic iconography of good and evil, with animals as signs of election or damnation. This is further complicated by the unstable nature of supernatural powers in her intertexts, and by her own representations of human-animal interactions and confusions, as we shall see.

WITCHES, FAIRIES, AND CHILDBIRTH

As Tucker points out, the "Fairy-Midwife-Witch" triad is present throughout d'Aulnoy's tales, as well as those of other authors (2003: 63–70). This association is the result of the representation of midwives as potentially diabolical in a number of witchcraft treatises, but particularly in the *Malleus maleficarum*, first published in 1487 and widely circulated for well over a century after that, which popularized this association. Witches are particularly seen as threatening birth, and midwives' access to the birthing room suggests the potential for diabolical intervention through them.[21] This is the result of the promulgation of the belief in diabolical witchcraft, that is, witchcraft undertaken with the aim of promoting the reign of Satan, and undermining the work of God; children dedicated to Satan or killed at birth would be lost to the kingdom of heaven. This fear of childbirth is reflected in the figure of the wicked fairy, who generally curses the royal child at birth, which we can see in Perrault's "Sleeping Beauty in the Woods" ("La Belle au bois dormant") and several of d'Aulnoy's tales, including her adaptation of Straparola's story of the Pig King.[22] As this first tale of the second night in Straparola's collection makes clear, fairies can use magic to benefit or trouble royal succession, as multiple fairies offer blessings and curses. In advance of the conception of this royal child, the first two bestow good looks and good character on the new baby, but the third condemns him to live as a pig until he has married three times (Straparola [1550–3] 2015: 92). Louveau stays close to the original in his version of this story, which inserts some characteristics of the diabolical midwife into the narrative of a royal birth.

The dedication of a newborn to the devil could be seen as one of the subtexts of the internal tale in d'Aulnoy's "La Chatte Blanche" ("The White Cat"). In this tale, the pregnant queen craves fairy-fruit, and promises her daughter, about to be born, to the fairies in exchange for that fruit (d'Aulnoy [1698] 2008b: 218–20); this plot is reminiscent of the story of Petrosinella in Basile's *Tale of Tales* (2.1), as the mother, craving parsley, promises her unborn daughter to the Ogress who has the herb. In Basile's tale, the Ogress shuts the girl into a tower, but she escapes by means of magic acorns that turn into wild animals. After inflicting extreme violence on the kingdom when they are refused the newborn girl, d'Aulnoy's fairies take her and shut her into a tower until she is old enough to marry. At that point, they offer her to a diabolical fairy king, Migonnet, whose monstrous form reflects his nature (d'Aulnoy [1698] 2008b: 235–6). When she refuses and tries to escape with the man she loves, he is killed, the princess is transformed into a white cat, and all of her father's subjects become cats as well. She can only be saved from this enchantment by a man who looks just like her deceased beloved.

The youngest son of a king, sent out to find treasures to win his father's throne, comes upon her palace and finds himself drawn to her, as she is lovely, learned, and kind. Her behavior marks her as human, but her appearance is almost entirely feline, even though she wears versions of human clothing. The prince repeatedly invokes this duality, as he wishes for it to be resolved: "Either you should become a girl, or you should make me a cat" (d'Aulnoy [1698] 2008b: 205).[23] Nonetheless, he senses something diabolical about her situation, and repeatedly compares the activities in this palace to a witches' sabbath. When he first enters and is greeted by hands without bodies that dress him and prepare him to greet the mistress of the house, he sees murals depicting stories of cats all around him, including those of sorcerers turning themselves into cats: "One saw all around the story of famous cats, Rodilardus hung by his feet at the council of rats, Puss in Boots, the Marquis of Carabas, the Cat who writes, the Cat who became a woman, sorcerers who became cats, the sabbath and its ceremonies" (199–200).[24] A few pages later, when the White Cat is surrounded by other courtly cats, some in flying chariots, all dressed magnificently and behaving like humans, he thinks that this is all just a bit diabolical: "it seemed to him that so much cattiness held a bit of the sabbath and the sorcerer" (205).[25] These direct references to the witches' sabbath suggest that the cat princess might in fact have been taken from her parents to serve the devil. And in fact, the charming prince has to cut off her head and tail for her to be restored to her human form, in a reminder of the human sacrifice that was said to result when witches offered the babies, stolen from their mothers, to Satan (217).

REPRESENTATIONS OF WITCHES AND FAIRIES: SHAPE-SHIFTING

Shape-shifting is a frequent characteristic of fairies in medieval tales. As noted above, Morgan le Fay was known for her capacity to change her form, and several of Marie de France's characters can change from one form to another. Shape-shifting is also a frequent characteristic of witches, as depicted in a woodcut from Ulrich Molitor's early treatise on witchcraft, *De lamiis et phitonicis muliebris* (Concerning Female Sorcerers and Soothsayers, 1489), in which the witches have transformed into a dog, a rooster or hen, and an ass (Figure 5.3). The belief in shape-shifting witches was fairly widespread in the sixteenth century, and was expressed not only in witchcraft treatises but also by authors such as Paré, who states in 1573: "Demons suddenly assume whatever form pleases them; and often one can see them transformed into animals, such as snakes, toads, owls, dunghill-cocks, crows, he-goats, asses, dogs, cats, wolves, bulls, and others" ([1575] 1982: 87).[26] In his work *On the Inconstancy of Witches*, published in 1612, Pierre de Lancre devotes a great deal of space to shape-shifting. This practice is frequently linked to travel to the witches' sabbath, as in Molitor's image.

FIGURE 5.3: "Witches Flying," from Ulrich Molitor, *De lamiis et phitonicis muliebris* (1489). Courtesy of the Division of Rare and Manuscript Collections, Cornell University Library. Public domain.

De Lancre devotes the fourth book of his treatise to these transformations and their historical and literary antecedents. He quotes Virgil's description of Circe changing Ulysses's companions into swine (*Eclogues* 8.7) and St. Augustine's statement that Diomedes's companions were transformed into birds as well as his claim that he knew a man who had been transformed into a pack-horse, and back into a man (*De Civitate Dei* 18.18). He also discusses Apuleius's claim to have been metamorphosed into an ass (Lancre [1612] 2006: 253–7). These evocative images lead, surprisingly, to a denunciation of the belief that humans and other animals can be transformed into animals of other species: "Thus the transformations of the magicians and witches that one reads about are not real and essential, but only illusions, done with diabolical magic and conjuring" (258). In this, he states, he differs from Jean Bodin: "Bodin, however, was of a different opinion, and believed that the transformation could occur in all types of bodies and that the demons could change the bodies of people into animals, and transform them into asses, dogs, and cats. But this is not true for the soul or for the mind, for it cannot be changed" (259). Thus, de Lancre enters into a heated theological debate over the nature of diabolical transformation. On the one hand, the transformation of humans into animals could serve as proof of diabolical activity. On the other, the idea that demons might have this ability attributes significant powers to them, including the possibility of the power of creation, which is supposed to be God's alone.

This debate over the reality as opposed to the illusory nature of diabolical transformation is a significant element in the collection of tales, *Della metamorfosi, cioè, Trasformazione del virtuoso* (*The Metamorphosis, or, Transformation of a Virtuous Man*), published by Evangelista Marcellino, under the pseudonym Lorenzo Selva, in 1582, and translated into French by Jean Baudoin in 1611, one year before de Lancre's work was published.[27] Using "a first-person Apuleian frame narrative" describing his "protagonist's metamorphosis, adventures as a snake, and eventual return to human form" to organize his work (Magnanini 2011: 332), Marcellino weaves Milesian-style tales of magic and theological debates together in a moralizing allegory. Particularly important for the connection between theologically oriented representations of witchcraft and fairy-tale transformations is the prominent discussion of "Church doctrine regarding both miraculous and demonic transformations" (332).

The poor protagonist, Acrisio, in love with the beautiful and inspiring Cloris but, urged by his mother to seek out his father's family, finds himself involved in this debate as he travels to discover his true origins and his fortune in the city of Naples. He encounters a group of religious men on pilgrimage, and, disgusted by his faithless and frog-like companions, joins the pious group (Marcellino 1611: 36). They discuss the myth of Circe, with its transformations of men into animals, and Moses's transformation of sticks into snakes, an act that was imitated by Pharaoh's magicians. But one of their number concludes that, for

Moses's works "There is no doubt ... that all of these transmutations were made by the divine all-powerful" (42–3).[28] Pharaoh's magicians could only recreate these transformations in appearance, but not in reality (45). If people appear to some as cats or horses, they only seem this way to certain people or to themselves because their minds are corrupted by the Devil (47). He mentions werewolves as an example of this type of transformation.

The plot of Selva's frame narrative is complicated when Acrisio himself is turned into a snake by a hideous cow-witch ("une grande vache hideuse," Marcellino 1611: 71–2), described as a savage monster ("un monstre sauvage," 73), after a series of strange ceremonial gestures (74–6). He will be freed only when he drinks the blood of his beloved. At this point, he remembers the discussion of transformations only in appearance, but finds he has become a snake, or at least appears as one to himself and others. When he is found by a group of young women, one of them thinks that he must be a fairy, and saves his life, keeping him as a pet. Over the course of his serpentine life, he hears a series of stories, some of which focus on tricks or jokes, but many of which return to the question of diabolical transformation.

Reminders of the limitations of the Devil's powers appear frequently in the discussions that follow these stories. The fifth story features a spurned lover, Gelanzio, who withdraws to a solitary place in an attempt to forget his bad fortune. A witches' daughter falls in love with him, and dies of heartbreak when he refuses her. Her mother then transforms the young man into an ass (Marcellino 1611: 177–87). He returns to his human form eventually, but dies miserably. As Acrisio ponders this possibility as his own potential fate, one of the group, Prudentio, warns the others that "You know well enough, my children, that these are only fables, and that the Devil would not know how to transmute a body" (183).[29] In the sixth story, two travelers encounter a fairy disguised as a snake, who rewards the one who helped her and punishes the one who harmed her (188–92). While a number of people in the group entertain the idea that Acrisio the serpent might be this fairy, a priest argues once more that "a form can be transmuted into another only in appearance" (192).[30] In the seventh story, a witch changes a man into an ass, but he is transformed back into his human form when he kneels before the Holy Sacrament. After this tale, the little group of storytellers debates the reality of diabolical transformation, one arguing that fairies can transform into serpents, but another countering that the Devil can only change things in appearance (193–6). In the eighth story, a man beats women who have taken the form of cats (197–8), but here, the storyteller takes the time to assert that "It is pure folly to believe that Fairies can be serpents, and this is only old wives' tales" (198).[31] The insistent refrain in the transformation tales is that the Devil can only achieve the appearance of bodily change, not the reality; only God has the power to change physical reality.

Ironically, Acrisio seems to be truly transformed back into a human shortly after this series of tales is told, when he returns home to his beloved Cloris and drinks her blood (334–5). Cloris does point out that this transformation might well have been divine punishment for Acrisio's own sins (340–1); after all, only God can transmute bodies from one form to another.

This debate provides subsequent generations of authors with a rich store of imagery and examples of human turned into beasts. It also transmits complex questions concerning this transformation and the nature of the relationship between humans and other animals, as well as the nature of the relationship between body and soul. In de Lancre's view, humans transformed into animals would not have animal souls, and thus there would be a disjunction between bodily appearance and the mind. Fairy tales from this period mine this wealth of imagery and concepts, and offer many variations on the theme of animals with human characteristics, such as Straparola's Pig King (night 2, tale 1), the snake sister Samaritana in the tale of Biancabella (3.3), the green bird in the tale of Serena (4.3), and the enchanted cat, a female precursor of Puss in Boots, of the tale of Costantino Fortunato (11.1). Basile's tales of the prince disguised as a serpent (day 2, tale 5) and the princess transformed into a she-bear to protect her from the incestuous advances of her father (2.6) add to this rich repertoire. These transformations are echoed by Selva's protagonist, Acrisio, who when transformed into a serpent retains his human sentience and rationality, as do most of the characters listed above, but is unable to speak. These serve as the sources for later versions or even new tales, such as Perrault's "Le Chat Botté" and d'Aulnoy's "La Chatte Blanche," "La Grenouille Bienfaisante," "L'Oiseau Bleu," and "Serpentin Vert," or humans with animal characteristics, such as "Le Prince Marcassin" (or "The Pig King").[32] Quite a few of these tales touch on complex moral questions raised by the intersecting identities of humans and animals, including the question of moral responsibility, that is, the question of whether humans in animal form still can be held responsible for their actions. This is a central issue in the tale of the Pig King, one that links it to the werewolf narratives of witchcraft lore. This link between fairy tales and witchcraft narratives is even more clear in Straparola's tale of Fortunio (3.4), who settles a dispute between an ant, an eagle, and a wolf, and gains the power to transform himself into any one of these animals as a reward. He uses this gift to transform himself into an eagle and court the princess Doralice, as well as to become a wolf and devour his stepmother and his brother. The lack of moral conclusion drawn concerning this behavior might suggest that humans should not be held responsible for what they do in their animal form, but this question is presented in a more unsettling manner in Straparola's tale of the Pig King, who kills his first two wives, the first in self-defense and the second without real justification.

The attribute of shape-shifting, first seen in *The Pleasant Nights* in the first tale of the seventh night, that of Ortodosio and Isabella, reappears in the fourth tale of the eighth night, when Dionigi learns magic from Lattanzio, the master tailor he has been apprenticed to, by spying on him. He turns himself into a horse, so his father can sell him and make some money. Unfortunately, Lattanzio buys him and mistreats him. Dionigi escapes, and transforms himself into a fish and then a ring, to avoid capture. The ring is given to a princess, and he reappears as human in her bedchamber, frightening and then intriguing her. Lattanzio, who disguises himself as a physician, cures the king and demands the ring in payment. Dionigi then becomes a pomegranate and as his former master transforms into a rooster to eat the pomegranate seeds, Dionigi transforms himself instantly into a fox, and eats the rooster. Once again, magic itself is not presented as good or evil, but only as potentially so, in that it can be used to help or harm others. And once again, Larivey modifies this representation of magic by calling Lattanzio's sorcery "his diabolical art" ("son art diabolique") and "his cabala" ("sa caballe," Straparola [1550–3] 1882: 3:177). These gestures seem quite minimal, however, and may indicate a desire to capitalize on the popularity of lurid tales of witches in France.

Straparola's tale seems to push the concept of shape-shifting to an extreme. This is partly a reflection of Dionigi's particular gift for witchcraft, and part for comic effect, particularly at the end, when seemingly ridiculous transformations come in rapid succession. The fact that Dionigi in essence cannibalizes his former master, at that point in the form of a rooster, is covered over by the clever transformations by which he outsmarts Lattanzio, who was seeking to destroy him. The shifting of forms thus allows the reader to accept violence that would not seem as amusing if inflicted on a human.

The strategy of using shape-shifting as a cover for violence is also evident in Straparola's tale of Fortunio (3.4), discussed above. After seeking his fortune and marrying a princess, he returns home to his stepmother and stepbrother, transforms himself into a wolf, and devours both of them (Straparola [1550–3] 2015: 156–63). The lack of moral condemnation of this act in the narrative suggests both that these relatives deserved this fate because of their harshness, and that wolf-Fortunio is merely ceding to his nature, which is quite different from that of human-Fortunio.

Yet the rapid shifting back and forth from one form to another in this tale and in some of d'Aulnoy's tales, raises a number of questions. First, are these transformations real, as Bodin would have us believe, or are they illusions, as de Lancre argues? The Green Serpent ("Serpentin Vert") moves back and forth between human and animal form, as does the Boar King ("Le Prince Marcassin"). They both speak, feel sorrow and remorse, and wish to overcome their animal natures, thus demonstrating a human consciousness that is covered over by animal skin. Are they then responsible for their actions, or excused due to the animal form which seems to affect them?

WEREWOLVES

In their unstable nature, Straparola's and d'Aulnoy's humans in the guise of animals evoke the most widely discussed shape-shifter of the early modern period, the werewolf. Werewolves are already present in ancient lore, discussed by Pliny in his *Natural History* ([77 AD] 2006: 58–61), and in medieval tales, of which Marie de France's *Bisclavret* ([12th c.] 2018: 144–61) might be the best known. In both of these sources, a human sheds his human clothing (werewolves are always male in ancient and medieval tales) and takes on a wolf's pelt. This transforms him from a civilized man into a violent monster.

De Lancre devotes the largest part of the fourth book of his treatise to lycanthropy, discussing both theories and cases of transformations of men into wolves ([1612] 2006: 267–341). This discussion raises once more the question of whether such transformations are real or merely illusions, and what the status of a werewolf actually might be. Is a werewolf merely a delusional human, a human soul with an animal's appearance, or a human completely transformed into an animal, with animal instincts and consciousness? The case of Jean Greinier, which is the particular focus of this book, raises some troubling questions about distinctions between the human and the animal.

Jean Greinier or Grainier is a young man of thirteen who likes to attack people and animals, and who is accused of killing and eating young children. He claims that "when he wants to run, he wears of wolf's skin, the one the Lord of the Forest brings to him when he wants him to run" (Lancre [1612] 2006: 272). This ambiguity of who generates the transformation is repeated throughout the narrative, raising the question of agency, and of who is responsible for the young man's violent behavior. Since this behavior includes cannibalism of young children, it is linked to the most disturbing aspects of witchcraft. But de Lancre introduces skepticism into his account, suggesting that some think these tales of lycanthropy are merely "fairy tales," and then focuses on this skepticism throughout the rest of his analysis of this case (276–85). This is reminiscent of the discussions in Selva's *Metamorphosis*, which deny the power of transmutation of bodies to the devil or to humans, and link such notions to fairy tales, as well as to the fallibility of human perception. Humans are portrayed as susceptible to being misled by demons and witches, and to all too easily believing the stuff of fairy tales. As skepticism arises concerning witchcraft, it seems that fairy tales, while using material similar to that in witchcraft narratives, must distance themselves from any facile belief in the magic that drives their narratives. One could imagine that the humorous aspects of the tales of Straparola and Basile, and the excesses of magical elements in their work as well as in that of later authors, signal the fictional nature of these stories. Arguably, the use of magic in fairy tales could constitute a subtle questioning of the belief in magic expressed by many witchcraft treatises, as Straparola and Basile, as well as their heirs, emphasize the absurd and fantastical nature of this magic.

De Lancre enumerates four types of transformation, making it clear that only the first two, divine and natural transformations, effect real change, and that the other two, imagination and witchcraft, only create the illusion of change. These last two causes are linked throughout his discussion of lycanthropy, which he ascribes to melancholy or an imbalance of humors as much as to demonic influences. He thus leaves in suspension whether this condition is an illness or a case of demonic possession, whether it originates in the mind of the individual affected or is imposed by external influences. At any rate, he suggests that even if a physical transformation were possible, and he denies demons the power to achieve such a transformation, it would not transform the soul. This conclusion points to a belief that the condition originates in the mind of the individual, something de Lancre might not have been able to openly declare at the time, without risking accusations of heresy ([1612] 2006: 296–341).

Werewolves resurface in fairy tales, most notably in Straparola's tale of Fortunio and Perrault's tale of "Little Red Riding Hood" ("Le Petit Chaperon Rouge"), which offers the most evident adaptation of the werewolf narrative. The wolf takes on human characteristics, particularly speech, but is driven by a voracious hunger for human flesh. But similar narratives appear in other tales that explore the complex divide between human and non-human animals, such as Straparola's story of the Pig King (2.1), in which the King Galeotto and his queen are condemned to have a son "completely covered with pig skin" (Straparola [1550–3] 2015: 92). This fate is imposed by a fairy, thus deflecting the diabolical influence into a less threatening figure. While he has some human characteristics, such as speaking a human language and responding to human forms of affection, he also, like a pig, rolls in mud and grunts. He kills his first two wives, on the pretext that they were planning to kill him; it is not clear whether this violence marks him as human or animal (93–4). He reveals to this third wife that he can take off the pig skin at night, but that he is condemned for the time being to wear it during the day. She shows great love and forbearance toward him, and eventually gives birth to a child who is fully human, to the relief of the king and queen. It is at this point that she reveals their son's secret to them, they destroy the pig skin, and the prince is restored to full humanity. This tale follows the narrative arc of de Lancre's werewolf story in a number of ways. Jean can put on or take off the wolf skin, but it is not entirely clear whether this is voluntary or imposed; once the skin is taken away from him, his animal existence seems to come to an end.

D'Aulnoy's version of the Pig King story, "Le Prince Marcassin," further complicates this narrative. The piglet prince has a voracious appetite, but his six nurses turn it toward fine wines, and he becomes a connoisseur. He is dressed and trained to appear as human as possible: "He had a harness with which he was supported, to train him to walk on his back legs; they put shoes with silk stockings attached to the knee, to make his leg look longer; they whipped him when he wanted to grunt; in sum, they eliminated, as much as possible, boar-like manners" (d'Aulnoy [1698] 2008b: 458).[33] This elaborate training is reminiscent of Jean Greinier's training by the monks in de Lancre's account of his lycanthropy.

Marcassin is dressed to cover his body as much as possible: "he wore long jackets that covered his legs, an English bonnet of black velvet to hide his head, his ears, and a part of his muzzle" (d'Aulnoy [1698] 2008b: 460).[34] He eats food preferred by boars, but plays musical instruments and rides horseback quite capably. One of his favorite pastimes is hunting, where he behaves as much like a boar as a human (460). While Straparola's Pig King murders his first two brides, Marcassin's behavior is more ambivalent. He impulsively wishes to marry his three wives, and seems somewhat threatening in his attempts to woo them. But Ismène, his first wife, kills herself in despair, and he kills the second only in self-defense, when she tries to kill him (470, 480).

In both Straparola's and d'Aulnoy's versions of these tales, however, the pig prince's use of his teeth to defend himself hints at the lycanthropic origins of his narrative. But d'Aulnoy pushes this possibility a bit further away by reducing Marcassin's responsibility for the deaths of his wives, and even further when it is revealed at the end of the tale that in fact no one has died, as the wives and other characters were always protected by a good fairy (d'Aulnoy [1698] 2008b: 493). In this way, the violence of the lycanthropic narrative is pushed further into the background, contained by the kind interventions of a superior force.

Marcassin, however, remains an equivocal character to the very end. He wears human clothes to cover over his animal hide and features; these traits in turn cover over a human body that is revealed only at night, and only to a faithful wife (d'Aulnoy [1698] 2008b: 488–92). His education enhances the human veneer that clothing affords him, but cannot completely efface an impulsive, animalistic nature that comes into conflict with the demands of court society. In short, in his very existence and in every action he takes, the prince constantly crosses over the imagined boundaries between animal and human, calling these very boundaries into question.[35]

HYBRID NATURES

The horror expressed at the birth of a pig prince in both Straparola's and d'Aulnoy's tales reflects narratives of monstrous hybrid births that circulated in the *histoires prodigieuses* as well as in medical treatises. In both versions of the fairy tale, the king contemplates killing his son by drowning him in the ocean; in d'Aulnoy's version, the father even calls his son a monster. There is a question in both tales of how this birth might reflect on the mother (d'Aulnoy [1698] 2008b: 457–8; Straparola [1550–3] 2015: 93). These details are not consonant with lycanthropy narratives, where the individual makes a pact with a demon and changes identity at will, but with the *histoires prodigieuses* stories of animal-human hybrids. In the 1561 edition of his collection of these tales, Boaistuau includes an account of a child born half-human, half-dog. The story is heavily moralized, with a long discussion of forbidden forms of sexuality (fornication, adultery, and bestiality, with a brief mention of sodomy), concluding with the tale of this child: "a child who was conceived and engendered by a woman and a dog" (Boaistuau 2010: 718).[36] This child is sent to the pope to be "expiated and purged" ("expié et purge," 719), mostly likely by being destroyed (Figures 5.4, 5.5, and 5.6). As a compiler, Boaistuau likely took this story from Conrad Lycosthenes (Conrad Wolffhart, 1518–61), an Alsatian humanist who authored an influential treatise on prodigies and marvels, although it had circulated widely in other forms by the time his collection was published.

Paré repeats this story in his chapter on "An Example of the Mixture or Mingling of the Seed," but adds in other tales, particularly those about pig-human hybrids (Paré [1575] 1982: 67–73; 1971: 62–8).[37] The assumption in these stories is that a human has been practicing bestiality, a belief that informs the reaction to the pig prince's birth in both Straparola's and d'Aulnoy's tales. What is extraordinary is the acceptance of this situation, albeit with some resistance and disgust, on the part of fairy-tale characters. This acceptance seems predicated on the assurance, coming from a supernatural source, that the situation will be rectified in the end, and the humanity of the child restored. In this detail, both stories thus join the unstable animality of the shape-shifter tales with the fixed hybridity of the *histoires prodigieuses* narratives. The dog-boy must be destroyed because he will always be dog-boy; his fate is to be trapped in an identity that is resolutely interspecies. The Pig King can move between human and animal, thus has a trans-species identity and has the potential to become (more) fully human, just as werewolves could be "cured" of their disease and become fully human again.

Similarly, the narrative of prohibited (monstrous?) human sexual conduct is suppressed in the fairy tales. Whereas bestiality mars the human in the *histoires prodigieuses*, no such behavior occurs in Straparola's or d'Aulnoy's narrations. As in the werewolf tales, only supernatural intervention can join human and animal natures; also, as in werewolf tales, because demonic or magical forces are involved, this union is not natural, in some sense not real, but rather a magical illusion or effect of the imagination.

THE WILD MAN

The figure of the wild man, related to the werewolf in its representations as an abject version of humanity and a prominent feature of the *histoires prodigieuses*, offers yet another version, with its own complications, of the monstrous human-animal interface. The medieval wild man comes in two main types: the man who has always lived in the forest, sharing characteristics

FIGURE 5.4: "Half-Human, Half-Dog Hybrid," from Pierre Boaistuau, *Histoires Prodigieuses* (1560). Courtesy of the Division of Rare and Manuscript Collections, Cornell University Library. Public domain.

FIGURE 5.5: "Animal-Human Hybrids," from Fortunio Liceti, *De Monstris* (1665). Courtesy of the Division of Rare and Manuscript Collections, Cornell University Library. Public domain.

FIGURE 5.6: "Half-Human, Half-Dog Conjoined Twins," from Fortunio Liceti, *De Monstris* (1665). Courtesy of the Division of Rare and Manuscript Collections, Cornell University Library. Public domain.

with the animals that make him both less civilized and more in tune with nature. The Lord of the Beasts (Seigneur des Bêtes) from Chrétien de Troyes's romance, *Yvain ou le Chevalier au Lion, (The Knight of the Lion (Yvain))*, is an excellent example of this type, controlling nature and capable of reasoning with King Arthur's knights ([12th c.] 1991: 298–300). Another type of wild man is the human punished for his arrogance by a loss of social status, the use of reason, and other attributes of civilization. Yvain himself, in his period of madness, is the perfect example of this type, irrational and deprived of the accoutrements of civilization (330–1). But he also evokes yet another type of wild man, the one driven mad by lost or unrequited love. Yvain goes mad when his wife Laudine repudiates him for not returning to defend the kingdom; he flees King Arthur's court after a lady sent by Laudine chastises him and takes back the ring his wife gave him to protect him from adversaries. This part of the tale might well have been a source for the origin tale of one of Straparola's wild men, as we shall see.

Boaistuau presents us with the second type, the fallen wild man, in the fourth chapter of his *Histoires prodigieuses*, presenting this condition as divine punishment of human arrogance, and offering, among other examples, the fate of Nebuchadnezzar:

> who (as it is written in fifth Daniel) felt the fury of divine justice so sharply that he was expelled and exiled from his kingdom for seven years, wandering through the deserts with the brute beasts, living on their food, and remained naked in such a state, beaten by heat, by cold, by hail and by dew, until his fur grew like that of an eagle and his nails like those of birds.
> (Boaistuau [1561] 2010: 383)[38]

Such punishment of royal arrogance could well be seen as a subtext for the dehumanization of royal offspring in so many fairy tales. Not only "Le Prince Marcassin," but also "La Biche au Bois" and "La Chatte Blanche" are good examples of this dynamic.

But the Wild Man can also be a truth-teller and a figure of a purer form of humanity, one not corrupted by court culture. In Boaistuau's thirty-eighth story, he recounts a story ostensibly told by Marcus Aurelius of a monstrous man ("un homme Monstrueux"), who travels to the Roman Senate to tell them of Roman cruelty toward their German provinces. This man is odd in appearance and strangely dressed:

> This peasant had a small face, thick lips, deep-set eyes, burnt skin, hair that stood on end, an uncovered head, shoes of porcupine leather, a cloak of goat skin, a belt of seaweed, a long and thick beard, eyebrows that covered his eyes, a stomach and neck covered with fur like a Bear's, and a staff in his hand; and since he was in this guise when we saw him enter the Senate,

we thought that it was some animal, having the face of a man; but after we heard the gravity of his speech, and the majesty of his phrasing, we judged that he was some deity, because if his look was monstrous, what he said was marvelous.

(Boaistuau [1561] 2010: 722–3)[39]

Both the man's own physical appearance, complete with bear-like body hair, and his choice of clothing underscore the intersection and interdependency of the human and the animal. At first, this appearance seems like a good reason to dismiss the man, but his command of language allows him to reenter the domain of the human, even that of the most powerful humans. In turn, he reduces the Romans to animality, accusing them of imposing "juges ... bestiaux" ("bestial judges") and of exercising inhuman cruelty on the people they have conquered (Boaistuau [1561] 2010: 723–8). His speech dominates this story, the third from the end of the collection. In this position, the story serves as a pendant to that of tyrants reduced to that state of wild men, the fourth story of the collection, and the resemblances between the two serve as a warning to the Romans: misuse of power can lead to a reversal of fortunes, where the wild man and the powerful human trade places. This process has already begun, as the German peasant speaks eloquent truth to power and reveals the corruption eating away at the Roman Empire.

Straparola's tales also feature some wild men. One, a satyr in the first tale of the fourth day, tells truth to power, revealing the queen's infidelity to the king, as well as the true gender of Costanza/Costanzo (Straparola [1550–3] 2015: 180). Another wild man narrative is the story of Guerrino (5.1), a prince who frees a wild man captured by his father. This wild man embodies both the fallen wild man type and the natural wild man, seen as morally superior to "civilized" humans. He is depicted as having been "a very handsome young man" who, unable to make the woman he loves reciprocate his feelings, chooses to live "among the woodland beasts, inhabiting the shadowy forests and thick woods, eating grass and drinking water like an animal." This alters his appearance: "Therefore, the poor wretch had grown thick fur, a very thick hide, and a thick, very long full beard, and on account of his feeding on the grasses, his beard, fur, and hair had become so green that he was a monstrous thing to behold" (216). Upon being freed by Guerrino in defiance of the king's orders, the wild man wanders until he is cured from his wildness by a fairy, and becomes a "handsome and charming young man" once more (217). Out of gratitude for his freedom, this young man saves Guerrino from almost certain death, and helps him to pass several tests required for marrying a king's daughter (217–23). He himself marries the king's other daughter, thus completing his rise in status because of his generous actions. As in the story of the Pig King, human and animal physical and moral qualities are mixed together in this figure until the end of the narration, when the wild man apotheoses into a superior human. Straparola's tale of three poor but gifted brothers (7.5) offers an even more positive description of the wild man that the youngest son becomes after he has lived in the woods for ten years: "He learned the language of the birds by dwelling constantly in such places for such a long time. He listened to them with great pleasure and he understood them and they recognized him as if he were the god Pan among the Fauns" (Straparola [1550–3] 2015: 306). Of course, the God Pan is generally portrayed as a human-animal hybrid, half-man and half-goat, thus enhancing the image of a man who has become something more than a mere mortal.

One could consider Marcassin to be a sort of wild man, but this figure is complicated in d'Aulnoy's tale. His speech, like his clothing, becomes a form of cover for his bestiality. He woos his wives eloquently, but cannot overcome his impulsive and violent nature as he demands wife after wife to replace the ones who have died in the wedding-chamber. It is, in fact, only when he accepts his animal nature, regretting the deaths he has caused and exiling himself from the court to prevent any further injury to others, that he begins to become human. He is accepted by Marthésie, his third wife, as he is, at first denying her observation that he takes on human form at night, and once she takes the pig skin, finding that he cannot put it back on because it has shrunk (d'Aulnoy [1698] 2008b: 480–92). Only when he loses his princely arrogance and embraces the wild man within himself is he finally allowed to become a human. Thus, in this case it seems that the ability to rise to a superior status depends upon recognizing one's own flawed and inferior nature.

CONCLUSION: FROM THE DIABOLICAL TO THE MAGICAL

Pierre Boaistuau's *Histoires prodigieuses* are largely focused on the deeply sinful and flawed nature of humanity and its weakness before diabolical influences. The gateway to this collection is a tale about the attributes and powers of Satan, including his demands for human sacrifice (Boaistuau [1561] 2010: 357–64). This sets the tone for the rest of the collection, which is dominated by a negative theological focus on the sins of mankind and divine retribution: the second chapter is about the destruction of Jerusalem, the third about earthly potentates punished for their sins by horrible deaths. The fourth chapter is about the humiliation of kings, and ends with the description of Nebuchadnezzar as a wild man. This focus informs Boaistuau's take on animal-human hybrids, as we have seen, as well as on other supernatural or marvelous events.

Fairy tales take these more menacing supernatural tales, whether found in witchcraft treatises or in the collections of *histoires prodigieuses*, and turn them to milder ends. But some more sinister aspects of the witchcraft tales linger, in both direct references to diabolical practices and in images that evoke the stereotypical appearance and behavior of witches. These aspects arise whenever royal individuals infringe on a strict but indeterminate code of conduct vis-à-vis the fairies, or whenever the fairies simply feel like being cruel; in this paradoxically arbitrary but extraordinarily codified and ceremony-oriented governance, the fairies resemble pagan gods such as Venus, as well as absolute monarchs. The supernatural elements in these tales, which hint at their diabolical origins, also hint at the violent subtext of benevolence exercised by those in power.

The afterlife of witchcraft in fairy tales evokes even larger questions that subtend this critique of power: what it means to be human and whether we can distinguish ourselves from other species; and whether we can possibly sort out the difference between what is true and what is merely illusory. These two aspects of human frailty are closely linked, as our capacity to understand the world around us and our place in it is closely linked to our belief in our own superiority. If this capacity is called into question by our repeated misperceptions or misunderstandings of the world and of ourselves, then we are no better, and possibly much worse, than the animals we claim as our subjects. As the witchcraft trials establish, these questions can be a matter of life and death. As fairy tales suggest, they are also the fruitful ground for endless speculation about our own, perhaps not entirely human, nature.

CHAPTER SIX

Space

Geographies of the Fairy Tale in Giambattista Basile's The Tale of Tales

DAVIDE PAPOTTI

Perhaps one of the best-known geographical manifestations of the fairy-tale tradition is the German Fairy Tales Route (*Deutsche Märchenstraße*). Established in 1975 to promote tourism, the 600 kilometer (370 mile) itinerary from Hanau to Bremen leads tourists to various attractions and sites that are related either to the lives of the Brothers Grimm or to their fairy tales. Dieter Richter recounts an amusing anecdote on how tales became associated with geographical points along the route. Richter writes:

> The points of contact between the fairy-tale world were understood in a very free and loose way: "We had a meeting in Bad Orb. Bad Orb is a very picturesque small town that had requested to be included on the German Fairy Tale Route. It is located quite close to the Fairy Tale Route and so it is obvious that they wanted a place at the table to attract tourists. My opposition was founded on the fact that in order to protect our credibility we had to find some reference [to a fairy tale] and not accept just any small town because it was picturesque ... I noted that the city had a good number of fountains, and even some particular monuments were fountains. And so I proposed, 'Why don't you take "The Frog Prince"?' 'The Frog Prince' was still free. And so Bad Orb was allowed to become a part of The Fairy Tale Route, and the Frog found his hometown."
>
> (1994: 83–4)[1]

If it is true that in some cases like this one physical geographies for fantastic fairy tales have been constructed long after the tales were written, it is equally true that the often fantastic geographies that we find in fairy tales were formed from elements drawn from the geographical realities of their authors or tellers.

The world of fairy tales, at first glance, might appear to be a world of mere fantasy. As Richter notes, "The fairy tale is the realm of the fantastic, for both anthropologists and in common perception" (1994: 79).[2] And yet, at the same time, all the magic and enchantment that we find in fairy tales, as well as the places where these tales unfold, are based on and begin in the real world. Fairy-tale plots are filled with geographical elements: forests trigger innumerable adventures; cities bustle with all kinds of activities that make possible different encounters and plot twists; rivers are either obstacles or instruments of travel; seas become an open world ready for adventurous navigators. Fairy tales possess a "geography" too. By "geography" we do not mean only a spatial location. The very existence of a geographical imagery in the tales, which can be related to specific spatial archetypes (such as deserts, forests, seas, rivers, mountains, etc.) is the mirror of the territorial experiences of a specific culture in a given historical time.

During the age of the marvelous, Italy was at the center of the Mediterranean trade routes along which people, goods, and ideas traveled. The various political powers occupying the Italian Peninsula had contacts and exchanges with all the other countries and regions in the area, from Morocco to the Holy Land, from Spain to Egypt, with the Republic of Venice as a key protagonist in the area. The age of the marvelous also witnessed the move of the European commercial "center of gravity" from the Mediterranean to the Atlantic context, with an increased flow of images, objects, and peoples coming from the new "marvelous possessions," and revealing the "wonder of the New World" for Europeans, to use the words from the title of Stephen Greenblatt's book (1991). In the two centuries of the age of the marvelous, 1450–1650, the geographical conscience of the Western world radically changed, by enlarging—in both a literal and a metaphorical sense—its perspectives. The age of the marvelous is therefore also an age of a geographical marvelous.

With the vivacity and curiosity of its characters toward the unknown, the world of fairy tales mirrors the unpredictable and the unexpected aspects of these epochal changes. Even though conveying spatial information is surely not the primary goal of this narrative genre, I believe it is possible to use the perspectives offered by an approach informed by cultural geography to provide a reading of the spatial components of fairy tales. Using geography in reading fairy tales does not only mean trying to address the issue of the location of a plot, or trying to answer the question, "Where does it take place?" Cultural geography can also shed light on the vocabulary that a society uses to indicate spaces, territories, and landscapes; it can help understand the practices of mobility through space; and it can identify the main landscape features that become visible in the narrative threads of fairy tales and the symbolic values associated with them.

In this chapter, I will explore the relationship between fairy tales and geographical space in Giambattista Basile's *Lo cunto de li cunti* (*The Tale of Tales*, 1634–6), a collection of tales written in Neapolitan dialect. As was typical of courtiers in this period, Basile traveled to and lived in different parts of Italy and the Mediterranean. Although he spent most of his adult life in courts in and around his native city of Naples, he was stationed on Crete as a young man while a soldier for the Venetian Republic and spent a year at the Gonzaga court in Mantua in northern Italy (Canepa [2007] 2016: xxxv–xl). Thus, like many of his protagonists, he traveled far from home and back again to seek his fortune. In the first part of the chapter, I will explain the concept of a "pre-landscape" society, a society that does not think of space in the way modern society does, with a consolidated aesthetic perspective with which the social gaze is imbued. The very word "landscape" does not exist in the literary sources of this period. To indicate "geographical space" a series of other varied terms are employed. As a second step, I will synthetically illustrate the ways in which landscape is represented in other literary genres in the period, paying particular attention to the topos of the *locus amoenus* prevalent in Italian collections of novellas, or realistic tales. Third, I will focus on the evocative power of geographical names, which represent one of the most evident geographical elements in the fairy-tale narrations. Then I will concentrate on one of the literary tropes most concerned with geography: travels and the specific features traveling protagonists encounter, mountains and woods. To conclude, I will mention the role of multisensorial perception in shaping the depiction of spaces. The perception of territories is surely a visual practice, but in Basile's tales it is intertwined with the information coming from other senses, such as touch, smell, and hearing.

A SOCIETY WITHOUT LANDSCAPE?

The chronological period (1450–1650) considered in this volume coincides with the very beginning of what we could call the "landscape era." Landscape is a quite recent acquisition in the array of the cultural concepts developed by Western societies to understand and appreciate the physical world. As many scholars have pointed out,[3] the concept of "landscape" was developed in the late Renaissance, together with the consolidation of a specific painting genre focused on depicting open-air settings. The very word "landscape" was born in this period, in the Dutch-German cultural context, to fix, in the linguistic imagery, the activity of contemplating a territorial scene, which was at the time becoming a new mode of viewing the world. In broader terms, therefore, the cultural contexts in which Italian fairy tales were born during the early modern period is a pre-landscape scenario, where the physical entity of the territory prevails, in its materiality, over the contemplating attitude and the aesthetic appreciation. In his book *Il paesaggio* (The Landscape, 2009), Michael Jakob sketches the evolution of the term during early modernity in Europe, assembling a chronology that spans from Francesco Petrarch's ascent of Mont Ventoux in the fourteenth century to the scientific focus of the eighteenth century and the Romantic attitude of the nineteenth century, to arrive to the contemporary "hypertrophy" of the landscape (2009: 8).

During the two centuries that span the age of the marvelous, we find crucial moments in the development of the concept of landscape. Even though landscape does not have a specific and univocal date of birth, it is possible to identify some potential periodization. Jakob distinguishes three stages of what he calls "proto-history of the landscape": the Greek, the Roman, and the end of the Middle Ages. "The third decisive era, that extends up until our own day, appeared for the first time at the end of the Middle Ages. It coincides, beginning in the fourteenth century, with the emergences of urban culture, of mercantile society, with the appropriation of space" (Jakob 2009: 53).[4] It is precisely during the years of the age of the marvelous that one can situate the beginnings of the development of "landscape consciousness," a period of transition that in painting, literature, and the social conscience sees the progressive advent of the idea of "landscape."

The birth and growth of the concept, its gradual diffusion across Europe, can be mapped in both temporal and spatial dimensions, as one of the most prominent French scholars of landscape studies within the disciplinary field of geography, Yves Luginbühl, states. He explains:

> It seems that the term [landscape] is first born in Dutch–*landskap*–in 1462, then in Germany (1480), in Portugal, France and in Italy. A little later in England and even later in Spain. Why this difference among the different countries? Why are there two hundred years between the word's appearance in Dutch and in Spanish? Because the word "landscape" is a form of representation of nature that distances itself from religion: landscape is a lay subject.
>
> (Luginbühl 2009: 66)[5]

Thus, when Basile penned his fairy tales in the first half of the seventeenth century, in a city under Spanish rule, the concept of "landscape" had not yet been fully developed.

Instead, the point of view adopted in the description of spatial information in early modern texts is mostly a horizontal one. The early modern period is far from the cult of the panoramic view that characterizes the modern era, as well as from the scientific zenithal (and apparently omniscient) gaze of our contemporary imagery imbued with images taken from the satellites. It is rather a world seen from below, or at street level, from a few recognized and recognizable points of view: "a land observed from the workshop, from the square, from the barnyard, from the tavern, from the refectory of the monastery" (Camporesi 1992: 13).[6] Literature follows painting, as far as landscape sensibility is concerned. As Piero Camporesi notes, commenting on Francesco Guicciardini's (1483–1540) travel diaries: "The landscape-land (*paesaggio-paese*), observed in a horizontal dimension deprived of spatial depth, of pictorial references, of emotional echoes, appears in pages written by Francesco Guicciardini and sixteenth-century travelers still quite far from the interpretive and reflective visualization of painting" (9).[7]

Consequently, in fairy tales written between 1450 and 1650, the territory that the characters traverse is seen in its spatial "thickness," so to speak. It is perceived and conceived in its concrete quantitative dimensions, in its productive capacities, in its physical characteristics, such as temperature, steepness, and distance. What today would be categorized as a "landscape," in the sixteenth century was:

> a space to comprehend through its essential geographic-economic characteristics, in its anthropic contours, almost with the professional sensibility of the merchant and the surveyor, rather than to contemplate distractedly for the soul's ineffable pleasure, to use for unnecessary *rêveries*, to consume in subdued, suggestive circuits, let alone to integrate in ways relevant to the sphere of the soul and religious meditation.
>
> (Camporesi 1992: 10)[8]

As we will see, the geographical content of early modern Italian fairy tales usually consists of simplified elements from a limited alphabet of spatial elements. The territorial background of the plot is usually sketched in brief and generic terms, if not totally absent. Compared to the attention given to the protagonists and the events of the narration, the geographical setting of the plot normally lies in the background of the tale. It remains, so to speak, slightly out of focus. If the general rule is that the geographical scenario does not warrant much of the narrator's attention, there are, of course, some notable exceptions, usually when a specific element of the landscape acquires some function in the development of the narrative thread. This can be described as "narrative utilitarianism," according to which landscape comes on stage only if it is functional to the development of the plot. There is no room for an aesthetic appreciation of the landscape, since the vision of the territory, at this chronological stage, is firmly rooted in a practical, "opportunistic" approach.

In sum, during the age of the marvelous we are still at the dawn of the modern conception of landscape. Even though we sometimes find an episode of increased attention to landscape elements and features in tales from this period, they are rarely at the center of the narrators' focus and attention. It will be necessary to wait for a progressive consolidation of the concept, both in the arts and in the wider public perception, to be able to pronounce the term "landscape" in the modern meaning of the word. Perhaps, then, as we begin to analyze fairy-tale depictions of geographical spaces, we can apply to literature what Piero Camporesi observed about the visual arts and treatises between the fifteenth and sixteenth centuries:

> In art and in the treatises of the fifteenth and beginning of the sixteenth centuries, the concept of landscape has not yet arrived at its full autonomy, nor does it possess the status of a rule in painting. Landscape may reach the high summit of very refined decoration, express itself with complex symbolic buildings without attaining complete liberation from the happy enslavement to detail.
>
> (Camporesi 1992: 35)[9]

THE LITERARY TRADITION OF REPRESENTING LANDSCAPE

Although there was not yet a well-developed concept of landscape in the age of the marvelous, there was a rich literary tradition and a repertoire of topoi for representing literary space and geography in texts. A few stereotypical categories of space had been consolidated and had become a part of a literary practice that concentrated more on drawing from earlier textual sources than on the firsthand observation of the surrounding environment: "learned literature traditionally focused on working with archetypes, with stylized effects, with centuries-old *topoi*, and was not always capable of reading and interpreting new realities that had not been considered in the literary laws" (Camporesi 1992: 30).[10]

One of the most typical geographical stereotypes found in medieval and early modern literature is the *locus amoenus*, an idyllic spot of land where the grace of nature offers a peaceful and harmonic refuge to humans, and where vegetation, water, temperature, and light find a perfect balance. The early modern *locus amoenus* finds its origins in classical Greek and Latin literature, and functions, as Mauro Varotto suggests, as a sort of idealized space detached from any real landscape. Varotto writes that in these early modern texts: "Landscape [is] understood as a synonym of *locus amoenus,* or an ideal, rhetorical background, devoid of any relationship to reality, created by the symbolic stylization of elements that have little to do with a real and concrete dimension" (2013: 2).[11] The stereotypical nature of this stylistic trope makes its passage through different historical epochs possible. One can find, for instance, the occurrence of *loci amoeni* in Boccaccio's fourteenth-century masterpiece, *Decameron*. Boccaccio's narrators, the ten young Florentines who flee their plague-ravaged city for the countryside, repeatedly find themselves in just such delightful environs as they move from villa to villa avoiding contact with the outside world. Seated in a lush green meadow (day 1), gathered in a blooming walled garden (day 3), or swimming in the pristine waters of the pond in Valley of the Ladies (day 6), Boccaccio's narrators tell tales to pass their time as they await the moment for a safe return to the stricken city of Florence. The authors of fairy tales, like almost all authors in this period who embraced prose narrative, found inspiration in Boccaccio's text, including in his representation of these idealized landscapes.

For example, the *topos* occurs in the *Proem* of *Le piacevoli notti* (*The Pleasant Nights*) by Giovan Francesco Straparola, one of the first Italian collections of tales to include a substantial number of fairy tales. In the overarching narrative, after a few days staying with friends in Venice, the political refugees, Ottaviano Maria Sforza and his daughter Lucrezia, who have fled their home in Lodi, begin to search for a home of their own and find one on the island of Murano. They rent an empty palace that possesses all the traditional features of the *locus amoenus* and is based on Boccaccio's description in the introduction to the third day of the *Decameron* (Pirovano 2000: 1:7n1):

> A marvelously beautiful palace that was empty at the time caught his eye and he went inside. Having seen the delightful location, the spacious courtyard, the splendid loggia, the agreeable garden full of joyful flowers, many different kinds of fruit, and an abundance of green plants, he praised it highly. When he climbed the marble steps, he saw the magnificent hall, the comfortable rooms, and a balcony above the water that commanded a view of the whole area.
>
> (Straparola [1550–3] 2015: 46–7)

The harmonic balance between the human construction, with its architectonic features (the courtyard, the loggia) and a domesticated nature is a key characteristic of the *locus amoenus*, or, to use Straparola's own words in his Proem, of the "vago e piacevol sito" (pretty and pleasant site).

While Basile's frame tale lacks such an extended homage to Boccaccio's *loci amoeni*, we do find examples of this topos in his tales. One example of this portrait of an uncontaminated corner of the world can be found in the tale "The Serpent." In this tale, the princess Grannoia is forced to marry a serpent. On their wedding night, after they have consummated the marriage, her father spies through the keyhole, expecting to see his daughter murdered by the beast. When he sees that the serpent has become a handsome prince, he opens the doors. Surprised by the intrusion, the serpent prince becomes a dove, but injures himself as he attempts to fly out a closed window. With her husband gravely injured and now in his human form, Grannoia sets out to find a cure to revive him. A fox, who will reveal the cure, joins Grannoia on her journey and it is at this point in the tale that we find the *locus amoenus*:

> And so they walked along until they came to a wood—where the trees, playing like children, made little houses to hide the shadows in—and since by then they were tired of walking and wanted to rest, they retired under the cover of the leafy branches, where a fountain played at carnival with the cool grass, pouring down pitchers full of water.
> (Basile [1634–6][2007] 2016: 155)

Besides through these literary commonplaces, how is landscape depicted in Basile's fairy tales?

THE EVOCATIVE POWER OF GEOGRAPHICAL NAMES

An important part of the geographical knowledge contained in fairy tales derives from geographical names. The mention of a specific toponym operates as a sort of synecdoche, which imparts geographical information to the reader. Since many fairy tales lack detailed descriptions of the landscape, of the place where the events occur, the geographical name stands out not only as a reference for the localization of a place but also as a concise source of information about the territory.

And yet, the information these fairy-tale toponyms might provide is necessarily limited and seeking "a real place" that corresponds to the literary geography is futile, no matter how much we desire to do so. In this regard, the amusing book *Die Wahreit über Hänsel und Gretel* (*The Truth about Hänsel and Gretel*, 2007), written by Hans Traxler, teaches us a good lesson. The "truth" in the title indicates the explanation contained in Traxler's book of the geographical setting that inspired the creation of the universally known fairy tale of the two siblings and the witch. Traxler explains in detail, with abundance of footnotes and learned references, why the setting of the narration should be identified precisely in a forest that lies near the highway that connects Franfurt and Würzburg (in Germany), not far from the rest area of Rohrbrunn. Although the book was meant by the author to be a parody of academic publications, it nonetheless was widely received as a serious academic study, in spite of the numerous statements made by the author denying the plausibility of his hypothesis. The exact localization of a narrative plot, in fact, is nearly inevitably associated to a sense of "truth"; and therefore it becomes particularly appealing.[12]

In the construction of this "likelihood," of this allure of "verisimilitude," geographical names play a crucial role. Their use can make reference to specific locations, and therefore add a layer of "realism" to the narration. In her book *From Court to Forest: Giambattista Basile's "Lo cunto de li cunti" and the*

Birth of the Literary Fair Tale (1999), Nancy Canepa observes in regard to the analysis of the points of departure of the protagonists of the tales: "The points of departure for Basile's heroes are of three types: real geographical locations, imaginary kingdoms, and unnamed places that, however, frequently have a realistic air to them. As noted previously, with the progression of the days the references to real towns decrease" (1999: 207). In Canepa's first type, we find many places that must have been familiar to Basile's first reading public, early modern Neapolitans and courtiers like himself, and can still be located on maps of the region. These include Marigliano ("The Tale of the Ogre"), Miano ("The Myrtle"), Aprano ("Vardiello"), Benevento ("The Flea"), and Cascano ("The Merchant"). And yet in the vast majority of cases (we will see one exception below), the naming of the locale does not result in a more profound understanding of the details and particularities of the space through which the protagonists move.

Still other toponyms refer to famous cities and places around the known world, which are employed to evoke exotic distances and proverbial abundance, such as Rome (Introduction, "Petrosinella"), Costantinople ("Rosella"), and Palermo ("Pretty as a Picture"). In these cases, the reference to specific geographical sites in distant, foreign countries often involves specific characteristics for which the place was universally known at the time. This is the case, for instance, for the reference to the fairy in "The Myrtle" as possessing "graces that rival those of Seville" to indicate that she is an astonishingly beautiful woman.

A second category of geographic names in Basile's tales, as Canepa notes, are those that convey an immediate perceivable meaning of a generic element. In this category, we can catalog Long Pergola ("The Enchanted Doe"), Strong Fortress ("The Old Woman Who Was Skinned"), Long Acres ("The Serpent"), Dry Rock ("The She-Bear"), Green Earth and Dry Rock ("Penta with the Chopped-Off Hands"), and Lovely Land, Long Furrow ("Pride Punished"). These geographical names do not indicate a specific location in the reader's mental map of the world. They are generic and are aimed at reinforcing the alluring undefined quality of a suspended narration. Their concrete and practical meaning makes reference to the tangible aspects of working life, to physical details of the territory, to the quality of the terrains, to chromatic qualities of the visual aspect of a land. Thus, even the invented geographical names reflect a kind of gaze that hardly elevates itself over a horizontal, concrete, practical observation of the surrounding world. At the same time, these toponyms often participate in the bawdy, and often scatological humor that runs throughout *The Tale of Tales*. As Canepa states:

> Almost every kingdom either playfully figures male or female genitalia or makes veiled reference to some aspect of the sexuality of the royal character who rules it. This is initiated in the frame tale itself, in which we encounter

two royal figures, the king of Valle Pelosa [Hairy Valley] (Zoza's father) and the prince of Campo Retunno [Round Field] (Tadeo). A sampling of other names includes the king of Automonte [High Mountain] of I.5, Rocca Forte [Strong Fortress] of I.10, Vallone Gruosso [Wide Ravine] of II.5, Surco Lungo [Long Furrow] of IV.10, and Grotta Nera [Black Grotto] of IV.1; the baron of Servascura [Dark Forest] of II.8; the king of Fuosso Stretto and the queen of Vigna Larga [Narrow Ditch and Wide Vineyard] of III.3; and the prince of Torrelunga [Tall Tower] of IV.9.

(1999: 208)

These metaphors, which are able to connect, in a sort of short circuit, the sphere of sex and the realm of landscape, are openly used in a passage in one tale where the person is compared to (and transformed into) a landscape:

> In "La serva d'aglie" [The Garlic Patch (III.6)], which is found at the exact center of *Lo cunto*, a hermeneutic key to the reading of all place-names is given. When attempting to discover the sex of an oddly feminine male servant, Narduccio's mother proclaims: "Volimmo fare qualche prova pe scoprire s'è femmena o mascolo, s'è campagna rasa o arvostata" [Let's try a few things to discover whether it's a woman or a man, whether it's flat country or woodland].
>
> (Canepa 1999: 208–9)

Related to these sexualized toponyms is a particularly interesting form of geographical "evocation," in which several places are mentioned as origins of specific products or qualities, and function as part of a laudatory description of beautiful women. We see this, for example, in the description of the beautiful fairy who hides inside a tree in a tale from the first day of *The Tale of Tales*, "The Myrtle." In this tale, the literary portrait of the different parts of the female body depends on geographical references to create a sort of vertiginous atlas of the wonders of the world mapped onto the lovely fairy's body. One morning the prince, who is visited nightly by a fairy who hides each day in a myrtle tree, desires to see his nighttime companion, like Apuleius's Psyche. After a servant has lit the candles, the prince spies the beautiful fairy and launches into a torrent of praise that concludes with

> From what India came the gold to forge this hair? From which Ethiopia the ivory to construct this forehead? From which Maremma the carbuncles to set in these eyes? From which Tyre the crimson to stain this face? From which Orient the pearls to string these teeth? And from which mountains the snow to sprinkle on this breast—snow that betrays nature, that nourishes flowers and warms hearts?
>
> (Basile [1634–6][2007] 2016: 25)

The use of the rhetorical figure of the enumeration, or list, comprised of geographical references, provides a sort of " atlas" of geographical imagery that delineates and maps the fairy's exotic beauty, for she is "a marvel of all woman" (Basile [1634–6][2007] 2016: 24). Thus, real toponyms are placed in the service of metaphor rather than conveying geographical information.

THE VOYAGE: TRAVELING THROUGH GEOGRAPHICAL SPACE

Travel, especially in the form of sea voyages and long overland journeys, is an essential motif of the fairy-tale genre. In his analysis of the morphology of Russian folktales, Vladimir Propp notes among the first few functions that he describes a departure from home: function I involves a family member leaving home, and function IX involves the hero being dispatched or allowed to depart ([1928] 1996: 26, 36). D. L. Ashliman argues that the structure of many, though not all, fairy tales follows the same basic outline: separation-initiation-return (2004: 41). Episodes of travel provide a chance for landscapes and spatial elements to move to the forefront of the narration. Naturally, when the protagonists are on the move, spatial descriptions become more common. Fairy-tale itineraries are often extremely simplified, and only a few main stereotypical elements are mentioned. We can see this in the "Introduction" to *The Tale of Tales,* when Princess Zoza, cursed by an old woman to marry Prince Tadeo, who lay in an enchanted slumber, must travel to the kingdom of Round Field to wake him. Zoza "per tanti paesi girò, tanti boschi e fiumane passò" ("traveled through so many countries and crossed so many woods and rivers," Basile [1634–6][2007] 2016: 7).

In regard to fairy-tale travels, Canepa observes:

> Fairy tale itineraries, both in *Lo Cunto* and in other collections, typically begin in the town or kingdom of the protagonist—the "civilized" world. Throughout the course of the tale the hero usually then departs from the home base: meets up with magical helpers and/or antagonists in a "foreign" place, which may be another town, unfamiliar but civilized, or a forest or other natural site; undergoes some sort of formative or initiatory experience; and then either returns back home or proceeds to a new home, usually a kingdom won or acquired through marriage.
>
> (1999: 207)

Canepa correctly indicates a central duality in the construction of fairy-tale space: the opposition between what is perceived as "home," a safe and familiar space, and the challenging experience of being "elsewhere," in an unknown territory. This is an archetypical distinction in the history of human presence on our planet, and makes its way directly into the narrative threads of the fairy tales.

As Basile's characters make their way through the world, one of the key questions asked to strangers encountered along the road is which *paese*, village or hometown, they come from. Together with the character's name and the profession, the place of provenance is a major component of identity in the tales. This is the case in "The Ignoramus," where characters' names are intimately linked to their geographic origins. In this tale, the idiot Moscione's father sends him to do business in the Orient, and so he travels on what was the typical trade route from Venice to Cairo. Along the way, he meets and befriends a number of extraordinarily gifted companions, each named for his talent: speedy Flash, Hare's-Ear, Sharpshooter, Blowboy, and Strongback. Together, they help him win a princess's hand in marriage and acquire great wealth. As he encounters each young man, Moscione issues a similar set of rapid-fire questions. To Hare's-Ear, who will help Moscione by overhearing important information, he asks: "What's your name, pal? What town are you from and what trade do you practice?" (Basile [1634–6][2007] 2016: 264). To Sharpshooter: "What name do you go by, my respectable man? Where were you born and what can you do in this world?" (265). To Blowboy: "What name do you go by by the life of my father? What land are you from? What is your profession?" (265). Each responds to the question of their place of birth with a different *paese* the name of which reflects a fundamental aspect of the character's identity: Hare's-Ear is from Curious Valley, Sharpshooter from Surefire Castle, and Blowboy from Windy Land. It is when Basile's fairy-tale characters venture far from home, though, that they encounter the topographic formations that form the physical geography of *The Tale of Tales*.

MOUNTAINS: SYMBOLIC ELEMENTS AND "ICONEMS"

Traces of the landscapes in the narrative thread of the fairy tales are rare, and mostly "casuali ed accessorie" ("random and ancillary," Camporesi 1992: 11). In most cases, the references to geographical elements are limited to a few specific territorial elements, those that we could call, using a term introduced by Eugenio Turri, "iconems." Turri defines an "iconem" as:

> a basic unit of perception, like a sign within an organic totality of signs, like synecdoche, where a part stands for the whole, or that expresses it with a primary hierarchical function, both as an element that better than others embodies the *genius loci* of a territory and inasmuch is a semantically highly charged visual referent to the cultural bond a society establishes with its own territory.
>
> (1998: 19)[13]

Iconems are "shortcuts" to the creation of a spatial setting, since they are able to evoke a spatial environment, whose details are unconsciously added by the reader. The essential geographical elements mentioned in the fairy tales, from this perspective, work as "bridges" toward the geographical imagery shared by the readers.

The elements encountered during travels and voyages depicted in Basile's tales, and in many European fairy tales of this period, normally belong to a quite simplified vocabulary of basic geographical features: mountains, rivers, lakes, seas, forests. This simple vocabulary was also shared by some cartographers of the period, as is evident in Figure 6.1, a map of the Kingdom of Naples created by Abraham Ortelius of Antwerp (1527–98).

On this map, which represents, at a small scale, the entire southern part of the Italian Peninsula, one can see that the geographical references to natural formations are reduced to few simple elements: the characteristic "molehills" to indicate mountains, and a few lines representing rivers. Mountains, as also evident in the cartography of this period, are a major element of the perception of the territory for many reasons. They are visible at a distance, they incarnate physical, evident borders among regions, and they are major obstacles during travels, as we find in Basile's tales. When the fool Antuono is thrown out of his mother's house, he journeys to "the foothills of a mountain so high that it butted horns with the clouds" (Basile [1634–6][2007] 2016: 14). It is there that

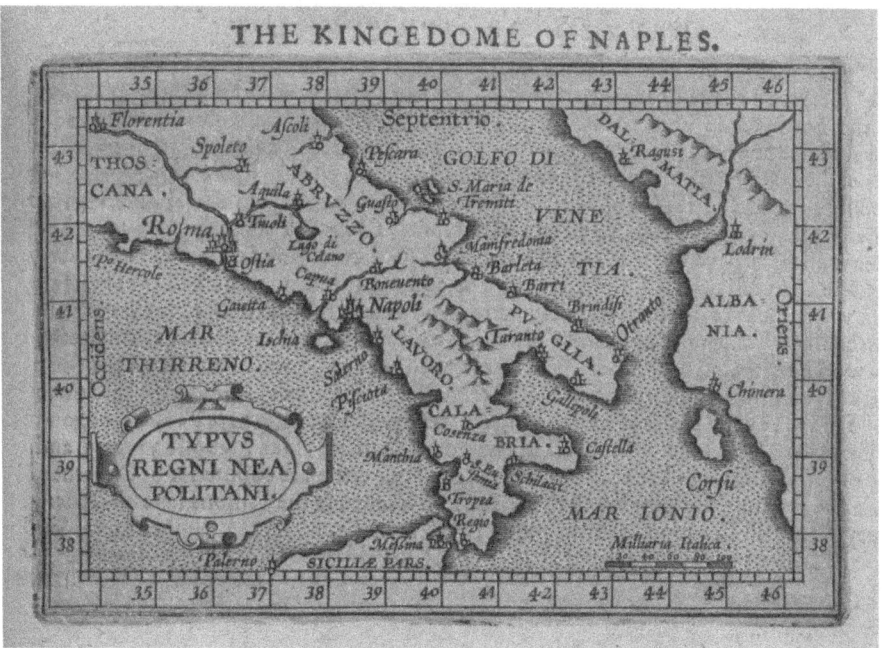

FIGURE 6.1: Abraham Ortelius's map of "The Kingedome of Naples" ("Typus Regni Neapolitani," 1603). From The New York Public Library, https://digitalcollections.nypl.org/items/510d47e4-6661-a3d9-e040-e00a18064a99. Public domain.

he meets the ogre who will teach him to be less of a fool and where he will learn the lessons that will allow him to return to his family in the village.

Mountains are also elements that, both from a physical and from a perceptive point of view, stand out from the rest of the territory, and are also often marked linguistically through Basile's baroque metaphors. On the opposite side of the same spatial axis, one can find caves, which five centuries later a creative speleologist, Andrea Gobetti (1986), defined as "the sky's roots." Caves are the spatial incarnation of the fight between light and darkness. And, as such, caves participate in Basile's exploration of this axis. As Canepa reminds us, Italo Calvino's (1982) reading of *Lo cunto de li cunti* was based on the relevance of the opposition between day and night, between light and darkness:

> Italo Calvino has brilliantly argued that the most striking metaphorical axis of Basile's work, the alternating representations of day and night, sunrise and sunset, is in itself a metaphor for a much more pervasive series of symbolic bipolarities: light and dark, beauty and ugliness, sexual acts and defecation, life and death, the royal and the common, Baroque culture and popular tradition; that there is an enduring dialectic between these opposites that contributes to the dynamism of *Lo cunto*; and that although the world of Basile's tales may appear at first reading to be a "morning world," the fusion of popular and Baroque produces its most memorable and dramatic effects when Basile puts his hand to describing the "darker" (and often more realistic) aspects of his fairy-tale cosmos.
>
> (1999: 209)

Basile explores the dark end of this axis in his tale "Goat-Face," in which a peasant digs at the foot of "a mountain—a spy for the other mountains which kept its head above the clouds to see what was going on in the air" (Basile [1634–6][2007] 2016: 75). There, he uncovers a correspondingly deep cave where the lizard, who wishes to raise his daughter in the lap of luxury, dwells. This space, which will turn out to hold marvelous wealth, is described as "a grotto so deep and dark that the Sun was afraid to enter" (75). For Canepa, this binary opposition is central in the description of the landscape characteristics as well:

> We find a similar dialectic between concrete extratextual realities and playful metaphorical constructions in the representation of the canonical topographies of the fairy tale, particularly in those of, or which emulate to some degree, the "natural" order. Forests, mountains, rivers, grottoes, gardens, and fountains all invariably trigger periphrastic outpourings that have been considered by Croce and others as the most effective examples of Basile's effervescent interpretation of Baroque poetics.
>
> (1999: 209)

As Canepa suggests, the physical elements of the territory that emerge in the narration are able to "trigger" further elements, by referring to the common geographical imageries that were potentially shared by the authors and his readers.

INTO THE (DARK) WOODS

Although most often literary scholars note the play of light and darkness in Basile's many metaphors describing the sunrise and sunset, his fairy-tale forests, the woods where so many plots unfold, are also a space where darkness prevails, but sometimes rays of illumination can penetrate the dense foliage. Woods are a central element of the geographical imagery of fairy tales, as Canepa notes: "The fairy-tale forest is generally a dark, wild, impenetrable place, and, at least in the popular folktale, is evoked in just as few, and absolute, words" (1999: 210). In many of Basile's tales, woods are the kingdom of obscurity that often inspire the sort of metaphorical play found in the descriptions of mountains. Basile's dragon slayer Cienzo travels through two woods before slaying a hydra. In the first, "a wood that kept its mule attended to outside its borders by the Sun, while it took its pleasure with the silence and the shadows" (Basile [1634–6][2007] 2016: 67), he finds a treasure in an abandoned tower. In the second, Cienzo "arrived in a solitary and deserted wood that was dark enough to make your mouth screw up" where he saves a fairy from an assault by a band of ruffians (68). Although woods can be a place of adventure, they are just as often spaces of isolation and imprisonment, especially for women. Basile's Rapunzel, named Petrosinella, is taken by an ogress to a tower in "a wood—where the Sun's horses never entered, so as not to pay rent on those pastures of shadow" (130). In "The Flea," Porziella is married to an ogre against her will and he drags her to his home in the forest, "into a wood—where the trees formed a palace for the meadow so that it wouldn't be discovered by the sun" (12). In some tales, the density of the vegetation, the size and intricacy of the trees create a world where light cannot enter, and yet paradoxically, in other tales the wood becomes the space where secrets are revealed, where characters are illuminated. In "The Serpent," Grannoia and a fox "came to a wood—where the trees, playing like children, made little houses to hide the shadows in" (155). Yet it is here that Grannoia learns from the fox that she can only bring her husband back to life with the blood of birds who know about the curse he is under. She is enlightened and sees the truth behind her husband's mysterious identity, not in her father's castle but in this dark forest.

As they climb mountains, cross streams, and venture into dark forests, how do Basile's characters experience the physical geography that surrounds them?

A MULTISENSORIAL PERCEPTION OF SPACE

Among the senses we use to perceive the world, we often grant an inordinate importance to the sense of sight. During the modern era, the myth of the panoramic view, as a tool that is able to satisfy aesthetic desire and at the same time the quest for a synthetic perspective over space, consolidated itself as a foundation of Western culture. Besides being a "pre-landscape" era, in the age of the marvelous we are also witnessing a literary world that is more attentive to other senses besides sight: touch, hearing, smell, even taste. These senses, which are an important integration to the visual component of perception, are able to amplify the sensorial connection with the surrounding environment: "It is an Italy of things and people, of trades and anti-trades, of business dealings and shady dealings, a long procession of objects, artifacts, products, activities, brought into focus and identified not by the noble sense of sight, but by the more popular sense of touch, taste, and smell" (Camporesi 1992: 13).[14]

The physical enjoyment of the surrounding environment is not predominantly based on a visual, detached experience but rather on a sensorial immersion in the "thickness" of the environmental component. This is clearly the case in Basile's story of Peruonto, the fool who uses wishes he obtained by helping the sons of fairy to impregnate a princess who has mocked him. The princess, much cleverer than he is, will use these same wishes to eventually turn the fool into a handsome man after she bears his child and is forced to marry him. When Peruonto finds the three young boys who will grant his wishes, he experiences the field where they lie in the sun, and the river that runs through it, via the sense of hearing. "And when he was in the middle of the meadow, where a river ran—chattering and murmuring about the scant discretion of the stones that blocked his way—he came across three boys who had made a little mattress out of grass and pillow out of flint" (Basile [1634–6][2007] 2016: 33).

This sort of physical immersion in the surrounding world was a characteristic feature of medieval existence, which was a continuously alternating between opposite poles, feast and famine, extreme wealth and abject poverty. As Yi-Fu Tuan elegantly summarizes:

> Europeans in the Middle Ages were insecure to a degree that is hard for us to envisage. Eighteenth- and nineteenth-century medievalism (from which we are not wholly free) tended to romanticize this bygone age, detecting in it a colorfulness, an intensity, and a range of feeling, a scope for the imagination, that shrank and faded with the appearance of modern life. But if the people of the Middle Ages feasted on color and beauty in their churches and festivities, they saw also utter drabness and filth in their daily surroundings; if they knew ecstasy and caught glimpses of heaven, they were far more familiar with toil and danger, acedia and fear.
>
> (1979: 71)

In a world characterized by extreme fluctuations in terms of access to food, in which a widely diffused condition of starvation coexists with legendary episodes of luxurious abundance, geographical affection for places is intertwined with alimentary imagery, as in the vertiginous farewell pronounced by Cienzo in Basile's "The Merchant," in which the urban structure and toponymy overlaps with culinary details. After accidentally killing the son of the king during a game of throwing rocks, Cienzo's father advises him to leave the Kingdom of Naples before the king kills him. In one of the rare exceptions in *The Tale of Tales* where a city is described in realistic detail, the narrator intertwines actual landmarks Basile's readers would have known well, with culinary details that create a new fairy-tale land of plenty that is grounded in realistic detail. Cienzo sets off from his father's home,

> But as soon as he had gone through Porta Capuana, he looked back and began to say, "Here I go, my beautiful Naples, I'm leaving you! Who knows if I'll ever be able to see you again, bricks of sugar and walls of sweet pastry, where the stones are manna in your stomach, the rafters are sugarcane, the doors and windows puff pastry? Alas! Separating from you, lovely Pennino, is like walking behind a funeral pennant! Taking leave of you, Piazza Larga, my spirit is squeezed narrow! Removing myself from you, Piazza dell'Olmo, I feel my soul split in two! Parting from you, Lancieri, is like being pierced by a Catalan lance! Where shall I find another Porto, sweet port of all the world's riches? Tearing myself away from you, O Forcella, my spirit tears itself away from the wishbone of my soul! Where is there another Gelsi, where the silkworms weave never-ending cocoons of pleasure? Where another Pertuso, resort to all virtuous men? Where another Loggia, where plenty is lodged and pleasure is refined? Alas, My Lavinaro, I cannot remove myself from you without a stream of tears flowing from my eyes! I cannot leave you, O Mercato, without a load of grief as merchandise! Beautiful Chiaia, I cannot part company with you without a thousand wounds tormenting my heart! Farewell, carrots and chard; farewell, fritters and cakes; farewell, broccoli and pickled tuna; farewell, tripe and giblets; farewell, stews and casseroles! Farewell, flower of cities, glory of Italy, painted egg of Europe, mirror of the world! Farewell, Naples, *non plus ultra* where virtue has set her limits and grace her boundaries! I leave you to become a widower of your vegetable soups, driven out of this dear village, O my cabbage stalks, I must leave you behind!"
>
> (Basile [1634–6][2007] 2016: 65–6)

The *topos* of food abundance described by Cienzo connects with the myth of the so-called "paese di cuccagna" (the land of plenty), a world where all the scarcity that characterized the everyday life in the real world disappears, leaving room for a never-ending feast and a world devoid of labor. The land of plenty makes an appearance in Boccaccio's *Decameron* and is called Bengodi ([*c*. 1353] 1966: 501). Its enticing abundance is used to capture the attention of Calandrino, a painter who will be duped by his friends into believing he has found a heliotrope that renders him invisible. This land of plenty, also called Cuccagna in Italian and Cockaigne in English, was also the subject of many chapbooks in verse as well as illustrations, such as Figure 6.2.

Without reaching the fantastic abundance of one of the two extreme poles, even real life offered abrupt shifts in food accessibility: "Food shortages, famines, and periods of relative well-being followed one another with demoralizing regularity" (Tuan 1979: 66). This reality of extreme hunger is seen by Yi-Fu Tuan as a trigger for imaginary travels into a legendary world of abundance: "Poor health, bad food, and bad eating habits no doubt played tricks on the imagination, making it easier for a person to hallucinate, have nightmares, and see visions. Overeating among the rich and undernourishment among the poor surely militated against a balanced view of life" (74).

The degree of verisimilitude in literary descriptions of abundance and scarcity varies accordingly, following the different social contexts in which a given text is created. Canepa notes that not only do the references to real places decrease as we move from day 1 to day 5 in the *The Tale of Tales*, but she also interprets the accuracy of geographical elements in light of the social hierarchy:

> The sites of misery and hunger from which they [the heroes and heroines of the fairy tales] set off on their own adventures are all too real, whereas the kingdoms where the luckiest of them end up are delightful but utterly fabulous realms, compensatory constructions of a marvelous "world upside down" where the social and economic constrictions of everyday life are suspended.
>
> (1999: 208)[15]

In this compensatory mode attuned to all the senses, not simply sight, Basile's fantastic geographies reflect the often harsh dualities of early modern Italy, where great abundance and devastating lack coexisted. This duality, together with the other binary oppositions that we have tried to illustrate (light vs. darkness, countryside vs. city), help frame the construction of space in the fairy tales. The perspective through which the environments surrounding the characters are observed is different from the aesthetic concept of "landscape" that permeates our perception of territory today. The world of the fairy tales is instead permeated by a concrete, physical sensoriality, by an unmediated openness to wonder and surprise, by an everyday contact with concrete environmental forces (such as darkness) and by the intervention of magical forces.

FIGURE 6.2: *Il Paese di Cuchagnia*, a fanciful eighteenth-century print of the land of plenty with capons that rain down from the sky, a mountain of cheese, and a wine-spouting fountain. The Miriam and Ira D. Wallach Division of Art, Prints and Photographs: Print Collection. From The New York Public Library, https://digitalcollections.nypl.org/items/fe061310-e6d6-0132-511c-58d385a7bbd0. Public domain.

Even though the depiction of space in Basile's fairy tales does not usually occupy the forefront of the narration, there are several "windows" through which the reader can glimpse the spatial and geographical imagery that lies behind his creative literary process. In Basile's fairy-tale world, literary traditions, cartographic imagery, and real-life experiences merge in a fascinating kaleidoscope of overlapping elements that allow us to speak of a geographical dimension in his tales.

CHAPTER SEVEN

Socialization

Civilizing the Fairy Tale in Early Modern Italy

SUZANNE MAGNANINI

In his seminal study *The Civilizing Process: Sociogenetic and Psychogenetic Investigations*, Norbert Elias argues that in the medieval and early modern periods, Western cultures underwent a socio- and psychogenetic process during which individuals acquired those habits, customs, and attitudes related to dress, diet, and comportment that rendered them civilized in the eyes of others (Elias [1939] 2000). The printed how-to guides that proliferated during the age of the marvelous (1450–1650) facilitated this evolution with advice for every aspect of public and private life. Some of these texts, such as Baldassare Castiglione's *The Book of the Courtier* (1528) and Juan Luis Vives's *The Education of a Christian Woman* (1523), would become early modern bestsellers, translated and reprinted in cities across Europe, and circulated amongst a multitude of popular handbooks and manuals governing all sorts of social interactions, household management, sexual and gender norms, and the education of children (Bell 1999: 5–11; Kelso 1956). Alongside such secular works, the Counter-Reformation Catholic Church published spiritual guides and didactic texts aimed at organizing and disciplining the inner lives of both men and women and eradicating heretical beliefs and superstitions (Bell 1999: 5–6; Zarri 1996). As such, Europe was awash in nonfiction texts aimed at civilizing and socializing adults, as well as their children. As authors, editors, and readers fully embraced Horace's adage from the *Ars poetica* that required poetry to serve the dual functions of educating and delighting, literature, too, played a role in these civilizing processes. Today fairy tales are considered by many to be primarily children's literature with one of the most recognizable features of the genre a didactic one, "the moral of the story." We might be tempted, then, to think that the genre played a major role in the educating and socializing of children in this period 1450–1650. This, however, was simply not the case. During these two centuries, children's literature as we now know it did not yet exist and the fairy tale and its tellers were considered poor conveyers of moral truths although the genre could be reframed and adapted to such ends, particularly by Catholic reformers.

Historians of children's literature who approach their field from the point of view of production, studying texts created exclusively or primarily for children, often argue that before children's literature could exist, Western societies needed to develop a concept of children as a group distinct from adults that required, for example, separate spaces in the household and a wardrobe that sartorially marked them as children. Citing the groundbreaking work by French historian Philippe Ariès, *Centuries of Childhood: A Social History of Family Life* ([1960] 1962), they often locate the origins of European and American children's literature at the end of the seventeenth century—and thus after the age of the marvelous—when economic, political, and social changes brought about this new perception of the child and need for a distinct literature that would nurture the child's social, emotional, and moral development (Conrad 2007: 182; Shavit [1983] 1999: 317). As historians of the family have refined Ariès's central thesis,[1] a number of scholars have examined children's literature by adopting an approach that privileges reception over production, and so deems "children's literature" texts that were read routinely by children, such as Aesop's fables, regardless of whether the texts were originally created for children (Lerer 2008; Reynolds 2011). Still others have uncovered medieval and early modern texts created specifically for children (Kline 2003). This reception-oriented approach is useful for the period under study here, a moment when literature written exclusively for children was scarce, and children read mostly works written for adults or for a heterogeneous audience comprised of children, youth, and adults. What, then, was the relationship between children and the fairy tale in the two centuries before children's literature as we know it today existed? Were fairy tales thought to delight and to instruct in equal measure? How did efforts at civilizing or socializing Italian society shape the literary fairy tale in the early modern period?

Through an analysis of literary representations of storytelling and the curricula of early modern Italian schools, I will demonstrate that in this period the fairy tale was a genre that was more closely associated with the amusement of children than with their education. In part, the association of fairy tales with narrators of questionable intellectual ability, crazy old crones and simple young girls, discouraged readers and pedagogues from accepting fairy tales as highly effective didactic texts. Thus, the fairy tale itself had to be socialized before it could begin to serve as a tool for encouraging readers to accept and embody social and moral norms. In the second part of the chapter, I will show how Counter-Reformation attitudes and censorial practices contributed to this process by shaping fairy tales into concisely written stories with explicitly stated morals that promoted the moral and social vision of the Catholic Church.

CHILDREN AND THE FAIRY TALE

The title of Giambattista Basile's *The Tale of Tales, Or Entertainment for the Little Ones* (1634–6), a seminal collection of the European fairy-tale tradition written in Neapolitan dialect, illustrates well the paradoxical relationship between children and the literary fairy tale during the age of the marvelous. The subtitle of Basile's collection of fifty tales directly suggests a ludic connection between children and fairy tales, a link highlighted at various points in the frame narrative in which the forty-nine tales of the collection are embedded, although children do not figure as the audience for the tales in the narrative frame tale. Instead, in Basile's overarching tale the obscene exchange between an old woman and the devilish court page who has smashed her oil jar provokes first melancholy Princess Zoza's laughter and then the old woman's curse upon her. Zoza is cursed to marry only Prince Tadeo, who lies as if dead in the far-off kingdom of Round Field and will rise up once again only if she fills a jar with her tears. When Zoza passes out from exhaustion after almost filling the jar, a clever black slave named Lucia completes the task, becomes Tadeo's wife, and is soon pregnant. Zoza instills the desire to hear stories in the slave by way of an enchanted doll she received from a fairy during her journey to Round Field. Lucia then threatens to abort by punching her belly should her desires not be satisfied. Prince Tadeo summons all the garrulous hags from his kingdom to his court, picks the ten best storytellers among them and commands them to tell tales "of the sort that old women usually entertain the little ones with" (Basile [1634–6] 2007: 42). Even though all the tales are told to a pregnant woman to preserve the life of a child yet to be born, and each tale told brings the struggle between two adult women for Prince Tadeo closer to a resolution, at other points in the frame tale the narrators describe their tales as children's stories, as tales recounted by grandmothers in nurseries (Canepa 2003: 38).

And yet, as Nancy Canepa persuasively argues, Basile's "sophisticated and complex" text was most likely never intended for young readers (Canepa 2003: 37). The flowery baroque prose of Basile's tales, as well as the dense enumerations of references to high and low culture, are unsuitable for the newly literate. Furthermore, those wishing to be instructed as well as entertained would find Basile's tales to be a puzzle, for "the moral vision of the tales is slippery when not evanescent" (39), with the introduction by the narrator, the recounted tale, and the concluding proverb often at odds. Basile's Cinderella, for example, is displaced in her father's heart by her stepsisters and must work in the ashes, but she also brutally murders her first stepmother. Nevertheless, she is never punished for this crime and achieves her happily ever after by marrying the prince (39). The narrator introduces the tale with a denunciation of envy and closes with a proverb on fate, "those who oppose the stars are crazy" (Basile [1634–6] 2007: 89). Talia, Basile's Sleeping Beauty, is impregnated with twins by a married king who rapes her as she sleeps; nonetheless, Talia marries him after he has killed his wife. Curiously, this is one of the few tales to lack an introduction and the narrator concludes with a proverb that comments uncomfortably on a tale featuring rape, "for those who are lucky, *good rains down even when they are sleeping*" (417, emphasis in original).

Michele Rak suggests that Basile's tales were more likely intended to be read or recited before educated, adult audiences that he encountered at the small courts around Naples, where he was employed for most of his adult life, rather than to entertain children (1986: 1057). Indeed, the word Basile uses for "entertainment," "*trattenemiento*," was most often employed to describe just such courtly diversions. For all these reasons, Canepa suggests that we should read Basile's subtitle metaphorically, as a reference to his adoption of a new genre, and our need as readers to approach the text with fresh eyes (2003: 44).

Despite the fact that Basile's tales never seem to have been intended for a puerile audience, by the latter half of the seventeenth century, Basile's text would come to be characterized as children's literature, appropriate for both amusing and educating young readers and their parents. At the conclusion of his foreword to his corrected 1674 edition of *The Tale of Tales*, Pompeo Sarnelli, writing under the pseudonym Masillo Reppone, issued an invitation to read the tales in the form of a sonnet, in which he addresses three distinct audiences for the text—"little ones," "youth," and "elders"—but suggests one common use for the text for all three groups, fun and entertainment, without ever emphasizing any moral utility of the work (Sarnelli [1674] 2012: 75). Just five years later, however, another editor of Basile's collection would argue for the moral utility of his fairy tales. In the dedicatory letter to his 1679 edition of *The Tale of Tales*, the Roman printer Bartolomeo Lupardi assures his dedicatee, the nobleman Giuseppe Spada, that Basile's text will both entertain and provide valuable lessons for Spada's sons. Lupardi both cites lines from Torquato Tasso's epic poem *Jerusalem Delivered* regarding the need to sweeten the cup of bitter medicine of moral truths with sugar so that children will ingest them, as well as Horace's claim that literature must both delight and instruct (Lupardi [1679] 2012: 82). In the moment when the fairy tale becomes part of the burgeoning corpus of children's literature, Lupardi reads Basile's subtitle literally and casts the Neapolitan tales as children's literature that might also provide moral instruction for their parents. In the two centuries preceding Lupardi's edition, the bonds joining fairy tales, children, and moral instruction were much more tenuous.

During the age of the marvelous, fairy tales were more likely to be associated with the amusement of children in domestic settings than with their education. Early modern Italians inherited their views of old wives spinning tales from the classical texts that were prized by Renaissance humanists, such as Plato's *Gorgias* and Apuleius's *The Golden Ass*, as well as from medieval authors (Warner 1994: 14). In his humanist defense of pagan literature for Christian readers in *The Genealogy of the Pagan Gods* (c. 1360), Giovanni Boccaccio wrote,

> Not even the craziest old crone keeping vigil around the hearth with the young serving girls and telling some tales about the Ogre, the Fairies, and Witches, which have been recited many times, thinks that she is not including some serious sentiment—to the degree that her feeble intellect permits—with which she wants to frighten the small children, or delight young ladies, or make fun of older folks or at least show the power of Fortune.
>
> ([c. 1360] 2012: 21)

Though Boccaccio admits that even the stories of old crones contain some "serious sentiment," and thus potentially could be instructive for children, stories of ogres, fairies, and witches rank far below other genres of classical literature, such as epic poetry, comedy, and tragedy, which more perfectly fulfill the requirements of educating and entertaining. Similarly, Boccaccio valued Apuleius's fairy tale of "Cupid and Psyche" recounted by the old woman in the robbers' cave for its power to comfort and restore young Charite, rather than for its power to impart wisdom (Boccaccio [c. 1360] 2012: 18). This belief in the unsuitability of the fairy tale as a didactic literature derived in part from the perception that the typical tellers of such fantastic tales, crazy old women or simple young girls, were intellectually inferior and ill-prepared to assume pedagogical responsibilities.

In the sixteenth century, fairy tales were also strongly associated with the routines of the nursery—putting children to bed, waking them, entertaining them—rather than with pedagogical or literary pursuits. It is precisely this association of fabulous stories of fairies with children that created great unease for the Florentine intellectuals assembled by Duke Cosimo I de' Medici and charged with rewriting Boccaccio's *Decameron* so that it would be acceptable to the censors of the Catholic Church, whose efforts I describe in greater detail below. Known as the "Deputati," this group of Florentine men of letters hesitated to introduce fairy-tale motifs into Boccaccio's realistic tales. They expressed their qualms in their exchanges with Rome concerning their rewriting of Boccaccio's tale of Frate Alberto (day 4, tale 2), in which lascivious Alberto seduces a foolish Venetian woman by telling her that the Angel Gabriel wishes to use Alberto's body to sleep with her. The reference to the Angel Gabriel had to be removed or substituted to eliminate the blasphemous tone of the tale. As the head of the Deputati, the Benedictine monk Vincenzo Borghini explained in a letter addressed to the Maestro del Sacro Palazzo in Rome, Tommaso Manrique, that replacing the angel with a pagan god was "a too obvious change of time periods," especially for a novella that was "very humble and very familiar" set in Christian Venice among merchants, not deities (Chiecchi 1992: 60).[2] At the same time, however, replacing the angel with "the king of fairies," is unsatisfactory because it pulls Boccaccio's realistic novella into the realm of the fantastic literature associated with the Knights of the Round Table and circulating in *cantari*, or chapbooks, also a primary mode for the circulation of fairy tales at this time.[3] Borghini saw few good options. They cannot use Demigorgo, a name sometimes used for the King of Fairies, because Boccaccio himself uses this for the progenitor of the pagan gods in his *Genealogy of the Pagan Gods*. Using simply "Orco" (Ogre) will infantilize this canonical Florentine novella, because ogres are typically found in tales for children (60). Ultimately, even though Manrique approved the change of the Angel Gabriel to the King of the Fairies, Borghini remained unhappy with it, primarily because he associated such fairy stories with children, clearly not the intended audience for this Florentine masterpiece. In a letter to Manrique's associate in Rome, the Domenican Eustachio Martelli, Borghini expressed that he was never satisfied with the change, in part because "in the first place it really looks like one of the evening tales [*novelle da veglia*], as we are wont to call them" (87).[4] Borghini went so far as to question his Roman superior's stance, noting that the substitution of "fantastic characters" would alter the novella in unacceptable ways: "where before it was a tale of a manly trick, it would become something for children" (94–5).[5] The Deputati even wrote to Duke Cosimo I to request that their expurgated *Decameron* be published initially in an incomplete form, removing certain novellas, like this one of Frate Alberto, until better solutions could be found. Since "no replacement was found that was not, to speak sincerely, insipid or puerile" the novella was "something for children rather than for reasonable men" (138).[6] To introduce a fairy in the Boccaccian novella would be to infantilize a canonical work.

Although, as Borghini suggests, Italian children might have been hearing fairy tales at home or reading them in chapbooks, from what we know about early modern curricula, they were not studying fairy tales in school, regardless of whether they attended reading, writing, and arithmetic schools or the humanist schools that taught Latin (Grendler 1989, 1995). Literacy beyond the ABCs was cultivated by reading brief narratives with clear, explicit morals, such as Aesop's fables in Latin or *Fior di virtù* (Flowers of Virtue) in Italian (Grendler 1989: 277). Attributed to a fourteenth-century Bolognese notary Tommaso Gozzadini but published anonymously in the fifteenth century, the *Flowers of Virtue* consisted of brief chapters either celebrating a virtue or denouncing a vice that were divided into four parts: a definition; an illustrative animal tale; relevant citations from famous authors or scripture; and then an exemplum, or illustrative story involving human characters. For example, the chapter on envy defines two sorts of this vice: the envy of seeing others flourish or the pleasure at seeing others fail. The definition is followed by the animal story of the *nibbio* or kite: "We may compare the vice of envy to the [kite] who is a bird so envious that when she sees her young getting fat in the nest, she hits them in the ribs with her beak so as to infect their flesh and make them thin" (*Fior di virtù* [fourteenth century] 1953: 19).[7] Citations concerning the evils of envy attributed to Seneca, Aristotle, Solomon, and Saint Gregory follow this brief tale. The chapter concludes with a concise summary of the Old Testament story of Cain and Abel: "Cain saw his brother Abel was prospering and that from day to day all his property was improving. This happened because he received these graces from God. Out of envy Cain slew his brother with a club" (21).

In his collection of fairy tales and realistic novellas, *The Pleasant Nights*, Giovan Francesco Straparola also denounces envy using the figure of the envious kite and its abused hatchlings. The narrator of the fourth tale on the first night of storytelling, a young woman named Eritrea, follows her fairy tale of the incestuous King Tebaldo who persecutes his daughter Doralice with a riddle in verse:

> There is born among the animals one so vile
> That it bears envy and hatred for its own seed.
> It naturally has such a wicked demeanor
> That, upon seeing its children grow fat, it laments.
> And with its beak it sharply
> Pecks and presses the tender flesh,
> So that all is left is bones and feathers.
> So much it is consumed by envy and hatred.
> (Straparola [1550–3] 2015: 81)

Certainly, like the envious kite, Tebaldo of Salerno harms his daughter. His incestuous desire causes her to flee in secret from Salerno. Doralice's nurse gives her a magic elixir that will keep her alive without eating and hides her in an elaborately carved chest, which is later sold to a merchant who in turn sells it to the king of England. When Tebaldo later discovers she has happily married and given birth to children, he dons a disguise, travels to England, and murders Doralice's sons, a crime for which she is condemned and brutally tortured. The narrator Eritrea attributes his actions to his unbridled sexual desire and begins the tale by lamenting the power of love over us: "I do not think there is not one of us who has not felt firsthand how great are the power of Love and the urges of the mortal flesh. He rules as a powerful lord and governs over his empire not with a sword, but with a single wave of his hand" (Straparola [1550–3] 2015: 74). Eritrea, however, later describes the sudden incestuous impulse that overtakes Tebaldo as he watches his daughter try on her mother's ring as a "diabolical thought," not love. Justice prevails in the story with the evildoer gruesomely executed at the end of the tale.

As with Basile's tales, extracting a concise moral from the story is no easy task because the introduction, the tale itself, and the concluding riddle offer different explanations for parents harming children: lust, devilish thoughts, envy. Perhaps such moral complexity is to be expected in the context of storytelling in *The Pleasant Nights*, where prominent literary figures of the day, such as Pietro Bembo and the poets Benedetto Trivigiano and Antonio Molino, mingle with young women known only by their first names to dance, sing, tell stories, and solve riddles during Carnival. If children are present and listening to the ludic diversions of adults during this pre-Lenten period when moral strictures are loosened, no mention is made of their participation. Like Basile's tales, Straparola's fairy tales are morally complex stories told by adults to other adults rather than tales aimed primarily at entertaining children. Only in the hands of a certain Catholic priest would Italian fairy tales become simple, morally unambiguous tales aimed at conveying a clear lesson.

CENSORSHIP AND THE FAIRY TALE DURING THE COUNTER-REFORMATION: STRAPAROLA'S *THE PLEASANT NIGHTS*

During the Catholic or Counter-Reformation, the literary fairy tale itself was socialized, or reshaped to conform to the new moral and spiritual standards promulgated by the Catholic Church in the wake of the Council of Trent (1545–63). At the meetings of the Council, clergymen debated and rearticulated the church's theological, doctrinal, and moral precepts and beliefs and devised various aesthetic and spiritual methods to inculcate these views in Catholics across the world. Having witnessed the power of printed texts to spread ideas and shape belief during the Protestant Reformation, the church sought to control the content of printed materials through various practices, including the creation of Indexes, or lists, or prohibited books that included rules governing permissible content and the censorship of books. These efforts led to the censorship of fairy tales already in print, such as Straparola's

The Pleasant Nights, while encouraging one author, Lorenzo Selva, to create tales that conformed to these strictures.

Now known as the Tridentine Index, the *Index of Prohibited Books* published in 1564 during the papacy of Pope Pius IV contained ten rules meant to explain more precisely the sort of printed material to be censored or banned. These rules would be carried forward in subsequent Indices. Scholars of sixteenth-century censorial practices often indicate rule number 7 as particularly threatening for literary texts because it expanded the prohibition of the printing and possession of heretical writings to include immoral texts.[8] But for early modern fairy tales, texts that literary critics often distinguish from other sorts of narrative by the presence of magic, rules number 8 and 9 appear to be equally, if not more, problematic. Rule 8 allowed the reading of books that possessed a positive moral message, as long as any references to heresy, wickedness, superstition, or divination were removed. Rule 9 banned all writings on divinatory practices, including pyromancy, necromancy, and palm-reading. It also broadly banned books that instructed readers in the magical arts, including love magic and other sorts of spells. Finally, negative portrayals of the clergy, so prevalent in the Boccaccian tradition, had to be eliminated or rewritten to recast monks, priests, and nuns as secular characters. These strictures served to "civilize" the literary fairy tale and transform the genre in two primary ways. First, Straparola's fairy tales that touched directly upon theological concerns or contained detailed representations of the practice of magic were heavily edited or eliminated. Second, some fairy tales written after the publication of the 1564 Index, such as those of Lorenzo Selva, more efficaciously conveyed the values of the church in concise, morally unambiguous narratives.

The censorial efforts of the Catholic Church reshaped the editions of Straparola's collection of tales published between 1565 and 1608 by requiring the editing or elimination of those tales that blatantly transgressed the rules set forth in the Tridentine Index. The censorship of subsequent editions of *The Pleasant Nights*, which has been meticulously documented by Donato Pirovano, focused heavily on eliminating the religious references in the text (Pirovano 2000: 2:805–10). Priests and monks became simply "giovani" (young men) or "signori" (men); churches became gardens or villas; and the citations of biblical passages with which the narrators sometimes introduce their tales were excised. In the 1601 edition, which was reprinted in 1604 and 1608, all references to the clergy, the church, and Catholic doctrine had been removed (2:809). Sexually explicit scenes were also shortened, removed entirely, or the characters' actions denounced as sinful, sometimes resulting in the elimination of entire paragraphs, sometimes just a few words. While passages depicting divinatory magic or witchcraft were censored if the magic proved efficacious in the plot, tales in which one character feigned using magic to dupe another remained uncensored. In this way, the censors were able to reposition the depiction of magic in *The Pleasant Nights* as a charlatan's hoax employed to trick gullible individuals rather than as an effective means for obtaining one's desires. The greatest effect that these interventions had on Straparola's *The Pleasant Nights* was to eliminate entirely certain tale types, while shoring up the division between the practice of magic outlawed by the church and more innocuous representations of fairy-tale magic.

Beginning with the 1601 edition, and continuing with the 1608 edition, three fairy tales were eliminated from Straparola's text: a sorcerer's apprentice tale of a necromancer who practices black magic, and two tales that deal with the afterlife. In tale 8.4, a tailor's apprentice spies on his master each night as he practices spells behind locked doors. Throughout the tale, the apprentice Dionigi and his master do battle, spell for spell, which culminates with a metamorphic showdown. In the final scene, the apprentice becomes a fox who devours his master who, moments before, had assumed the form of a chicken. Dionigi then returns to his human form and marries the princess (ATU 325 "The Magician and His Pupil"). In a story from the Fourth Night (4.5), Flamminio Veraldo seeks Death, but finds Life who teaches him a stern lesson about wanting to know the future (ATU 326 "The Youth Who Wanted to Learn What Fear Is"). The third tale eliminated, 11.2, is a ghost story, in which the soul of a man whose body was properly buried thanks to the generosity of kind Bertuccio, returns the favor by helping Bertuccio to marry the king's daughter (ATU 505 "The Grateful Dead").

Despite these many editorial interventions, *The Pleasant Nights* would appear on four different Indexes of Prohibited Books: in 1580, 1590, 1596, and 1600 (Beecher 2012: 1:78). Of course, the church's efforts at censoring fairy tales was never completely effective. Editions continued to be printed after these bans. Moreover, earlier, less- or uncensored editions of *The Pleasant Nights* continued to circulate alongside the highly redacted seventeenth-century editions, and the censorship did not always extend to images, leaving visual traces of magical practices in the text. For example, tale 7.1 was not eliminated from the 1608 edition, but highly censored. In this tale, abandoned by her merchant husband who has taken up with a prostitute in Bruges, a Florentine wife named Isabella buys the help of a witch named Gabrina when fasting and prayers in the Church of Santissima Annunziata prove ineffective in bringing back her wayward husband. In the seventeenth-century editions, the long passage in which Gabrina has Isabella strip and enter a magic circle that the witch has drawn on the ground while she recites incantations to summon a devil from hell to transport the spurned wife to Bruges in one night has been removed, mutilating the tale and making it difficult to follow. The image of the devil, witch, wife, and magical inscriptions, however, remains (Figure 7.1). Although we can question the success of the church's program of censorship, we do not find the three ATU tale types (325, 326, and 505) in the later collections of Italian fairy tales by Selva and Basile. While the majority of Straparola's fairy

FIGURE 7.1: Gabrina casts a spell over Isabella as a devil enters the room, from *Le tredici piacevolissime notte* (1608). Courtesy of the University of Colorado Boulder Libraries. Public domain.

tales do not undergo radical rewriting at the hands of censors, their textual interventions did reduce the diversity of tale types in his collection and distance fairy-tale magic from the actual, contemporary practice of magic.

When scenes of magic in fairy tales did not directly contain references to the practice of witchcraft, they were left mostly unchanged. In one tale, a wild man regains his human form by making a fairy laugh and thus curing her of her illness (5.1); in the fairy tale of King Pig, the fairy still curses the queen (2.1). Enchanted animals also persist in the 1608 edition. A clever fairy cat aides Costantino Fortunato in Straparola's Puss in Boots tale (11.1); Livoretto receives a talking horse from his mother (3.2); Pietro Pazzo's wish-granting tuna impregnates a princess (3.1). Magical metamorphoses remain intact: Fortunio will change into a wolf and devour his jealous family (3.4); Biancabella's amputated hands will grow back thanks to a fairy (3.3). It seems that the censors were willing to allow the depiction fairy-tale magic and intervened only when it approached the sorts of practices prohibited in rules 8 and 9 of the Tridentine Index. For example, in the 1608 edition, the rubric for the tale of Pietro Pazzo, which features a wish-granting tuna fish that impregnates the princess who has mocked the protagonist, eliminates the word "incantesimo" (spell), which might suggest that the tuna used witchcraft.[9]

Ultimately, these changes could not keep *The Pleasant Nights* in print. Straparola's complete collection of tales would not be reprinted again until the late nineteenth century (Beecher 2012: 1:78–9).

CIVILIZING APULEIUS: LORENZO SELVA'S *DELLA METAMORFOSI*

The Franciscan preaching friar Evangelista Marcellino was well aware of the rules of the 1564 Tridentine Index when he took up the pen to write his Christian adaptation of Apuleius's *The Golden Ass*, titled *Della metamorfosi, cioè, trasformatione del virtuoso* (*The Metamorphosis, or, Transformation of a Virtuous Man*), which he published under his pseudonym, Lorenzo Selva, in 1582. In Selva's hands, fairy tales became pointedly didactic texts with unambiguous morals aimed at instilling the values of the Counter-Reformation Church, and thus tools for the moral and spiritual acculturation of Catholics. While still the provenance of young or old female narrators in Selva's text, after these fairy tales are told, authoritative male characters always mediate the women's words to ensure that the proper interpretation is conveyed to readers and that magic is presented according to church doctrine.

Born in 1530 in the Tuscan village of San Marcellino near Pistoia, Lorenzo Gerbi entered the Franciscan order at thirteen and took the name Evangelista Marcellino. After studying and teaching theology in Paris, he settled in Rome, where he preached at various churches and delivered weekly sermons to the city's Jewish community in an effort to convert its members, although his duties also took him to other Italian cities to preach. A prolific author, he published more than thirty-five religious works as Evangelista Marcellino, including sermons and commentaries on numerous books of the Bible. He died in Rome in 1593.[10]

First printed allegedly without his consent in Orvieto in 1582, *The Metamorphosis, or, Transformation of a Virtuous Man* would be reprinted six times over the next thirty-five years and translated into French in 1611.[11] In explaining his use of a pseudonym in the author's letter to his readers in the 1583 edition of *The Metamorphosis*, Selva claims that his novel, the product of his younger, secular self, was no longer appropriate for him to publish under his name now that he was ordained. This literary disguise allowed him to maintain two distinct authorial identities, one religious and the other secular. And yet, Selva and Marcellino shared similar moral and didactic goals. Citing the ancient poet Horace's adage in the proem to the novel, Selva depicts his text as a decorous form of amusement that will also instruct his readers. But unlike Straparola's editor Orfeo della Carta, who vaguely gestures toward the moral utility of *The Pleasant Nights* in his letter to the readers, Selva supplies a precise allegorical reading of the novel that reinforces Christian doctrine in his Proem. The protagonist Acrisio's post-metamorphic snake form symbolizes prudence and his return to his beloved, chaste Clori, after encountering city women, who represent speculative virtue, and the women of the country villas, who represent moral virtue, signifies that only divine grace can grant us our divine image (Selva 1583: Proemio). In providing an allegorical reading for his protagonist's transformation, Selva follows the Christian interpretive tradition of his classical model.

Apuleius's *The Golden Ass*, which includes the tale of Cupid and Psyche, had been read as a Christian allegory for centuries before Selva chose it as a model. In her article "Allegorizing Apuleius," Julia Haig Gaisser reviews the long tradition of reading the Latin novel, and particularly the tale of Cupid and Psyche, as a Christian allegory (2003).[12] Fulgentius, for example, emphasizes Psyche's error in wanting to gaze upon her sleeping spouse, Cupid, and reads Psyche as the Soul who is undone by desire or Cupid. Because Fulgentius skips over the happy ending Apuleius affords her, Psyche is, for him, akin to Adam: she gazes on Cupid and is expelled from his house, just as Adam is driven from the Garden of Eden with Eve after he eats the forbidden fruit (Gaisser 2003: 23–7). Boccaccio took a more positive view of the Cupid and Psyche tale, interpreting Cupid as God and Psyche as the soul who seeks union with the divinity, but cannot gaze upon the face of the divine (29–31). Although the humanist Filippo Beroaldo's widely read sixteenth-century commentary on Apuleius focused on the historical context for *The Golden Ass*, he also provided a reading less pointedly religious than those of Fulgentius and Boccaccio. For Beroaldo, Pleasure, the daughter of Cupid and Psyche, is born from "the desire and love of the soul" and "we turn into asses" when we let bestial pleasure overrun our reason and virtue (Gaisser 2003: 39).

Despite the prominence of these readings, I believe that Selva subscribes to an interpretation of the Latin novel that Gaisser describes as an isolated, loose strand in the chain of interpretation. This allegorical reading of the novel is written in the margins of a fourteenth-century manuscript of the Third Vatican Mythographer found in the Biblioteca Nazionale in Florence. The author "reads Apuleius's *Apology* [in which he defends himself against charges of witchcraft] and *Metamorphoses* together, as virtually a single work, and takes the novel as Apuleius's personal testimony of the dangers of magic, written in order to deter others from his mistakes" (Gaisser 2003: 35–6). This interpreter views Lucius's sufferings as a "necessary penance," almost a purgatory, in Gaisser's assessment, rather than a lively, comic adventure aimed at getting us to renounce our bestial, vice-ridden ways, or as an allegory for the mystical comingling of the soul and the deity. Selva, too, reads *The Golden Ass* as autobiography, as is clear when his protagonist, already changed into a serpent, confesses as he waits to hear a tale: "I resolved to make every effort to be able to hear it, yearning no less to hear tell of this vanity, than Apuleius, changed into an ass, was to write the tale of Psyche narrated to Charite by the old woman, as he himself writes in his *The Golden Ass*" (Selva 1583: 80).[13] Reading his source text as an autobiographical renunciation of magic facilitates Selva's adaptation and transformation of Apuleius's work into a post-Tridentine denunciation of witchcraft (Figure 7.2).

Like Apuleius's Lucius, Selva's protagonist Acrisio is a highly mobile first-person narrator who recounts adventures in animal form after a witch casts a spell on him. Acrisio does not, however, dabble in magic and enjoys none of the sexual adventures afforded to Apuleius's Lucius in both his human and asinine forms. Instead, Selva rewrites Lucius's picaresque and bawdy adventures as a chaste pastoral romance reminiscent of Jacopo Sannazaro's *Arcadia*. In book 1, Acrisio's mother informs him that he is not really a poor shepherd but the son of a deceased Neapolitan nobleman. She urges him to return to Naples to claim

FIGURE 7.2: Master of the Die (1530–60), Lucius the ass overhears the old woman recounting the tale of Cupid and Psyche, sixteenth-century engraving. Courtesy of the Metropolitan Museum of Art. Public domain.

his family's wealth. Despite his beloved Clori's laments and his own reticence to leave her, Acrisio sets off for the city.

In book 2, while traveling south toward Naples, Acrisio meets up with a group of pilgrims traveling from Santiago de Campostela to Rome. As in *The Golden Ass*, the protagonist's metamorphosis is preceded by a debate on the efficacy of witchcraft in which an elderly pilgrim authoritatively asserts the position of the Catholic Church on witchcraft and transformation: true metamorphoses occur only through divine intervention, as is the case with transubstantiation, and explains that those phenomena we take to be transformations of the physical state of a being are actually cases of diabolical illusion.[14] After he parts ways with the pilgrims in Rome, Acrisio arrives in Naples and is welcomed into his ancestral home. There Acrisio's cousin tries to seduce him, but he, still pining for Clori, refuses her advances. Seemingly in a dream, the spurned girl brings an old woman to his room who puts a spell on him. If he drinks from a spring in the Apennines, he will become a snake for seven moons and recuperate human form only if he drinks the blood of his beloved.

The longest of the four books, book 3, contains Acrisio's adventures as a snake that overhears thirteen tales as it moves about the Italian countryside. Still in serpentine form at the end of book 3, Acrisio arrives once again in his village where he encounters the grieving Clori. Pulling out her hair and beating her chest, she laments the loss of her lover. Although mute, the snake Acrisio tries his best to reveal his true identity. Grabbing the snake to her breast, she faints, thus allowing Acrisio to lap up some of her blood and reacquire his human form.

In the fourth and final book, Acrisio will hear one more tale on the importance of persistence in love and will eventually reconcile with Clori after admitting his sins. Tragically, in the very same moment a poisonous spider bites Clori and she dies. Acrisio then commits himself to living a virtuous life.[15] In keeping with Selva's didactic goals, the thirteen novellas Acrisio overhears while slithering about the Italian countryside in book 3, include moralizing *beffe*, or tales of tricks, that upbraid avaricious and lustful characters; chaste love stories that end tragically; anti-Protestant propaganda; tales condemning witchcraft; and three fairy tales. In rewriting Apuleius's text, Selva eliminates the tale of Cupid and Psyche, which stretches across chapters 4, 5, and 6 of the eleven chapters of the Latin novel, and inserts a palimpsest in miniature of Apulieus's entire novel roughly at the center of his own text. Two stories of men turned into asses through witchcraft, tales 5 and 7 of the thirteen novellas in book 3 of Selva's novel, circumscribe a fairy tale, tale 6 in book 3, that offers a simple moral lesson rather than an allegory of the soul.

At this point in the overarching narrative, Acrisio in snake form pauses to listen to a young woman named Placida sing as she hangs her laundry. Suddenly a young man arrives and begins to assault her. Acrisio saves the woman's chastity by wrapping himself around the scoundrel's neck, forcing him to run away. When sometime later Placida's brother finds Acrisio in a tree and begins to stone him, Placida comes to the serpent's aid because she recognizes it as the beast that defended her. She wonders aloud whether the creature is a fairy. Her friends, Anna and Eugenia, are excited by the idea since they have learned by reading Ludovico Ariosto's *Orlando Furioso,* a chivalric epic featuring the fairy or sorceress Alcina, that this would be a lucky find. Placida and her friends decide to test their theory empirically: if they call the snake and it comes to them, then it is a fairy. The experiment works. That night the adults return to the house and Placida's father encourages an old woman called Mon'antonia to tell of the funeral she has just attended. Her story is a tale of witchcraft and metamorphosis. Mon'antonia recounts the tragic tale of two young lovers, Ersilia and Gelanzio, who are separated when the girl's father marries her to the son of a wealthy farmer. Mad with grief, Gelanzio wanders about and eventually passes out in front of a witch's house. The witch plans to kill him to use his fat for her diabolical unguents, but her daughter falls in love with Gelanzio and saves him. When Gelanzio rejects the daughter's love, the girl hangs herself. In revenge, the witch strikes Ersilia dead by simply looking at her and casts a spell on Gelanzio so that he becomes a donkey for eight years. Upon returning to human form, he stays in his sick bed and eventually dies.

When Mon'antonia has finished her tale, a priest present intervenes, immediately telling those present that such transformations are nothing more than diabolical illusions that affect the appearance but not the essence of beings, thus articulating the position of the church, that Selva presented in book 2 through the character of the elderly pilgrim. He promises to explain himself further when the group travels to a feast the following day. That night, the three girls share a room with Mon'antonia and ask her whether she believes that fairies exist and that they can take the form of snakes. As we saw earlier, the girls believe in fairies based on the authority of Ariosto's poem, a text most educated people read allegorically rather than literally. Mon'antonia assures them that such fairies exist, stating that they are named for the Roman goddess Fatua. To Placida's questions as to whether fairies can become snakes, the old woman replies that, like Persephone who was condemned to spend six months a year in the underworld, "so they say about Fairies, that for six months they must stay in the shape of a snake, and another six in their own shape." When asked whether anyone has ever seen a fairy in both forms, the old woman recounts the following fairy tale saying, "Yes, it has happened and I remember that when I was a girl, it must be seventy years ago, the following novella was recounted as if it were quite true" (Selva 1583: 139).

One day two nameless travelers spy a snake staring at them as they rest by a spring. While one wishes to stone it to death, the other traveler restrains him from killing the beast. His compassion is rewarded that night when during a violent storm the two travelers take refuge in a cave on a mountaintop. While his companion sleeps, a fairy appears to the compassionate traveler, reveals that she was the snake he had saved earlier, takes him to her underground palace, and showers him with riches. When he asks that his companion be permitted to share this wealth, the fairy initially balks at the suggestion. Later she instructs the man to bring a golden jar to his companion ordering him to open it only when he is alone. The two travelers separate and when the evil companion opens the jar, poisonous fumes kill him. The old woman ends her tale with a clear moral message: "And so, daughters of mine, try to do good even towards brute beasts, remembering either later on or on time good is always remunerated and evil punished" (Selva in Magnanini 2011: 339–40).

Mon'antonia's confident assertions regarding fairies and their metamorphic nature are challenged the very next day as the girls travel with relatives to a festival with their snake in tow. As promised, the priest returns to the subject of metamorphosis and tells another donkey tale taken, however, from the inquisitor's handbook on witchcraft, *The Hammer of Witches* (*Malleus Maleficarum*, 1486). A woman on Crete gives six hard-boiled eggs to a young sailor who asks her for food. When he eats the eggs, he is turned into a donkey and his companions, unable to recognize him, refuse to let him board their ship. Desperate, the donkey enters a church during Communion and seems to kneel down in prayer. Genovese merchants present at the Mass view this as a miracle and when the woman returns with a club to claim the poor beast, the merchants have her seized. Under torture, she confesses, reverses the enchantment, and is burned at the stake. The priest concludes his tale by noting that although such transformations are visible to others, they are not visible to the individual who has experienced them. Though witches exist, fairies do not. As if he overheard Mon'antonia's fairy tale, the priest later concludes, "Regarding what they say, that snakes are fairies, these are the stupid thoughts and foolishness of the common people" (Selva 1583: 146). With these words the priest dismisses the fairy tale recounted by Mon'antonia as superstitious foolishness. In doing so, he discredits the sources of her tale, the oral tradition by which she heard the text, and the classical myth with which she supports her arguments.

As in Apuleius's Latin novel, Selva's narratives about human-to-donkey metamorphosis frame a fairy tale recounted by an old woman to a group of girls that appear roughly at the center of the Italian novel. However, the moral—good will be rewarded and evil punished—is so generic as to avoid any complicated theological interpretation. Allegorically speaking, it is no Cupid and Psyche tale. And yet, we can discern remnants of Apuleius's fairy tale in Selva's story of the snake fairy, just as Armando Maggi finds traces of motifs from Cupid and Psyche utilized in new ways in Basile's tales.[16] Like Psyche's envious sisters, the protagonist's companion seeks to harm the snake and is jealous of his friend's good fortune. Psyche falls into an enchanted sleep after opening a box containing Proserpina's beauty that Venus has sent her to fetch in the underworld. The good man's companion falls dead after opening the golden jar. The fairy takes the form of a serpent, the same shape Psyche's sisters suggest her monstrous bridegroom possesses; however, there is no sexual encounter between the fairy and the good traveler. Despite the presence of these motifs, the allegory of the soul becomes a straightforward exemplum. Psyche's complex character has been simplified by being neatly divided between the good and bad companion, making the simplified moral even easier to comprehend.

In his post-Tridentine adaptation of Apuleius, Selva, like Basile, isolates and redeploys motifs from Cupid and Psyche for his own purposes, which align with the proscriptions in the Index of 1564. Selva's asses are not protagonists impelled by a burning curiosity for magic who take a circuitous, and often sexy, path to enlightenment and piety. Instead, Selva's humans-turned-beasts are passive, the victims of female witches who practice magic but who in turn, as a consequence, suffer dearly by being deprived of loved ones and their lives. His palimpsest in miniature of Apuleius's novel functions as a theological denunciation of witchcraft aligned with the teachings of the Reformed Catholic Church that reduces the fairy tale to a simple morality tale. This fairy tale of Selva's closely resembles the brief tales in *Fior di virtù* with their simple plots and straightforward morals.[17]

Much more complex, but equally unambiguous, is the allegorical reading of Selva's third fairy tale, the thirteenth and final tale told in book 3, provided by a male character who hears it and reinforced by paratextual glosses printed in the margin of the text. As Acrisio the snake listens attentively, a young woman named Lisabetta tells a tale to a company of men and women gathered in her family's home about the two sons of a king in the Indies in the New World—one legitimate and good and the other illegitimate and sinful—who have divided their father's subjects and created brawling factions in the kingdom. When civil war appears imminent, the king threatens his legitimate son who immediately brings his followers in line, but the illegitimate son and his faction persist in their wicked ways. Upon the advice of his barons, the king decides to send the both sons on quest for the herb pistis ("faith" in Greek), reasoning that they will have to toil virtuously to obtain it. The legitimate son, however, only pretends to depart and sets snares for his brother.

The illegitimate son then begins his quest and encounters a woman in a valley who reveals everything he must do to obtain the magic herb. Her complex directions include the interdiction that he must not stop and look at the tree with the golden leaves in the garden where the pistis grows, for it will awaken in him a lustful appetite that will spur him to eat the fruit of the tree and then fail in his quest. At this point, the narrator interjects a moralizing apostrophe, "Oh human fragility, if you don't overcome evil at it beginning, how will you overcome it when it has grown so? Wretched is he who thinks of ignoring the advice of one who knows more than he!" (Selva in Magnanini 2011: 346). Confident he will not succumb, the young man sits in front of the tree and then eats the fruit, which leads to his immediate arrest by guards who take him to the ruler of the land. Advised not to sully his hands with the blood of a lowly thief, the ruler sends the young man to the Kingdom in the South to capture the beautiful maiden Agape ("love" in Greek). After many days of traveling, he meets an old man to whom he recounts his past adventures.

Convinced that the young man has learned his lesson, the old man provides him with the correct answers to the questions that will be posed to him before he enters Agape's castle. Once inside, he must love her with all humility and renounce his own will, only then will she give herself to him and go away with him. All goes as planned, until the young man breaks the one interdiction to not take anything but Agape when leaving the castle: he fails by taking a cameo with his own portrait. After Agape berates him for loving something besides her, he is then seized by guards and imprisoned. As he is being marched to his execution, the old man appears again and after hearing the young man's humble confession, suggests he might return to Agape's good graces if he can capture the flying horse. This time, after selflessly helping fellow travelers who in gratitude reveal how to capture the winged horse, the young man succeeds in his quest, flies to Agape's castle, and then returns to his father's kingdom with the seeds of the pistis plant. The king rejoices, but the legitimate son, filled with envy, leaves the kingdom never to return, despite his father's entreaties. The most authoritative character who hears the young woman's tale, a preacher and renowned theologian, provides an allegorical reading of the tale:

> He had arrived precisely when the novella began and listened to it paying close attention until the end. He praised her greatly on account of the mystical meanings she gave the tale. Showing that that seed was a symbol of faith, the beautiful woman charity, and the horse prayer, which must be made without the stink of sin, without the weight of the love of earthly goods, and with much sureness and confidence, so rightly the horse had these conditions. And from these three things that our soul must have in order to join with God, he came to speak about the nobility of the soul, by saying that it is very noble and superior to these things down here, just as the spirit dominates the body, it was perverted that the soul be subject to those things, especially to the brute passions which transformed it from the image of God into a Beast.
> (Selva in Magnanini 2011: 352)

Similarly, the many marginal glosses for this tale supply allegorical readings which encourage readers to interpret it as an antisemitic parable. The opening lines are glossed with "Consider whether this king symbolizes God for us with the Hebrew and Gentile people." The legitimate son is "The Hebrews the first born of God," while the illegitimate son represents the Gentiles: "The Gentiles who were not in the city, since like beasts they went wandering in the desert." The legitimate son is criticized for not accepting his father's command when he sets snares for his brother "Confident in his own legal justice, the Hebrew turned away from God's justice." And the legitimate son's refusal to enter the kingdom after his brother's return is seen as the Jewish people's refusal to convert: "Blindness fell upon Israel, says the Apostle, since she did not want to save herself with the people (Selva in Magnanini 2011: 353)." Through both the commentary of the theologian and the paratextual glosses, the fairy tale becomes both didactic religious literature and antisemitic propaganda. As such, this tale appears to be a fictional reformulation of themes and antisemitism common to Selva's sermons that he delivered to both Catholics and Jews (Michelson 2012).

Selva "civilizes" the fairy tale in a number of ways to make the genre conform to the post-Tridentine morality and theology preached by the Catholic Church. In Selva's hands, fairy tales become a form of religious allegory aimed at conveying general morals (be good to all creatures) or articulating specific theological concepts (the importance of prayer). The fairy tale also becomes a means for communicating Selva's, and the Catholic Church's, antisemitism and to articulate the belief in the superiority of Christian belief and the imperfection of Judaism. While in the fiction of the frame tale, fairy tales are still the narrative provenance of old women or young girls, the women's words are always interpreted by an authoritative male voice, by way of a male character's comments or the marginal glosses that readers would naturally attribute to the author or male editor of the text. Although all narrated by women, Selva's three fairy tales all feature male protagonists. In the stories female characters function as benevolent helpers who are themselves enchanted or bestow enchanted objects upon worthy men, or as the wives who are part of the reward provided to the men to facilitate the happy ending of the tale. These female characters operate as civilizing forces who help the young men develop into functioning, successful adults by providing moral instruction or monetary support. Like female saints, they intercede to protect, guide, and promote the interests of worthy men. Thus unlike Straparola's and Basile's female characters, who often act boldly, Selva's women are reduced to supporting roles more attuned with post-Tridentine gender mores. Ultimately, Selva's concisely written tales offer unambiguous, explicitly stated morals and thus function more clearly as efficacious tools for socialization than Straparola's or Basile's morally complex tales ever did, providing readers were willing to accept and conform to their message.

CONCLUSION

The textual repression enacted after the Council of Trent created two seemingly opposed tendencies in the Italian fairy-tale tradition although both, however, served to "civilize" tales according to church doctrine. Some fairy tales, like those in Straparola's *The Pleasant Nights*, were emptied of all Christian content, while in Selva's *Metamorphosis*, the fairy tale was recast as Christian allegory. The secularizing of the fairy tale also occurred in Giambattista Basile's *The Tale of Tales*, a work written and published in the wake of the sixteenth-century *Indices of Prohibited Books*. In fact, in the preface to a nineteenth-century German translation of *The Tale of Tales*, Jacob Grimm noted with surprise the complete lack of references to Christian figures in Basile's fairy tales. This absence contrasted sharply with the German tales he and his brother collected, edited, and published in 1812, for in what today we call *Grimms' Fairy Tales*, German stories of angels, devils, and the Virgin Mary appear alongside tales featuring ogres and fairies (Maggi 2015: 66). Despite these civilizing efforts, neither Straparola's and Basile's secularized fairy tales nor Selva's Christian allegories became primarily children's literature during the age of the marvelous (1450–1650). It would take another two hundred years for these tales truly to become "entertainment for the little ones" when John Taylor published a highly expurgated English translation of Basile's tales adorned with drawings by renowned children's book illustrator George Cruikshank (Basile [1634–6] 1848).[18]

CHAPTER EIGHT

Power

Abuse of Power, Gender, and Race in Tales by Straparola and Basile

ARMANDO MAGGI

The concept of power lies at the core of the fairy-tale genre, both in its literary and oral forms. Although we have learned to associate the fairy tale with a flight from reality, the essence of the fairy tale is the staging of an injustice and/or abuse of power reflecting a historical reality and the wishful resolution of such conflict. Some of the most cherished tales of the Western tradition, such as "Beauty and the Beast" and "Cinderella," are premised on a social and/or cultural inequality. The mysterious Beast is an affluent nobleman who abuses an impoverished merchant, Belle's father, by accusing him of a preposterous crime; "Cinderella" recounts the unutterable violence occurring in the secrecy of the household. In particular, gender discrimination and social marginalization have been the objects of some insightful studies, such as, for example, Ruth Bottigheimer's "Fertility Control and the Birth of the Modern European Fairy-Tale Heroine" in the provocative volume *Fairy Tales and Feminism* (2004), whereas the crucial figures of the ogre and the fool as the embodiments of social ostracism have been the object of a thoughtful essay by Nancy Canepa on Giambattista Basile's seventeenth-century *The Tale of Tales* in the collective volume *Monsters in the Italian Literary Imagination* (2001).

As we shall see in this chapter centered on the first European collections of fairy tales, we don't need to look to modern or postmodern retellings of classic tales to find conscious allusions to and representations of deeply unsettling instances of historically determined abuses of power. The act of contaminating the illusory backdrop of the fairy tale with the basest instances of reality is not foreign to Giovan Francesco Straparola's *Le piacevoli notti* (*The Pleasant Nights*, 1550–3) and Giambattista Basile's *Lo cunto de li cunti* (*The Tale of Tales*, 1634–6), the two first seminal books of this genre. If "breaking the spell," in the sense of exposing the cultural background of classic fairy tales, is the catchphrase of our contemporary attitude toward classic tales from Jacob and Wilhelm Grimms' or Charles Perrault's collections, it is essential to understand that, despite their significant temporal and cultural distance (Straparola was from Lombardy and lived during the apex of the Italian Renaissance; Basile was a Neapolitan baroque intellectual), the two early modern Italian writers were less interested in casting a benign spell over their readers, as we would expect from a book of children's literature, than in portraying a reality in which societal biases or abuses and their fictional, magical dissolution don't bring about a sense of comforting reassurance.[1] Straparola and Basile in fact seem to revel in the injustices or even atrocities they depict and some of their most powerful tales have happy, but puzzling and mystifying, endings.

A regrettably modern approach to fairy tales is to read them as single narrative entities disengaged from their broader textual context. This attitude is particularly deleterious when analyzing *The Pleasant Nights* and *The Tale of Tales*, since both echoed the structure of Boccaccio's *Decameron* (c. 1353) with a frame tale and a sequence of stories told in separate days, mostly by female narrators. In such a complex narrative structure, the single tales are not isolated monads but rather narrative units that echo and affect each other and the frame in which they are located. This is easily understandable when considering the hybrid nature of *The Pleasant Nights*, a medley of realistic and crudely salacious short stories à la Boccaccio and undisputable "fairy tales," although all the narratives in Straparola's book are called *favole*, which Boccaccio considers as one of the possible ways to define his tales, "novelle, o favole, o parabole, o istorie che dire le vogliamo."[2] In book 14 of *The Genealogy of the Pagan Gods*, Boccaccio (1313–75) had openly associated them with "crazy old women."[3] It is worth stressing that Boccaccio's massive work, which borrowed from several ancient and medieval literary sources to create a comprehensive synthesis of Greek and Roman mythology, exerted an invaluable influence on the European imagination and thus also on the first volumes of fairy tales, especially Basile's *The Tale of Tales*.

STRAPAROLA: POWER, GENDER, AND SOCIAL CLASS

In the Preface to the *Decameron*, Boccaccio posits the issue of power at the center of his collection of stories. He envisions his book as an expression of "gratitude" for the support he received from friends during a painful love experience. If he can't "provide some relief" to the people who helped him, he wishes to "offer" it to those who most need it, namely, the "delicate ladies" whose freedom is severely "restrained" by their families and who, unlike men, must bear the most agonizing love feelings in the solitude of their rooms (Boccaccio [c. 1353] 2013: 2–3). With his stories Boccaccio thus aims to empower his female readers by giving them not only some temporary solace but also some "good advice" about what to "avoid" and what to "pursue" (3).

In the preface to the first part of *The Pleasant Nights*, the mysterious editor Orfeo della Carta makes an initial allusion to Boccaccio and the Italian literary tradition of the *novella* by repeating the trope of the "pleasure" (*diletto*) and "instruction" (*ammaestramento*) women receive from reading entertaining stories. However, whereas in introducing his *Decameron* Boccaccio emphasized the text's healing quality with no reference to its literary merits, the editor of *The Pleasant Nights* shifts the emphasis from its alleged female readers to the book itself, whose problematic nature and questionable results Orfeo attributes to the inferiority of its original sources, women themselves. After claiming that Straparola's style is both "elegant" and "learned," Orfeo begs his female interlocutors not to "despise" and "reject" these tales because of their unusual "subject matter" and, contradicting what he stated a few sentences earlier, stresses that their "humble and lowly style" is not Straparola's fault, because he claims to have simply jotted down what he had heard from some female storytellers, who in his introduction to the second volume of *The Pleasant Nights* he identifies as the ten female fictional storytellers at the Venetian gathering, even though a few of the tales were purportedly told by some renowned male intellectuals, such as Pietro Bembo. Thus, according to Orfeo della Carta, women are at once the real authors and the target readers of Straparola's book, but only if we approach the text as the product of an oral storytelling. Speaking of readership, it is worth recalling that starting from the late fifteenth century Venetian society was divided into three social classes, the patriciate or nobility, the so-called *cittadini* (citizens), who were not noble but held important bureaucratic positions, and artisans or lower classes (*popolo*). Wearing similar clothes and sharing a similar cultural background, the citizens and the aristocracy alike were Straparola's target audience, and his tales reflect this multilayered and complex societal structure.[4]

Rather than being the recipients of an uplifting book of instructive tales, in *The Pleasant Nights* female characters are the original authors of tales that may neither suit nor comfort female readers. These tales are "elegant" if seen from the standpoint of their male "transcriber" Straparola and "humble and lowly" if considered as examples of women's own storytelling. Reminiscent not only of the *Decameron* but also of Baldassare Castiglione's *The Courtier* (1528), the frame tale of *The Pleasant Nights*, set on the island of Murano, seemingly reiterates the centrality of both its female characters in charge of the daily entertainments and its female readers, the "gracious ladies" whom Lauretta, the first narrator, openly addresses in the first tale of the entire volume, the misogynist story of Salardo, who disregards the first "sensible and reasonable" rule imparted by his dying father, that he should never reveal any secret to his wife (Straparola [1550–3] 2015: 51, 53).[5] To test his wife Teodora, Salardo tries to force her to eat the falcon that, he falsely claims, was very dear to the marquis who treats him and his family with great affection and respect. Enraged, Teodora scolds her husband and refuses to eat it, and as a response he raises his hand and gives her such a violent slap on her face that leaves "her right cheek all red" (54). Dismayed by her husband's unexpected violence and immoral behavior, Teodora reports him to the marquis. We could say that Straparola's first tale stages the negotiations of power in the public (Salardo vs. the Marquis) and the private (Salardo vs. his wife) sphere. The tropes of a husband testing his wife with all sort of abuses (the well-known tale of Griselda from the tenth day of the *Decameron* comes to mind) and women's alleged unreliability are not new and show up in numerous other classic, medieval, and early modern narratives and also again in *The Pleasant Nights* (see night 2, tale 1). But what is relevant in this context is its prominent position within the collection, which contributed to make it one of Straparola's "most widely disseminated tales" (Beecher 2012: 106).[6]

The paradoxical aspect of Straparola's collection is that the act of self-transformation to improve one's social status is presented as an almost exclusively male experience, despite the allusion to the hypothetical instructions female readers may receive from *The Pleasant Nights*. Female characters tend to be either pious and stoic, as, for example, Princess Doralice (night 1, tale 4) who rejects her father's incestuous advances, or more frequently cunning and/or deceptive. Nevertheless, despite these contrasts among female characters, throughout the collection they are often static figures with immutable psychological and moral traits and whose positive or negative destiny is dictated by their immutable character, regardless of their social conditions. Let us consider the famous tale of the pig prince (night 2, tale 1). Isabella, the storyteller, opens her narration by stressing the special place man enjoys in God's eyes since He didn't create him a "brute beast" and then moves on to introduce the wonder tale of King Galeotto who had a son who, born a pig, eventually turned into a handsome young man (Straparola [1550–3] 2015: 92). Based on the narrator's initial remarks, the reader would expect a sort of moral tale, an allegorical narrative of self-discovery. However, at first the tale seems to concern more the virtuous and beautiful queen Ersilia who, while asleep in a garden, is visited by three fairies who, impressed by her "gracefulness," decide to make her *inviolabile* (inviolable) and *affatata* (enchanted) (Straparola 1927: 63). Each fairy grants the queen two gifts, the first for her and the second for her future son. As far as the three gifts for the queen are concerned, the first fairy makes her "inviolable," the second won't allow anyone to harm her, and the third wants her to become "the wisest" and "richest" woman in the world. Whereas the fairies' three rewards for the future prince are essential to the rest of the tale (the prince will be handsome, virtuous, but at birth he will have the look and manners of a pig and only after three marriages will he be able to acquire a human form), the gifts granted to the queen mother play no role in the story and are never mentioned again. This incongruity could be simply dismissed as a "blunted motif," which, however, as Max Lüthi underscores, is never a meaningless detail but rather an allusion to a deeper, and less visible, narrative coherence (Lüthi 1987: 65).

It is interesting to note that the adjective "inviolable," which is repeated twice to indicate the main gift given to the queen by the three fairies, certainly can't be applied to the three destitute girls who are forced to marry the bestial prince. The pig's three wives are first and foremost "violable" women and as such they enter the narrative. He gores the first two to death when they plot to kill him rather than to yield to his beastly sexual advances. Each of them, including the third and luckier one, is violated by the pig covered in "stinking dung." Whereas thanks to the fairies the queen can't be harmed, the pig prince's third wife, Meldina, survives her ordeal only because she literally embraces her degrading experience: she welcomes the "filthy" pig in her bed (Straparola [1550–3] 2015: 95). Unlike Marie-Catherine d'Aulnoy's late seventeenth-century rewriting "Prince Marcassin" that connects the prince's transformation to a process of acculturation, no moral message is explicitly detectable at the end of Straparola's tale, apart from the predictable allusion to love's transformative power. The key to the tale is in Meldina's cryptic justification for marrying the pig. When the queen tries to convince her to refuse her son's request, Meldina recites a brief poem stressing the importance of modesty, honesty, and meekness ("The precious and rare gift / that you have in your hands, hold tight").[7] As an indigent young woman, she can't say no to a prince's offer even if he is a beast who previously murdered her two sisters. At the end of the tale, what lingers in a modern reader's mind is the insistence on the violability of the female characters, including the queen, whose safety (no one will be able to violate her, says the second fairy) is nothing but an act of magic, a fairy's precious gift. Thus, we could infer that whereas male characters articulate a natural dominance, female characters' power can only have a "supernatural," magical connotation.

The riddles following each of Straparola's tales are usually dismissed as unnecessary addenda and usually omitted from anthologies of classic fairy tales also because of their often crude and vulgar content.[8] In a few instances, however, the riddles are succinct and powerful texts that may even enlighten the meaning of the tale they follow. The third tale of the second night, for instance, ends with a riddle in which a mysterious "refined and beautiful" female speaker states that she responds to innumerable abuses with meek kindness. Even though a "mother" and a "daughter" take turns in whipping her she covers "everyone's shoulders and hips," and everyone can "use" her (Straparola [1550–3] 2015: 112–13). When she finally reaches old age, the riddle continues, she is "beaten and mistreated" by men. Before learning from the narrator, Lionora, that the poem in fact regards a fine piece of cloth that women first "beat" with scissors and needles and then men use as paper to write on, we can't help but perceive the short poem as a brief and effective summary of a modest woman's biography, from her childhood to her senior years, and the power relations between women and men that underpin this biography. It is worth mentioning that this riddle follows the story of a young woman, Teodosia, who only thanks to God's intervention is able to stave off the sexual demands of a man who, when she "miraculously disappears," satisfies his physical urge by groping and kissing the pots, pans, and brushes lying in the kitchen (111).

Particularly puzzling seems Straparola's choice to pair up the famous tale of the enchanted cat (usually known as Puss in Boots, night 11, tale 1) with a riddle that celebrates the beauty and harmony of the created world, which is accompanied by the sun, moon, and stars, like a garden is "adorned with pretty flowers" and an oak with twelve branches, which stand for the year and the twelve months (Straparola [1550–3] 2015: 397). This is unquestionably the most poetic riddle of the entire volume. It describes the world as a perfectly balanced and welcoming "earthly machine." How can we possibly reconcile this reassuring and conflict-free view of the world with the fairy-tale genre that emphasizes abuses and injustices that can only be healed through unnatural, unreal, and miraculous interventions? What is striking in Straparola's story of the "enchanted" cat is how naturally she moves through the human world, how easily she exerts her power over her human interlocutors. Unlike Perrault's Puss in Boots, Straparola's cat doesn't derive her authority from sophisticated oratorial skills.[9] In the French rewriting, the cat is not enchanted; he is only an astute "rascal" who knows how to play "cunning tricks" and pretends not to hear his poor master's plan to kill and eat him (Perrault [1697] 2001: 398–99). For his plan to succeed, in Perrault the cat first of all needs a pair of boots and a pouch to walk into the woods and catch the prey he will offer the king; later, when presenting the rabbit to the king, he makes up a name for his poor master, "The Marquis of Carabas," a title used by both the third-person narrator and the characters throughout the rest of the tale. By contrast, the Italian cat's magical power is so overwhelming that, when she is allowed to offer a hare to the king on behalf of her master, she can call him by his real name "Costantino" without attributing to him a false title and a false name. While describing her master to the king, the cat defines Costantino simply as "messer," a vague and common title used to indicate a respectable man, and instead emphasizes that Costantino is a man of great "goodness, beauty, and power" (Straparola [1550–3] 2015: 394).[10]

As the tale makes clear, the only thing that Costantino really lacks is power. The true magic accomplished by the Italian tale and its following riddle on the harmony of the world is to offer a deeply humane and uplifting view of the human condition (unlike his French counterpart, Costantino never contemplates the idea of eating his cat who helps him only out of pity for his miserable conditions) by making the wishful claim that the world is naturally benign toward those who are downtrodden, abused, and powerless, not only from a political but also from a legal standpoint, if we consider that in her will his dying mother had left Costantino, the youngest of the three brothers, her (apparently) least useful property, the female cat (Figure 8.1).

Such a hopeful perspective is to be expected from a wonder tale, but let us remember that Straparola's stories are not isolated units; they are inserted

FIGURE 8.1: Costantino Fortunato and his enchanted cat, from *Le tredici piacevolissime notte* (1608). Courtesy of the University of Colorado Boulder Libraries. Public domain.

into a broader narrative based on Boccaccian realism within a frame that is instead reminiscent of the Neoplatonic tone of Pietro Bembo's *Asolani* (1505) and Castiglione's *The Courtier*. Bembo's *locus amoenus* is a beautiful garden enclosed in an isolated castle and Castiglione's ideal court of Urbino where noble men and women debate how to achieve spiritual love become in Straparola the exotic island of Murano with its fairy-tale-like palace. This hybridism of *The Pleasant Nights* makes the contrast between real and imaginary particularly jarring. Wonder tales in which a poor man succeeds in marrying a princess clash with more genuine and detailed depictions of social tensions, as for example in the fifth tale of the third night entirely centered on an inappropriate social interaction between a noble and a commoner. The tale opens with the vivid description of the conversation between two noble brothers, Emilliano and Lucaferro, and some friends of theirs, which is however disturbed by the arrival of Emilliano's faithful cowherd Travaglino. Disregarding the most basic social norms, Emilliano gets up, leaves his aristocratic companions, and joins his cowherd for a long conversation. "Inflamed with rage," Lucaferro confronts his brother and questions his cowherd's loyalty to his master (Straparola [1550–3] 2015: 166). After a heated discussion, the two brothers agree to wager their estates on Travaglino's honesty. Lucaferro's attractive wife seduces the cowherd and demands that he bring her the head of Emilliano's beloved bull with golden horns. Travaglino complies with her request but, torn by remorse, confesses his crime to his master, thus confirming his moral rectitude. The noble Emilliano's seemingly minor faux pas in fact offers a brief but sharp glimpse into the all-too-real rules separating social classes in early modern Italy, which are easily overcome or inexistent in the wondrous world of fairy tales. In *The Pleasant Nights* issues of social and cultural inequality become particularly pronounced when its fairy tales are read next to tales following the tradition of the realistic Italian novella.

BASILE: SOCIAL INEQUALITY, FEMALE IDENTITY, AND SLAVERY

In Giambattista Basile's *The Tale of Tales*, published some eighty years after Straparola's collection of tales, reality in its most unsettling instances becomes the very fabric of the fairy tale. In Basile's volume, which unlike Straparola's contains only fairy tales and is subtitled "Entertainment for the Little Ones," the baroque emphasis on a grim view of the human condition and the created world, often depicted in its decaying physicality and ruthless abuses of power, results in a form of fairy tale in which magic and wonder don't offer conclusive solutions to cases of discrimination and injustice. In their insightful comments on the historical backgrounds of Straparola's and Basile's volumes, Suzanne Magnanini and Nancy Canepa stress the lack of social "mobility" within the

Venetian and Neapolitan societies despite the significant temporal lapse between the two seminal Italian books (Canepa 2007: 13; Magnanini 2008: 94). Unlike the Brothers Grimm's world ruled by a natural providence that spontaneously mends all wrongs, Basile's universe is an inscrutable and hostile mystery unconcerned with human beings' ordeals and social and private traumas.

Basile posits the issue of social hierarchy at the very core of his book. *The Tale of Tales* opens as follows: "A seasoned proverb of ancient coinage," Basile writes, "says that those who look for what they should not find what they would not, and it's clear that when the monkey tried putting on boots it got its foot stuck, just like what happened to a ragged slave girl who although she had never worn shoes on her feet wanted to wear a crown on her head ... and however steep her climb up was, her tumble was even greater. It happened in the manner that follows" (Basile [1634–6] 2007: 35). From this opening sentence it is evident that Basile's collection rejects one of the basic narrative conventions of the fairy-tale genre, magic's ability to redistribute power and subvert social inequality. Whereas, as Suzanne Magnanini points out, *The Pleasant Nights* doesn't seriously address the issue of slavery, *The Tale of Tales* places slavery as the fundamental narrative engine of the whole collection of tales. The pivotal character of the first European collection of fairy tales is a dark-skinned female slave, whose name is Lucia.

Comprised of fifty stories divided into five days, the frame tale of *The Tale of Tales* recounts the initial crime and nauseating punishment of a black woman who dared to ascend to a higher social level. After the initial reference comparing the slave to a monkey, the frame narrative turns to the misadventures of Princess Zoza who, suffering from melancholy, is unable to laugh. Her father the king has an oil-spouting fountain built in the middle of the main square in the hopes that seeing people slipping and falling while trying to get some oil will cheer up his daughter. Zoza bursts out in sonorous laughter only when an elderly woman, who had striven to fill a jar with oil, counters the attack of a boy who had shattered her jar with a stone by lifting up her skirt and showing him her aged genitals. Offended by the princess's laughter, the old woman curses her, saying that the only man she will be able to marry is Prince Tadeo, who, however, lies dead because of a fairy's evil spell and can be brought to life only by a woman capable of filling up a jar with her tears. The princess goes on a solitary journey and eventually finds the prince's tomb, but right before completing her task, exhausted, she falls asleep and the black slave picks up the jar and quickly completes the task by shedding just a couple of tears. The resurrected prince feels compelled to bring "that mass of black flesh" to his royal palace and marry her (Basile [1634–6] 2007: 39). The dismayed princess moves into a house across from the prince's residence and shows the now pregnant slave three magical objects granted by three fairies, the last being a hazelnut that contains a doll spinning gold. Lucia threatens to kill the fetus she carries in her belly (his name is "Little Georgie") unless she receives those magical objects, but before giving the doll to the slave princess Zoza "beg[s] the little piece of clay to instill in the slave's heart the desire to hear tales" (40, 41). To satisfy his wife's demand, Prince Tadeo hires ten expert female storytellers, who are as physically repulsive as the ladies in the *Decameron* and *The Pleasant Nights* were gracious and attractive.

Before analyzing the abhorrent demise of the black slave Lucia, which coincides with the "happy ending" of the entire book, it is necessary to approach the issue of gender and power in *The Tale of Tales*, because in the character of Lucia, Basile blends a derogatory view of female identity with a disturbing depiction of slavery. A deplorable cliché of fairy-tale studies is to assume that a female author, teller, or collector of oral fairy tales has inevitably a "better," more openminded view of female identity. By simply reading my above short summary of the first part of Basile's frame tale, it would be reasonable to conclude that *The Tale of Tales* offers an intentionally demeaning and insensitive, to say the least, view of women's conditions in seventeenth-century southern Italy. However, as stated at the beginning of this chapter, neither Straparola nor Basile make an overt and consistent denunciation of social abuses, even though some of their tales offer disturbing depictions of the miserable conditions of the lower classes. As our analysis will show, some of Basile's most complex tales are more pro-woman, so to speak, than their retellings in Laura Gonzenbach's nineteenth-century collection *Sicilian Fairy Tales*, which banalize Basile's inventive and innovative narrative twists.

An additional aspect to bear in mind in approaching Basile's often shocking tales is the key concept of "marvel" (*meraviglia* or *maraviglia*), which characterizes the Italian literary baroque. In *Moral Philosophy* (1673), Emanuele Tesauro, the author of the most extensive treatise on metaphor ever written in Western Europe, explains that marvel is a "brief rapture" that awakes us to the sudden recognition of something overwhelmingly new and unexpected. "Ignoring its origin," Tesauro claims, we feel compelled to learn its secret nature (1673: 554–5). Rephrasing Tesauro's words, we could say that the baroque marvel is a device that, aiming primarily at startling readers, may however also lead them to a sudden insight about reality. As far as *The Tale of Tales* is concerned, Basile shuns any predictable expectation we may harbor about central issues such as abuse of power, slavery, and female identity. In seventeenth-century Italy, marvel is at once what we expect from this term (marvel indicates what is majestic and stunning) and its opposite, that is, the most horrific and revolting manifestation of nature and social interactions. It is worth recalling that, as Walter Benjamin stresses in *The Origins of the German Tragic Drama*, the baroque saw nature not "in bud and bloom, but in the over-ripeness and decay of her creations" ([1928] 1990: 179). In Basile's book, marvel is simultaneously the morbid and derisive lingering on the reality of the aging female body and the denunciation of female oppression and even the shocking celebration of female social independence. In Basile, the marvelous has a multilayered function, at once shocking the readers with its pyrotechnic effects and compelling them to reflect upon the abhorrent abuses of power against those who were considered inferior because of their gender, social class, or physical deformities.

Let us examine a few tales that exemplify this paradox. The baroque's obsession with the decaying of nature and the human body in particular, along with a culturally ingrained bias against female aging, finds in *The Tale of Tales* unforgettable representations, as for example in the gruesome "The Old Woman Who Was Skinned," the tenth tale of the first day.[11] According to the female narrator Iacova's introductory remarks, this tale is about women's "accursed vice … of wanting to look beautiful" through the excessive use of cosmetics that end up damaging their faces and bodies. If women's "vanity" is reproachable in girls, it is "even more worthy of punishment" in old women who try to compete with young ladies (Basile [1634–6] 2007: 115). The tale concerns two poor old sisters who live beneath a king's house. Basile describes in detail these women's numerous physical "deformities," which they hide by remaining at home the whole day (116). The elderly women, however, repeatedly complain to the king, who has never seen them, about his most insignificant actions, such as throwing a torn-up letter or a flower's petal out of the window, which they claim, hurt them (the torn-up letter had dislocated their shoulders, for instance). Overcome by his imagination, the king becomes convinced that the complainer must be a delicate young lady and, rushing to the women's door, begs "her" to show him her beauty. One of the sisters lets the king, who can hardly control his sexual arousal, kiss one of her fingers through the keyhole, which doesn't appease the licentious king who, reminding the "girl" of his absolute power, begs the lady to satisfy his lust. Knowing that "when a superior begs for something that he's actually issuing a command," she tells him that she will sleep with him only if he receives her at night and in complete darkness (119). In a reversal of the Cupid and Psyche myth, which Basile uses in several of his tales, after possessing her the king lights a candle, realizes that a naked old woman is lying next to him, and disgusted has her thrown out of the window.[12] The woman doesn't fall to her death because her hair gets entangled in the branches of a fig tree. Some fairies, who had never laughed, happen to walk by and find the spectacle so comical that, enjoying a good laugh for the first time thanks to the woman's pitiful condition, they turn her into a beautiful girl. When the king goes to the window to see what happened to the old woman, he sees the beautiful girl and, utterly shaken and confused, rushes downstairs and begs her to marry him. At the wedding party, the young queen's envious sister insists that the queen tell her how she became so young and beautiful. Annoyed by the old woman's obstinacy, the young queen tells her that she skinned herself. The old sister convinces a barber to skin her and then bleeds to death.

Two first conclusions can be drawn from this brief summary. First, in Basile's tale power has no connection with any moral conduct. The lucky sister turned into a young woman doesn't deserve this special treatment; it's only chance and her laughable situation that bring about her transformation. What could have been her well-deserved punishment (she hangs from a tree because she lied to the king) turns into good fortune. Second, the tale depicts female identity as a result of male fantasy, something that the two old women use to profit from the king's wild imagination. As I explain in an essay on Matteo Garrone's adaptation of this story in his film *The Tale of Tales* (2015), the two old "deformed" women, hiding their repulsive bodies in the basement of the king's palace, become visible only when the king fantasizes that they are one young girl (Maggi 2017: 7). His erroneous conclusion, we should add, results from the two women's seemingly inexplicable complaints. Despite their destitute condition, the two sisters had dared to express repeated objections to the king's behavior.

As the existentialist philosopher Gabriel Marcel points out in "Ego and Its Relation to Others" written in 1941, a human being's "consciousness of existing" is strictly "linked up with the urge to make ourselves *recognized*" by others (Marcel 1962: 15; emphasis in original). Before being the object of the king's misguided lust, the two indigent and elderly sisters had learned to survive in secrecy by serving as mirror images of each other.[13] By sharing their "shameful" condition of pariahs, the two old women helped each other tolerate what Marcel calls "the wound," that is, the vague feeling, common to all human beings, of not being there or of not being totally there (16). At the same time, however, we shouldn't overlook the fact that the two women drew the king's attention by standing up to him and insisting on their alleged delicate bodies, which the king misread as an allusion to a young and graceful lady. As a result of the king's imagination, the two old women become present as one inexistent beautiful girl and their deepest desire is to embody this phantasmatic identity.

One might go so far as to say that, after dispatching the old woman to her likely death, the bewildered king returns to the window and looks down because he can't accept the discrepancy between the reality he knew (the imaginary girl who dared to criticize his actions) and the reality he saw when he lit the candle (the old woman). In both Apuleius's myth and Basile's tale, the lighting of the candle unsettles and weakens the beholder regardless of his/her social level (the powerless Psyche and the powerful king in Basile) and grants a paradoxical elevated status to the one who is exposed to the candle's light: Cupid is caught off guard and flees saddened and dismayed; however, he triggers an even deeper longing in the young Psyche who runs after him in despair. The old woman is thrown out of the window, but the result of this ruthless violence is her magical transformation into such a seductive lady that the king can't help but beg her to marry him.

This tale eloquently elucidates the complex rapport between power and chance, power and magic in Basile's collection of fairy stories. It is also crucial, however, to keep in mind the dynamics that take in a world in which power is distributed unevenly between the genders. In his film adaptation, Matteo Garrone modifies the ending, choosing a conclusion that reestablishes the just order of social and gender norms. At a royal wedding at the end of the film, the young queen suddenly realizes that the skin of her hands is rapidly deteriorating, returning to its original, and "real," condition. Realizing that the fairy's enchantment is wearing off quickly, the distressed queen hurries out of the palace and disappears from the film. Apart from being a statement of poetics about the illusory nature of any magic—his previous films, such as *The Embalmer* (2002) and *Gomorrah* (2008) exposed the grim reality of contemporary southern Italy infested by organized crime and political corruption—Garrone's interpretation also introduces a fair and just conclusion. Based on a fundamental unwritten rule of the contemporary fairy tale, we expect a (young) woman to be blessed because of her beauty and honesty, not because of a random and deceptive act of magic. In Garrone's *The Tale of Tales*, whereas the quickly aging queen runs away ashamed, her old sister doesn't die as we read in Basile, but bleeding from numerous wounds on her face and arms slowly walks up the steps leading to the main square of their village. Unlike her devious sister, the skinned old woman almost parades her "real" condition, not necessarily accepting it but certainly showing it as the obscene spectacle of her own real suffering, her inner "wound" (according to Marcel's definition), which she had previously hidden with her sister in their miserable basement.

Unlike the Italian film director, in his baroque tale Basile at once displays the incomprehensible, meaningless vagaries of human existence and shows no regard for an elderly poor woman's disquiet, while granting her lucky sister the joy of youth and beauty, the two forms of fleeting power traditionally granted to women. In another beautiful and mysterious fairy tale, however, Basile offers a radically different view of female power and female identity. In "The Three Crowns," the sixth tale of the fourth day, Basile tells the seemingly odd story of a disconsolate king who "could not have children" (Basile [1634–6] 2007: 337). Based on a sequence of subtle and overt gender-role reversals, this tale deserves a slightly more detailed summary. Basile writes that once, while in a garden, the despondent king cries out, "Oh heavens, send me an heir to my state, so that my house won't remain desolate!" and then hears a voice coming out of the bushes: "King, would you rather have a daughter who runs away from you or a son who will destroy you?" (337).[14] After consulting with the wise men of his court, the king decides that, even though honor does not usually reside among women, a daughter wouldn't be a danger for his life and his kingdom. That night, after having answered "woman, woman" (*femmena femmena*) to the voice in the bushes (Basile [1634–6] 1998: 754), the king sleeps with his wife and "after nine months he ha[s] a beautiful daughter" whom he locks up in a sturdy palace so as to protect her from her "sad destiny" (Basile [1634–6] 2007: 337, 338). The king even arranges a marriage for her with a king but when his daughter, named Marchetta, comes out of her confinement to join her future husband, a strong wind picks her up and takes her to the house of a cannibal ogress. There the girl finds an elderly lady, whom the ogress left to guard her things. The old woman tells the girl that she should hide from the cannibal but could ingratiate herself with the monster by cleaning her house and cooking a good meal, and finally warns her to show herself to the ogress only if she swears by the three crowns that she won't hurt the person who has worked hard for her. When the girl finally reveals herself, the grateful ogress promises her that she will give her a good marriage. She also gives the girl the keys to all the rooms of her house but asks her not to open the last room, because that would make her furious. Disregarding the ogress's order, Marchetta opens the door and sees three sleeping girls dressed in gold and sitting on three royal chairs. They are the daughters of "the fairy" who enchanted them because they would run a great risk unless a princess came to wake them.[15] When Marchetta walks into the room the three sleeping girls wake up hungry and Marchetta cooks some eggs for them. When the ogress comes back she becomes so angry at Marchetta that she slaps her in the face. The girl is so offended that she decides to leave despite the ogress's contrite apologies.[16] Before leaving, the girl receives two gifts from the ogress: a ring that she should wear with the stone inside of her hand and should look at it only when, in a moment of great danger, she hears her name repeated by an echo. The second gift, which the girl herself requests, are male clothes. Dressed as a man, in a forest she meets a king who is so impressed with the good manners of this youth that he takes him as his page. At court, the king's wife, the queen, falls in love with this page but since he doesn't respond to her advances, she tells her husband that the page made a pass at her. Condemned to death, while being dragged to the place of her execution Marchetta cries out: "Who will free me from the gallows [*forca*]?" (Basile [1634–6] 2007: 343; [1634–6] 1998: 766). "Orca" (the ogress), the echo replies, and Marchetta, remembering the ring she received from the ogress, looks at the stone for the first time (Basile [1634–6] 1998: 768). At this point a mysterious voice is heard saying three times: "Let her go, she is a woman!" The king demands that she tell the truth and Marchetta recounts her true story and finally the evil queen is executed and the king marries Marchetta.

"The Three Crowns" is a gender- and power-bending tale that intentionally questions the clichéd traits associated with what have become conventional fairy-tale characters. The baroque "marvel" effect is extraordinary in this tale. At the outset, it is a distressed king, and not a queen or the royal couple together, who laments his inability to have children as if giving birth were a male prerogative. Moreover, both the mysterious voice's offer in the garden and the king's response are puzzling because, if the king's concern is to find an heir to his kingdom, how will a girl who runs away solve his problem? Even though he believes that women are not honorable creatures, the king chooses a girl only to save his life because, according to the oracle, a son would murder him. Finally, the king tries to prevent his daughter from running away by locking her up. Why would her flight be her "sad destiny"?

An enlightening element in the first part of the tale is the sudden gust of wind that snatches the girl away, a clear allusion to the Cupid and Psyche myth. Marchetta's "sad destiny" equals Psyche's sacrifice to the allegedly horrendous deity before being brought from Zephyr to Cupid's abode. It is worth adding that Basile uses Apuleius's trope of the wind kidnapping the female heroine only in this tale. Marchetta's "sad destiny" is thus a journey of self-discovery similar to Psyche's, even though instead of a handsome male deity Marchetta is led to a female cannibal. In the monster's house, the girl first behaves according to societal demands (she cleans up the house and cooks) but then turns into a brave prince, rescuing three sleeping beauties (the three crowns) from their enduring slumber brought about by their mother, the ogress, who, like Marchetta's father, wishes to protect them from some sad destiny.

Marchetta's gender fluidity responds to the shifting power balance in the tale. She is female when she is asked to improve a female cannibal's living conditions according to society's most conventional demands on women (cooking and cleaning), but then acts as a man when she is expected to break the spell imposed on three sleeping beauties. Basile's intentional reversal of the reader's narrative and societal expectations leads to an additional twist when Marchetta asks the apologetic ogress for male clothes because, in the world outside the ogress's protective abode, a woman can't travel or live on her own. The king's benevolence toward Marchetta as a gentle page, whom Basile always identifies as "he" and not "she," and the queen's infatuation are well-known motifs of the fairy-tale tradition, including the false page's rejection of the queen's illicit request. The tropes of gender bending and cross-dressing had already found a very similar treatment in Straparola's famous tale of Princess Costanza (night 4, tale 1) who pursued both a traditionally female and male education: she learned to "embroider, sing, play music" but she also "devoted herself to the art of war" (Straparola [1550–3] 2015: 174). Refusing to marry below her status, Costanza leaves her father's palace, dresses as a man and, calling herself Costanzo, enters a king's service, where the queen lusts after her but, being rejected by Costanzo, convinces her husband to subject him to a number of dangerous challenges that the page/princess successfully overcomes.

It is in the finale, however, that the tale reveals its deepest originality. What saves Marchetta from being unjustly executed is the fact that she is a woman, as the disembodied voice repeats three times ("She is a woman!"). Her salvation lies in the resounding affirmation of her truthful gender identity, supported by a terrifying female creature's magical power. Basile's tale ends with this salvific truth, which is at once powerful and liberating. In this tale, Basile gives the baroque marvel a truly unique and unexpected treatment.

The originality of Basile's storytelling becomes even more evident if we take a look at the retellings of this story present in Luigi Pitrè's and Laura Gonzenbach's nineenth-century collections of Sicilian fairy tales.[17] Although these volumes supposedly gather oral narratives, their versions of Basile's literary tales are more coherent and polished, but also more conventional, especially in their depiction of female identities. One of the first tales of Giuseppe Pitrè's vast collection of Sicilian folk and fairy tales first published in 1875 is "My Three Beautiful Crowns," which is the story of a poor orphan girl who wanders alone until she reaches a palace "completely draped in black ... as though someone were being mourned" (Pitrè 2009: loc. 2303).[18] This is the residence of an empress whose three sons have gone missing. In desperation she cries out "my three beautiful crowns!" without knowing that her sons are sound asleep in a forgotten room of her large palace. Like Marchetta, the Sicilian girl wakes them up one after the other and feeds them. Instead of eggs, she gives them some chicken broth (loc. 2336). This oral version of Marchetta's story is much clearer than its baroque, and literary, predecessor.[19] Not only is the expression "three crowns" clearly directed at three princes and not at an ogress's daughters, the sexual and social roles are also clarified. She is a poor young woman and behaves as such throughout the tale. She works like a respectful maid whose kind and moral conduct is rewarded. At the end one of the princes deigns to marry her.

The tale "Zafarana," from Gonzenbach's *Sicilian Fairy Tales* (1870) primarily based on transcriptions of female narrators' accounts, answers several of the unresolved incongruities and mysteries of Basile's original story, first of all the identity of the disembodied voice (Gonzenbach 1870: 47–54). Whereas the central focus of Basile's "The Three Crowns" was the journey of its female main character through the oppressive restrictions of a male-dominated society and her final self-realization, in Gonzenbach's rendering the emphasis shifts from the female heroine to the identity of the mysterious voice, which turns out to be a cursed prince, who right before the girl's execution appears accompanied by his royal court, shouts "Stop it! Stop it!" (*Haltet ein! Haltet ein!*) and explains why the girl shouldn't be punished (53). In Gonzenbach's collection of fairy tales hailed by some misguided critics as a more "feminist" view of fairy tales, the girl Zafarana is deprived of all agency and is saved by the benign intervention of the usual prince of so many fairy stories, whereas in Basile the girl's redemption comes from her sexual identity and a caring female monster. Whereas Basile's tale empowers his heroine, Gonzenbach's and Pitrè's versions confirm Max Lüthi's opinion that the (noble) male subject tends to be the fundamental subject of European fairy tales (1976: 137). However, Lüthi's sweeping conclusion should also consider the historical evolution of the literary fairy-tale genre, especially its becoming, starting from the eighteenth century, a vehicle for conventional gender norms in modern European culture.

POWER AND ENSLAVEMENT IN BASILE'S FRAME TALE

It is time now to return to the frame tale of *The Tale of Tales* and examine its unsettling closure to explore the disturbing issue of slavery. After listening to forty-nine tales, Prince Tadeo, despite the slave's (Lucia, his wife) objections, invites Princess Zoza to tell one additional tale, in which she narrates her ordeal and the slave's deception.

Wasting no time, the prince brings the matter, and the book, to a swift conclusion: "After giving Lucia a worse dressing-down than he would have given a donkey and making her confess to the betrayal with her own mouth, he immediately ordered that she be buried alive, with only her head above ground, so that her death would be more tortured" (Basile [1634–6] 2007: 444). The slave's gruesome execution coincides with the book's happy ending. Prince Tadeo marries Princess Zoza while Lucia and her baby die a slow and excruciating death. As Steven Epstein stresses in *Speaking of Slavery*, countless medieval and early modern Italian literary works mention slavery "in passing," but in several texts, such as *The Tale of Tales*, "slaves are important to the argument or story being told" (2001: loc. 817). As Epstein correctly underscores, slaves' social role in medieval and early modern Italian literature have received scant critical attention. In Basile's collection of fairy tales slaves play both a peripheral and a central role. For example, in "The Little Slave Girl" (day 2, tale 8) the noble Lisa is turned into a slave by her jealous aunt but eventually regains her liberty. In "The Padlock" (day 2, tale 9), one of Basile's rewritings of the Cupid and Psyche myth, a poor girl encounters "a handsome slave" (*un bello schiavo*) who leads her to a marvelous underground palace where she will sleep with a mysterious lover (Basile [1634–6] 1998: 413; Basile [1634–6] 2007: 200). Despite the frequent presence of slaves (see day 3, tale 2; day 4, tale 8; day 5, tale 4), in *The Tale of Tales* the black slave Lucia stands out not only because her crime and her craving for stories set the volume in motion but also because of her disquieting execution.

In the *Motif-Index of Folk Literature,* the motif of a young woman buried alive falls into the section "S. Unnatural Cruelty," and alludes to multiple motifs under the rubric "S100–S199. Revolting murders or mutilations," especially the section "S.123," all variations of the theme "Buried alive."[20] The motif of a woman buried alive with her head above ground is already present in Straparola's *The Pleasant Nights*. In the fourth tale of the first day, we read the story of Princess Doralice who flees her father, the king of Salerno, who wants to marry her, and lands in England where she becomes the king's spouse. Reaching her in England, her resentful father stabs her two children sleeping next to her with her dagger. Her husband accuses her of murdering their children and orders that she be buried alive with her head above ground so as to make her death more painful. Her nurse travels from Salerno to England where she reveals Doralice's innocence and her father is subsequently executed. A fundamental difference between Straparola's and Basile's treatment of the motif of the lady buried alive is its location in the story. Whereas in Straparola Doralice is innocent and her unjust punishment is placed in the middle of the tale, in Basile the slave Lucia is guilty and her horrendous punishment represents the happy ending of the entire book. Moreover, Lucia doesn't die alone; she is pregnant and her fetus "Little Georgie," who had been his father's main concern at the beginning of the book (Prince Tadeo hired the ten storytellers to save his life because Lucia threatened to kill the baby by punching her belly), is not even mentioned when his mother is led to her abhorrent death.

Even before entering Basile's volume as a character, Lucia, who despite her noble marriage is almost always referred to as "the slave," appears in the first page of the book in the allusion to the obscene dance "Lucia canazza" (Lucia the Bitch), one of the unsuccessful entertainments used by the king to relieve Princess Zoza's melancholia (Basile [1634–6] 1998: 10).[21] As Canepa explains, quoting the ethnographer Roberto De Simone, this Carnival dance was very popular in early modern Naples and "derived from the ecstatic dances of possession characterized by continuous spinning" (Canepa in Basile [1634–6] 2007: 36n6; see De Simone 2002: 7). In Canepa's words, the performer, a "man in blackface, dressed as an Oriental woman," mimed a female body in a sexual act followed by "birth, death, and resurrection." Keeping in mind that "Lucia" was one of the most frequent names given to female slaves, we understand that in *The Tale of Tales* Lucia, unlike all the other characters' names in *The Tale of Tales* (Zoza, Tadeo, etc.), is not a merely fictional presence, because in her historicity she conjures up the stunning image of a female body, or better yet a female slave's body, reduced to its sexual functions and exposed to public derision (Epstein 2001: loc. 586). In the creation of the character of the pregnant slave, Basile triggers a staggering baroque effect of dialectical confrontation between reality and fiction. Lucia is first of all the subject of a public performance (the dance "Lucia the Bitch"). From being a mere spectacle in *The Tale of Tales* she acquires a fictional identity and biography (she is the character who marries a prince who had died because of a fairy's curse). Lucia is also the name of an enslaved black woman who marries a prince by displacing his intended bride, a white fairy, in the penultimate tale of the collection, "The Three Citrons." At the same time, however, her name alludes to a real historical presence, since in Naples women slaves were often given the name Lucia (Figure 8.2).

Throughout the book Lucia's very humanity is questioned, as she is often compared to animals (monkey, cricket, and donkey). Her inability to speak

FIGURE 8.2: A second slave named Lucia, from Basile's "The Three Citrons," mistakes the fairy's image for her own in the fountain, by Warwick Goble in *Stories from the Pentamerone* (1911). Courtesy of the University of Colorado Boulder Libraries. Public domain.

proper Italian makes her the object of constant derision and alludes to her subhuman identity, even though reporting a slave's alleged linguistic limits for comical effects is a trope not unique to Basile, as Michele Rak points out.[22] Throughout the book Lucia repeats one eloquent, albeit ungrammatical, sentence in which she shows no emotional or moral concern for the well-being of her unborn baby, whose life she is ready to end in the most brutal manner: "Se ... me pugni in pancia dare e Giorgiettino ammazzare" ("If ... me punch belly and little Georgie kill," Basile [1634–6] 1998: 18; [1634–6] 2007: 40). In Giorgio Agamben's words, in Western culture slaves had a "special status" because they were "at once excluded from and included in humanity, as those not properly human beings who make it possible for others to be human" (2015: 20). Adopting a well-known epithet for North African captives, Basile introduces Lucia as a "cricket-legged slave girl" (*schiava gamme-de-grillo*), thus hinting at her almost bestial appearance (Basile [1634–6] 1998: 16; [1634–6] 2007: 39). It is Prince Tadeo himself who makes the nastiest remark about the young slave. When he first lays eyes on her after being resurrected by her tears, he is shocked by "that mass of black flesh" (*quella massa de carne negra*), thus presenting Lucia as a sort of "stain" on the text, a repulsive and dark "something" that has not reached a recognizable human form.

Basile's brutal treatment of this character is unacceptable for a modern reader. It is important to underscore this essential point because for centuries the readers of Basile's masterpiece paid no substantial attention to the slave's race and the abominable treatment to which she and her unborn child were subjected, probably because her death was read as the well-known fairy-tale motif of the final punishment of the villain and the particularly cruel choice of her execution was dismissed as a bleak instance of baroque marvel. However, these facile interpretations are insufficient today and Basile's gruesome appropriation of a fairy-tale motif already present in Straparola (the honest lady unjustly punished) demands a new approach. The philosopher Alphonso Lingis rightly asks us at the beginning of *The Community of Those Who Have Nothing in Common*: "Is there not a growing conviction, clearer today among innumerable people, that the dying of people with whom we have nothing in common—no racial kinship, no language, no religion, no economic interests—concern us?" (1994: loc. 53). The image of the pregnant black woman slowly decomposing with her unborn baby is a radical departure from the fairy-tale genre's demand for unreality as Jack Zipes underscores ("fairy tales are preoccupied with removing listeners and readers from the world of reality"), reflecting instead seventeenth-century culture's emphasis on reality's most physical and repulsive manifestations (Zipes 2012: loc. 688). *The Tale of Tales*, the first European book of literary fairy tales, we could say, ends with an overwhelming irruption of reality.

Let us remember that the horror of Lucia's execution involves her child. "When a woman steps to the front of the stage of horror," the philosopher

Adriana Cavarero underscores, "the scene turns darker and, although more disconcerting, paradoxically more familiar. Repugnance is heightened, and the effect is augmented, as though horror ... required the feminine in order to reveal its authentic roots" (2009: 14). It is essential to bear in mind, however, that the book ends announcing the execution of the pregnant slave with no explicit allusion to her, and her baby's, actual death. This is not to say that *The Tale of Tales* is an unfinished text, something to be continued. The book does end and Lucia and her unborn baby are supposed to die. However, we can't help but perceive that something unresolved still lingers when the happy ending is announced and the social order is restored with the marriage of Prince Tadeo and Princess Zoza. We can't help but remember that the whole book rested on the survival of Tadeo's and the slave Lucia's son Little Georgie. Little Georgie suddenly disappears from the text and his pending death is not mentioned. Little Georgie, we could argue, is a truncated motif à la Lüthi. Let us recall that for Lüthi a truncated motif hints at a deeper narrative cohesion and calls for a closer textual analysis.

Basile's closing marvel effect lies in a horrific ending that we, the readers, can't help but perceive as a non-ending. Basile's choice of making a "mass of black flesh," as he calls the slave, the core of his entire volume is in itself a phenomenal act of baroque marvel. The black slave is the ultimate other, a subhuman human being, a sort of real monster familiar to Basile's seventeenth-century readers. However, choosing to let this monster die while pregnant added an additional layer of horror also because her fetus already has a name and ensuring his survival becomes the narrative engine of the whole book. It is at this point that, we would argue, the basic concept of hope becomes central for a correct appreciation of *The Tale of Tales*. "The world-improving imagination," the philosopher Ernst Bloch writes in the first volume of *The Principle of Hope*, "projects its images into the future" (1986: 1:98, 99). "The never-forgotten spirit of fairytale," Bloch continues, "works in the dreams of a better life, but also, and this must finally be understood, suo modo in works of art" (98). Bloch contends that "every great work of art, besides its manifest essence, is also carried towards a *latency of its coming side*, that is: towards the contents of a future which had not yet appeared in its time, in fact ultimately towards the contents of an as yet unknown final state" (98, emphasis in the original).

One might claim that Basile is essentially a racist author. "Racist" would be its audience as well, both the noble Neapolitans listening to the live performance of his tales and his contemporary readers. It is essential to understand, however, that Basile's "marvelous" finale worked in so far as it triggered in its baroque readers/listeners that "brief rapture" mentioned in Tesauro's *Moral Philosophy*, that is, a destabilizing feeling that could even manifest itself as laughter in accordance with the book's comical tone, bearing in mind however that laughter is often a coping mechanism for what we perceive as excessive and unbearable. The "latency" of Basile's seventeenth-century literary masterpiece lies in its aborted ending, in the sense that we end our reading convinced that something has remained unsaid, that the death of the baby can't be processed, can't be accepted and is thus suspended, and that the baroque *The Tale of Tales*, which repeatedly stages the horrors of an unjust and sadistic society, achieves its highest marvel by refusing to end.

The concept of "power" in early modern fairy tales is a cluster of contradictory and thought-provoking elements, which challenge many of our received ideas about this literary genre. "Power" in fact lies at the core of the fairy-tale genre and calls for a closer analysis of a variety of additional notions, such as gender biases, social inequality, and race discrimination. Straparola's and Basile's tales at once depict imaginary settings and allude to disturbing aspects of their contemporary societies. Placed in dialogue with their subsequent retellings and rewritings, they turn into powerful and unforgettable commentaries on the human condition.

NOTES

Introduction

1. I borrow "Age of the Marvelous" from Joy Kenseth's exhibition catalog (1991). I base my discussion here on my own book (Magnanini 2008) and a number of literary and historical studies of the marvelous (Campbell 1999; Daston and Park 1998; Findlen 1994; Greenblatt 1991; Hathaway 1968).
2. The discussion of the hydra here is based on Magnanini (2008: 117–43).
3. For an insightful reading of this frontispiece, see Snyder (2016: 78–9).
4. For early theoretical discussions of the genre, see Bottigheimer (2012).
5. See the notes to Donato Pirovano's edition of *Le piacevoli notti* (Straparola 2000) for more information on Straparola's borrowings from Boccaccio and other authors.
6. For more examples of *cantari*, see Segarizzi's lavishly illustrated bibliography of the holdings of popular imprints at the Marciana Library in Venice (Segarizzi 1913).
7. "Cum certi contrapesi sepe fare,/conciò la pistarola ad un segnazo/ed ambe due le mane via dal brazo."
8. "È del poeta il fin la meraviglia."
9. "Maistrata de più arte e più mestere,/e perchè non potëa laborare/maestrava le pucelle a recamare."
10. For variants and antecedent on this tale-type, see Beecher (2012: 1:571–603).
11. "E quei cagnoli se gli misse al lato, / Gridando forte con parole strane, / Dicendo, putana, con chi hai generato? / Che in adulterio sei stata con un cane / Io ti prometto per l'alto Dio beato / Che 'l ti convien morir per le mie mane, / In modo, tal che così arrabbiata / Gridando for di camera fu andata."

Chapter 1

1. For accounts of the significance of Straparola in the advent of the modern European fairy tale, see Bottigheimer (2002) and Magnanini (2008). Ziolkowski (2010) significantly dissents from Bottigheimer's assignation of the origin of the fairy tale to Straparola.
2. For a survey of the role of Boccaccio's plots, primarily from *The Decameron*, on the drama of the sixteenth and seventeenth centuries, see Wright (1957: 175–88,

196–260). On Shakespeare's relationship to both Italian prose and theater, see Clubb (2002: 32–46). For a more recent reading of the Italian novella and Shakespeare, see Walter (2019).

3. To take one example, Artese (2015: 173–209) examines the oral, folktale sources for *Cymbeline*, and Valerie Wayne (2009: 163–87) explores the written, romance tradition behind the same play. In neither case can it be said with any certainty that Shakespeare had heard or read most of the materials. However, together they suggest the richness of the romance and folktale traditions that lie somewhere in the background of the play.

4. "Written for noble players [the Queen's Men], who, fallen on evil days, gave it to country audiences, an Induction which shewed country folk entertaining strayed courtly players supplied a looking glass or mirror for actual performance" (Bradbrook 1962: 328).

5. Ser Giovanni's version is similar to the much earlier story in Johannes de Alta Silva's *Dolopathos* (Esposito 1974: xix), written in France around the end of the twelfth century, itself a later revision of the tales of the Seven Sages, which circulated from India to Europe. *Dolopathos* also contains a version of "The Maiden Seeks Her Brothers" tale, which appears to be related to parts of *Cymbeline* (Artese 2015: 182).

6. For instances of the sleeping potion in the early Italian fairy tale, see Straparola, night one, tale four (1.4); Basile, day three, story five (3.5).

7. For folktale variants of the casket trial in which the woman makes the choice, see Artese (2015: 104). Walter (2019: 50–5) provides two instances of male choice: the story of Barlaam and Josaphat, a Christianized version of the life of the Buddha in the *Golden Legend*, and *The Decameron* 10.1.

8. By contrast, both Straparola (8.4) and Basile (3.4, 4.1) construct stories around rings with magical powers. There is also, of course, the longer of tradition of rings of great power in the romance tradition, which Shakespeare would have known from, among other places, Canace's ring in Chaucer's *The Squire's Tale* and Spenser's use of Canace's ring in the second part of *The Faerie Queene* (1596).

9. See also Karen Newman (1987) for a feminist account of the play's "traffic in women" that emphasizes the difference made by a woman's manipulation of the tokens of exchange, the ring in particular, at the end of the play.

10. See Artese (2015: 122–5) on folktale analogues for the woman as royal physician, which can be also found in early modern fairy tales including Straparola (5.2) and Basile (2.2, 2.5, 2.6, and 5.1).

11. "I cannot reconcile my heart to Bertram; a man noble without generosity, and young without truth; who marries Helen as a coward, and leaves her as a profligate: when she is dead by his unkindness, sneaks home to a second marriage, is accused by a woman whom he has wronged, defends himself by falsehood, and is dismissed to happiness" (Johnson 1968: 7:404).

12. Gorfain names Diana's riddle as a "neck riddle." It "demonstrates a link between the riddle, redemption and pregnancy, for the expectant Helena is called the riddle answer and also Diana's bail" (Gorfain 1977: 155).

13. Valerie Wayne intriguingly argues that the medieval *Book of Taliesin* contains the wager plot, the emphasis on Welsh, and thus British identity, and a version of the Queen-Cloten relationship (2009: 174–5). It is possible that Shakespeare knew of the stories at second hand during a period when Welsh-British identity was of importance to him, partly due to conflict between Prince Henry Frederick and his father, James I, over the son's desire to be invested with the title of Prince of Wales. (There had been no Prince of Wales since the death of Prince Arthur in 1502.)

Chapter 2

1. On the establishment of an Ottoman canon, see Kuru (2007), and on the possibilities of different approaches, see Kuru (2014).
2. *Mesnevi* (*mesnevī/mathnawi*) is a poem that consists of rhymed couplets (aa bb cc …); its length and topic is not predetermined. Both in Persian and Ottoman literature, it was a favorite form to narrate stories. For a discussion of the genre, see Aynur et al. (2016).
3. Yet another reason for this bias is the available sources of Ottoman literary history. One of the primary sources is the poets' biographies, which by definition favor poetry over prose. For example, in her overview of Ottoman literature, Aynur states that, "when surveying the collections of authors' biographies that Ottoman literati also produced, there is no doubt that the status of poetry was higher than that of the other two [i.e., works in prose and a mixture of verse and prose]" (Aynur 2006: 487). Özön argues that the poets' biography collections cause prose to be dismissed in sources (see Özön n.d.: 31).
4. For an overview of Ottoman prose fiction and its canonical examples, see Kavruk (1998).
5. In *Eski Türk Edebiyatında Mensûr Hikâyeler* (Prose Stories in Classical Turkish Literature), Kavruk provides an overview of different attempts at categorization (1998: 12–14). Kavruk's own work is categorized into "Translated Stories," "Original Stories," "Adaptations," and "Stories in Verse Turned into Prose," and reflects general trends in the scholarship on prose stories.
6. For a canonical approach to "Turkish" fairy tales, see Boratav (1969). For an overview of the establishment of fairy-tale stories within folklore studies with an emphasis on their Turkishness, see Oğuz (2010).
7. See, for example, the canonical work by İnalcık (1973).
8. For an overview of the period and some of the canonical works, see Kuru (2013b).
9. For a discussion of the establishment of an "Ottoman/Rūmī" style, see, for example, Kuru (2013b: 548–92).
10. The question of Ottoman decline has been one of the significant discussions in Ottoman historiography. For an overview of the different discussions on the topic, see Sadji (2008: 1–40).
11. On the shared literary culture and circulation in Anatolia, see Pifer (2020).
12. The discussion of what is "original" and what is not is an ongoing one in studies of Ottoman literature, and will be discussed in detail in the following pages.
13. The reasons thereof may be many, but the criteria of modern literary production and its emphasis on originality, as well as nationalistic historiography's emphasis on "our" literary production (read Ottoman or Turkish, depending on the time period or political inclinations of the authors) versus "others" (read Persian and Arabic) should be considered as the primary motivations.
14. See also Paker (2014). For a recent study on *nazire*, see İnan (2017).
15. Layla and Majnun, Yusuf and Zulaikha, Khusraw and Shirin are stories of love and can be compared to romances. There are many translations and adaptations emphasizing different aspects (love, desire, mysticism) of these multilayered stories. For instance, for a comparative perspective on the story of Yusuf and Zulaikha and its possible readings, see Merguerian and Najmabadi (1997).
16. For a thorough discussion of translations in the Ottoman context, see Paker (2015). She also distinguishes between the terms *terceme*, which she translates as "translation," and its modern Turkish equivalent, *çeviri*, which she translates as

"translation proper." Accordingly, Paker argues that the Ottoman activity should be regarded as *terceme*, not *çeviri*, which prioritizes loyalty to the source text (2015: 31–2).

17. For the rich terminology used in adaptation studies, see Sanders (2016: 18). A similar fluidity between translations and adaptations can also be observed in the European fairy-tale tradition. See, for example, Suzanne Magnanini's work on Lorenzo Selva's *Della metamorfosi* (1582) (2011: 331–7).
18. Paker refers here to the study of Demircioğlu (2005: 109–32).
19. On the use of Rūm and Rūmī, see, for example, Kafadar (2007).
20. I am thankful to Serpil Bağcı for her help in locating this image and her insights on this paper.
21. It is remarkable that the scholarship in Turkish tends to refer to the work as a translation, while articles in English commonly refer to it as an adaptation or free adaptation. For a very detailed discussion of the work in comparison with ʿAṭṭār work, see Shepherd (1979). On different aspects of Gülşehrī and his work, see, for example, the recent works of Kuru (2013a), Yıldız (2015), and Pifer (2020). I am very grateful to Michael Pifer for his generosity in discussing with me Gülşehrī and the recent scholarship on him.
22. There is no consensus in the scholarship as to how many stories are taken from ʿAṭṭār work. According to Shepherd, the number is ten (1979: 101). For a comparative list of stories in both works, see also Shepherd (1979: 74–99). According to Kuru, there are nine stories (2013a: 282), and according to Yıldız and Sak, there are seven shared stories (Yıldız 2015: 338; Sak 2012: 658–9).
23. Sanders builds her argument on the discussion of Susan Bassnett (2014: 3).
24. For an overview on *majlis* and its importance in literary culture, see Andrews and Kalpaklı (2009). For *majlis* in the Arabic context, see Ali (2010).
25. See the section *te'līf* stories in Kavruk (1998: 70–102).
26. All translations are mine unless otherwise noted.
27. In the biography of poets by ʿAşıq Çelebi, one can find a reference to this story under Vahdī Çelebi: "His story of Anabacı, which is famous, is his edition, his invention and creation" ([1568] 2010: 349). Remarkably, ʿAşıq Çelebi does not use the word *te'līf* with reference to the story. As a further observation, while we cannot say if this is the first original, its title attracts attention. Although some story collections give titles to stories, the "title" in Ottoman storytelling seems to have another function. In many compilations, the stories are generically titled thematically, for instance, the story on women's wiles. In other collections, the titles are simply giving the plotlines or main characters. These titles seem to have functioned as references to readers or storytellers, as they usually tell the end in advance.
28. For the transliteration of the story, Kavruk (1998: 171–85).
29. For detailed information on the story, see Marzolph, van Leeuwen, and Wassouf (2004: 370–6).
30. For translations of *The Thousand and One Nights* in Ottoman Turkish, see Birkalan (2004). For a discussion of the Turkish sources of the Nights, see Karateke (2015).
31. The collection is published by Osman Ünlü with an introduction as a critical edition, see Cinānī ([16th c.] 2009).
32. "Do you see, my wife, if I were deficient in intellect [*nāqiṣetü'l-ʿaql*] like you, I would have said that you are having intercourse in front of my eyes. I would have slandered you as you did to me. But I know that this situation is a peculiarity of this

tree's natural abilities. Based upon this, I do not accuse you falsely, and remain calm and silent" ([sixteenth century] 2009: 121–3).

33. The earlier versions of this story will be discussed shortly below. I was able to locate a later version of this story in a story collection. There it is generically titled "Hikāyet-i Mekr-i Zenān" ("The Story of Women's Wiles") (17b–20a). The manuscript, titled "Ḥikāyāt" (Stories), is located at the Milli Kütüphane in Ankara, in the collection of Ankara Adnan Ötüken İl Halk Kütüphanesi, under catalog number 06 HK 3208 (*Ḥikāyāt* [Stories] n.d.). The manuscript is not dated but its last page records the 1754 earthquake, so one may presume it was compiled before this date. The story echoes Cinānī's version, and the emphasis on women's deficiency in intellect is a key part of the plot. However, the language is simpler and more colloquial, as to be expected from a lower quality manuscript—presumably one circulating among lay people. The latest reference to this story is recorded in 1944–5, in Bergama in field research conducted by one of the students of Boratav. Unfortunately, I only have access to the motif index of the frame tale, and this tale is one of the tales told by the women who are engaged in a competition as to who can cheat on their husband more successfully. However, the summary provided shows clearly that it is a retelling of this story—although in this version the woman claims that the husband has seen his own shadow, and does not ascribe magical properties to the tree (Eberhard and Boratav 1953: 322).

34. The collection of the *Forty Viziers* is believed to be based on an Arabic text (*Ḥikāyāt-ı Erbaʿīn-i Ṣubḥ u Mesā*) that has been lost. For detailed information on the source, see "Kırk Vezir Hikâyeleri İnceleme-Metin-Sözlük" ("The Story of Forty Viziers, Analysis, Text, Dictionary," 2012).

35. For a general overview of women's wiles in Islamicate literature, see Najmabadi (1999), Mills (1999, 2001), and Sayers (2014).

36. The Story of the Widow of Ephesus has been in circulation since roughly the first century and has famously been told by many different authors, among them Petronius and La Fontaine. For a general overview of the story and versions, see Goldberg (1975–2015: 860–4). For a preliminary bibliography of Widow of Ephesus, see "Bibliography of *Widow of Ephesus*" (n.d.; in the Western context). For a detailed discussion of the Ottoman versions of this story, see Cora (2020).

37. Under Islamic law, a dowry is paid to the wife in two installments. The first installment is given to the bride upon marriage, and the second installment is due upon the husband's death or divorce (Spies 2012).

38. For the symbolic significance of the beard in the Ottoman context, see Cora (2020).

39. I discuss this story within the context of the stories set in faraway lands in the last chapter of my dissertation, Cora (2018).

40. See, for example, *Ferec baʿd eş-şidde, "Freud nach Leid"* (Hazai and Tietze 2006).

41. Frenk is a complex term referring commonly to the "Western other." Baki Tezcan defines *Frenk* "as the term that corresponds to the Western use of the 'Turk' most precisely," as a "blanket term" used in reference to any Western European Christian (Tezcan 2011: 269).

42. The dog-headed people were referred to in Turkish translations of Qazwīnī's famous thirteenth-century book, *The Wonders of Creation* (see Figure 2.2). They are also familiar characters to the readers of Pliny or Heredotus. For an introduction to the depiction of the "marvelous east" see, for example, Wittkower (1942). Further research would reveal the intertextualities between different depictions of

dog-headed people. I am also thankful to Günseli Gürel for her help in navigating images of the dog-headed people in Islamicate manuscripts.
43. Actually, he is not a crown prince anymore, as he is the sole ruler of the lands. However, the original story continues to refer to him as *şehzāde* and I will also do so to avoid any confusion.
44. "Bir şehzāde otuz sene seyyāḥ olub cefā ve ezādan ṣoñra pādişāh oldugu" (TDK A 142, see Untitled Manuscript n.d.: 330b16–335a4).
45. For further information on his edition, see "Habicht, Maximillian," in Marzolph, van Leeuwen, and Wassouf (2004).
46. I am grateful to Anne Duggan for pointing out this version and its translation.
47. For a very brief overview of the fantastic elements and fairy tales, see Nikolajeva (2000: 150–4).
48. The males are instead defined "by their parentage (the miller's son), by their station in life (the prince), by their relationship to siblings (the youngest brother), by their level of intelligence (the simpleton) or by physical deformities" (Tatar 1987: 85).

Chapter 3

1. Although in early modern Italy women writers didn't immediately embrace the literary fairy tale the way writers such as Marie-Catherine d'Aulnoy and Henriette-Julie de Murat did in seventeenth- and eighteenth-century France, a few Italian women wrote texts that include features typical of fairy tales. For example, Moderata Fonte's tale of Lioncorno and Biancarisa appeared in *The Worth of Women* (1600) and Giulia Bigolina's prose romance *Urania* (1569?) includes fairy-tale motifs.
2. "Il racconto fiabesco è un'invenzione della Modernità in cui confluiscono molti antichi materiali e tecniche di una tradizione narrativa delle donne e per le donne" (my translation).
3. For more on this and other old women in Basile's book, see Ansani (1997).
4. On the connections between Basile and Apuleius, see Maggi (2015: 25–67).
5. On this story in the context of early modern science and society, see Magnanini (2008: 93–143).
6. Examples may be found in the essays cited in my first paragraph as well as in the contributions included in Haase (2004).
7. On this tale-type in connection to gender and the history of fairy tales, see Bottigheimer (1993).
8. On the changing story of Rapunzel, see Warner (2010).
9. For more about this belief see Mazzoni (2002: 11–59) and Magnanini (2008: 70–92).
10. For more on these two tales in relation to twentieth-century representation of dolls in children's literature by women, see Mazzoni (2012).
11. On this film, see Mazzoni (2017).

Chapter 4

1. An earlier anthology of medieval tales translated by Virginia Skord Waters, *Tales of Tears and Laughter: Short Fiction from Medieval Japan* (1991), contains one story involving animal-human romance and will be of use to readers seeking greater acquaintance with medieval Japanese fiction in general. Japanese-language sources on animals and animal-human marriage in Japanese literature include Nakamura Teiri, *Nihonjin no dōbutsukan: Henshintan no rekishi* (1984); Fukuda

Akira, *Mukashibanashi kara otogizōshi e: Muromachi monogatari to minkan denshō* (2015); and Saitō Maori, *Irui no utawase: Muromachi no kichi to gakugei* (2014).

2. Scholars believe that the early eighteenth-century printing of *Otogi bunko* reused woodblocks originally produced in the latter half of the seventeenth century. It is not known what title was given to this earlier printing or who its intended audience was.
3. *Otogi bunko* was first printed with the title *Otogizōshi* in 1891. However, this term had already been applied to *Otogi bunko* nearly a century earlier: *Otogi bunko* is listed with the alternate title *Otogizōshi* in *Gunsho ichiran*, a catalog of books compiled by Ozaki Masayoshi in 1801.
4. Common alternatives to "*otogizōshi*" include "*chūsei shōsetsu*," or "medieval stories," and "*Muromachi monogatari*," or "Muromachi-era tales." Japan's medieval period is generally considered to fall between 1185 and 1603, while the Muromachi era lasted from 1336 to 1573; those who object to these designations point out that not all of the tales called such were actually produced between these dates.
5. Fairy tales may also be referred to as *mukashibanashi* (old tales) and *dōwa* (nursery tales). Like the English "fairy tale," all of these terms lack a precise, universally accepted definition. Although there is much that has been and could be said on this subject, this chapter does not aim to define the term "fairy tale" or interrogate its usefulness as a category, either within a specific cultural context or cross-culturally.
6. The story about a monkey abducting a human bride is *The Wisteria Basket* and the story about a woman marrying a giant serpent is *The Seventh Night* (also known as *The Tale of Amewakahiko*) both of which are discussed extensively in this chapter. The tale of a fox-demon seducing the emperor is *Lady Tamamo*. The latter two tales are translated in Haruo and Kimbrough (2018).
7. The fisherman who catches a turtle-goddess in his net is Urashimako (later known as Urashimatarō). Versions of this tale appear in three eighth-century texts: *The Chronicles of Japan* (*Nihon Shoki*), *The Tango Province Records of Wind and Earth* (*Tango no Kuni no fudoki*), and *Ten Thousand Leaves* (*Man'yōshū*). Although the story has changed somewhat over the centuries, it numbers among the best-known fairy tales in modern Japan.
8. The term "medieval misogyny" was coined by R. Howard Bloch in his scholarship on European literature; Tonomura argues for the extension of this concept, with modifications, to Japanese literature. Tonomura's analysis focuses on *Tales of Times Now Past*, a twelfth-century *setsuwa* collection; her discussion includes several *setsuwa* involving relationships between a human man and an animal woman, some of which would later be retold as *otogizōshi*.
9. The emperor is also more famously the descendant of the sun goddess Amaterasu.
10. The text states that Amewakahiko's father throws 苽, a variant form of the character 菰, meaning "wild rice." However, based on both the illustrations and comparison with oral folklore, it is highly likely that 苽 should instead be read as a variant of 瓜, or "melon." In a variant textual lineage of *The Seventh Night* (see note 11 below), the Milky Way is formed from the tears of Amewakahiko's wife.
11. Like many *otogizōshi*, *The Seventh Night/The Tale of Amewakahiko* is not a single text but rather a cluster of textual variants that do not necessarily share a single title. *The Seventh Night* is a literal translation of the Japanese title *Tanabata*; another, less literal possibility is "The Star Festival," a common English gloss for the holiday

celebrated on this date. The tale exists in at least twenty manuscripts, which are divided into two lineages—the scroll lineage and the bound-book lineage—each of which is largely consistent within itself. Although both lineages tell broadly the same story and have extremely similar illustrations, the bound-book lineage is almost four times as long. The oldest surviving manuscript (by a significant margin) belongs to the scroll lineage, but there is some dispute as to which lineage is closest to the urtext.

12. The less common female equivalent of *nandai muko* is *nandai nyōbō*, or "the wife's tasks."
13. One of the differences between *The Seventh Night* and "The Tale of the Rich Man Qian Luwei" is that the former is set either in Japan or an unspecified location (depending on the textual lineage) while the latter is set in China. Accordingly, I have romanized Qian Luwei as a Chinese name; the Japanese reading of the same characters would be Kan Rikugo. Qian Luwei does not appear in any Chinese sources.
14. Astronomically speaking, Altair and Vega remain at a fixed distance year-round, but in the Northern Hemisphere they are most visible at midsummer. The seventh month in the lunar calendar corresponds to August in the Gregorian calendar, but in Japan the Star Festival is now commonly celebrated in July.
15. Arguably, swan maidens need not even be birds. For instance, the selkies of Scottish folklore—seals rather than swans—fulfill essentially the same motific function.
16. Stories about human men forcibly taking heavenly maidens as wives appear in two eighth-century provincial gazetteers, *The Ōmi Province Records of Wind and Earth* (*Ōmi no Kuni no fudoki*) and *The Suruga Province Records of Wind and Earth* (*Suruga no Kuni no fudoki*). Other tales of heavenly maidens appear in different provincial gazetteers.
17. More information on Chinese variants of feathered robe tales and star-festival tales can be found in Nai-Tung Ting, *A Type Index of Chinese Folktales: In the Oral Tradition and Major Works of Non-Religious Classical Literature* (1978).
18. In the version of "Rich Man Mudsnail" most commonly told to children today, the dilemma of the interspecies marriage is resolved without any violence on the part of the wife; the mudsnail groom is smashed open and thus transformed into a human after being attacked by a crow. The theme of spousal violence has likewise dropped out of currently popular renditions of "The Frog King" in the West.
19. Unlike the scroll lineage, the bound-book lineage of *The Seventh Night* attaches a superficial Buddhist gloss to the story.
20. Vladimir Propp, father of the morphological school of folklore analysis, uses the term "lack" to describe the initial need that compels the hero to set out on his or her quest.
21. Twentieth-century ethnographers have recorded variants of "The Monkey Bridegroom" all across Japan; it is one of the country's most geographically widespread folktales and is believed to be of considerable if uncertain age.
22. *Otogizōshi* in which an inhuman bride brings wealth to her husband's household before eventually departing include *The Tale of the Wife from Inari* (*Inarizuma no sōshi*), *The Tale of the Feathered Robe* (*Hagoromo no sōshi*), *The Tale of the Crane* (*Tsuru no sōshi*), and *The Tale of the Clam* (*Hamaguri no sōshi*). The latter is translated in Haruo and Kimbrough (2018).
23. Fox wives are typically benevolent, but less uxorially inclined fox women are mischievous, even malicious.

Chapter 5

1. In his introduction to the volume on *Monster Theory* "Monster Culture (Seven Theses)," Jeffrey Jerome Cohen elaborates on the complexity of these categories and their transgressions by the monstrous, as well as the creative and critical potential of the monstrous (1996: 3–25).
2. See Tucker, "Fairy-Midwife-Witch" in the chapter "Fairies and Midwives" (2003: 63–70).
3. Paré, *On Monsters and Marvels* ([1575] 1982), ch. 9, "An Example of the Monsters that are Created through the Imagination" (38–42), and ch. 20, "An Example of the Mixture or Mingling of Seed" (67–73) (*Des Monstres et prodiges* [1971], ch. 9, "Exemple des monstres qui se font par imagination" [35–8], and ch. 19, "Exemple de la commixtion et meslange de semence" [62–8]). Kathryn A. Hoffmann (2005), examines the intersection of these medical accounts of human "anomalies" and the various spectacles of physiological difference, providing an important insight into the effect of these means of presenting and representing monstrosity. Nancy L. Canepa analyzes the reassignment of the ogre into "a realm of relative, ambivalent monstrosity in which he—or she—becomes part of a general critique of social and literary institutions" (2001: 222). This happens in part by means of an association of the ogre with the medieval/early modern fool.
4. Louveau published his translation of the first five nights as *Les Facecieuses Nuictz du Seigneur Jan François Straparole, avec les Fables et Enigmes, racontées par deux jeunes gentilzhommes et dix Damoiselles* (1560). His translation was republished in 1573 in Paris by Mathurin Martin.
5. First published as *Le second et dernier livre des facecieuses nuicts du Seigneur Jehan François Straparole: contenant plusieurs belles fables, & plaisans énigmes, racontées par dix damoiselles, & quelques gentilshommes* (1576).
6. As Bottigheimer makes clear, the French translations, published under the title *Les facecieuses nuicts*, were also quite popular, and along with the original printings of 1560, 1573 (for Louveau's translation of the first part), 1576 (for Larivey's translation of the second), and 1581/2 (for Larivey's revised and augmented edition of the full text), the collection was reprinted at least three times after that, in 1595, 1596, and 1611. See Bottigheimer (2005: 22). Straparola's tales were republished continuously throughout the second half of the sixteenth century and into the seventeenth century.
7. For information on the presentation manuscript created for Elizabeth I of England in 1559, see the Wellcome Collection (n.d.).
8. The initial printing of Boaistuau's collection was followed by subsequent editions in 1561, 1564, and 1566. Then, the collection is augmented by fourteen stories contributed by Claude de Tesserant, published separately in 1567 but joined by material from Belleforest in 1571. The collection continued to grow, reaching six volumes of material by various contributors in its 1598 iteration. Consultation of the catalog of the Bibliothèque nationale de France shows editions from 1560, 1561, 1564, 1566, 1567, 1571, 1575, 1578, 1594, 1595, 1598, and 1608.
9. In fact, Boaistuau's *Histoires tragiques* first appeared in 1559, as he was preparing his collection of *histoires prodigieuses*.
10. Belleforest took up the mantle of translator and adaptor of Bandello's tragic tales in 1564 and continued to publish these tales and many of his own (adapted from other sources) until his death in 1583, with a number of posthumous editions. Perhaps

the most popular and extensively published such tales were François de Rosset's *Les Histoires tragiques de nostre temps*, first published in 1614, augmented in 1619 and 1623, and published continuously well into the eighteenth century. Consultation of the catalog of the Bibliothèque nationale de France shows editions from 1614, 1623, 1632, 1648, 1651, 1653, 1654, 1662, 1665, 1685, 1688, 1700, 1701, and 1721. These are of Rosset's work only, and do not account for similar tales by other authors, which were also prevalent in the form of collections or individual tales that would circulate in pamphlet form.

11. "Evidence suggests that the spread of the specific conception of diabolical witchcraft across Europe originated from the Council of Basel (1431–49)" (Broedel 2013: 32).
12. See also Hudson (2018: 33–50), for a detailed analysis of witchcraft persecutions during the period in which Malory was writing.
13. See Mackay's introduction to *The Hammer of Witches* (Kramer and Sprenger 2009: 19–24), for a discussion of Satanism and sorcery.
14. For an analysis of Weyer's work, see Wilkin (2008: 7–52).
15. Rosset's stories, among others, reflect the contemporary obsession with sorcery and demonic activity. His first story, about the fall of Leonora Galigaï, focuses on her witchcraft, used to control the queen; the third, on a case of sorcery in Marseille, well known at the time; the tenth, on a disastrous demonic apparition; the twentieth, on a pact with the Devil. See the François de Rosset, *Histoires tragiques* (2001), "Histoire I: Des enchantements et sortilèges de Dragontine, de sa fortune prodigieuse et de sa fin malheureuse" ("Story I: The Enchantments and Witchcraft of Dragontine, her Prodigious Fortune and Unhappy End," 2001: 37–72); see also "Histoire III: De l'horrible et épouvantable sorcellerie de Louis Goffredy, prêtre de Marseille" ("On the Horrible and Terrifying Witchcraft of Louis Goffredy, a priest in Marseille," 102–32); "Histoire X: D'un demon qui apparaissait en forme de demoiselle au lieutenant du chevalier du guet de la ville de Lyon. De leur accointance charnelle, et de la fin malheureuse qui en succéda" ("On a Demon who Appeared in the Form of a Young Lady to a Lieutenant of the Knights of the Watch in the City of Lyon. On their Carnal Union, and the Unhappy End that Followed," 251–61); "Histoire XX: Des horribles excès commis par une religieuse à l'instigation du diable" ("The Horrible Excesses Committed by a Nun at the Instigation of the Devil," 428–42).
16. *Metamorphoses*, book 10, verses 717–20, 115: "Borne through the middle air by flying swans on her light car, Cytherea had not yet come to Cyprus, when she heard afar the groans of the dying youth and turned her white swans to go to him" (Ovid 1977). She was also represented as having her chariot pulled by sparrows, see Cyrino (2010: 122).
17. See Ovid's *Metamorphoses*, book 7, verses 234–6 (1977: 358–9), 350–51 (366–7), 398–9 (370–1).
18. d'Aulnoy, *Contes nouveaux*, "La Biche au bois": "Chacune avait son chariot de différente manière; l'un était d'ébène tiré par des pigeons blancs, l'autre d'ivoire que de petits corbeaux traînaient, d'autres encore de cèdre et de calembour. C'était là leur equipage d'alliance et de paix; car lorsqu'elles étaient fâchées, ce n'était que des dragons volants, que couleuvres qui jetaient le feu par la gueule et par les yeux; que lions, que leopards, que panthers, sur lesquels elles se transportaient d'un bout du monde à l'autre, en moins de temps qu'il n'en faut pour dire bonjour ou bonsoir" ([1698] 2008b: 117; translations of d'Aulnoy's tales are my own).
19. Another example is the evil fairy king of "La Chatte Blanche," who arrives to claim the princess in a chariot of fire, in a scene that is not propitious (d'Aulnoy [1698] 2008b: 236).

20. The best-known representation of this scene is Raphael's fresco of "Venus on the Chariot Pulled by Doves," in the Loggia of Cupid and Psyche in the Villa Farnesina.
21. See Kramer and Sprenger, "Question Eleven: That in Various Ways Midwife Sorceresses Kill the Fetuses in the Womb and Cause Miscarriages, and When They do not do this, They Offer the New-borns to Demons" (2009: 211–12).
22. d'Aulnoy, *Contes nouveaux*, "La Biche au bois" ([1698] 2008b); *Contes des Fées*, "La Princesse Printanière," "Serpentin Vert" ([1697–8] 2008a).
23. "Ou devenez fille ou rendez-moi chat."
24. "On voyait autour l'histoire des plus fameux chats, Rodilardus pendu par les pieds au conseil des rats, Chat botté, marquis de Carabas, le Chat qui écrit, la Chatte devenue femme, les sorciers devenus chats, le sabbat et toutes ses cérémonies."
25. "il lui semblât que tant de chatonnerie tenait un peu du sabbat et du sorcier."
26. "les Demons se forment tout subit en ce qu'il leur plaist, et souvent on les voit transformer en bestes, comme serpens, crapauds, chats-huans, huppes, corbeaux, boucs, asnes, chiens, chats, loups, toreaux et autres" (Paré 1971: 82).
27. For background on this work, see Magnanini (2011: 331–8).
28. "Il n'a a point de doute, respondit alors un jeune homme des nostres, que toutes ces transmutations furent faictes par la Toute-puissance divine" (Marcellino 1582; translations from this text are my own).
29. "Vous sçavez assez, mes enfans, que ce ne sont que fables, & que le Diable ne sçauroit transmuer un corps."
30. "Qu'une forme peut estre transmuee en l'autre par la seule apparence."
31. "Que les Fees sont des serpens, c'est une pure folie de croire, & ce ne sont que contes de vieilles."
32. For more on animals in fairy tales, see Verdier (1991).
33. "Il avait une lisière avec laquelle on le soutenait, pour lui apprendre à marcher sur les pieds de derrière; on lui mettait des souliers et des bas de soie attachés sur le genou, pour lui faire paraître la jambe plus longue; on le fouettait quand il voulait gronder; enfin on lui ôtait, autant qu'il était possible, les manières marcassines."
34. "Il portait de longues vestes qui lui couvraient les jambes, un bonnet à l'anglaise de velours noir pour cacher sa tête, ses oreilles, et une partie de son groin."
35. For a different, but very important, analysis of Marcassin's hybrid nature, see Seifert (2011: 252–8). Seifert underscores the uncertainty of the outcome in "Le Prince Marcassin," in ways that echo the dilemma faced by authors of treatises on lycanthropy: "Has his hybridity really been dissolved, or does the fairies' exception cover this possibility? More generally, are we to conclude that animal appearances are not always animal essence and, contrariwise, that human appearances are not always human essence? If so, can there ever be a clear divide between humans and animals?" (2011: 257).
36. "Un enfant qui fut conceu et engendré d'une femme et d'un chien."
37. Both Boaistuau's and Paré's tales are taken for the most part from Conrad Lycosthenes's collection, *Prodigiorum ac ostentorum chronicon* (1557), particularly 397 for one of the pig stories and 656 for the dog-boy.
38. "Lequel (ainsi qu'il est écrit en Daniel cinquiesme) sentit la fureur de la justice divine si aspre, qu'il fut l'espace de sept ans chassé et exilé de son royaume, vagant par les deserts avec les bestes brutes, vivant de semblable pasture, et demeura nud en tel estat, battu du chaud, du froid, de la gresle et rousée, jusques à ce que le poil luy creut comme celuy de l'Aigle, et ses ongles comme ceux des oyseaux" (all translations of Boaistuau's stories are my own).

39. "Ce villain avoit le visage petit, les levres grosses, les yeux profondz, la couleur aduste, les cheveux herissez, la teste descouverte, les souliers de cuir de porc-espic, le saye de poil de chevre, la ceinture de joncz marins, la barbe longue et espoisse, les sourcilz qui luy couvroyent les yeux, l'estomac et le col couvert de poil comme un Ours, et un baston en la main: et estant en cest equipage quand nous le vismes entrer au Senat, nous pensions que ce fust quelque animal, ayant figure d'homme: mais apres que nous eusmes entendu la gravité de ses propos, et majesté de ses sentences, nous jugeasmes que c'estoit quelque deité: Car si la figure estoit monstrueuse, ses propos estoient prodigieux."

Chapter 6

1. All translations are my own unless otherwise noted. The original reads: "I punti di contatto con il mondo fiabesco possono essere intesi in maniera molto libera e tollerante: 'Avevamo un incontro a Bad Orb. Bad Orb è una località molto pittoresca che aveva chiesto l'ammissione alla Via delle Fiabe: sorge proprio in prossimità del percorso fiabesco e quindi è ovvio che desiderasse un posto al 'banchetto turistico'. La mia opposizione si fondava sul fatto che per salvaguardare la nostra credibilità dovevamo cercare dei riferimenti [alla fiaba, nota dell'A.] e non accogliere una località qualsiasi solo in quanto 'pittoresca'… Notai che la cittadina aveva un gran numero di fontane, e anche alcuni particolari monumenti erano fontane. Allora proposi: "Perché non vi prendete *Il Re Ranocchio*?" Il Re Ranocchio era ancora libero.' Così Bad Orb fu ammessa a far parte della Via delle Fiabe, e Ranocchio trovò la sua patria."
2. "Tanto per gli antropologi quanto nella concezione commune, la fiaba è il regno del fantastico."
3. Among the many possible references, see Jakob (2018) and Roger (2008).
4. "La terza epoca decisiva, che si prolunga fino ai nostri giorni, debutta alla fine del Medioevo. Coincide, a partire dal XIV secolo, con l'emergere della cultura urbana, della società, della cultura urbana, della società mercantile, con l'appropriazione dello spazio."
5. "Sembra che il termine [paesaggio] nasca per la prima volta in olandese—landskap—nel 1462, poi in Germania (1480), in Portogallo, Francia e in Italia. Un po' più tardi in Inghilterra e più tardi ancora in Spagna. Perché questa differenza tra i paesi? Perché intercorrono due secoli e mezzo tra l'apparizione della parola in olandese e in spagnolo? Perché la parola 'paesaggio' è una forma di rappresentazione della natura che prende la distanza dalla dimensione religiosa: il paesaggio è un soggetto laico."
6. "un paese osservato dalla bottega, dalla piazza, dall'aia, dall'osteria, dal refettorio conventuale."
7. "Il paesaggio-paese, osservato in una dimensione orizzontale priva di spessore spaziale, di rimandi pittorici, di echi affettivi, appare nelle pagine di Francesco Guicciardini e dei viaggiatori del Cinquecento ancora molto lontano dalla visualizzazione interpretativa e riflessa della pittura."
8. "Spazio da cogliere nei suoi essenziali tratti geografico-economici e nei suoi profili antropici, quasi con la sensibilità professionale del mercante e dell'agrimensore, piuttosto che da contemplare disinteressatamente per gli ineffabili piaceri dello spirito, da usare per ingiustificate *rêveries*, da consumare in morbidi circuiti suggestivi, o tanto meno da integrare in implicazioni attinenti alla sfera dello spirito e della meditazione religiosa."

9. "Nell'arte e nella trattatistica del Quattro e del primo Cinquecento, il paesaggio non arriva ad una sua piena autonomia, né possiede dignità di statuto pittorico. Può raggiungere preziose vette di raffinatissima decorazione, articolarsi in complessi edifici simbolici senza approdare ad una completa affrancazione dalla felice schiavitù del particolare." On the parallel path of landscape painting and cartography in the "age of marvelous," see also Farinelli (2013: 228–30) and Tosco (2007: 24–33).
10. "la grande letteratura tradizionalmente intenta a lavorare su archetipi, su effetti stilizzati, su *tópoi* secolari, non sempre capace di leggere e interpretare realtà nuove non contemplate negli statuti letterari."
11. "Il paesaggio inteso quale sinonimo di *locus amoenus*, ovvero sfondo ideale, retorico, privo di rapporto con la realtà, prodotto dalla stilizzazione simbolica di elementi che poco hanno a che fare con una dimensione reale e concreta."
12. Richter (1994: 82–4) correctly reminds us of the potential economic consequences of a "geo-localized" piece of literature, analyzing the success story of the *Deutsche Märchenstrasse* (German Fairy Tale Route), a German association for tourism promotion that stretches for nearly 600 kilometers from Hanau to Bremen.
13. "unità elementare di percezione, come segno all'interno di un insieme organico di segni, come sineddoche, come parte che esprime il tutto, o che lo esprime con una funzione gerarchica primaria, sia in quanto elemento che meglio d'altri incarna il genius loci di un territorio sia in quanto riferimento visivo di forte carica semantica del rapporto culturale che una società stabilisce con il proprio territorio."
14. "È un'Italia di cose e genti, di mestieri e di anti-mestieri, di affari e di malaffari, una lunga sfilata di oggetti, manufatti, prodotti, attività, messa a fuoco e identificata non dal nobile senso della vista ma da quelli più popolari del tatto, del gusto, dell'olfatto."
15. On the concept of the "upside down world" and its meaning and role in the medieval collective imaginaries, see Cocchiara (1980).

Chapter 7

1. On the fortune and debates surrounding Ariès's arguments, see King (2007).
2. All translations are my own unless otherwise noted. The Italian reads: "uno scambiamento di tempi troppo apparente" and "umilissimo e familiarissimo."
3. For more on *cantari*, see the Introduction, this volume.
4. The Italian reads "in prima giunta ha veramente viso d'una di queste novelle da veglia, come noi sogliamo dire."
5. The Italian reads: "persone favolose" would alter the novella in unacceptable ways: "dove prima ell'era una burla da uomini, ella non sia doventata da fanciulli."
6. The Italian reads: "non si è trovato scambio che non sia (per dire sinceramente) scipito e puerile," the novella was "cosa da fanciulli più che da uomini sensati."
7. Fersin translates "nibbio" as magpie, a related species.
8. I base my discussion here on Sorrentino (1935), Chiecchi and Troisio (1984), and Fragnito (2005).
9. The phrase "che prima per incantesimo di lui era gravida" becomes "che prima per lui era gravida."
10. On Selva's life and preaching, see Mazzara (1721), Piladi (1944), Zawart ([1928] 1944), and Michelson (2012, 2013: 154–6).
11. As I explain in my article in which I translate Selva's fairy tales (Magnanini 2011: 337n3), "*The Metamorphosis* was published by the Giunti press in Florence in

1583, 1591, 1598, 1608, and 1615 and in Venice in 1616 by Pietro Farri. See Piladi's bibliography of Selva's published and manuscript works (74–6). The French translation by J. Baudoin was printed in Paris in 1611 with the title *La métamorphose du vertueux, livre plein de moralité, tiré de l'italien de Laurens Selva, et mis en françois par J. Baudoin* (Mancini 1975: 205–6). In 1818, the printer Giovanni Parolari published an abridged version of *The Metamorphosis* that focuses on the plot of the romance. In a letter to his readers, Parolari explains that he has cut many of the tales because they are 'licenziose' (licentious) and excised other 'digressioni' (digressions) which 'non potrebbero lette senza sbadigli' ('cannot be read without yawning'; Selva [1582] 1818: 8)."
12. On this tradition, see also Maggi (2015: 33–4).
13. Apuleius's first-person protagonist Lucius, in donkey form, exclaims: "This was the story the boozy little dame in her dotage told the captive girl. Standing close by and listening, I was sorry, by Hercules, that I didn't have a notebook and pen so that I could take down such a charming little yarn" (Apuleius 2011: 130).
14. For more on this, see Kathleen P. Long's chapter, this volume.
15. The book concludes with Acrisio, suspecting Clori's last word was "teco" (she only manages to utter te), citing three lines from Petrarch's *Trionfo della morte*, "Cosi del mondo il piu bel fiore scelse, Non già per odio ma per dimostrarsi, Piu chiaramente nelle cose eccelse."
16. Maggi writes "Basile appropriates the classic tale and brings to the surface additional hidden possible plots lying dormant within Apuleius's myth. For Basile, the Latin tale is not a fixed, immutable message that has something to do with human soul" (2015: 33).
17. No such moral is appended to Selva's second fairy tale. The female narrator of this story, which is the eleventh tale in book 3, states that she will explain the origins of both a local proverb ("eat, drink, or scram") and the name of a fortress near Selva's home town of San Marcellino. The poor but clever protagonist Marcello acquires through hard work three magic objects that he uses to defeat a corrupt magistrate, marry the magistrate's daughter, and save his family from poverty: a cloth that produces feasts which he received from a baroness whom he served well, a flask containing ten soldiers who will do his bidding, and phial that becomes an impenetrable tower when buried.
18. See Figure 3.2, this volume, for Cruikshank's illustrations.

Chapter 8

1. On the notion of breaking the magic spell, see Zipes (1980).
2. Wayne A. Rebhorn has translated this passage as "Stories, or fables or parables or histories, or whatever you wish to call them" (Boccaccio 2013: 3).
3. Cited in Magnanini (2008: 39). As Magnanini aptly points out, fairy tales correspond to Boccaccio's fourth, and most untruthful and thus unreliable, category of storytelling (*favola*), although he was willing to identify an allegorical and thus educational meaning in some of these modest tales.
4. For an analysis of the Venetian class of "citizens," see Schmitter (2004).
5. In the "Proem" Straparola briefly describes how the gatherings took place. The host, Lady Lucrezia, decrees that first the participants would dance; then, five young girls sing a song; and finally each of the five would tell a story followed by a riddle that would be solved before moving the subsequent tale (Straparola [1550–3] 2015: 49).

6. Additional examples of contemporary tales with such trope are Matteo Bandello, *Novelle* (1554), part 1, tale 21 (the story of Ulrico) and Giraldi Cinzio, *Ecatommiti* (1565), "Deca" 5, tale 9 (the story of Parteneo and Pognira).
7. Straparola: "il dono prezioso e raro/c'hai nelle mani, fa che'l tenghi caro" ([1550–3] 1975: 1:68).
8. It is telling that in his important 1927 edition Giuseppe Rua cuts off the riddles altogether from the text and lumps them at the end of the book.
9. Louis Marin has magisterially shown this point in his essay on the transformative power of language in Perrault's tale. See Marin (1989).
10. On the Italian title "messer," see Treccani (n.d.: s.v. "Messere").
11. For an analysis of this tale, see Canepa (2003).
12. I study the myth of Cupid and Psyche in Basile in *Preserving the Spell* (Maggi 2015: 25–67).
13. For the similarities between Marcel's view and Lacan's mirror-stage, see Maggi (2017: 6). It is worth mentioning that Marcel wrote his essay during the Nazi and Fascist eras. He aimed to elucidate the link between man's uprooted condition and Fascism. He comes to the following conclusion: "The obscure consciousness that after all I am nothing but an empty void" leads us to see others as "a means of resonance or an amplifier" (Marcel 1962: 23).
14. It is worth mentioning that in their summary of Basile's tale, the Brothers Grimm simplify the voice's offer: "King, which do you want, a daughter or a son?" (Maggi 2015: 328).
15. The Italian text calls them "figlie de la fata" (Basile [1634–6] 1998: 762) although no fairy is mentioned in this tale. The distinction among the various fantastic figures typical of fairy tales (witch, fairy, ogress, etc.) is murky in Basile and it is incorrect to change "the fairy" into "a fairy" because "fairy" in Basile mainly indicates a more-than-human creature, often similar to a "witch." The ogress is a magical being, and as such can be defined as "fairy."
16. Marchetta's firm reaction to the ogress's slap recalls Salardo's wife in the first story of Straparola's book. Both women react to power when it turns into physical violence. When Salardo hits her in the face, his wife reports his crime to the marquis.
17. Luisa Rubini stresses the connection between the two tales in her note to "Zafarana" (see Gonzenbach 1999: 486–7).
18. For the tale in Italian, see Pitrè (1875: 1:93–9).
19. Pitrè does not mention Basile's "Three Crowns" as a variant of this Sicilian tale (see Pitrè 1875: 4:372–3). Pitrè finds interesting connections with early modern Italian poets, such as Torquato Tasso and Giambattista Marino.
20. *Motif-Index of Folk Literature. Electronic Edition.* Volume 5: L–Z. "S100–S199. Revolting murders or mutilations." The nineteenth-century Sicilian folktale "The Beautiful Maiden With the Seven Veils" in Laura Gonzenbach in *Sicilianische Märchen* closely echoes Basile's frame tale but the gruesome ending is replaced by a more common motif: similar to the wicked king Tebaldo's in Straparola's *The Pleasant Nights*, the deceitful slave is thrown into a cauldron with boiling oil and then tied to the tail of a horse and dragged throughout the city (Gonzenbach 1870: 73–84). For an analysis of this tale in light of Basile's frame tale, see Maggi (2015: 88–107).
21. Lucia is called "prencepessa" (princess) twice in the introduction to the fifth day (Basile [1634–6] 1998: 878 and 882). This dance is also mentioned at the beginning of the third day of *The Tale of Tales* (Basile [1634–6] 1998: 458).

22. For the trope of slaves' imperfect Italian, see Rak's footnote 17 in Basile ([1634–6] 1998: 29). See also Ferrara (1950: 320–8). Ferrara studies a fifteenth-century comic poem by Alessandro Braccesi that reports the words of a female (maybe Tartar) slave in a garbled Italian. Ferrara's article is cited in Epstein (2001: loc. 1288).

REFERENCES

Agamben, Giorgio (2015), *The Use of Bodies*, trans. Adam Kotsko, Stanford, CA: Stanford University Press.
Aldrovandi, Ulisse (1640), *Serpentum ac draconum historiae*, ed. Bartolomeo Ambrosini, Bologna: Clementem Ferronium.
Ali, Samer M. (2010), *Arabic Literary Salons in the Islamic Middle Ages Poetry, Public Performance, and the Presentation of the Past*, Notre Dame, IN: University of Notre Dame Press.
Andrews, Walter and Mehmet Kalpaklı (2009), "Toward a Meclis-Centered Reading of Ottoman Poetry," *Journal of Turkish Studies*, 33 (1): 309–18.
Ansani, Antonella (1997), "Beauty and the Hag: Appearance and Reality in Basile's *Lo cunto de li cunti*," in Nancy L. Canepa (ed.), *From Court to Forest: The Origins of the Literary Fairy Tale in Italy and France*, 81–98, Detroit, MI: Wayne State University Press.
Apuleius, Lucius (1977), *The Golden Ass: Being the Metamorphoses of Lucius Apuleius*, trans. W. Adlington, rev. S. Gaselee, Cambridge, MA: Harvard University Press, Loeb Classical Library.
Apuleius, Lucius (2011), *The Golden Ass*, trans. and ed. Sarah Ruden, New Haven, CT: Yale University Press.
Ariès, Philippe ([1960] 1962), *Centuries of Childhood: A Social History of Family Life*, trans. Robert Baldick, New York: Random House.
Artese, Charlotte (2015), *Shakespeare's Folktale Sources*, Newark: University of Delaware Press.
Ascham, Roger (1570), *The Scholemaster*, London. Available online: http://www.gutenberg.org/cache/epub/1844/pg1844-images.html (accessed July 13, 2019).
Ashliman, D. L. (2004), *Folk and Fairy Tales: A Handbook*, Westport, CT: Greenwood Press.
ʿAşıq, Çelebi ([1568] 2010), *Meşâʿirüʾş-şuʿarâ*, ed. Filiz Kılıç, Istanbul: İstanbul Araştırmaları Enstitüsü.
Aynur, Hatice (2006), "Ottoman Literature," in Suraiya Faroqhi (ed.), *The Cambridge History of Turkey*, vol. 3, 481–520, Cambridge: Cambridge University Press.

Aynur, Hatice, Müjgan Çakır, Hanife Koncu, Selim Kuru, and Ali Emre Özyıldırım, eds. (2016), *Mesnevi, Hikayenin Şiiri* [Mesnevi: The Poetry of the Story], Istanbul: Turkuaz.

Bağcı, Serpil (2000), "From Translated Word to Translated Image: The Illustrated Şehnâme-i Türkî Copies," *Muqarnas*, 17: 162–76.

Bandello, Matteo ([1554–73] 1890), *The Novels of Matteo Bandello Bishop of Agen Now First Done into English Prose and Verse by John Payne*, 6 vols, London: Villon Society.

Basile, Giambattista ([1634–6] 1848), *The Pentamerone, or The story of stories, fun for the little ones*, trans. John Edgar Taylor, illus. George Cruikshank, London: David Bogue.

Basile, Giambattista ([1634–6] 1911), *Stories from the Pentamerone*, selected and ed. E. F. Strange, illus. Warwick Goble, London: Macmillan.

Basile, Giambattista ([1634–6] 1986), *Lo cunto de li cunti*, ed. Michele Rak, Milan: Garzanti.

Basile, Giambattista ([1634–6] 1998), *Lo cunto de li cunti*, ed. Michele Rak, Milan: Garzanti.

Basile, Giambattista ([1634–6] 2007), *The Tale of Tales, or Entertainment for Little Ones*, trans. with an Introduction and Notes by Nancy L. Canepa, illus. Carmelo Lettere, Foreword by Jack Zipes, Detroit, MI: Wayne State University Press.

Basile, Giambattista ([1634–6][2007] 2016), *The Tale of Tales or Entertainment for Little Ones*, trans. with an Introduction and Notes by Nancy L. Canepa, illus. Carmelo Lettere, Foreword by Jack Zipes, New York: Penguin.

Bassnett, Susan (2014), *Translation*, London: Routledge.

Battistini, Andrea (1997), "La cultura del Barocco," in Enrico Malato (ed.), *Storia della letteratura italiana*, 14 vols., vol 5, 463–559, Rome: Salerno Editrice.

Beecher, Donald, ed. (2012), *The Pleasant Nights*, by Giovanni Francesco Straparola, ed. with an Introduction and Commentaries by Donald Beecher, trans. W. G. Waters thoroughly revised and corrected by editor, Lorenzo Da Ponte Italian Library, 2 vols, Toronto: University of Toronto Press.

Bell, Rudolph (1999), *How to Do It: Guides to Good Living for Renaissance Italians*, Chicago: University of Chicago Press.

Belsey, Catherine (2007), *Why Shakespeare?*, Basingstoke: Palgrave Macmillan.

Benjamin, Walter ([1928] 1990), *The Origin of German Tragic Drama*, trans. John Osborne, New York: Verso.

Bettelheim, Bruno (1976), *The Uses of Enchantment: The Meaning and Importance of Fairy Tales*, New York: Alfred Knopf.

"Bibliography of *Widow of Ephesus*" (n.d.), University of Saskatchewan. Available online: http://homepage.usask.ca/~jrp638/widow/widowframes/bibliof.html (accessed August 8, 2019).

Bigolina, Giulia ([1569?] 2005), *Urania: A Romance*, ed. and trans. Valeria Finucci, Chicago: University of Chicago Press.

Birkalan, Hande A. (2004), "*The Thousand and One Nights* in Turkish: Translations, Adaptations, and Issues," *Fabula*, 45: 221–36.

Bloch, Ernst (1986), *The Principle of Hope*, vol. 1, trans. Neville Plaice, Stephen Plaice, and Paul Knight, Cambridge: Cambridge University Press.

Boaistuau, Pierre (1560), *Histoires prodigieuses*, Paris: Pour Vincent Norment et Jehanne Bruneau.

Boaistuau, Pierre (2010), *Histoires prodigieuses (edition de 1561)*, ed. Stephen Bamforth, Geneva: Droz.

Boccaccio, Giovanni ([fourteenth century] 1966), *Opere*, ed. Cesare Segre, Milan: Mursia.

Boccaccio, Giovanni ([*c*. 1353] 1993), *The Decameron*, trans. Guido Waldman, ed. Jonathan Usher, Oxford: Oxford University Press.

Boccaccio, Giovanni ([*c*. 1360] 2012), "Giovanni Boccaccio's *The Genealogy of the Pagan Gods*," trans. and ed. Suzanne Magnanini, in Ruth B. Bottigheimer (ed.), *Fairy Tales Framed: Early Forwards, Afterwords, and Critical Words*, 13–21, Albany: State University of New York Press.

Boccaccio, Giovanni ([*c*. 1353] 2013), *Decameron*, ed. and trans. Wayne A. Rebhorn, New York: W. W. Norton and Company.

Boccadamo, Giuliana (2010), *Napoli e l'Islam: Storie di musulmani, schiavi, e rinnegati in età moderna*, Naples: M. D'Auria Editore.

Bonomo, Giuseppe (1958), "Motivi stregonici in una novella dello Straparola," *La rassegna della letteratura italiana*, 62: 365–9.

Boratav, Pertev Nail (1969), *Az Gittik Uz Gittik*, Ankara: Bilgi Yayınevi.

Boratav, Pertev Nail (1982), "Halk Masalları," in Pertev Nail Boratav (ed.), *Folklor ve Edebiyat 2*, 271–5, Istanbul: Adam Yayıncılık.

Bottigheimer, Ruth B. (1989), "Cupid and Psyche vs. Beauty and the Beast: The Milesian and the Modern," *Merveilles & Contes*, 3 (1): 4–14.

Bottigheimer, Ruth B. (1993), "Luckless, Witless, and Filthy-Footed: A Sociocultural Study and Publishing History Analysis of 'The Lazy Boy,'" *Journal of American Folklore*, 106 (421): 259–84.

Bottigheimer, Ruth B. (2002), *Fairy Godfather: Straparola, Venice, and the Fairy Tale Tradition*, Philadelphia: University of Pennsylvania Press.

Bottigheimer, Ruth B. (2004), "Fertility Control and the Birth of Modern European Fairy-Tale Heroine," in Donald Haase (ed.), *Fairy Tales and Feminism*, 37–52, Detroit, MI: Wayne State University Press.

Bottigheimer, Ruth B. (2005), "France's First Fairy Tales: The Restoration and Rise Narratives of *Les facetieuses nuictz du Seigneur François Straparole*," *Marvels & Tales*, 19 (1): 17–31.

Bottigheimer, Ruth B. (2009), *Fairy Tales: A New History*, Albany: State University of New York Press.

Bottigheimer, Ruth B., ed. (2012), *Fairy Tales Framed: Early Forewords, Afterwords, and Critical Words*, Albany: State University of New York Press.

Bottigheimer, Ruth B. (2014), *Magic Tales and Fairy Tale Magic from Ancient Egypt to the Italian Renaissance*, New York: Palgrave.

Bradbrook, M. C. (1962), "Peele's *Old Wives' Tale*: A Play of Enchantment," *English Studies*, 43: 323–30.

Broedel, Hans (2013), "Fifteenth Century Witch Beliefs," in Brian P. Levack (ed.), *The Oxford Handbook of Witchcraft in Early Modern Europe and Colonial America*, 32–49, Oxford: Oxford University Press.

Bullough, Geoffrey, ed. (1957–75), *Narrative and Dramatic Sources of Shakespeare*, 8 vols, London: Routledge and Paul.

Burckhardt, Sigurd (1962), "*The Merchant of Venice*: The Gentle Bond," *ELH*, 29 (3): 239–62.

Butler, Martin ([2005] 2012), "Introduction," in Martin Butler (ed.), *Cymbeline*, 1–74, Cambridge: Cambridge University Press.

Calvino, Italo (1982), "La mappa delle metafore," in Giambattista Basile, *Il Pentamerone*, ed. and trans. Benedetto Croce, Bari: Laterza.

Campbell, Mary (1999), *Wonder and Science: Imagining Worlds in Early Modern Europe*, Ithaca, NY: Cornell University Press.

Camporesi, Piero (1992), *Le belle contrade: Nascita del paesaggio italiano*, Milan: Garzanti.

Canepa, Nancy L., ed. (1997), *Out of the Woods: The Birth of the Literary Fairy Tale in Italy and France*, Detroit, MI: Wayne State University Press.

Canepa, Nancy L. (1999), *From Court to Forest: Giambattista Basile's 'Lo cunto de li cunti' and the Birth of the Literary Fairy Tale*, Detroit, MI: Wayne State University Press.

Canepa, Nancy L. (2001), "Ogres and Fools: On the Cultural Margins of the Seicento," in Keala Jewell (ed.), *Monsters in the Italian Literary Imagination*, 222–46, Detroit, MI: Wayne State University Press.

Canepa, Nancy L. (2003), "Entertainment for the Little Ones?: Basile's *Lo cunto de li cunti* and the Childhood of the Literary Fairy Tales," *Marvels and Tales*, 17 (1): 37–54.

Canepa, Nancy L. ([2007] 2016), "Introduction," in Giambattista Basile, *The Tale of Tales, or Entertainment for the Little Ones*, illus. Carmelo Lettere, Foreword by Jack Zipes, xxxiii–lxvi, Detroit, MI: Wayne State University Press.

Carney, Jo E. (2018), "The Queen's Deathbed Wish in Early Modern Fairy Tales: Securing the Dynasty," in Anna Riehl Bertolet (ed.), *Queens Matter in Early Modern Studies*, 123–40, London: Palgrave MacMillan.

Cavarero, Adriana (2009), *Horrorism*, trans. William McGuaig, New York: Columbia University Press.

Chiecchi, Giuseppe (1992), *Dolcemente dissimulando: cartelle Laurenziane e* Decameron *Censurato (1573)*, Padua: Editrice Antenore.

Chiecchi, Giuseppe and Luciano Troisio (1984), *Il* Decameron *sequestrato: Le tre edizioni censurate nel Cinquecento*, Milan: Edizioni Unicopli.

Chrétien de Troyes (1991), *Arthurian Romances*, trans. William Kibler, London: Penguin.

Cinānī ([16th c.] 2009), *Bedāyi ü'l-āṣār*, ed. Osman Ünlü, Cambridge, MA: Department of Near Eastern Languages and Civilizations, Harvard University.

Clubb, Louise (2002), "Italian Stories on the Stage," in Alexander Leggatt (ed.), *The Cambridge Companion to Shakespearean Comedy*, 32–46, Cambridge: Cambridge University Press.

Cocchiara, Giuseppe (1980), *Il Paese di Cuccagna e altri studi sul folklore*, Turin: Bollati-Boringhieri.

Cohen, Jeffrey Jerome (1996), *Monster Theory: Reading Culture*, Minneapolis: University of Minnesota Press.

Como, Michael (2009), *Weaving and Binding: Immigrant Gods and Female Immortals in Ancient Japan*, Honolulu: University of Hawai'i Press.

Conrad, JoAnn (2007), "Childhood and Children," in Donald Haase (ed.), *The Greenwood Encyclopedia of Folktale and Fairy Tales*, vol. 1, 181–5, Westport, CT: Greenwood Press.

Cora, Nazlı İpek Hüner (2018), "'The Story Has It': Prose, Gender and Space in the Early Modern Ottoman World," PhD diss., University of Chicago.

Cora, Nazlı İpek Hüner (2020), "'Isn't She a Woman?': The 'Widow of Ephesus' in the Ottoman Empire," *Journal of Near Eastern Studies*, 80: 245–65.

Corna, Francesco da Soncino ([1487] 1998), *Historia della Regina Oliva*, ed. Silvia Marchi, Pisa: Isitituti editoriali e poligrafici internazionali.

Cyrino, Monica S. (2010), *Aphrodite*, New York: Routledge.

d'Aulnoy, Marie-Catherine Le Jumel de Barneville, Comtesse ([1697–8] 2008a), *Contes des fées*, ed. Nadine Jasmin, Paris: Champion.

d'Aulnoy, Marie-Catherine Le Jumel de Barneville, Comtesse ([1698] 2008b), *Contes nouveaux ou fées à la mode*, ed. Nadine Jasmin, Paris: Champion.

D'Ancona, Alessandro, ed. (1863), *La rappresentazione di Santa Uliva*, Pisa: Fratelli Nistri.

Darnton, Robert (1984), *The Great Cat Massacre and Other Episodes in French Cultural History*, New York: Basic Books.

Daston, Lorraine and Katherine Park (1998), *Wonders and the Order of Nature 1150–1750*, New York: Zone Books.

De Simone, Roberto (2002), *Il cunto de li cunti nella riscrittura di Roberto De Simone*, Turin: Einaudi.

Demircioğlu, Cemal (2005), "From Discourse to Practice: Rethinking 'Translation' (terceme) and Related Practices of Text Production in the Late Ottoman Literary Tradition," PhD diss., Boğaziçi University, Istanbul.

Desens, Marliss C. (1994), *The Bed-Trick in English Renaissance Drama: Explorations in Gender, Sexuality, and Power*, Newark: University of Delaware Press.

Eberhard, Wolfram and Pertev Naili Boratav (1953), *Typen türkischer Volksmärchen*, Wiesbaden: F. Steiner.

Elias, Norbert ([1939] 2000), *The Civilizing Process: Sociogenetic and Psychogenetic Investigations*, trans. Edmund Jephcott, ed. Eric Dunning, Johan Goudsblom, and Stephen Mennell, Malden, MA: Blackwell Publishers.

Epstein, Stephen (2001), *Speaking of Slavery: Color, Ethnicity, and Human Bondage in Italy*, Ithaca, NY: Cornell University Press.

Esposito, Enzo (1974), "Introduzione," in Enzo Esposito (ed.), *Il Pecorone*, vii–xxxiii, Ravenna: Longo Editore.

Farinelli, Franco (2013), "Paesaggio: senso e significato," in Gianluigi Baldo and Elena Cazuffi (eds.), *Regionis Forma Pulcherrima. Percezioni, lessico, categorie del paesaggio nella letteratura latina*, 227–41, Florence: Olschki.

Fass-Leavy, Barbara (1994), *In Search of the Swan Maiden: A Narrative on Folklore and Gender*, New York: New York University Press.

Feng, Aileen A. (2017), *Writing Beloveds: Humanist Petrarchism and the Politics of Gender*, Toronto: University of Toronto Press.

Ferrara, Mario (1950), "Linguaggio di schiave nel Quattrocento," *Studi di filologia italiana*, 8: 320–8.

Ferraro, Joanne (2008), *Nefarious Crimes, Contested Justice: Illicit Sex and Infanticide in the Republic of Venice, 1557–1789*, Baltimore: Johns Hopkins University Press.

Findlen, Paula (1994), *Possessing Nature: Museums, Collecting, and Scientific Culture in Early Modern Italy*, Los Angeles: University of California Press.

Fior di virtù ([14th c.] 1953), trans. Nicholas Fersin, Washington, DC: Library of Congress.

Fiume, Giovanna (2009), *Schiavitù mediterranee: Corsari, rinnegati e santi di età moderna*, Milan: Bruno Mondadori.

Fonte, Moderata ([1581] 2006), *Floridoro: A Chivalric Romance*, ed. Valeria Finuuci, trans. Julia Kisacky, Chicago: University of Chicago Press.

Fonte, Moderata ([1600] 1997), *The Worth of Women: Wherein is Clearly Revealed Their Nobility and Superiority to Men*, ed. and trans. Virginia Cox, Chicago: University of Chicago Press.

Fox, Adam (2000), *Oral and Literate Culture in England, 1500–1700*, Oxford: Oxford University Press.

Fragnito, Gigliola (2005), *Proibito Capire: La Chiesa e il volgare nella prima età moderna*, Bologna: Il Mulino.

Fries, Maureen (1994), "From the Lady to the Tramp: The Decline of Morgan le Fay in Medieval Romance," *Arthuriana*, 4 (1): 1–18.
Frisch, Andrea (2015), *Forgetting Differences: Tragedy, Historiography, and the French Wars of Religion*, Edinburgh: Edinburgh University Press.
Fujikake Kazuyoshi (1982), "Kyōhōki ni okeru Shibukawa-han no 'Otogizōshi' no ichi," *Nihon bungaku*, 31 (7): 25–36.
Fukuda Akira (1997), *Kamigatari, mukashigatari no denshō sekai*, Tokyo: Daichi Shobō.
Fukuda Akira (2015), *Mukashibanashi kara otogizōshi e: Muromachi monogatari to minkan denshō*, Tokyo: Yayoi Shoten.
Gaisser, Julia Haig (2003), "Allegorizing Apuleius: Fulgentius, Boccaccio, Beroaldo, and the Chain of Reception," in Rhoda Schnur et al. (eds.), *Acta Conventus Neo-Latini Cantabrigiensis*, 23–41, Tempe: Arizona Center for Medieval and Renaissance Studies.
Gesner, Konrad (1558), *Historia Animalium*, vol. 3, Basel: C. Froschoverus.
Gobetti, Andrea (1986), *Le radici del cielo*, Turin: Centro di Documentazione Alpina.
Goldberg, Christine (1975–2015), "Witwe von Ephesus," in Kurt Ranke, Hermann Bausinger et al. (eds.), *Enzyklopädie Des Märchens: Handwörterbuch Zur Historischen Vergleichenden Erzählforschung*, vol. 14, 860–4, Berlin: Walter de Gruyter.
Goldberg, Christine (1997), "The Donkey Skin Folktale Cycle (AT 510B)," *Journal of American Folklore*, 11 (435): 28–46.
Gonzenbach, Laura (1870), *Sicilianische Märchen*, Leipzig: Verlag von Wilhelm Engelmann.
Gonzenbach, Laura (1999), *Fiabe siciliane*, ed. Luisa Rubini, Rome: Donzelli.
Gorfain, Phyllis (1976), "Riddles and Reconciliation: Formal Unity in *All's Well That Ends Well*," *Journal of the Folklore Institute*, 13 (3): 263–81.
Gorfain, Phyllis (1977), "Remarks Toward a Folkloristic Approach to Literature: Riddles in Shakespearean Drama," *Southern Folklore Quarterly*, 40: 143–57.
Greenblatt, Stephen (1991), *Marvelous Possessions: The Wonder of the New World*, Chicago: University of Chicago Press.
Grendler, Paul F. (1989), *Schooling in Renaissance Italy*, Baltimore: Johns Hopkins University Press.
Grendler, Paul F. (1995), *Books and Schools in the Italian Renaissance*, London: Variorum.
Haase, Donald (2004), "Preface," in Donald Haase (ed.), *Fairy Tales and Feminism: New Approaches*, vii–xiv, Detroit, MI: Wayne State University Press.
Habicht, Max, F. H. van der Hagen, and Karl Schall, eds. (1826), "Geschichte des Prinzen von Karisme und der Prinzessin von Georgien" ["The Story of the Prince of Khwarazm and the Princess of Georgia"], in *Tausend und Eine Nacht, Arabische Erzählungen, Zum ersten Mal aus einer Tunesischen Handschrift*, vol. 2, 3–33, Vienna: A. v. Haykul.
Haruo Shirane and Keller Kimbrough, eds. (2018), *Monsters, Animals, and Other Worlds: A Collection of Medieval Japanese Tales*, New York: Columbia University.
Hathaway, Baxter (1968), *Marvels and Commonplaces: Renaissance Literary Criticism*, New York: Random House.
Hatto, A. T. (1961), "The Swan Maiden: A Folk-Tale of North Eurasian Origin?," *Bulletin of the School of Oriental and African Studies*, 24 (2): 326–52.
Hazai, György and Andreas Tietze, eds. (2006), *Ferec ba'd eş-şidde, "Freud nach Leid"* (Ein frühosmanisches Geschichtenbuch), Berlin: K. Schwarz.

Hebert, Jill M. (2013), *Morgan le Fay, Shapeshifter*, New York: Palgrave MacMillan.
Herzig, Tamar (2013), "Witchcraft Prosecutions in Italy," in Brian P. Levack (ed.), *The Oxford Handbook of Witchcraft*, 249–67, Oxford: Oxford University Press.
Ḥikāyāt [Stories] (n.d.), National Library in Ankara, manuscript number: 06 HK 3208.
Historia della Regina Stella et Mattabruna, Nuovamente Ristampata (16th c.), Available online: https://books.google.com/books?id=Y-b5vgEACAAJ&printsec=frontcover&source=gbs_ge_summary_r&cad=0#v=onepage&q&f=false (accessed December 16, 2020).
Hoffmann, Kathryn A. (2005), "Of Monkey Girls and a Hog-Faced Gentlewoman: Marvel in Fairy Tales, Fairgrounds, and Cabinets of Curiosities," *Marvels & Tales*, 19 (1): 67–85.
Holt, Mack (2005), *The French Wars of Religion, 1562–1629*, Cambridge: Cambridge University Press.
Hudson, Claire (2018), "Women and Witchcraft in Thomas Malory's Le Morte D'Arthur," *Postgraduate Perspectives on the Past*, 3 (1): 33–50. Available online: https://search.informit.com.au/documentSummary;dn=692351017857524;res=IELHSS-ISSN:2397-6918 (accessed July 23, 2020).
Hunter, G. K. (1962), "Introduction," in G. K. Hunter (ed.), *All's Well That Ends Well*, xi–lix, London: Methuen.
Hutcheon, Linda (2006), *A Theory of Adaptation*, London: Routledge.
Ichiko Teiji (1955), *Chūsei shōsetsu no kenkyū*, Tokyo: Tokyo Daigaku Shuppan.
İnalcık, Halil (1973), *The Ottoman Empire: The Classical Age, 1300–1600*, trans. Norman Itzkowitz and Colin Imber, New York: Praeger Publishers.
İnan, Murat Umut (2017), "Rethinking the Ottoman Imitation of Persian Poetry," *Iranian Studies*, 50 (5): 671–89.
Istoria della Regina Stella e Mattabruna (early 19th c.), Naples.
Jakob, Michael (2009), *Il paesaggio*, Bologna: il Mulino.
Jakob, Michael (2018), *What Is Landscape?*, Trent: LISt Lab.
Johnson, Samuel (1968), *The Yale Edition of the Works of Samuel Johnson*, vols 7–8, Johnson on Shakespeare, ed. Arthur Sherbo, intro. by Bertrand Bronson, New Haven, CT: Yale University Press.
Jolles, André ([1929] 2017), *Simple Forms*, trans. Peter J. Schwartz, London: Verso.
Jorgensen, Jeana (2012), "Sorting Out Donkey Skin (ATU 510B): Toward an Integrative Literal-Symbolic Analysis of Fairy Tales," *Cultural Analysis*, 11: 91–120.
Kafadar, Cemal (2007), "A Rome of One's Own: Reflections on Cultural Geography and Identity in the Lands of Rum," *Muqarnas*, 24: 7–25.
Karateke, Hakan (2015), "The Politics of Translation: Two Stories from the Turkish Ferec ba'de Şidde in Les mille et une nuit, contes arabes," *JNES*, 74 (2): 211–24.
Katsumata Takashi (1997), "Chūsei shōsetsu 'Tanabata' to senkō bunken no kankei ni tsuite," *Nagasaki Daigaku kyōikubu jinbun kagaku kenkyū hōkoku*, 50 (4): 17–22.
Kavruk, Hasan (1998), *Eski Türk Edebiyatında Mensûr Hikâyeler* [Prose Stories in Classical Turkish Literature], Istanbul: Ministry of National Education (MEB).
Kawai Hayao (1982), *Mukashibanashi to Nihonjin no kokoro*, Tokoyo: Iwanami Shoten.
Kawamori Hiroshi (2000), *Nihon mukashibanashi no kōzō to katarite*, Suita-shi: Ōsaka Daigaku Shuppankai.
Kelso, Ruth (1956), *Doctrine for the Lady of the Renaissance*, Urbana: University of Illinois Press.
Kenseth, Joy, ed. (1991), *The Age of the Marvelous*, Hanover, NH: Hood Museum of Art.

Kepler, Johannes ([1634] 1965), *Kepler's Dream*, ed. John Lear, trans. Patricia Freuh Kirkwood, Berkeley: University of California Press.

Kieckhefer, Richard (2013), "The First Wave of Trials for Diabolical Witchcraft," in Brian P. Levack (ed.), *The Oxford Handbook of Witchcraft*, 159–78, Oxford: Oxford University Press.

Kimijima Hisako (1967), "Chūgoku no hagoromo setsuwa: sono bunpu to keifu," *Geibun kenkyū*, 24: 20–42.

Kimijima Hisako (1969), "Hagoromo oboegaki: hishō to henshin," *Geibun kenkyū*, 27: 411–22.

Kimijima Hisako (1999), "Hagoromo setsuwa no seigyō keitai ni kansuru ichishiron," *Gifu Seitoku Gakuen Daigaku kiyō: Kyōiku Gakubu, Gaikokugo Gakubu*, 37: 272–90.

King, Margaret L. (2007), "Concepts of Childhood: What We Know and Where We Might Go," *Renaissance Quarterly*, 60 (2): 371–407.

"Kırk Vezir Hikâyeleri İnceleme-Metin-Sözlük" ["The Story of Forty Viziers, Analysis, Text, Dictionary"] (2012), ed. Aziz Birinci, PhD diss., Istanbul University, Istanbul.

Kline, Daniel T. (2003), "Medieval Children's Literature: Problems, Possibilities, Parameters," in Daniel T. Kline (ed.), *Medieval Literature for Children*, 1–11, London: Routledge.

Knight, G. Wilson ([1947] 1966), *The Crown of Life: Essays in Interpretation of Shakespeare's Final Plays*, London: Methuen.

Komatsu Kazuhiko (1995), *Ijinron: minzoku shakai no shinsei*, Tokyo: Chikuma Shobō.

Komatsu Kazuhiko (2003), *Ikai to Nihonjin: emonogatari no sōzōryoku*, Tokyo: Kadokawa Shoten.

Kramer, Heinrich and Jacob Sprenger (2009), *The Hammer of Witches*, trans. Christopher S. Mackay, Cambridge: Cambridge University Press.

Kuru, Selim S. (2007), "Sex in the Text: Deli Birader's *Dâfi'ü'l-gumûm ve Râfi'ü'l-humûm* and the Ottoman Literary Canon," *Middle Eastern Literatures*, 10 (2): 157–74.

Kuru, Selim S. (2013a), "Gülşehrī The Seventh Sheikh of the Universe: Authorly Passions in Fourteenth-Century Anatolia," in Selim S. Kuru and Baki Tezcan (eds.), "Defterology: A Festschrift in Honor of Heath Lowry," special issue *of Journal of Turkish Studies/Türklük Bilgisi Araştırmaları*, 40: 280–7.

Kuru, Selim S. (2013b), "The Literature of Rum: The Making of a Literary Tradition (1450–1600)," in Suraiya Faroqhi and Kate Fleet (eds.), *The Cambridge History of Turkey*, vol. 2, 548–92, Cambridge: Cambridge University Press.

Kuru, Selim S. (2014), "Anadolu'da Türkçe Edebiyatın Büyük Dönüşümü" ["The Great Transformation of Turkish Literature in Anatolia"], *Journal of Turkish Studies = Türklük Bilgisi Araştırmaları: Yusuf Oğuzoğlu Armağanı*, 42: 137–50.

LaFleur, William (1983), *The Karma of Words: Buddhism and the Literary Arts in Medieval Japan*, Berkeley: University of California Press.

Lancre, Pierre de ([1612] 2006), *On the Inconstancy of Witches (Tableau de l'inconstance des mauvais anges et demons)*, ed. Gerhild Scholz Williams, associate eds. Michaela Giesenkirchen and John Morris, trans. Harriet Stone and Gerhild Scholz Williams, Tempe: Arizona Center for Medieval and Renaissance Studies.

Lee, A. C. ([1909] 1966), *The Decameron: Its Sources and Analogues*, New York: Haskell House.

Lerer, Seth (2008), *Children's Literature: A Reader's History, From Aesop to Harry Potter*, Chicago: University of Chicago Press.

Lewis, Franklin (2012), "One Chaste Muslim Maiden and a Persian in a Pear Tree: Analogues to Boccaccio and Chaucer in Four Earlier Arabic and Persian Tales," in Ali Ashgar Seyed-Gohrab (ed.), *Metaphor and Imagery in Persian Poetry*, 137–203, Leiden: Brill.

Liceti, Fortunio (1665), *De Monstris*, Amsterdam: A. Frisius.

Lieberman, Marcia R. (1972), "'Some Day My Prince Will Come': Female Acculturation through the Fairy Tale," *College English*, 34 (3): 383–95.

Lingis, Alphonso (1994), *The Community of Those Who Have Nothing in Common*, Bloomington: Indiana University Press.

Lippi, Lorenzo ([1676] 1748), *Il Malmantile racquistato*, ed. Anton Maria Biscioni, Venice: Stefano Orlandini.

Luginbühl, Yves (2009), "Rappresentazioni sociali del paesaggio ed evoluzione della domanda sociale," in Benedetta Castiglioni and Massimo De Marchi (eds.), *Di chi è il paesaggio? La partecipazione degli attori nella individuazione, valutazione e pianificazione*, 61–9, Padua: CLEUP.

Lupardi, Bartolomeo ([1679] 2012), "Dedicatory Letter to Signor Giuseppe Spada," trans. and ed. Suzanne Magnanini, in Ruth B. Bottigheimer (ed.), *Fairy Tales Framed: Early Forwards, Afterwords, and Critical Words*, 81–3, Albany: State University New York Press.

Lurie, Alison (1970), "Fairy Tale Liberation," *New York Review of Books*, December 17: 42–4.

Lüthi, Max (1976), *Once Upon a Time: On the Nature of Fairy Tales*, trans. Lee Chadeayne and Paul Gottwald, Bloomington: Indiana University Press.

Lüthi, Max (1987), *The Fairytale as Art Form and Portrait of Man*, trans. Jon Erickson, Bloomington: Indiana University Press.

Lycosthenes, Conrad (1557), *Prodigiorum ac ostentorum chronicon*, Basil: Henricum Petri.

Maggi, Armando (2015), *Preserving the Spell: Basile's "The Tale of Tales" and Its Afterlife in the Fairy Tale Tradition*, Chicago: University of Chicago Press.

Maggi, Armando (2017), "Identity and Hope in Matteo Garrone's Adaptation of Giambattista Basile's Tale 'The Old Woman Who Was Skinned' Read in the Light of Gabriel Marcel's and Ernst Bloch's Philosophy," *Between, Journal of the Italian Association for the Theory and Comparative History of Literature*, 7 (14): 1–11.

Magnanini, Suzanne (2008), *Fairy-Tale Science: Monstrous Generation in the Tales of Straparola and Basile*, Toronto: University of Toronto Press.

Magnanini, Suzanne (2011), "Between Straparola and Basile: Three Fairy Tales from Lorenzo Selva's *Della metamorfosi* (1582)," *Marvels and Tales*, 25 (2): 331–69.

Magnus, Olaus (1555), *Historia de gentibus septentrionalibus*, Rome: Icannem Mariam de Viottis Parmensem.

Mallette, Karla (2014), "Seven Sages of Rome: Narration and Silence," in Marion Uhlig and Yasmina Foehr-Janssens (eds.), *D'Orient en Occident: Les recueils de fables enchâssées avant les Mille et une Nuits de Galland*, 129–46, Turnhout: Brepols Publishers.

Malory, Sir Thomas (1967), *The Works of Sir Thomas Malory*, ed. Eugene Vinaver, Oxford: Clarendon Press.

Mancini, Albert N. (1975), "Il romanzo italiano nel Seicento: Saggio di bibliografia delle traduzioni in lingua straniera (Francia, Germania, Inghilterra e Spagna)," *Studi secenteschi*, 16: 183–217.

Marcel, Gabriel (1962), "The Ego and Its Relation to Others," in *Homo Viator*, trans. Emma Craufurd, 13–28, New York: Harper Torchbooks.

Marcellino, Evangelista [pseud. Lorenzo Selva] (1582), *Della metamorfosi, cioè, Trasformazione del virtuoso*, Orvieto: Rosato Tintinnassi.

Marcellino, Evangelista [pseud. Lorenzo Selva] ([1582] 1611), *La metamorphose du vertueux: Livre plein de moralité*, trans. Jean Baudoin, Paris: Charles Sevestre.

Marchi, Silvia, ed. (1998), "Introduction," in Francesco Corna da Soncino, *Historia della Regina Oliva*, 18–33, Pisa: Istituti editoriali e poligrafici internazionali.

Marie de France ([12th c.] 2018), *The Lais of Marie de France: Text and Translation*, ed. and trans. Claire M. Waters, Ontario, CA: Broadview Editions.

Marin, Louis (1989), "Recipes of Power ("Puss-in-Boots")," in *Food For Thought*, trans. Mette Hjort, 148–61, Baltimore: Johns Hopkins University Press.

Marinello, Giovanni (1562), *Gli ornamenti delle donne*, Venice: Francesco de' Franceschi.

Marzolph, Ulrich (2000), "Oriental Fairy Tales," in Jack Zipes (ed.), *Oxford Companion to Fairy Tales*, 370–4, Oxford: Oxford University Press.

Marzolph, Ulrich, Richard van Leeuwen, and Hassan Wassouf, eds. (2004), *The Arabian Nights Encyclopedia*, Santa Barbara, CA: ABC-CLIO.

Mazzara, Benedetto (1721), "Vita del Beato Evangelista di S. Marcello Min. Oss.," in *Legendario francescano*, 12 vols, vol. 1, 27–31, Venice: Domenico Lovisa.

Mazzoni, Cristina (2002), *Maternal Impressions: Pregnancy and Childbirth in Literature and Theory*, Ithaca, NY: Cornell University Press.

Mazzoni, Cristina (2012), "Treasure to Trash, Trash to Treasure: Dolls and Waste in Italian Children's Literature," *Children's Literature Association*, 37(3): 250–65.

Mazzoni, Cristina (2017), "Violence in Fairy Tales: Basile's *Lo cunto de li cunti* and Garrone's *Il racconto dei racconti*," *Annali d'Italianistica*, 35: 177–92.

Merguerian, Gayane Karen and Afsaneh Najmabadi (1997), "Zulaykha and Yusuf: Whose 'Best Story'?," *International Journal of Middle East Studies*, 29 (4): 485–508.

Michelson, Emily (2012), "Evangelista Marcellino: One Preacher, Two Congregations," *Archivio italiano per lo studio della pietà*, 25: 185–202.

Michelson, Emily (2013), *The Pulpit and the Press in Reformation Italy*, Cambridge, MA: Harvard University Press.

Miller, Alan L. (1987), "The Swan-Maiden Revisited: Religious Significance of 'Divine-Wife': Folktales with Special Reference to Japan," *Asian Folklore Studies*, 46: 55–86.

Mills, Margaret A. (1999), "Whose Best Tricks? Makr-i Zan as a Topos in Persian Oral Literature," *Iranian Studies* 32 (2): 261–70.

Mills, Margaret A. (2001), "The Gender of the Trick, Female Tricksters and Male Narrators," in *Asian Folklore Studies*, 60: 237–58.

Mitani Eiichi (1952), *Monogatari bungakushiron*, Tokyo: Yūseidō Shuppan.

Mitchell, David T. and Sharon L. Snyder (2000), *Narrative Prosthesis: Narrative and the Dependencies of Discourse*, Ann Arbor: University of Michigan Press.

Molitor, Ulrich (1489), *De lamiis et phitonicis muliebris*, Strassburg: Johann Prüss.

Monter, William (2013), "Witchcraft Trials in France," in Brian P. Levack (ed.), *The Oxford Handbook of Witchcraft*, 218–31, Oxford: Oxford University Press.

Mukasa, Shun'ichi (2008), "Saru muko wa naze korosareta no ka: mizugoi mukoiri-tan no saikōsatsu," *Jinbun ronsō*, 25: 29–40.

Nai-Tung Ting (1978), *A Type Index of Chinese Folktales: In the Oral Tradition and Major Works of Non-Religious Classical Literature*, Helsinki: Suomalainen Tiedeakatemia Academia Scientiarum Fennica.

Najmabadi, Afsaneh (1999), "Reading and Enjoying: 'Wiles of Women' Stories as a Feminist," *Iranian Studies*, 32 (2): 203–22.

Nakamura, Teiri (1984), *Nihonjin no dōbutsukan: Henshintan no rekishi*, Tokyo: Kaimeisha.

Nakamura Tomoko, Yumira Himiko, and Mamiya Fumiko (2001), "Irui kon'intan ni tōjō suru dōbutsu: dōbutsu muko to dōbutsu yome no baai," *Kodomo to mukashibanashi*, 7: 84–102.

Newman, Karen (1987), "Portia's Ring: Unruly Women and Structures of Exchange in *The Merchant of Venice*," *Shakespeare Quarterly*, 38 (1): 19–33.

Niditch, Susan ([1987] 2000), *A Prelude to Biblical Folklore: Underdogs and Tricksters*, Urbana: University of Illinois Press. (Original title *Underdogs and Tricksters: A Prelude to Biblical Folklore*.)

Nikolajeva, Maria (2000), "Fantasy Literature and Fairy Tales," in Jack Zipes (ed.), *Oxford Companion to Fairy Tales*, 150–4, Oxford: Oxford University Press.

Oğuz, Öcal (2010), "Türkiye'de Mit ve Masal Çalışmaları veya Bir Olumsuzlama ve Tek-Tipleştirme Öyküsü," *Millî Folklor*, 85: 36–45.

Olrik, Axel ([1909] 1965), "Epic Laws of Folk Narrative," in Alan Dundes (ed.), *The Study of Folklore*, 131–41, Englewood Cliffs, NJ: Prentice-Hall.

Ovid (1977), *Metamorphoses*, trans. Frank Justus Miller and G. P. Goold, Cambridge, MA: Harvard University Press.

Ozawa Toshio (1989), "Mukashibanashi ni okeru shūshi kinō," *Bungei gengo kenkyū: bungei hen*, 16: 27–39.

Ozawa Toshio (1994), *Mukashibanashi no kosumorijii: hito to dōbutsu no kon'in-tan*, Tokyo: Kōdansha.

Özön, Mustafa Nihat (n.d.), *Türkçe'de Roman* [Novel in Turkish], Istanbul: Remzi Kitabevi.

Paker, Saliha (2002), "Translation as *Terceme* and *Nazire*: Culture-bound Concepts and Their Implications for a Conceptual Framework for Research on Ottoman Translation History," in Theo Hermans (ed.), *Crosscultural Transgressions: Research Models in Translation Studies II, Historical and Ideological Issues*, 120–43, Manchester: St. Jerome Publishing.

Paker, Saliha (2014), "Tercüme, Te'lif ve Özgünlük Meselesi" ["On Translation, Te'lif and Originality"], in *Metnin Halleri: Osmanlı'da Telif, Tercüme ve Şerh* [*Te'lif*, Translation and Commentaries in Ottoman Empire], 36–71, Istanbul: Klasik Yayınları.

Paker, Saliha (2015), "On the Poetic Practices of 'a singularly uninventive people' and the Anxiety of Imitation: A Critical Re-appraisal in Terms of Translation, Creative Mediation and 'originality'," in Şehnaz Tahir Gürçağlar, Saliha Paker, and John Milton (eds.), *Tradition, Tension and Translation in Turkey*, 27–52, Amsterdam: John Benjamins Publishing.

Paré, Ambroise ([1575] 1982), *On Monsters and Marvels*, trans. and intro. Janis L. Pallister, Chicago: University of Chicago Press.

Paré, Ambroise (1971), *Des Monstres et prodiges*, ed. Jean Céard, Geneva: Droz.

Perrault, Charles (2001), "The Master Cat; or, Puss in Boots," in *The Great Fairy Tale Tradition: From Straparola and Basile to the Brothers Grimm*, ed and trans. Jack Zipes, 397–401, New York: W. W. Norton & Company.

Philips, Ambrose and François Pétis de La Croix, trans. (1708), *Turkish Tales: Consisting of Several Extraordinary Adventures, with The History of the Sultaness of Persia and the Viziers*, London: J. Tonson.

Pifer, Michael (2020), *Kindred Voices: A Literary History of Medieval Anatolia*, New Haven, CT: Yale University Press.

Piladi, Angelico (1944), *Il P. Evangelista Marcellino insigne Predicatore ed Ecclesiaste del secolo XVI*, Florence: A. Vallecchi.

Pirovano, Donato (2000), "Nota al testo," in Giovan Francesco Straparola, *Le piacevoli notti*, 2 vols, 2:805–26, Rome: Salerno Editrice.
Pitrè, Giuseppe (1875), *Fiabe, novelle e racconti popolari siciliani*, vol. 4, Palermo: Luigi Pedone Lauriel.
Pitrè, Giuseppe (2009), *The Collected Sicilian Folk and Fairy Tales of Giuseppe Pitrè*, trans. Jack Zipes and Joseph Russo, New York: Routledge.
Pliny (2006), *Natural History*, vol. 3, trans. H. Rackham, Cambridge, MA: Harvard University Press.
Propp, Vladimir ([1928] 1996), *Morphology of the Folktale*, 2nd edn., ed. and preface Louis A. Wagner, intro. Alan Dundes, Austin: University of Texas Press.
Quiller-Couch, Arthur ([1926] 1969), "Introduction," in Arthur Quiller-Couch and John Dover Wilson (eds.), *The Merchant of Venice*, vii–xxxii, Cambridge: Cambridge University Press.
Rak, Michele (1986), "Il racconto fiabesco," in Giambattista Basile, *Lo cunto de li cunti*, ed. Michele Rak, 1057–1111, Milan: Garzanti.
Rak, Michele (2007), *Da Cenerentola a Cappuccetto rosso: Breve storia illustrata della fiaba barocca*, Milan: Bruno Mondadori.
Reynolds, Kimberley (2011), *Children's Literature: A Very Short Introduction*, Oxford: Oxford University Press.
Richter, Dieter (1994), *La luce azzurra: Saggi sulla fiaba*, Milan: Mondadori.
Roger, Alain (2008), *Court traité du paysage*, Paris: Gallimard.
Ronco, Daniele (n.d.), *Il maggio di Santa Uliva: Origine della forma, sviluppo della tradizione*, Pisa: University of Pisa. Available online: http://eprints.adm.unipi.it/357/1/uliva.pdf (accessed December 16, 2020).
Rosset, François de (2001), *Histoires tragiques*, ed. Anne de Vaucher Gravili, Paris: Livre de Poche.
Rowe, Karen E. (1979), "Feminism and Fairy Tales," *Women's Studies*, 6: 237–57.
Rubini, Luisa (2007), "Fiabe in ottava rima: il cantare fiabesco a stampa (1475–1530)," in Michelangelo Piccone and Luisa Rubini (eds.), *Il cantare italiano tra folklore e letteratura*, 414–40, Florence: Olschki.
Ruch, Barbara (1971), "Origins of the Companion Library: An Anthology of Medieval Japanese Stories," *Journal of Asian Studies*, 30 (3): 593–610.
Ryūsawa Aya (2005), "'Fujibukuro sōshi emaki' ni tsuite," *Biyō*, 2: 37–60.
Sadji, Dana (2008), "'Decline' and its Discontents and Ottoman Cultural History: By Way of Introduction," in Dana Sadji (ed.), *Ottoman Tulips, Ottoman Coffee: Leisure and Lifestyles in the Eighteenth Century*, 1–40, New York: I.B. Tauris.
Saitō Maori (2014), *Irui no utawase: Muromachi no kichi to gakugei*, Tokyo: Yoshikawa Kōbunkan.
Sak, Vesile Albayrak (2012), "Eski Türk Edebiyatı'nda Tercüme Geleneği ve Bu Gelenekte Mantıku't-Tayr Tercümeleri" ["The Tradition of Translation in Classical Turkish Literature and the Translations of Mantıku't-Tayr"], *Turkish Studies*, 7 (4): 655–69.
Salisbury, Joyce E. (1994), *The Beast Within: Animals in the Middles Ages*, New York: Routledge.
Sanders, Julia (2016), *Adaptation and Appropriation*, 2nd edn., London: Routledge.
Sarnelli, Pompeo ([1674] 2012), "Forward to Giambattista Basile's *Pentamerone* (1674) and Foreward to *An Outing to Posillipo* (1684)," trans. and ed. Nancy L. Canepa, in Ruth B. Bottigheimer (ed.), *Fairy Tales Framed: Early Forwards, Afterwords, and Critical Words*, 71–9, Albany: State University of New York Press.

Sasaki Kōichi (1982), "Reiraku shita kamigami no denshō," *Nihon bungaku*, 31 (4): 36–46.
Sayers, David Selim (2014), "The Wiles of Women in Ottoman and Azeri Texts," PhD diss., Princeton University, Princeton.
Schedel, Hartmann (1493), *Liber chronicarum*, Nuremberg: Anton Koberger.
Schmiesing, Ann (2014), *Disability, Deformity and Disease in the Grimms' Fairy Tales*, Detroit, MI: Wayne State University Press.
Schmitter, Monika (2004), "'Virtuous Riches': The Bricolage of Cittadini Identities in Early-Sixteenth-Century Venice," *Renaissance Quarterly*, 57 (3): 908–69.
Segarizzi, Arnaldo, ed. (1913), *Bibliografia delle stampe popolari italiane della R. Biblioteca Nazionale di S. Marco di Venezia*, Bergamo: Istituto Italiano D'Arti Grafiche Editore.
Seifert, Lewis (1996), *Fairy Tales, Sexuality, and Gender in France, 1690–1715: Nostalgic Utopias*, Cambridge: Cambridge University Press.
Seifert, Lewis (2011), "Animal-Human Hybridity in d'Aulnoy's 'Babiole' and 'Prince Wild Boar,'" *Marvels & Tales*, 25 (2): 244–60.
Seifert, Lewis (2015a), "Introduction: Queer(ing) Fairy Tales,'" *Marvels & Tales*, 29 (1): 15–20.
Seifert, Lewis (2015b), "Queer Time in Charles Perrault's 'Sleeping Beauty,'" *Marvels & Tales*, 29 (1): 21–41.
Seki Keigo (1943), "Hagoromo kō," *Minzokugaku kenkyū*, 8 (4): 441–59.
Seki Keigo (1953), *Nihon mukashibanashi II: Honkaku mukashibanashi*, Tokyo: Kadokawa Shoten.
Selva, Lorenzo ([1582] 1583), *Della metamorfosi, cioè trasformazione del virtuoso*, Florence: Giunti.
Selva, Lorenzo ([1582] 1818), *La metamorfosi di Lorenzo Selva*, Venice: Giovanni Parolari.
Shakespeare, William (1999), *The Winter's Tale*, ed. Frances E. Dolan, New York: Penguin.
Shakespeare, William (2000a), *Cymbeline*, ed. Peter Holland, New York: Penguin.
Shakespeare, William (2000b), *The Merchant of Venice*, ed. A. R. Braunmuller, New York: Penguin.
Shakespeare, William (2001), *All's Well That Ends Well*, ed. Claire McEachern, New York: Penguin.
Shavit, Zohar ([1983] 1999), "The Concept of Childhood and Children's Folktales: Test Case—Little Red Riding Hood," in Maria Tatar (ed.), *The Classic Fairy Tales*, 317–32, New York: W. W. Norton & Company.
Shepherd, Vanessa Margaret (1979), "The Turkish Mystical Poet Gulsehri, with Particular Reference to His Mantiq Al-Tayr," PhD diss., University of Cambridge.
Shinoda Chiwaka (2007), "'Tennin nyōbō' to sekai no ruiwa," *Hiroshima Journal of International Studies*, 13: 93–119.
Skord Waters, Virginia (1991), *Tales of Tears and Laughter: Short Fiction from Medieval Japan*, Honolulu: University of Hawaii Press.
Snyder, Jon R. (2016), "Art and Truth in Baroque Italy, or the Case of Emanuele Tesauro's *Il cannocchiale aristotelico*," *MLN*, 131 (1): 74–96.
Snyder, Susan ([1993] 2008), "Introduction," in Susan Snyder (ed.), *All's Well That Ends Well*, 1–65, Oxford: Oxford University Press.
Sorrentino, Andrea (1935), *La letteratura italiana e il Sant'Uffizio*, Naples: Libreria Editrice Francesco Perella.
Speroni, Sperone (1558), *Dialoghi*, Venice: Domenico Gigli.

Spies, O. (2012), "Mahr," in P. Bearman, T. Bianquis, C. E. Bosworth, E. van Donzel, and W. P. Heinrichs (eds.), *Encyclopaedia of Islam*, 2nd edn., Lieden: Brill.

Stone, Kay (1975), "Things Walt Disney Never Told Us," *Journal of American Folklore*, 88 (347): 42–50.

Straparola, Giovanni Francesco ([1550–3] 1975), *Le piacevoli notti*, ed. Manlio Pastor-Stocchi, 2 vols., Rome: Laterza.

Straparola, Giovan Francesco ([1550–3] 1560), *Les Facecieuses Nuictz du Seigneur Jan François Straparole, avec les Fables et Enigmes, racontées par deux jeunes gentilzhommes et dix Damoiselles*, trans. Jean Louveau, Lyon: Guillaume Rouille.

Straparola, Giovan Francesco ([1550–3] 1576), *Le second et dernier livre des facecieuses nuicts du Seigneur Jehan François Straparole: contenant plusieurs belles fables, & plaisans énigmes, racontées par dix damoiselles, & quelques gentilshommes*, trans. Pierre de Larivey, Paris: Abel l'Angelier.

Straparola, Giovan Francesco ([1550–3] 1608), *Le tredici piacevolissime notti*, Venice: Zanetti.

Straparola, Giovan Francesco ([1550–3] 1882), *Les Facétieuses Nuits du Seigneur J.-F. Straparole*, 4 vols, trans. Jean Louveau and Pierre de Larivey, Paris: Librairie des Bibliophiles.

Straparola, Giovan Francesco ([1550–3] 1927), *Le piacevoli notti*, 2 vols, ed. Giuseppe Rua, Bari: Laterza.

Straparola, Giovanni Francesco ([1550–3] 2000), *Le piacevoli notti*, ed. Donato Pirovano, 2 vols, Rome: Salerno Editore.

Straparola, Giovan Francesco ([1550–3] 2015), *The Pleasant Nights*, ed., trans., and intro. Suzanne Magnanini, Toronto: Iter, Center for Reformation and Renaissance Studies.

Tatar, Maria (1987), *The Hard Facts of the Grimms' Fairy Tales*, Princeton, NJ: Princeton University Press.

Tatar, Maria (2019), "What Is a Fairy Tale?," in Nancy L. Canepa (ed.), *Teaching the Fairy Tale*, 15–23, Detroit, MI: Wayne State University Press.

Tatar, Maria, ed. and intro. (2017), *Beauty and the Beast: Classic Tales about Animal Grooms and Brides from around the World*, New York: Penguin.

Tesauro, Emanuele ([1654] 2000), *Il cannocchiale aritstotelico*, Cuneo: Editrice Artistica Piemontese.

Tesauro, Emanuele (1673), *La filosofia morale*, Venice: Pezzana.

Tezcan, Baki (2011), "The Frank in the Ottoman Eye," in James G. Harper (ed.), *The Turk and Islam in the Western Eye, 1450–1750: Visual Imagery before Orientalism*, 267–96, Burlington, VT: Ashgate.

Tonomura, Hitomi (1994), "Black Hair and Red Trousers: Gendering the Flesh in Medieval Japan," *American Historical Review*, 99 (1): 129–54.

Topsell, Edward (1608), *The History of Serpents*, London: Laggard.

Tosco, Carlo (2007), *Il paesaggio come storia*, Bologna: il Mulino.

Traxler, Hans (2007), *Die Wahrheit über Hänsel und Gretel: Die Dokumentation des Märchens der Brüder Grimm*, with photographs by Peter von Tresckow and Wilkin H. Spitta, Ditzingen: Reclam.

Treccani (n.d.), s.v. "messère." Available online: https://www.treccani.it/vocabolario/messere/#:~:text=messere%20%5Bdal%20provenz.,%E2%89%88%20_region._ (accessed January 9, 2021).

Tucker, Holly (2003), *Pregnant Fictions: Childbirth and the Fairy Tale in Early Modern France*, Detroit, MI: Wayne State University Press.

Turri, Eugenio (1998), *Il paesaggio come teatro. Dal territorio vissuto al territorio rappresentato*, Venice: Marsilio.

Ünlü, Osman (2009), "Introduction and Analysis," in Cinānī ([16th c.] 2009), *Bedāyi'ü'l-āṣār*, Cambridge, MA: Department of Near Eastern Languages and Civilizations, Harvard University.

Untitled Manuscript (n.d.), Türk Dil Kurumu El Yazması ve Nadir Eserler Kütüphanesi (TDK) [The Manuscript Library and Special Collections of Turkish Language Association], manuscript number: A 142.

Uther, Hans-Jörg (2004), *The Types of International Folktales: A Classification and Bibliography Based on the System of Antti Aarne and Stith Thompson*, FF Communications 284–6, Helsinki: Suomalainen Tiedeakatemia, Academia Scientiarum Fennica.

Varchi, Benedetto ([1548] 1858), *Opere*, 2 vols, Trieste: Sezione letteraria-artistica del Lloyd Austriaco.

Varotto, Mauro (2013), "Oltre il *locus amoenus*: le diverse geografie del paesaggio latino," in Gianluigi Baldo and Elena Cazuffi (eds.), *Regionis Forma Pulcherrima: Percezioni, lessico, categorie del paesaggio nella letteratura latina*, 1–18, Florence: Olschki.

Verdier, Gabrielle (1991), "From Dragons to Dragonflies: A Taxonomy of Creatures in the Literary Fairy Tale," *Cahiers du dix-septième*, 5 (2): 163–76.

Voragine, Jacobus de ([13th c.] 2012), *The Golden Legend: Readings on the Saints*, trans. William Granger Ryan, Intro. Eamon Duffy, Princeton, NJ: Princeton University Press.

Walter, Melissa Emerson (2019), *The Italian Novella and Shakespeare's Comic Heroines*, Toronto: University of Toronto Press.

Warner, Marina (1994), *From the Beast to the Blonde: On Fairy Tales and Their Tellers*, New York: Farrar, Straus & Giroux.

Warner, Marina, ed. ([1994] 2004), *Wonder Tales: Six French Stories of Enchantment*, trans. Gilbert Adair, John Asherby, Ranjit Bolt, A. S. Byatt, and Terence Cave, Oxford: Oxford University Press.

Warner, Marina (2010), "After Rapunzel," *Marvels & Tales*, 24 (2): 329–35.

Warner, Marina (2014), *Once Upon a Time: A Short History of Fairy Tale*, Oxford: Oxford University Press.

Warren, Roger (1998), "Introduction," in Roger Warren (ed.), *Cymbeline*, 1–77, Oxford: Oxford University Press.

Wayne, Valerie (2009), "Romancing the Wager: *Cymbeline*'s Intertexts," in Mary Ellen Lamb and Valerie Wayne (eds.), *Staging Early Modern Romance: Prose Fiction, Dramatic Romance, and Shakespeare*, 163–87, New York: Routledge.

Wellcome Collection (n.d.), s.v. "Elizabeth I Histories Prodigieuses," Library Catalogue. Available online: https://wellcomecollection.org/works?query=ELIZABETH+I+his toires+prodigieuses (accessed January 9, 2021).

Wesselofsky, Alessandro (1866), *La figlia del re di Dacia: Testo inedito del buon secolo della lingua*, Pisa: Tipografia Nistri.

Weyer, Johann (1563), *De praestigiis daemonum, et incantationibus ac veneficiis, libri V.*, Basel: Joannem Oporinum.

Weyer, Johann (1567), *Cinq livres de l'imposture et tromperie des diables: des enchantements et sorcelleries*, Paris: Jacques du Puys.

Wilkin, Rebecca (2008), *Women, Imagination, and the Search for Truth in Early Modern France*, Burlington, VT: Ashgate.

Wittkower, Rudolf (1942), "Marvels of the East: A Study in the History of Monsters," *Journal of the Warburg and Courtauld Institutes*, 5: 159–97.
Wright, Herbert G. (1957), *Boccaccio in England from Chaucer to Tennyson*, London: Athlone Press.
Yamamoto Yōko (2008), "Tennin kara tennyo e: naze gosui no tennin ga josei to sareru yō ni natta no ka," *Meisei Daigaku kenkyū kiyō: Nihon Bungakubu, Gengo Bungaku Gakka*, 16: 89–98.
Yi-Fu Tuan (1979), *Landscapes of Fear*, Minneapolis: University of Minnesota Press.
Yıldız, Sara Nur (2015), "Battling *Kufr* (Unbelief) in the Land of Infidels: Gülşehri's Turkish Adaptation of ʿAṭṭār's Manṭiq al-Ṭayr," in A. C. S. Peacock, Bruno De Nicola, and Sara Nur Yıldız (eds.), *Islam and Christianity in Medieval Anatolia*, 329–47, London: Ashgate.
Yoshida Mikio (2009), "Irui kon'intan no tenkai: irui to no wakare o megutte," *Nihon bungaku*, 58 (6): 12–19.
Zambelli, Paola (2007), *White Magic, Black Magic in the European Renaissance: From Ficino, Pico, Della Porta to Trithemius, Agrippa, Bruno*, Leiden: Brill.
Zarri, Gabriella (1996), *Donna, disciplina, creanza cristiana dal XV al XVII: Studi e testi a stampa*, Rome: Edizioni di storia e letteratura.
Zawart, Anscar ([1928] 1944), *The History of Franciscan Preaching and of Franciscan Preachers (1209–1927): A Bio-Bibliographical Study*, New York: Joseph F. Wagner.
Ziolkowski, Jan M. (2010), "Straparola and the Fairy Tale: Between Literary and Oral Traditions," *Journal of American Folklore*, 123 (490): 377–97.
Zipes, Jack (1980), *Breaking the Magic Spell: Radical Theories of Folk and Fairy Tales*, 1st edn., Austin: University of Texas Press.
Zipes, Jack (2000a), "Approaches to the Literary Fairy Tale," in Jack Zipes (ed.), *Oxford Companion to Fairy Tales*, 17–22, Oxford: Oxford University Press.
Zipes, Jack (2000b), "Introduction: Towards a Definition of the Literary Fairy Tale," in Jack Zipes (ed.), *Oxford Companion to Fairy Tales*, xv–xxxii, Oxford: Oxford University Press.
Zipes, Jack (2012), *The Irresistible Fairy Tale: The Cultural and Social History of a Genre*, Princeton, NJ: Princeton University Press.
Zipes, Jack, ed. (2000c), *The Great Fairy Tale Tradition: From Straparola and Basile to the Brothers Grimm*, New York: W. W. Norton.

CONTRIBUTORS

N. İpek Hüner Cora is Assistant Professor of Turkish Literature at the Bogazici University, Istanbul. Her research interests include the history of Ottoman literature in the early modern era, gender, and sexuality as well as the history of reading. She is especially interested in tracing stories featuring women across centuries and geographies. Among her publications is "'Isn't She a Woman?': The 'Widow of Ephesus' in the Ottoman Empire," which appeared in the *Journal of Near Eastern Studies* in 2020.

Kathleen P. Long is Professor of French in the Department of Romance Studies at Cornell University. Her publications include *Hermaphrodites in Renaissance Europe* (2016), and the edited volumes *High Anxiety: Masculinity in Crisis in Early Modern France* (2002), *Religious Differences in France* (2006), and *Gender and Scientific Discourse in Early Modern Europe* (2016). She is preparing a translation into English of *The Island of Hermaphrodites* (*L'isle des hermaphrodites*), a book on literature of the French Wars of Religion, and one on *The Premodern Postnormal*. She is coeditor for a series on *Monsters and Marvels: Alterity in the Medieval and Early Modern Worlds*.

Armando Maggi is the Arthur and Joann Rasmussen Professor of Western Civilization at the University of Chicago. His latest book is *Preserving the Spell: Basile's The Tale of Tales and Its Afterlife in the Fairy-Tale Tradition* (2015). He has published numerous volumes and essays on early modern culture, with a special focus on demonology, Neoplatonic philosophy, epic poetry, mysticism, and fairy tales. Among his current interest is a study of the concept of "ruins" in contemporary culture.

Suzanne Magnanini is Associate Professor and President's Teaching Scholar in the Department of French and Italian at University of Colorado, Boulder, who studies and teaches early modern Italian fairy tales, women's writing, and Boccaccio's *Decameron*. Her publications include *Fairy-Tale Science: Monstrous Generation in the Tales of Straparola and Basile* (2008) and she is the editor and translator of Giovan Francesco Straparola's *The Pleasant Nights* (2015).

Cristina Mazzoni teaches at the University of Vermont, where she holds the Wolfgang and Barbara Mieder Green and Gold Professorship in Romance Languages. She has published widely about holy women writers, food studies, and fairy tales. Her latest book, *Golden Fruit: A Cultural History of Oranges*, won the 2018 AAIS Book Prize for Renaissance, eighteenth, and nineteenth centuries, and her anthology *The Pomegranates and Other Modern Italian Fairy Tales* is forthcoming in 2021.

Laura Nüffer is Assistant Professor at Colby College in Maine in the Department of East Asian Studies. Her research interests included animal studies, Japanese folklore, and medieval and early modern Japanese fiction. She has translated *otogizōshi* for the volume *Monsters, Animals, and Other Worlds: A Collection of Short Japanese Medieval Tales* (2018), edited by Haruo Shirane and Keller Kimbrough, and has contributed an essay on Japanese fairy tales to *The Wiley Blackwell Companion to World Literature* (2020), edited by Ken Seigneurie.

Davide Papotti is Professor of Geography at the University of Parma. His research interests include the relation between geography and literature, the geography of tourism, and the cultural geography of rivers. His publications include *L'altro e l'altrove. Geografia, antropologia, turismo*, with Marco Aime (2012), and a coedited volume with Marco Aime, *Piccolo lessico della diversità* (2018).

Kevin Pask is Professor of English at Concordia University, Montreal. He has published on the history of literary biography from the Renaissance onward, ideas of literary fantasy and the imagination, and the history of nationalism. His works include *The Emergence of the English Author: Scripting the Life of the Poet in Early Modern England* (1996) and *The Fairy Way of Writing: Shakespeare to Tolkien* (2013).

INDEX

Note: *n* = endnote.

Aarne-Thompson-Uther (ATU) Tale
    Type Index 1–2, 8, 30, 76, 79, 87–8,
    91, 178
Abé no Seimei (historical/legendary
    figure) 99
adaptation(s) 7–8, 25, 38, 49–69
    overlap with translation 26, 53–5
Aesop 175
"Affair of the Poisons" (1677–82) 130
Agamben, Giorgio 210
Aldrovandi, Ulisse 4
Alexander of Hales 16
"All Stick Together" tale type 91
All's Well That Ends Well (Shakespeare)
    26–7, 32–9, 36
    theme of resurrection 38–9
    theme of riddling 34–5, 37–8
    theme of rings 35–7, 38
    treatment of healing powers 33–4
    use of 'bed trick' 32, 34, 35–7
Alta Silva, Johannes de, *Dolopathos*
    214*n*5
Altair and Vega, myth of 101, 102–3,
    220*n*14
animals
    animal-human hybrids 62–4, 63, 121,
        141–2, 143–4, 217–18*n*42
    flying 128–31
    helpful 121–2, 179
    witches' familiars 128
    see also cross-species pairings

Apuleius (L. Apuleius Madaurensis),
    Metamorphoses, or The Golden Ass
    8, 26, 121, 131, 135, 173, *182*,
    226*n*13
    adaptation by Selva 180, 181–2, 183, 186
    "Cupid and Psyche" 75–8, 85, 102,
        158–9, 181, 186, 202, 205
Arabian Nights see The Thousand and One
    Nights
Ariès, Philippe, *Centuries of Childhood:*
    A Social History of Family Life 170
Ariosto, Ludovico, *Orlando Furioso* 29, 184
Aristotle 5, 175
    Poetics 2
Armin, Robert, *The Italian Tailor and His*
    Boy 9, 26
Artese, Charlotte 27, 35, 214*n*3, 214*n*10
Ascham, Roger, *The Scholemaster* 26
Ashliman, D. L. 159
'Aṭṭār, Ferīdūn 53–5, 216*n*22
Atwood, Margaret 72
Augustine of Hippo, St, *Of the City of God*
    (De Civitate Dei) 135
Aulnoy, Marie-Catherine d' *see* d'Aulnoy
Aynur, Hatice 215*n*3

Bağcı, Serpil 53
Bandello, Matteo 26, 33, 221–2*n*10
    Novelle 227*n*6
Basel, Council of (1431–49) 124, 125, 126,
    222*n*11

Basile, Giambattista, *Lo cunto de li cunti (The Tale of Tales)* 4–5, 6, 71–93, 139, 151, 152, 155–68, 176, 178, 185
  "Cagliuso" (Day 2, Tale 4) 74, 121
  "The Cinderella Cat" (Day 1, Tale 6) 74, 83–5, 88
  "The Enchanted Doe" (Day 1, Tale 9) 91–2, 157
  "The Flea" (Day 1, Tale 5) 91, 157, 163
  "Goat-Face" (Day 1, Tale 8) 162
  "The Golden Trunk" (Day 5, Tale 4) 77–8, (aka "The Golden Root"), *84*
  "The Goose" (Day 5, Tale 1) 74, 91
  "The Ignoramus" (Day 3, Tale 8) 160
  "Introduction" (frame tale) 19–20, 74–5, 159, 171
  "The Little Slave Girl" (Day 2, Tale 8) 20–1, 40, 85, 88, 207
  "The Merchant" (Day 1, Tale 7) 4–5, 157, 163, 165–6
  "The Myrtle" (Day 1, Tale 2) 157, 158
  "Nennillo and Nennella" (Day 5, Tale 8) 74, *84*
  "The Old Woman Who Was Skinned" (Day 1, Tale 10) 91, 157, 201–3
  "The Padlock" (Day 2, Tale 9) 77, 82, 207
  "Penta with the Chopped-off Hands" (Day 3, Tale 2) 7–8, 10–13, 15, 18–23, 157
  "Peruonto" (Day 1, Tale 3) 74, 87–8, 164
  "Petrosinella" (Day 2, Tale 1) 74, 88–9, 132, 157, 163
  "Pretty as a Picture" (Day 5, Tale 3) 86–7, 88, 157
  "Pride Punished" (Day 4, Tale 10) 157
  "Rosella" (Day 3, Tale 9) 157
  "The Serpent" (Day 2, Tale 5) 102, 137, 155–6, 157, 163
  "The Seven Little Doves" (Day 4, Tale 8) *84*
  "The She-Bear" (Day 2, Tale 6) 74, 79–81, 82, *84,* 85, 137, 157
  "Sun, Moon, and Talia" (Day 5, Tale 5) 74, 92–3, 172
  "The Tale of the Ogre" (Day 1, Tale 1) 157, 161–2
  "The Three Citrons" (Day 5, Tale 9) (20, 21, 23, 75, 82, 208, *209*, 227*n*14, 227*n*16
  "The Three Crowns" (Day 4, Tale 6) 90, 203–7
  "Vardiello" (Day 1, Tale 4) 157
  active role of women 82–7, 88–9, 188
  biographical background 151
  creation of sense of wonder 11–12, 201
  depictions of slaves/race relations 18–21, 199–200, 207–12
  film adaptation (2015) 91–2, 202, 203
  handling of social status/power structures 198–212
  influence of Boccaccio 7, 25–6, 192
  lack of religious content 189
  later (Italian) editions 172–3
  misogyny 82–3, 200
  moral dubiety 6, 172
  narrative framework 74–5, 155, 199–200, 207–12, 227*n*22
  narrator-figures 75, 171, 200
  personal names 160
  role of forests 163
  role of mountains 161–3
  significance of title 171–2
  social context 192, 198–9
  sources 73, 76–8
  target readership 171–3
  theme of voyage 159–60
  treatment of female characters 73–93, 200–7
  treatments of landscape 155–68
  use of place names 156–9
  violence of plots 6, 83–6, 200
Basnett, Susan 55
Baudoin, Jean 135, 225–6*n*11
beauty
  importance, in hero/heroine 86–7
  whiteness equated with 20–1
"Beauty and the Beast" (tale/theme) 6, 72, 76–9, 107
  social milieu 191
"bed trick" 32, 34, 35–7, 201
La Belle Hélène de Constantinople (anon.) 8
Belleforest, François de 221–2*n*10, 221*n*8
Belsey, Catherine 30
Bembo, Pietro, Cardinal 6, 176
  Asolani 198

Benjamin, Walter, *The Origins of the German Tragic Drama* 200
Berkeley Witch (legendary figure) 128, *129*
Beroaldo, Filippo 181
bestiality, allegations/supposed offspring of 15–16, 99, 121, 141–2, 147
Bettelheim, Bruno 108
Bigolina, Giulia, *Urania* 218*n*1
births, deformed/hybrid *see* monsters/monstrosities
Bloch, Ernst, *The Principle of Hope* 211
Bloch, R. Howard 219*n*8
Boccaccio, Giovanni 27, 51, 59, 177, 226*n*3
  Genealogy of the Pagan Gods 173, 174, 181, 192
  see also Decameron
Bodin, Jean 135, 138
Boiardo, Matteo Maria, *Orlando Innamorato* 17
Boiastuau, Pierre, *Histoires Prodigieuses* 3–4, 122, 142, 145–6, 147, 221*n*8, 223*n*37
Borghini, Vincenzo 174
Bottigheimer, Ruth B. 120, 122, 191, 214*n*1, 221*n*6
Braccesi, Alessandro 228*n*23
Broedel, Hans 124–5
Buddhism 99, 100, 109, 220*n*19
Bullough, Geoffrey 40
Burckhardt, Sigurd 30
burial alive, as punishment 23, 75, 80, 207–8
Butler, Martin 40

Calvino, Italo 162
Camporesi, Pietro 153, 154, 164
Campriano (trickster character) 9
Canepa, Nancy L. 12, 172, 191, 198–9, 208, 221*n*3
  From Court to Forest: Giambattista Basile's "Lo cunto de li cunti" (ed.) 156–8, 159, 162, 166
Carter, Angela 72
  "The Bloody Chamber" 82
cartography *161*, 161–2
Castiglione, Baldassare, *The Book of the Courtier* 169, 193, 198
Catholic Church

Index of Prohibited Books 177, 189
  censorship by 176–80, 188–9; limited effectiveness 178–9; Rules of 177, 179–80
  pamphlets issued by 169–70
Cavarero, Adriana 210–11
Çelebi, ʿAşıq 216*n*27
Çelebi, Vahdī, "Anabacı" 56–7, 216*n*27
censorship 176–80, 188–9
  areas not touched by 179–80
  limited effectiveness 178–9
  specific targets 177–8
chapbooks 9, 13–16
Chaucer, Geoffrey 29, 51
  "The Merchant's Tale" 59
  "The Squire's Tale" 214*n*8
children's literature
  amusement *vs.* educative aims 170–1, 173
  association of fairy-tales with 172–4
  educative aims 169–70
  relationship with fairy tale 170–1, 189
  role in basic education 174–5
Chrétien de Troyes, *Yvain ou le Chevalier au Lion* 145
Christian mythology, (contested) use of 173–4
Christianity, attitudes to animals 99
The Chronicles of Japan (Nihon shoki) 107
Cinānī, *Bedāyi'ü'l-āṣār (Embellished Works)* 57–61, 217*n*33
"Cinderella" (tale/theme) 6, 72, 74, 79, 97, 191
  moral dubiety 172
  personality of heroine 83–5
Cinzio, Giraldi, *Ecatommiti* 227*n*6
Cockaigne (magical land) 9, 166, *167*
Cohen, Jeffrey Jerome 221*n*1
'Constance' saga 8
Corna da Soncino, Francesco, *Historia della Regina Oliva* 7, 10–11, 12–13, 18
Croce, Benedetto 162
cross-species pairings 80–1, 95–118, 218–19*n*1
  arranged *vs.* spontaneous 116
  husband as non-human figure 103
  and imperial lineage 98, 99
  introduction of non-traditional animals 114–18

religious context 98–9
resolved by transformation 78–9, 99
variations on theme 114–18
Western *vs.* Japanese views 99
"Crown Prince" story 61–8
differences between versions 61, 65–8, 69
Cruikshank, George 84, 189
cultural geography 150–1
Cupid and Psyche, myth of 8, 26, 75–6, 181, 185–6, 201, 202, 205
see also Apuleius
Cymbeline (Shakespeare) 26–7, 39–47, 43, 45, 214*n5*
handling of 'resurrection' plot 43–4
significance of rings/keepsakes 40–3, 44–6
sources 40, 214*n3*

Dante (Alighieri), *Inferno* 11
Darnton, Robert 68
d'Aulnoy, Marie-Catherine 218*n1*
"The Beneficent Frog (La Grenouille bienfaisante)" 122, 137
"The Blue Bird (L'Oiseau bleu)" 122
"The Doe in the Woods (La Biche au bois)" 130–1, 145, 222*n18*
"The Green Serpent (Serpentin Vert)" 122, 137, 138
"Le Prince Marcassin" 132, 137, 138, 140–1, 142, 145, 147, 195, 223*n35*
"La Princesse Carpillon" 128–30
"The White Cat (La Chatte blanche)" 132–3, 137, 145, 222*n19*
De Simone, Roberto 208
Decameron (Boccaccio) 6–7, 9, 25–6, 32–3, 74–5, 166, 192
establishment disapproval 173–4
Frate Alberto (Day 4, Tale 2) 174
Griselda (Day 10, Tale 10) 9, 194
Masetto (Day 3, Tale 1) 9
preface 192–3
as source for Shakespeare 25–6, 32–3, 34, 35–6, 40–2
use of *locus amoenus* 154–5
della Carta, Orfeo 180, 193
"Deserted Wife" plot 35
Disney, Walt Disney Studios ix, 6, 71
donkeys, transformations into 183–6

dragons 106
alleged real-life sightings 2, 4–5
slayings 5, 163
Dürer, Albrecht 128

Elias, Norbert, *The Civilizing Process: Sociogenetic and Psychogenetic Investigations* 169
Elizabeth I of England 221*n7*
The Embalmer (2002) 203

fairies 227*n15*
and childbirth 132–3
discussions in Selva 183–5
impact of witches on portrayals of 128–31, 147–8
medieval representations 123–4
Fairy Tale Route 149–50, 225*n12*
farfariello (little devil), character of 11, 128
feathered-robe tales 98, 103–6, 109–10, 220*n16*
Ferec Bad'eş-Şidde (Relief After Hardship) 50–1
Ferrara, Mario 228*n23*
La figlia del re di Dacia (The Daughter of the King of Dacia, anon.) 10, 20
The Fishes' Chronicle of the Great Pacification (Uo Taiheiki) 97
Florence, intellectual/cultural movements 173–4
Flowers of Virtue (Fior di virtù, attrib. Gozzadini) 175
Fonte, Moderata
Floridoro 17
Il merito delle donne (The Worth of Women) 9, 218*n1*
forests, role in tales/public imagination 163
Forty Viziers 50–1, 58–60, 61–8, 217*n34*
Fox, Adam 27
Francis I of France 3
Frederyke of Jennen (anon.) 40–2
Frenk (Ottoman term for non-Turk) 62, 217*n41*
Fries, Maureen 124
Frisch, Andrea 123
Fulgentius, Fabius Planciades 181

Gaisser, Julia Haig 181
Galileo Galilei 2

Galland, Antoine 66
Garrone, Matteo 91, 202, 203
   see also *The Embalmer* (2002),
      Gomorrah (2008), *The Tale of Tales*
      (2015)
gender/sexuality 71–93
   and animal forms/metamorphoses 78–9,
      80–1, 95–6, 97–8, 139
   and female autonomy 81–7, 88–9
   and incest 79–80
   and melancholy 77, 82
   and power structures 112–13, 191–207
   and queer theory 89–93
   same-sex attractions 90, 92
Geoffrey of Monmouth, *Life of Merlin* 124
Gesner, Konrad 4
Gesta Romanorum (anon.) 29
Go-Hanazono, Emperor 102
Gobetti, Andrea 162
Goble, Warwick *209*
Gomorrah (2008) 203
Gonzenbach, Laura (ed.), *Sicilian Fairy*
   Tales 200, 206, 227*n*20
Gorfain, Phyllis 30
Gosson, Stephen, *The Schoole of Abuse* 26
Gozzadini, Tommaso 175
   see also *Flowers of Virtue*
"Grateful Dead" tale-type 178
Greenblatt, Stephen, *Marvelous Possessions:*
   The Wonder of the New World 150
Greene, Robert, *Pandosto* 27
Gregory, St 175
Greinier, Jean 139, 141
Grien, Hans Baldung 128
Grimm, Jacob/Wilhelm, *Children's and*
   Household Tales ix, 6, 10–11, 192,
   199, 227*n*14
   "The Frog King" 78, 79, 107–8, 109, 149
   "The Golden Goose" 74, 91
   "The Handless Maiden" 74
   "Hans My Hedgehog" 74
   "Hansel and Gretel" 74
   "Rapunzel" 74, 88
   "Simple Hans" 74
   "Snow White" 74, 85
   religious content 189
   sources 72–3, 74
   tourist trail 149–50, 225*n*12
Guicciardini, Francesco 153

Guise, François de Lorraine II, duc de 123
Gülşehrī 53–5, 216*n*21

Haase, Donald 72
   Fairy Tales and Feminism (ed.) 191
Habicht, Maximilian, *One Thousand and*
   One Nights (trans.) 66–8
hands, severed, as theme of tales 7–13,
   18–23
   magical restoration 13, 18, 23, 179
   as source of wonder 12–13
Heliodorus of Emesa *Aethiopica* 40
Henry Frederick, Prince 214*n*11
Hercules (mythical figure) 3, *3*
Herodotus 68, 217–18*n*42
Herzig, Tamar 126
"Hikāyet-i Mekr-i Zenān" (The Story of
   Women's Wiles) 217*n*33
Hirochika, Tosa *101, 102*
histoires prodigieuses 122–3, 126, 147–8
histoires tragiques 122–3, 126, 221–2*n*10
Historia della Regina Stella e Mattabruna
   (anon.) 7, 13–18, *14*
Historie von vier Kaufmännern (anon.) 40
Hoffmann, Kathryn A. 221*n*3
Holt, Mack 123
Hopwood, James *36*
Horace (Q. Horatius Flaccus), *Ars poetica*
   170, 172–3, 180
Hutcheon, Linda 9
   A Theory of Adaptation 55, 68
hydras, sightings/slayings 3–5, *4*, 163

Ichiko Teiji 97
iconems, definition/significance 160–1
incest, as theme of tales 7–8, 11, 73,
   79–80, 175–6
Index of Prohibited Books see under
   Catholic Church
Islamic literature/culture 53, 217*n*37
Italian Wars (1494–1530) 126
Italy
   as centre of fairy-tale production 5–7
   children's education 174–5
   cultural trends 173
   origination of popular tales 6
   as political/trading hub 150
   verse epics 5
   violence of plots 6

Jacobus de Voragine, *Legenda aurea (The Golden Legend)* 5, 214*n*7
Jakob, Michael, *Il paesaggio (The Landscape)* 152
James VI of Scotland/I of England 214*n*11
Japanese literature 8, 95–118
    feathered-robe tales 98, 103–6, 109–10
    oral tales 104–5, 108
    terminology 219*nn*4–5
    timing of medieval period 95, 219*n*4
Johnson, Samuel, Dr 37, 214*n*11
Jolles, André 34–5

Kavruk, Hasan 215*n*5
Kawai Hayao 110–11
Kepler, Johannes 2
    Somnium (Dream) 5
Kieckhefer, Richard 126
Kimbrough, Keller *see* Shirane, Haruo
King Kong (1933/2005) 113
"King Lindworm" (Danish folk tale) 108–10
Knight, G. Wilson 46
Komatsu Kazuhiko 105–6, 112

la Fontaine, Jean de 51
la Force, Charlotte-Rose de Caumont, "Persinette" 88
Lacan, Jacques 227*n*13
Lancre, Pierre de, *On the Inconstancy of Witches* 133–5, 138
    treatment of lycanthropy 139–40, 141
landscape(s) 151–6
    coinage of term 151, 152
    development of concept 152, 153–4
    literary traditions of representation 154–6
    mountainous 161–3
    wooded 163
Larivey, Pierre de 122, 127–8, 138, 221*nn*5–6
"Lazy Boy" tale type 87
Leonardo da Vinci 10
Leprince de Beaumont, Jeanne-Marie, "Beauty and the Beast" 72
Lewis, Franklin 58, 59–60
Lieberman, Marcia 71
Lingis, Alphonso, *The Community of Those Who Have Nothing in Common* 210
Lionbruno (chapbook character) 9

Lippi, Lorenzo, *Il Malmantile racquistato (Malmantile Reconquered)* 5
Little One-Inch (Issun bōshi) 97
"Little Red Riding Hood" (tale/theme) 72, 140
locus amoenus, trope of 154–6, 198
Louis XIV of France 130
Louveau, Jean 122, 132, 221*n*4, 221*n*6
Luginbühl, Yves 152
Lupardi, Bartolomeo 172–3
Lurie, Alison 71
Lüthi, Max 195, 206–7, 211
Lycosthenes, Conrad 3, 4, 142, 223*n*37

Maggi, Armando 6, 185, 226*n*16
    Preserving the Spell 10–11
magic realism 32–3
"Magician and His Pupil" tale type 9, 138, 178
Magnanini, Suzanne 120, 198
Magnus, Olaus, *History of the Northern Peoples* 128, 130
Mallette, Karla 55
Malleus maleficarum (The Hammer of Witches) 125, 132, 185, 222*n*13
Malory, Thomas, *Le Morte d'Arthur* 124
Manrique, Tommaso 174
Marcel, Gabriel 202, 227*n*13
Marcellino, Evangelista *see* Selva, Lorenzo
Marcus Aurelius, Emperor 145–6
Marguerite of Navarre 26
Marie de France 133
    "Bisclavret (The Werewolf)" 139
    "Lanval" 123–4
    "Yonec" 124
Marin, Louis 227*n*9
Marinello, Giovanni, *Gli ornamenti delle donne* 20
Marino, Giambattista 11
Martelli, Eustachio 174
Medici, Cosimo I de', Duke 173–4
Medici, Lucrezia Tornabuoni de' 17
melancholy, of principal characters 29, 77, 81–2, 87, 199
The Merchant of Venice (Shakespeare) 26–7, 28–32
    significance of rings 29–30, 31–2, 35, 38, 40
    treatment of marriage 30, 31–2

mesnevi (verse genre) 62, 215*n*1
metamorphosis/es 99, 121–2, 132–3, 179, 183–6
  censorship of tales involving 178
  reversal 78–9, 107–8, 109, 133, 183
  on violation of taboo 99–100, 107
  voluntary 80–1
  see also animal-human hybrids; shape-shifters; werewolves
The Metamorphosis, or, Transformation of a Virtuous Man (Selva) 26, 135–7, 139, 180–8, 226*n*17
  'Agape' episode 186–8
  allegorical readings 180–1, 186–8
  handling of metamorphosis 135–7, 183–6
  moralistic aims 180–1, 183, 185–6, 188, 189
  Proem 180–1
  publishing history 180, 225–6*n*11
  transformation of source material 181–2, 183, 186
  treatment of female characters 188
Mitchell, David T. 21
Molino, Antonio 176
Molitor, Ulrich, *Concerning Female Sorcerers and Soothsayers* 133, *134*
"The Monkey Groom" (*Saru mukoiri*) 112, 113, 220*n*21
monkeys, in cross-species pairings 111–14, 115
monsters/monstrosities 119–48
  alleged real-life sightings 3–5
  births 121, 141–2; blamed on maternal misconduct 15–16, 142
  range of forms 119–20
  tale genres 122–3
  travel stories involving 62–5, 67–8
  see also werewolves; witches/witchcraft
Monter, William 125
Morgan le Fay (legendary figure) 124, 133
mountains, role in tales/public imagination 161–3
Murad III, Sultan 57
Murat, Henriette-Julie de Castelnau, comtesse de 74, 122, 218*n*1
murder, acceptability in fairy-tale setting 6, 86, 172, 195
Murtaza Pasa, Vizier 63

non-human characters *see* animals; cross-species pairings; monsters/monstrosities

Old Testament 30–1, 175
Olivia of Palermo, St 19
One Thousand and One Nights 50–1, 56–7
  German translations 61, 66–8
Ortelius, Abraham 161, *161*
Otogi bunko (*The Companion Library*) 96, 219*nn*2–3
otogizōshi ("companion tales") 95–118, 219*n*4
  etymology 96
  generic range 96–7
Ottoman Empire, literature/culture 49–69
  adaptations/translations into 52–5
  definition of fairy tales 50–1
  differences between Ottoman versions 65–6
  differences from Western versions 60, 61, 66–8
  literary epochs 51–2
  narrative forms 50
  "original," difficulty of establishing 55–7
  similarities to Western storylines 51, 59–60
Ovid (P. Ovidius Naso), *Metamorphoses* 121, 128–30, *131*, 222*n*16
Ozawa Toshio 110

Painter, William, *The Palace of Pleasure* 26, 32
Paker, Saliha 56, 215–16*n*16
Paré, Ambroise, *On Monsters and Marvels* 13, 120, 126, 133, 142, 221*n*3, 223*n*37
Parolari, Giovanni 225–6*n*11
'pear tree' story 51, 58–60, 68
Peele, George, *The Old Wives' Tale* 27–8
Perrault, Charles 72–3, 122, 192
  "Cinderella" (Cendrillon ou la petite pantoufle de verre) 74
  "Donkey Skin" (Peau d'âne) 74, 79
  "Little Red Riding Hood (Le Petit chaperon rouge)" 140
  "Puss in Boots (Le Chat botté)" 74, 121, 137, 196

"The Sleeping Beauty (La Belle au bois dormant)" 74, 92, 132
   sources 74
"persecuted maiden" tales 7–23
   variations on theme 8–9
Pétis de la Croix, François 66, 68
Petrarch, Francesco 11, 152, 226*n*15
Petronius 51
Pirovano, Donato 177
Pitrè, Giuseppe 206, 227*n*19
Pius IV, Pope 177
place names, significance of 156–9
   sexual implications 157–8
Plato, *Gorgias* 173
Pliny the Elder (C. Plinius Secundus)/
   Plinian races 2, 139, 217–18*n*42
power, representations of 191–212
   and social class 191
Propp, Vladimir 1, 159, 220*n*20
Pulci, Luigi, *Morgante* 11, 17
"Puss in Boots" (tale/theme) 6, 74, 121, 133, 137, 179, 196–7, *197*

queer theory 89–93
querelle des femmes 23, 90

race, and social status 18–21, 211–12
   see also slaves/slavery
Rackham, Arthur *45*
Rak, Michele 19, 73, 172, 210
rape, as acceptable/precursor to happy ending 6, 77, 92–3, 172
Raphael 223*n*20
La rappresentazione di Santa Uliva (anon.) 10
"Rapunzel" (tale/theme) 6, 72, 74, 88–9, 163
The Rare Triumphs of Love and Fortune (anon.) 40
"rash promise" motif 111
"The Rat-Snake Groom" (Korean folk tale) 108
Rebhorn, Wayne A. 226*n*2
Records of Ancient Matters (Kojiki) 98, 102
Remi, Philippe de, *Le Roman de la manekine* 8
Reppone, Masillo *see* Sarnelli, Pompeo
resurrection, of (apparently) dead 38–9, 43–4, 86

Rhead, Louis *43*
"Rich Man Mudsnail" *(Tanishi chōja)* 108, 112, 220*n*18
Richardson, Samuel, *Pamela* 32
Richter, Dieter 149–50, 225*n*12
riddles 34–5, 195–6
rings, symbolic significance/magical powers 29–30, 31–2, 35–7, 38, 40–1, 73, 214*n*8
Rosset, François de 221–2*n*10, 222*n*15
Rowe, Karen 71–2
Rua, Giuseppe 227*n*8
Ruch, Barbara 96, 112
Rūmī 53, 59–60

Saint Bartholomew's Day massacres (1572) 123
Sanders, Julia 55
Sannazaro, Jacopo, *Arcadia* 182
Sarnelli, Pompeo 172
Schmiesing, Ann 21
"Search for the Lost Husband" tale type 76
Segarizzi, Arnaldo 213*n*6
Şehnāme (Persian epic) 53, *54*
Seiemon, Shibukawa 96
Seifert, Lewis 89–90, 92, 120, 223*n*35
Seki Keigo 104
Selva, Lorenzo (Evangelista Marcellino) 135, 177, 178
   biography 180
   see also The Metamorphosis, or, Transformation of a Virtuous Man
Sensca, L. Annaeus 175
Ser Giovanni Fiorentino, *Il Pecorone* 28–9, 214*n*5
setsuwa (Japanese short story genre) 98
The Seventh Night (Tanabata) 8, 95, 100–11, *101*, 114, 115, 118, 219–20*nn*10–13, 220*n*19
   links with feathered-robe tales 104–6, 109–10
   plot summary 100–1
   (possible) sources 102
   significance of snakeskin 106–8, 109–10
Sforza, Ottaviano Maria/Lucrezia 74, 155
Shakespeare, William 25–47
   King Lear 33, 41
   Macbeth 26
   Measure for Measure 32, 38–9

INDEX

A Midsummer Night's Dream 26, 32
Othello 33
Pericles 39
The Taming of the Shrew 28
The Tempest 26, 39
The Winter's Tale 27, 39, 40
see also *All's Well That Ends Well*; *Cymbeline*; *The Merchant of Venice*
shape-shifters 103, 120, 121, 124, 133–8, 134
    belief in 133–5
    see also metamorphosis/es; werewolves
Shinto 99
Shirane, Haruo and Keller Kimbrough, *Monsters, Animals, and Other Worlds* 96
silence, linked to melancholy 77, 82
slaves/slavery 18–21, 199, 200, 207–12
    representation as subhuman 208–10
    use of patois 19–20, 208–10, 228n23
"Sleeping Beauty" (tale/theme) 6, 72, 74, 92–3, 172
snakes, as principal characters
    in cross-species pairings 95, 100–3, 106–11, 115
    magically transformed 183–6
    shedding of skin 100, 104, 106–7, 109–10
"Snow White" (tale/theme) 43–4, 74, 85, 89
Snyder, Sharon L. 21
Snyder, Susan 32
society/socialization 169–89
    educative texts 169–70
space, treatments of 149–68
    characters' experiences of 164–8
    early modern perspective 152–3
    travels through 159–60
    see also landscape; place names
Spada, Giuseppe 172
Spenser, Edmund, *The Faerie Queene* 29, 214n8
Speroni, Sperone 16
Stone, Kay 71
Straparola, Giovanni Francesco, *Le piacevoli notti (The Pleasant Nights)* 6, 11, 23, 34–5, 71–93, 139, 176, 188
    "Adamantina's Magical Doll" (Night 5, Tale 2) 91

"Ancilotto, King of Provino" (Night 4, Tale 3) 137
"Biancabella" (Night 3, Tale 3) 74, 90–1, 121–2, 137, 179
"Costantino Fortunato" (Night 11, Tale 1) 74, 121, 137, 179, 196–7, *197*
"Costanzo-Costanza" (Night 4, Tale 1) 90, 122, 146, 205
"Crazy Pietro (Pietro Pazzo)" (Night 3, Tale 1) 87–8, 179, 180
"Fortunio" (Night 3, Tale 4) 137, 138, 140, 179
"Guerrino and the Wild Man" (Night 5, Tale 1) 146–7
"Isotta and Travaglino" (Night 3, Tale 5) 198
"Livoretto" (Night 3, Tale 2) 86, 179
"Maestro Lattanzio and His Apprentice Dionigi" (Night 8, Tale 4) 138, 178, 214n8
"Ortodosio and Isabella" (Night 7, Tale 1) 37, 126–8, 138, 178, *179*
"The Pig King" (Night 2, Tale 1) 74, *78*, 78–9, 99, 132, 137, 141, 142, 146–7, 179, 194–5
Proem (frame tale) 155, 226n5
"Salardo" (Night 1, Tale 1) 194
"Tebaldo and Doralice" (Night 1, Tale 4) 73–4, 75, 76–7, 79–80, 81–2, 175–6, 194, 207–8, 210, 227n21
"Teodosia" (Night 2, Tale 3) 196
"The Three Brothers" (Night 7, Tale 5) 147
censorship 176–80; specific removals 177–8
editor's preface 180, 193
French translations/adaptations 6, 122, 123, 127–8, 132, 138, 221n6
handling of social status/power structures 193–8, 212
influence of Boccaccio 7, 25–6, 192–3
narrative framework 74, 192, 193–4, 197–8, 226n5
riddling conclusions 34–5, 175, 195–6
social/religious context 126–8, 192, 212
sources 73, 76–8
target readership 75, 193, 194
treatment of female characters 194–5
violence of plots 6

The Stuck-on Bowl (Hachikazuki) 97
swan maidens 103–4, 220*n*15

The Tale of Amewakahiko see *The Seventh Night*
Tale of Tales (2015) 91–2, 202, 203
The Tale of the Cat (Neko no sōshi) 97
The Tale of the Clam (Hamaguri no sōshi) 220*n*22
The Tale of the Crane (Tsuru no sōshi) 98, 100, 220*n*22
The Tale of the Feathered Robe (Hagoromo no sōshi) 220*n*22
The Tale of the Jewel Beetle (Tamamushi no sōshi) 97
The Tale of the Mouse (Nezumi no sōshi) 115–18
  departure from traditional animal forms 115–16
  social milieu 116–17
"The Tale of the Rich Man Qian Luwei" 102–3, 105–6, 220*n*13
The Tale of the Wife from Inari (Inarizuma no sōshi) 220*n*22
The Tale of the Wild Goose (Kari no sōshi) 106, 114–18
  departure from traditional animal forms 115–16
  social milieu 116–17
The Tale of the Wisteria Basket (Fujibukuro no sōshi) 111–14, 115–16
  gender hierarchy 112–13
  surviving manuscripts 113–14
Tales of Things Transformed (Bakemono no sōshi) 114–18
  departure from traditional animal forms 115–16
  social milieu 116–17
Tameie, Fujiwara, *Poems Ancient and Modern* 102–3
Tarleton, Richard, *News Out of Purgatory* 26
Tasso, Torquato
  Aminta 29
  Jerusalem Delivered 172
Tatar, Maria 2
Taylor, John 189
Tesauro, Emanuele
  The Aristotelian Telescope 5, 11–12
  Moral Philosophy 200, 211–12

Tesserant, Claude de 221*n*8
te'līf ('original') 56–7
third siblings, special characteristics 77, 95, 102
Thomas Aquinas, St 16
Thompson, Stith, *The Motif-Index of Folk Literature* 207
"Tom Thumb" (tale/theme) 97
Tonomura, Hitomi 219*n*8
Topsell, Edward 4
translation
  in Ottoman Empire 49–50
  of Italian tales 26, 122
  of stories from *Forty Viziers* 64–8
  overlap with adaptation 53–5
Traxler, Hans, *Die Wahreit über Hänsel und Gretel* 156
Trent, Council of (1545–63) 188
Trivigiano, Benedetto 176
Tuan, Yi-Fu 164, 166
Tucker, Holly 120, 131, 132
Turri, Eugenio 160

Uther, Hans-Jörg 1–2, 8

Varchi, Benedetto 16
Varotto, Mauro 154
Villeneuve, Gabrielle-Suzanne de, "Beauty and the Beast" 107
Virgil (P. Vergilius Maro), *Eclogues* 135
Virgin Mary 10, 12, 15, 189
virgin offerings 112
virginity, significance of 33, 37
Vives, Juan Luis, *The Education of a Christian Woman* 169
voyage, theme of 159–60

Waldensian heresy 125
Walter, Melissa Emerson 38, 214*n*7
Warner, Marina 9, 18
  From the Beast to the Blonde 73
  Wonder Tales: Six French Stories of Enchantment 2
Warren, Roger 27, 40
Waters, Virginia Skord (trans.), *Tales of Tears and Laughter* 218–19*n*1
Wayne, Valerie 214*n*3, 214*n*11
werewolves 120, 139–41
  alleged real-life cases 139–40

Weyer, Johann, *On the Illusions of Demons* 126
"Widow of Ephesus" story 60–1, 68–9, 217*n*36
wild man, figure of 142–7
    "fallen" 145, 147
    as truth-teller 145–7
    types of 142–5
witches/witchcraft 2–3, 124–38, 185
    airborne transport 128–31, *129, 130, 134*
    artistic depictions 128, *129, 130*
    censorship of tales involving 177–80
    and childbirth 132–3
    impact on portrayal of fairies 128–31, 147–8
    real-life persecutions/fear of 120–1, 124–6, 130
    and shape-shifting 133–8
women
    active agency, as lead characters 81–7, 88–9
    bonds between sisters 90–1
    old/ugly, mockery of 75, 199, 200, 201–2
    physical attributes 86–7
    reduced agency 88, 188
    as storytellers 72–3, 75, 93, 180, 185, 188, 200
    as target readership 75, 193, 194
    violent behaviour 83–6
    "women's wiles," as plot theme 56–7, 58–61, 217*n*33
wonder tales see *histoires prodigieuses*
Wonders of Creation 63

Yanagita Kunio 104
Yıldız, Sara Nur 55
"Youth Who Wanted to Learn What Fear Is" tale type 178

Ziolkowski, Jan M. 213*n1*
Zipes, Jack 210